The Injustice System

The Injustice System

A Murder in Miami and a
Trial Gone Wrong

Clive Stafford Smith

VIKING

VIKING
Published by the Penguin Group
Penguin Group (USA) Inc., 375 Hudson Street, New York, New York 10014, U.S.A. • Penguin Group (Canada), 90 Eglinton Avenue East, Suite 700, Toronto, Ontario M4P 2Y3, Canada (a division of Pearson Penguin Canada Inc.) • Penguin Books Ltd, 80 Strand, London WC2R 0RL, England • Penguin Ireland, 25 St. Stephen's Green, Dublin 2, Ireland (a division of Penguin Books Ltd) • Penguin Group (Australia), 707 Collins Street, Melbourne, Victoria 3008, Australia (a division of Pearson Australia Group Pty Ltd) • Penguin Books India Pvt Ltd, 11 Community Centre, Panchsheel Park, New Delhi – 110 017, India • Penguin Group (NZ), 67 Apollo Drive, Rosedale, Auckland 0632, New Zealand (a division of Pearson New Zealand Ltd) • Penguin Books, Rosebank Office Park, 181 Jan Smuts Avenue, Parktown North 2193, South Africa • Penguin China, B7 Jiaming Center, 27 East Third Ring Road North, Chaoyang District, Beijing 100020, China

Penguin Books Ltd, Registered Offices: 80 Strand, London WC2R 0RL, England

First American edition
Published in 2012 by Viking Penguin, a member of Penguin Group (USA) Inc.

10   9   8   7   6   5   4   3   2   1

Published in Great Britain as *Injustice: Life and Death in the Courtrooms of America* by Harvill Secker, an imprint of Random House Group Limited.

LIBRARY OF CONGRESS CATALOGING IN PUBLICATION DATA
Smith, Clive Stafford.
   The injustice system : a murder in Miami and a trial gone wrong / Clive Stafford Smith.
      p.   cm.
   Includes bibliographical references and index.
   ISBN 978-0-670-02370-7
   1. Maharaj, Kris—Trials, litigation, etc.   2. Trials (Murder)—Florida.   3. Criminal justice, Administration of—United States.   I. Title.
   KF224.M2115S65 2012
   345.759'02523—dc23
   2012019068

Printed in the United States of America

PEARSON

This book is dedicated to Marita Maharaj,
whose dedication to her husband
through the quarter century
of his incarceration is an inspiration to us all.

The concept of justice as a lady with a blindfold and a pair of scales someone else may lay a decisive finger on without her noticing has often struck me as questionable. It presupposes a readiness in those among whom she dispenses her gifts to keep their hands to themselves. You must agree that would be a perfect world, and in such a world she would be a redundant figure. Keep the figure, by all means, as a symbol of what might be achieved. Keep the illusion of detachment. Cultivate its manner. But admit it cannot be a controlling force without compromising itself.

—Paul Scott, *The Day of the Scorpion*

Our justice system makes two promises to its citizens: a fundamentally fair trial and an accurate result. If either of those two promises is not met, the criminal justice system itself falls into disrepute.

—Pascal Calogero, former chief justice, Louisiana Supreme Court

PREFACE

It is often said that human beings are fallible—that, notwithstanding our best efforts, we are bound to make mistakes. One of the most dissonant experiences of my life has been to represent someone at trial who I am sure—to the extent a fallible human being can be—is innocent, only to hear twelve jurors announce *beyond a reasonable doubt* that he or she is guilty.

After two or three years of investigation, I often know more about the circumstances of the crime than anyone else, sometimes more than the person on trial—especially if he or she is innocent. Terrified at making a mistake that could cost someone his life, I try to investigate and analyze every angle. I write up a long document about each case, hundreds of pages, that takes account of every possible theory of guilt or innocence. Sometimes I'm confident that I know who really committed the murder.

And yet twelve jurors file back into the courtroom and say that the wrong person is guilty beyond a reasonable doubt. Perhaps they even decide he should be executed.

Such results are inevitable, no matter how vigorous the defense. But to say that all human endeavor is imperfect is merely a truism. If that were the sum of it, the question would be relatively simple—we know that mistakes are inevitable, so roughly what error rate are we willing to accept, in light of the value of our goal?

"Despite precautions," argues the death penalty advocate Ernst van den Haag, "nearly all human activities, such as trucking, lighting, or construction, cost the lives of some innocent bystanders. We do not give up these activities, because the advantages, moral or material, outweigh the unintended losses. Analogously, for those who think the death penalty just, miscarriages of justice are offset by the moral benefits and the usefulness of doing justice."[1]

Arguments may rage—particularly in academia—over what the benefits of the death penalty may be. But the debate obscures the real problem: most of the "lapses" do not simply happen by accident. Rather, the system is structured in such a way that it inevitably fails—it is almost as if it were designed to fail. Even the most superficial analysis reveals how the legal procedure we use for sending people to prison is deeply flawed. Politicians and judges do not discuss the system's faults; instead, they write and rewrite rules that are designed to convince us that the emperor before us is not naked after all.

Lawyers and judges will tell you that it is better that one hundred guilty people go free than that one innocent person should suffer imprisonment. Many of these jurists, however, do not translate this precept into practice. Of course, they might act differently if they themselves, or someone they knew and loved, were the innocent person being sent to prison. Suddenly the debate would involve not a faceless statistic but rather a human being, who has only one life, which is being wrenched from him for a crime he did not commit. But the rules are not written by people who expect to live by them.

Jurists would also have us believe that the American legal process is the best in the world. Perhaps it is. Perhaps America delivers merely the least-worst justice. But to cling to mediocrity because it is superior to catastrophe would be a sorry ambition.

Most people would agree that the purpose of the legal system is to make society safer by ensuring that those who commit crimes are incapacitated and punished. So let us consider whether each actor in the legal system is contributing to this goal. Charles Darwin spoke of the survival of the "fittest" or the "best adapted." In the legal system, we must examine whether each player is "best adapted" to his or her role—whether he or she brings the right talents to achieve the stated objective.

For nearly thirty years, I have been representing defendants in capital cases mainly in the South, based first in Atlanta and then in New Orleans. My aim is to help provoke a debate that is, unfortunately, not currently taking place. We have to recognize our predicament before we can pose solutions. Two simple rules should guide all efforts toward reform: first, we must clearly identify where we are trying to go; and second, we must be sure that every incremental change that we make takes us closer to that destination rather than farther from it. It is emphatically not sufficient to try to sweep the problems under the carpet, as all three branches of the U.S. government are wont to do.

This book traces the life, and death sentence, of Krishna (Kris) Maharaj, a British businessman, born and raised in Trinidad, who was tried and convicted for committing a double murder that took place at the DuPont Plaza Hotel in downtown Miami very close to the noon hour on October 16, 1986. The victims were a Jamaican businessman, Derrick Moo Young, and his son Duane.

Please try not to prejudge Krishna Maharaj as either innocent or guilty. By the end, no doubt you will have formed an opinion; only at that point I ask that you act on it. By then, you may have reached a verdict on our criminal justice system as well.

In the meantime I will cede the floor, as is customary at the start of every trial, to the prosecution.

Clive Stafford Smith

CONTENTS

1

The Trial

The prosecutor is clean-cut, with close-cropped dark hair and a long, thin face that advertises its sincerity. He walks toward the podium and nods to the jury. Twelve men and women are sitting attentively in their places. His job is to lay out the evidence that they will hear over the next several days.

"May it please the court," John Kastrenakes begins. "Counsel for the defense. And ladies and gentlemen of the jury. This case is about hate. This case is about vengeance of the highest order. This case is about stalking and lying in wait to murder a victim. This case is about the manipulation of witnesses and the fabrication of an alibi.

"The victims in this case are Derrick Moo Young, a Jamaican businessman, father of four, who died in a hail of gunfire in room 1215 at the DuPont Plaza Hotel in downtown Miami, on October 16, 1986. And his son, his eldest son, Duane Moo Young, twenty-three years old, was executed to eliminate him as a witness, by the defendant, Krishna Maharaj."

The defendant is in his late forties, heavyset, with thick black hair and a dark complexion. He is a Trinidadian of Indian descent who has been living in Miami off and on for the last three years. A self-made millionaire, he has business interests in England, America, and his native Trinidad. His Portuguese wife, Marita, sits in the front row. She is well dressed, her glamour muted by sober attire. The strain shows as she shifts nervously on the wooden pews that ensure no courtroom observer ever gets too comfortable.

"Before I talk about what the evidence will reveal to you in this case, I would like to tell you about the types of evidence you will hear," the prosecutor continues. "You will hear from witnesses, you will hear scientific evidence regarding fingerprints, ballistics evidence, business records, and the statements that this defendant made to the police. All of that points to this defendant, nobody else, as the killer of Derrick Moo Young and Duane Moo Young.

"Well, as with all brutal, evil acts, there is a beginning. And the beginning was not on October 16, 1986. In the beginning, Derrick Moo Young and the defendant, Krishna Maharaj, were business partners in KDM, which was a corporation that dealt primarily with export and import. They were more than business partners; they were friends. But the business broke up and the friendship came to an end in April 1986."

The prosecutor briefly introduces the victims in the case. Derrick Moo Young was effectively retired, and semidisabled. He was trying to support his family on a limited income, no more than $24,000, helping Krishna Maharaj with his property investments. Duane was seemingly collateral damage in the quarrel between his father and the man on trial for murder.

"The disputes began with the breakup of the business," Kastrenakes continues. "Suits and countersuits were filed at Broward County Circuit Court, in Fort Lauderdale, and the defendant then initiated the war that culminated in the murder of Derrick Moo Young and his eldest son, Duane.

"The war began, interestingly enough, in the newspaper known as the *Caribbean Echo*. You will hear from the editor of that newspaper, Eslee Carberry. You will hear that in April 1986 the defendant—not satisfied with the progress of his civil suit against Derrick Moo Young—paid for a newspaper article exposing Derrick Moo Young as a swindler. And you will see that newspaper article.

"And Mr. Carberry published that article, but refused to publish follow-up articles from Krishna Maharaj presenting his side of the story. Because Derrick Moo Young came to Eslee Carberry and said, 'Hey, there's another side to this story. Let me show you some documents concerning this guy Maharaj.'

"Sure enough, starting in June 1986, the paper began to publish—relentlessly—articles exposing Krishna Maharaj as a swindler, as a forger, as a manipulator. And things began to get very, very dirty.

"What did the defendant do? Well, the defendant offered to buy the *Caribbean Echo*, but Mr. Carberry refused to sell it to him. He offered other articles against Derrick Moo Young, but Carberry refused to publish them.

"So what did Krishna Maharaj do next? He started his own newspaper and began to hire away the people from the *Caribbean Echo*, lure them away with money and other promises of wealth that they would receive with his paper. And he vowed to destroy the *Caribbean Echo* and to destroy Derrick Moo Young.

"Well, he did hire those people away, but Eslee Carberry continued publishing his articles, exposing Krishna Maharaj as a money launderer from Trinidad, a scamster, a fraudster. And one thing led to another, and the papers in Trinidad began to pick this up." The prosecutor can see that he has the jury's attention. He has framed his narrative and will now begin to set the stage for the crime and introduce his witnesses.

"One of the people the defendant hired away from the *Echo* was a person by the name of Tino Geddes. Mr. Tino Geddes will testify in this case. Mr. Tino Geddes was taken into the defendant's confidence, and shortly, when the articles got intensive from the *Echo*, Mr. Geddes was recruited to assist the defendant in a plan. A plan that consumed Krishna Maharaj's every waking moment, from July 1986 to the murder, the hail of bullets at the DuPont Plaza. And that plan was the elimination, the murder, of Derrick Moo Young and Eslee Carberry, the editor of the *Caribbean Echo*.

"This hatred, which consumed his life, became an obsession and led to what I would call—and what the evidence will show to have been—almost comical attempts that failed to murder these people. The evidence will show that the defendant purchased crossbows, Chinese throwing stars, camouflage gear, weapons of various sizes and sorts, including a nine-millimeter pistol. The pistol will be very important in the case because it is a murder weapon. You are going to hear that this equipment was purchased by the defendant for one reason only. Mr. Geddes will tell you it was purchased to murder Derrick Moo Young.

"What are the comical types of failed attempts to murder these people? Well, you are going to hear from Mr. Geddes that they waited for

Mr. Carberry late at night on a lonely road, hoping to catch him. But as fate would have it, they got hungry and went and got a sandwich and they missed Mr. Carberry and didn't get a chance to murder him up at West Palm Beach. You will hear about a Ryder rental truck in late July 1986. Lying in wait out on U.S. Route 27 in camouflage gear with a crossbow, waiting to take out Derrick Moo Young when he happened along the road. They were expecting him. He never showed up.

"You will hear some of the most bizarre plans that came from the mind of this defendant, obsessed as he was with the murder of Derrick Moo Young. He was going to even shoot up the wedding of Derrick's son Paul Moo Young as one of the plans.

"Mr. Geddes will tell you about another plan, and this one is important, because it relates to what actually happened. Geddes knew, and the defendant knew, that Derrick Moo Young wanted nothing to do with the defendant and would never agree to a meeting with him alone, anywhere, anytime, anyplace. So the plan was to lure him to a place where he wasn't expecting to see the defendant.

"As a matter of fact, Mr. Geddes was recruited to make a phone call to Derrick Moo Young to lure him to the DuPont Plaza Hotel. This took place sometime in the late summer of 1986. Mr. Geddes was there at the hotel and made a phone call to Derrick Moo Young, who happened to be out of town.

"Also, he called Eslee Carberry to have him come in to meet a fictitious Trinidadian lawyer. . . . Mr. Carberry will testify he got a call from Mr. Geddes, wanting him to come to this hotel tomorrow, and he didn't think anything of it. But when you hear the testimony, it will mean a lot to you. And he said, 'I am not going down there. I really don't feel well. Forget it.'

"Well, that plan failed also. But the important thing about that plan was that it was to occur at the DuPont. It was to lure the victims there to meet somebody else, and the defendant would be waiting there.

"And also Mr. Geddes saw the defendant with a bag, which was a zippered bag. And in this bag he had a nine-millimeter silver gun. And a glove that he had in one hand, his right hand. The evidence will show he is a right-handed man. You will hear from Mr. Geddes, and you will ask yourselves, 'How can a man with his journalistic background'—and you will hear he is a broadcaster for RJR in Jamaica—'a well-respected journalist, how could he have gotten himself involved?'"

The prosecutor has rehearsed his story well, and the parts are beginning to fall into place. He needs to convince the jury that even though his witness participated in these plots, Geddes is still credible. So he tells the jury that at some point Geddes had enough. He decided he wanted nothing more to do with these crazy plots and pulled out.

"Well, does that end the defendant's manipulation of other people for his evil work?" Kastrenakes asks rhetorically. "The answer is no. Because this is when Mr. Neville Butler comes into the picture. He is a Trinidadian national who worked under the pen name of 'Crossley West' at the *Caribbean Echo*. And as with the other people at the *Echo,* the defendant lured him away from the *Echo* to work for his own newspaper, the *Caribbean Times,* and destroy the *Echo*.

"But the defendant set one condition before Butler could work for the *Times*—one condition. And that condition, in October 1986, was—'You've got to set up a meeting between me and Derrick Moo Young and Mr. Carberry.'

"Mr. Butler said, 'Why, you know Moo Young will never meet you under any conditions.'

"He said, 'Yes, that is why I need you to set it up, to have somebody used as bait to get him to this location, so I could meet you here.'

"Butler says, 'Why me?'

"'Well,' the defendant says. 'Well, your name has come up as being involved in this extortion attempt down in Trinidad, and I want to clear up your name. What we are going to do is get Derrick Moo Young in there, and have him write out a confession that he has been the one extorting the money—and we may rough him up a little bit, tie him up. But nobody is going to get killed or really hurt.'

"Butler, naïve Butler, agrees, and that sets off the chain of events that will lead to the murders, including the murder, planned for months, of Derrick Moo Young." The prosecutor has now successfully introduced his second eyewitness, who was also involved in the plot.

"Well, the plan takes root with Mr. Butler," the prosecutor says.

"Butler knows two people from the Bahamas, Prince Ellis and Eddie Dames. They are unwittingly used in this case. Mr. Dames is an air traffic controller, now the manager of the airport in Nassau. And Prince Ellis, he is a caterer and runs Lucky Five Catering Service in Nassau. As a matter of fact, they had been making plans during this period of time to open a nightclub, a business in Nassau, which they needed equipment for. And the defendant asks Butler if he knows anybody who could possibly lure the Moo Youngs.

"'I know these two people are coming over here, and they need restaurant things. . . .'

"The defendant said, 'Good. It is a great idea, play them up really big. The Moo Youngs will bite on that.'

"Butler agrees." The prosecutor has identified his key characters. Now the time has come to supply the material evidence underpinning his case.

"Phone calls. You will see the evidence of phone calls going between Butler and the Moo Youngs and the defendant, minutes apart, a couple of days before the murder. The Moo Youngs know that Mr. Dames is coming to Miami. Butler hooks them up, saying the Moo Youngs are big importers, exporters. Says Dames and Ellis need large amounts of restaurant equipment, and they also need music equipment.

"They arrive in Miami. Mr. Dames arrives in Miami on October 15, which is a Wednesday. Thursday is the murder, October 16.

"What the evidence is going to show is that the defendant registers in a room at the DuPont Plaza, room 1215. Is he registered under the name of Krishna Maharaj? Of course not! He calls himself Eddie Dames. And it is him saying this to the people at the DuPont Plaza. You will hear those people testify.

"He says, 'Well, there is—I want a room—the penthouse suite upstairs, and it is going to be paid for in cash.' Mr. Butler comes in shortly afterward—the guy gives $110 in cash for the two days that they are going to be there. And Eddie Dames is registered at the room. As a matter of fact, Mr. Dames flies in on the fifteenth and doesn't stay in the room that night. Nobody stays there. So the base is set up, the plan is ready to roll." The prosecutor describes how Dames and his friend, Prince Ellis, are out all morning, spending hours at the Ace Music Studio, looking at equipment for Dames's disco back in Nassau. The prosecutor then returns to the crime scene and Maharaj's latest plot.

"Is this one going to fail like every other one that has failed? Tragically no. And that is the reason you folks are here, because Mr. Carberry is alive, because they couldn't set up the meeting with Mr. Carberry. But Derrick Moo Young is dead, and his son, who wasn't expected to be there, just went along with his dad that day. He is dead because he was with his father." We have come at last to the day of the crime.

"What happens on the sixteenth? Well, as planned, they all show up at the DuPont Plaza. Outside, early in the morning. Maharaj is waiting outside, and Neville Butler shows up. The maid cleans the room. And then they go up to the room, make a phone call to Mr. Moo Young, and confirm that the meeting is on.

"And Mr. Moo Young arrives, along with his son—who is unexpected, but it doesn't faze the defendant that somebody else came along, because as you will picture from all the other evidence, that has always been the game plan. If somebody else comes along, they have to die, too.

"So Butler calls the people up to the room. They come in the room expecting to meet Eddie Dames, the man who wants to import and export. Who do they find? They see him—the defendant. He comes out of the bathroom with a glove on his right hand and a nine-millimeter pistol in his right hand, and a pillow—which will be important also—in his left hand.

"He begins shooting at the victim, shooting at Derrick Moo Young. . . . First, he shoots him in the knee, right there in the room. In the kneecap. Shows him that he means business. You will see pictures of the room, and you will see that the room had been rearranged by the defendant. Fingerprint evidence will also tell you that. Pay very close attention to that, and you will see legal pads that were there for a confession, and you will see heating elements, which were used, and the heating cords—they were used—they were bought the morning of the sixteenth by the defendant at the hotel."

The prosecutor gets a little lost in his presentation at this point. Later he will explain what he means—there were two immersion heaters, short eighteen-inch cords with metal spirals on the end that could be dipped into water to boil it. They were quite common in the 1980s but went out of fashion when coffee makers took over and became standard issue in most hotel rooms.

"Neville Butler—Neville Butler knew they were going to use those two to tie them up. As a matter of fact, they were tied up at various points during the shooting. Well, instead of writing a confession, do you think that Mr. Moo Young bravely makes an attempt to save his own life? He charges the defendant, dives, and is mortally wounded by a hail of gunfire.

"You will hear evidence that he was shot six times in the chest and through his body. And you will hear the testimony by the medical examiner that he didn't die immediately. And that is important, because somehow he is able to crawl while the defendant is interrogating his son concerning monies, and getting a confession. He is able to crawl and throw himself out into the hallway.

"You will hear testimony that nobody in that entire hotel heard gunfire, and that was due to a few reasons. You will hear that the hotel was very sparsely populated on October 16. As a matter of fact, three rooms were occupied only, and during the time of the murder, nobody was there. Also, on the eleventh floor below, there was an entire reconstruction going on, remodeling. The normal noises, with hammers banging and moving furniture, that kind of stuff.

"There was no silencer used by the defendant. When he told Mr. Geddes about the possible attempt at the DuPont, Mr. Geddes asked, 'What about the gunfire? What are the people going to hear at the hotel?'

"The defendant says, 'Don't worry. This hotel is well built. The walls are soundproof.' And that shows you why he thought there would be no problem. As a matter of fact, he was right. He is right that nobody heard the gunfire. Nobody heard it. But the blood of Derrick Moo Young out in the hallway is the thing that alerted people that something was going on.

"You will hear testimony from the security people and the house people of the hotel, how they responded. I will get that to you through the testimony of the people there, what happened. Somebody saw the blood, and they brought somebody else up, and they noticed that the door had a pin out, which means that somebody double-locked the door from the inside, live people. Because the only way you can double-lock that room is to have somebody who is alive inside.

"They even have a conversation with the defendant, the security guard from the outside. And he asks if everything is okay in the room. And the defendant responds that everything is okay. They go back downstairs, leaving the door unlocked—excuse me, unguarded. For five minutes or so. And come back up and the pin is back out—excuse me, back in—which means that they have left. They open the door and discover the bodies. In that five-minute period of time, the defendant was able to flee along with Neville Butler.

"Also the people who walked up there did not see a 'do not disturb' sign initially on the door, a typical 'do not disturb' sign. When they came back the second time, it was there. Whose fingerprints were on the 'do not disturb' sign? Right there—the defendant. Whose blood was right next to the defendant's prints on the 'do not disturb' sign? The blood of Derrick Moo Young, trying to get away outside. The blood-spattered area. The scene is crucial."

The prosecutor has described what happened in room 1215. Now he will buttress the lay witnesses with experts, and explain the curious sequence of events leading up to the defendant's arrest.

"There is going to be an eyewitness, Neville Butler, who will tell you what happened in the room. But the physical evidence from the scene is also very important. You will hear testimony about that, as I told you, of the fingerprints in places that only the killer would have left them. Listen carefully to that testimony.

"Also, there will be a gun scientist's testimony, a ballistics expert, and there were nine-millimeter casings that were fired over projectiles, and only one gun was used, and the gun was never recovered. But if you listen closely to the testimony of the gun expert, as well as the other evidence in the case, he will say it was a nine-millimeter semiautomatic pistol. You will hear that the nine-millimeter pistol was sold to this defendant by another person, and you will see the person who sold it. You will hear the testimony of who he sold that gun to.

"As a matter of fact, you will hear testimony from a trooper who stopped the defendant for a minor traffic infraction back on July 25, 1986. What did that trooper find on the defendant? It wasn't important then, but for this trial, it is crucial that he found the nine-millimeter pistol, silver in color. The same gun that Neville Butler says, the same gun that matches the scientific evidence—the murder weapon.

"What else did the trooper find in the car? Camouflage equipment, Chinese throwing stars, crossbows, he found all these things.

"Well, the murder happens. What happens then? The defendant flees the room, leaves his fingerprints, his left-hand fingerprints— remember, the glove is on his right hand—in all the crucial places, some right-hand fingerprints and things when he first arrived in the room with a soda can, reading a newspaper. Fingerprints were there in more than ten places, ten places where fingerprints were found. But this is crucial about the left-hand fingerprints, remember that.

"He goes downstairs with Neville Butler, and they wait out in the car for three hours while medical emergency people are arriving. The bodies are found. The body of Derrick Moo Young is found—and his son Duane is taken out upstairs. Mr. Butler will tell you that the defendant couldn't leave any witnesses and took Duane upstairs and shot him right in the head, murdered him.

"The bodies are found, and they wait downstairs. Mr. Butler is telling the defendant that they are waiting there because they have to find out what Eddie Dames knows.

"What does Dames know? He is going to be coming back—he was told to leave by Neville Butler, he went to a music store, and he doesn't come back to the hotel until one o'clock. Eddies Dames is in the dark, and he was just used as the bait, but they have to wait for him.

"In waiting for him, the defendant admits to Butler the concerns that he has about the police officer who sold him the gun. You will hear from the lieutenant from the Miramar Police Department that he sold the defendant the gun, the nine-millimeter. The defendant is concerned about that and concerned about how to get rid of the gun. And he talks about throwing the gun in the river, that kind of stuff.

"Waiting for Eddie Dames, they miss him, and he gets in and asks for messages for his room. And you can imagine the number of police who grab him saying, 'What do you mean? Why are you asking for messages for your room, 1215?'

"He says, 'That is my room and I want to see if there are any messages.'

" 'Well, I have to talk to you at the police station.'

"On his way to the police station, Neville Butler sees him from the car. He gets out of the car and he goes and speaks to Eddie Dames. One thing leads to another, and Eddie Dames and Neville Butler get away from the defendant. The defendant has told Butler, 'From now on, we are going to stay together. You can trust me, and I am going to promise that I am going to take care of you. I am going to buy a car for you. We have to get our stories straight.'

"Butler gets away and flees from the defendant.

"The defendant in the next few hours—they are unaccounted for. But we do know from the actual records, from telephone records, that he found his way to the airport around five o'clock in the afternoon on October 16 and makes a certain number of calls. You will see that he was calling his newspaper. And as a matter of fact, Mr. Geddes will tell you that he was at the newspaper that afternoon, and he was asked by his boss to go to the airport immediately.

"Ms. Daphne Canty, a young lady who is Neville Butler's girlfriend— her sister, excuse me, his girlfriend's sister—she was there and said that there was some guy who kept calling. He wants Butler to meet him or talk to him, and Neville Butler gets this message around five or six o'clock. Then he picks up his girlfriend, he goes to the police.

"Neville Butler goes to the police that afternoon and tells the police what happened in the room. He says, 'By the way, this guy wants to meet—he wants me to meet him at the Denny's by the airport.' So Neville Butler goes to the Denny's and talks with Detective John Buhrmaster, who is the lead homicide investigator in this case, and they go in there. Well, at Denny's, Neville Butler sees the defendant and the defendant sees him, and Buhrmaster arrests the defendant.

"The defendant goes to the police station and agrees to talk to the police. You will hear that he has a conversation with the police. Sure, he wants to talk about his case. And what does he tell the police? He tells the police that never has he been inside the DuPont Plaza Hotel on October 16 and, what's more, in his life he has never been on the twelfth floor. Nobody said that he had ever been on the twelfth floor. Unfortunately, Detective Buhrmaster doesn't have the results of the fingerprints at that time and doesn't confront him with that evidence. He gets it a few days later.

"The defendant also says, 'I have never owned any handguns.' You are going to hear evidence that the handgun was sold to him by a police officer.

"Also, he says: 'By the way, I couldn't have done it, because I was with Tino Geddes at the Kenyon Press in Fort Lauderdale,' which is a printery for the paper. In the morning through lunchtime. The murder occurred around lunchtime. He said, 'I wasn't up there. I was at the printery with Tino Geddes.'

"Well, that is bunk. Tino Geddes never saw the defendant that day until six o'clock at the airport. Never saw him. Geddes will come in here and tell you that when he met him at the airport that night, he agreed that he would lie for him initially. And he did initially give a statement to the defense attorney in the case, like 'I was with him that morning.' As a matter of fact, Geddes will tell you that at the defendant's request he fabricated—actually fabricated—an alibi in manipulating innocent people to be mistaken and say they were with the defendant that morning. They actually did that. Well, Geddes isn't going to lie anymore. He is not going to lie for him, the defendant, anymore. He is going to come in here and tell you like it is, set the record straight."

The prosecutor's review of the crime has been succinct, given the number of characters and the sensational nature of the crime—a murder in a major Miami hotel. Now he concludes with a summary, revisiting all the highlights before his plea for justice.

"The fingerprints, the ballistics evidence, the trooper who stopped that man, the police officer who sold him the gun—overwhelming evidence. The motive is overwhelming. The State of Florida is asking you to do some thinking in this case. Please pay very close attention to the witnesses, observe their demeanors, assess for yourselves whether they are telling you the truth. I am going to ask you at the closing of the case to dispense justice, because justice cries out for conviction in this case, which is one of first-degree murder, in two counts. Brutal first-degree murder. The most coldly, mechanically planned type of first-degree murder. The blood of Derrick Moo Young and Duane Moo Young is still on his hands. I am going to ask you folks to do the right thing and listen to the evidence, do your duties. And I am confident that you will return a verdict that speaks the truth, that the defendant is guilty of two counts of first-degree murder, kidnapping, and terrorizing these two people before they died.

"Thank you for your time."[1]

With that, John Kastrenakes, the assistant state attorney, takes his seat beside his senior partner Paul Ridge, who is working with him on the case. The two men whisper briefly while Judge Howard Gross invites the defense attorney, Eric Hendon, to present his opening statement. Hendon is very brief. He merely asks the jurors to keep an open mind as they listen to the prosecution's case. He presents no alternative account of events and does nothing to undermine the prosecutor's depiction of his client's motive or character. He has every right to do this, of course. The burden of proof rests with the prosecution, and the defense is not required to present any evidence at all.

Over the next several days, the case proceeds with only minor turbulence along the way. The prosecution's presentation runs very close to the script promised in the opening comments, fleshed out in various details. Neville Butler is a key witness. He admits to lying and to claiming originally that he had been kidnapped by the defendant. He says he did this out of fear, as he thought he might himself be guilty of something. He then had pangs of conscience and came forward to the police and the prosecution to change certain details of his story. He remains true to the central theme of his story, however: that he saw Kris Maharaj kill Derrick and Duane Moo Young.

On the morning before the third day of evidence, midway through Neville Butler's testimony, Judge Gross does not appear on the bench. Chief Judge Klein does not tell the members of jury what has happened; he sends them home and tells them to come back at the start of the next week to continue the trial. Judge Gross is then replaced by Judge Harold Solomon. Eric Hendon is asked if he would like to declare a mistrial, but he urges the prosecution to continue; he says that he and his client want to proceed with the case.

When the trial resumes, Butler inadvertently adds a few details that contradict the prosecutor's account of events. He says that Eddie Dames knew the basic outlines of the plot to lure the Moo Youngs to the DuPont Plaza, and that Kris Maharaj briefly met Eddie Dames and Prince Ellis in the hotel lobby—but overall he corroborates the prosecution's story. An attentive defense attorney might have picked up on these variations and pressed to see why Dames's version of events was inconsistent—or why Neville Butler had so substantially changed his story. Hendon lets both points slide by unremarked.

Next up, Eslee Carberry testifies about the series of articles he published in the *Caribbean Echo*. The first one claimed that Maharaj had forged a $243,000 check to Derrick Moo Young. Derrick had supposedly sued him over it, and the story ran under the headline 'Alleged Fraud and Conversion Case Filed Against Maharaj.' In the second article, Kris's younger brothers, Ramesh and Robin, were accused together with Kris of being part of a scam described as 'irregular, illegal and possibly fraudulent.' The scam involved a complex operation whose aim was to get currency out of Trinidad and into the United States. At the time, the government of Trinidad set strict limits as to how much money one could take out of the country. This meant that rich people could spend only a limited amount of money when they went abroad. The article suggested that the Maharaj brothers' scheme enabled wealthy Trinidadians to purchase equipment in the United States and pay twice the asking price. Half of the money would go toward the actual machine, which would be shipped back to Trinidad and properly declared at customs; the other half would go into an offshore U.S. account that they could then use on their travels.

This story ran twice, once under the headline '$1.5 Million Shared by Three.' "Numerous persons," says Carberry, quoting to the jury from the article he had run in his paper, "including Carl Tull, a top Trinidad trade unionist, seem anxious to clarify many financial dealings involving Krishna Maharaj." What was that about? The jury is left to speculate.

Hendon does not object; he does nothing to cast doubt on the veracity of these claims.

The scandals escalate, and new ones emerge with every new edition of the *Echo*. Week upon week, Carberry publishes Derrick Moo Young's devastating and damaging pieces about Krishna Maharaj. Little wonder that the defendant should want revenge. Next there is a story about a threat to kill Carberry himself, made in a crowded restaurant. "I could have killed you a long time ago!" an unhinged Krishna Maharaj is said to have shouted. "I *will* kill you!"

Carberry tells the jury that he also ran a piece about Krishna Maharaj's criminal record in Britain. As he does with each story, he tells the jury in general terms what it is about and then reads from the article. "I did secure a comment from a Scotland Yard spokesperson," he says. And he quotes from the statement as it appeared in his article: "'While we need the man for questioning in connection with alleged criminal activities, it is far too costly for us to implement extradition proceedings so we will therefore bide our time.'" The jury is left to assume that Maharaj left London for Florida because he was wanted by the British authorities.

Eric Hendon, rotund in his dark polyester suit, sweats in the air conditioning. He makes a single desultory point on cross-examination: Carberry admits that perhaps Maharaj did not threaten to kill him— only to destroy his paper. But Hendon allows the other stories to stand. By now, the jury must have a dark picture of his client: a swindler and a liar wanted on two continents.

It gets worse when Tino Geddes takes the stand. Geddes had taken a job as a journalist with the *Caribbean Times*, the rival publication Maharaj set up to compete with the *Echo*. He testifies that his new boss told him that Derrick Moo Young was "not an honest person." Geddes soon gets to the meat of his testimony: Maharaj's elaborate plots for revenge. He tells the stories with relish. He says he was present when the defendant bought crossbows, two hunting knives, and camouflage gear. The first plot was aimed at Eslee Carberry. Geddes describes how he and his employer drove to West Palm Beach together to stake out Carberry while he was at the *Town Crier*, the publisher that printed the *Echo*.

"Maharaj said he would do Carberry damage on the lonely stretch of road that runs from Wellington down to Fort Lauderdale," Geddes testifies. "Maharaj told me that he was going . . . to blow away Mr. Carberry." Geddes says he saw a shotgun case in the car.

The two men got bored waiting for Carberry; they decided to take a break and get some food. When they returned, they found that Carberry had already gone home. The threat of violence bothered him, Geddes says, but he did not protest as he did not want to have to walk back to Fort Lauderdale.

Geddes then describes how a few days later his boss rented a Ryder truck from West Broward Boulevard "to get at" Derrick. The idea was that they would go to Griffin Road, near where both the Maharaj and Moo Young families lived, and Kris would run Derrick off the road. "It's the end of Griffin Road, where Griffin Road comes out to the expressway," he specifies, lending more credence to his testimony through this detail.

Later, the prosecution will call a man from Ryder to prove that the two men did indeed rent a truck. This plot failed, Geddes says, because Derrick did not show up.

The last plot is—as Kastrenakes promised—the most relevant to the trial at hand, a dry run of the murders that would take place on October 16. Geddes describes how his boss called him one day and told him to come alone to the DuPont Plaza Hotel. He is not sure about the date; it was "a couple" weeks before the Moo Youngs died.

Maharaj met him at the hotel bar beforehand and gave him a key. "Did he say anything?" the prosecutor asks, prodding his witness.

"No, he made no comment at all," Geddes says. But this sounds odd. "It was a limited conversation," he corrects himself.

Was there a witness? Yes, a bartender was there, but Geddes cannot describe him. "What I do know is that he was bilingual," he says.

When Geddes entered the hotel room, he found Kris there, wielding an automatic pistol with a light chrome finish. "He had a glove on one hand," Geddes says. "He asked me how would I feel to see two guys laid out in here."

Geddes remembers that the gun had no silencer. "He said the rooms were soundproofed and you couldn't hear an explosion from outside," Geddes says.

What if other people showed up? the prosecutor prompts again. Geddes explains that his boss told him he could take care of up to three himself. If there were more, Geddes would have to help him.

Now comes the crux of the story. Geddes was to call Derrick Moo Young and Eslee Carberry. "There is this man from Trinidad who has booked into this hotel wanting to see him," he should say. There were two rooms with a door between the adjoining suites, and Maharaj would come in from the second room once Derrick had arrived.

Geddes made four calls to Carberry and one to Derrick from the hotel room that day. He reached Derrick's wife, who said that Derrick was out of the state. So that plan failed as well.

Now that he has warmed up his witness, the prosecutor asks him to turn to the day of the crime and to focus, in particular, on the defendant's alibi. Geddes describes how, after the murder, his boss asked him to cobble together a story placing him elsewhere. This was easy to do, as the day before the murders—Wednesday, October 15, 1986—they had gone together to visit the *Times* printing press in Fort Lauderdale. It was simple enough to get everyone there to think that the meeting had taken place on the next day, Thursday. He tells the jury that later he felt guilty for covering up the crime, so he changed his story and told the state's attorneys that he had been lying to protect his boss.

During cross-examination, Hendon does not think of asking some obvious questions. Did the other "alibi" witnesses agree that the story was concocted? Who were they, and how could they all have independently misremembered the date? What proof did Geddes have to corroborate his fanciful stories of midnight ambushes? Where, precisely, were these homicidal attacks meant to take place? Geddes nonetheless volunteers some assistance unbidden. For one thing, he throws Carberry's credibility into question.

"Carberry uses his paper as a gossip column to lash out at anyone he isn't particularly fond of," Geddes says at one point. "Eslee Carberry has some sort of vendetta against Mr. Maharaj."

Hendon does raise one serious question. Originally, Geddes was going to testify to an alibi, proof that Kris Maharaj might be innocent. Is Geddes testifying now—and has he reversed his story—because of threats or promises made by the prosecution? Hendon reveals that Geddes received help back home in Jamaica, where he was caught smuggling ammunition into the country. This could have drawn a heavy sentence, since crime was out of control on the island and punishments were severe. Both prosecutors, Paul Ridge and John Kastrenakes, traveled to Jamaica to put in a good word for Geddes and to confirm that he had bought a gun legally in Florida. Geddes received the lightest possible sentence as a result.

Geddes is ready when Eric Hendon questions him on this point.

"I purchased that gun because I had become involved in these escapades that I have already described with Mr. Maharaj," he says. "And I was, in fact, fearful for my own safety, and this is why I purchased this firearm."

Hendon presses further—if Geddes changed his story once, what is to say he is now telling the truth?

"If I am lying to this jury," Geddes concludes dramatically, "I would pray to God He would punish me in the worst way possible. Everything I have said to this jury has been the truth."

Hendon, fatefully, lets him have the last word.

Perhaps Geddes is a bit over the top, but much of his story seems to be corroborated by the scientific evidence that a series of witnesses for the prosecution present next. First there is the matter of the murder weapon. Some months earlier, Krishna Maharaj bought a nine-millimeter Smith & Wesson pistol from a police officer. No murder weapon was ever found on Maharaj or at his house—perhaps, as Butler hypothesized, he threw it into one of Florida's many waterways.

The state ballistics expert, Thomas Quirk, testifies that the gun used to commit the crime was a nine-millimeter semiautomatic with six right-hand twists in the barrel. Quirk says he can narrow down the murder weapon to six types of guns—Browning, Leyte, Llama, Sig Sauer,

Smith & Wesson, or Star, all nine-millimeter pistols. He runs through the standard bullets fired from each of these and says that while he cannot be sure, he thinks a Smith & Wesson was the most likely of the six. The jury has already heard that Krishna Maharaj owned a Smith & Wesson gun. This is not conclusive, as there would be more than 270,000 Smith & Wessons at large in the United States, but why can't he account for the whereabouts of his gun?

Ivan Almeida, the prosecution fingerprint expert, testifies that twenty-one prints in the room were matched to Krishna Maharaj. As Kastrenakes promised, two left-hand prints were found on the "do not disturb" sign. The prosecutor made a big deal in his opening statement about the difference between the right- and left-hand prints found at the scene. This supposedly corroborates Neville Butler's story that Maharaj wore a glove on his right hand only. To be sure, there are left-hand prints on the bathroom door, the desk, the glass table, the telephone receiver, the top of the television, and the plastic wrappers that were taken off a cup and the heater cords. But there are right-hand prints on the soda can and a Miami newspaper. A right-palm print is also found on a copy of *USA Today*. And both left- and right-hand prints are on the outside of the door to the room.

Butler's prints are in the room as well, but Kastrenakes assures the jury that this is to be expected, as Butler admits to being there. Pressed by the prosecutor, the fingerprint expert testifies that there can be no question but that Krishna Maharaj was in the room also.

At this point, the prosecutor asks the lead homicide detective on the case, John Buhrmaster, to take the stand. Buhrmaster has dark hair and a narrow, smooth face and is roughly the same age as Kastrenakes. Policing is his life. He has risen through the ranks, married another law enforcement officer, and even raised his daughter to want to join the force. He is already well into the years required for retirement, but he has no plans to go. Life outside the Miami-Dade Police Department has little appeal for him. He arrested Krishna Maharaj at Denny's restaurant and began to question him at 1:23 in the morning.

"Did you have any discussion with the defendant concerning guns?" Kastrenakes asks.

"Yes, I did," replies the detective.

"What kind of conversation did you have with the defendant concerning his ownership of guns?"

"When I asked him if he owned any, he told me that the only guns that he owned were two shotguns and they were at his house now."

"Did you have any conversation with the defendant as to whether or not he owned any handguns?" Kastrenakes presses on, since this is not quite the answer he wants.

"Yes, sir, I asked him if he owned any handguns, and he indicated that no, he had never owned any."

The prosecutor then asks the homicide detective to tell the jury whether Maharaj admitted to being at the scene of the crime. Buhrmaster says that without prompting, the defendant denied ever being in room 1215 of the DuPont Plaza Hotel. He testifies that he had not even mentioned the room number to the defendant before then. While the detective has plenty more to say, these are the key points. With twenty-one of his fingerprints in the room, Krishna Maharaj is clearly lying.

Hendon sallies into a few areas in his cross-examination but does not make any headway. A Colombian businessman, Jaime Vallejo Mejia, was registered in room 1214, directly across the hall from the murders. Mejia claimed he was elsewhere in the building at the time of the murders. The lawyer asks what Buhrmaster did to corroborate this.

"He said he was on the sixth floor, and I believed him," the homicide detective says dismissively.

Hendon asks what this man Mejia's business consisted of.

"I don't recall," says Buhrmaster. He sees no relevance to Hendon's suggestion that he should have searched the man's room or taken his fingerprints. Hendon is made to look as if he is thrashing around in the water polo pool, trying to obscure the view of the goal.

As the other expert witnesses appear, Hendon is able to point out that Kastrenakes slightly overstated his case on the blood evidence. David Rhodes, a Metro-Dade County police officer working as a serologist, testifies that the blood on the "do not disturb" sign was insufficient to match to anyone. But this is a minor victory, as few could doubt that it belonged to Derrick Moo Young. There was no evidence that anyone else had bled anywhere near the sign.

Some holes in the story are filled in. Prince Ellis testifies that he and Eddie Dames had been out trying to purchase music equipment for their planned nightclub when the murder took place. Ellis had stayed in the DuPont Plaza on the night of the fifteenth, but he never went up to room 1215. On the day of the murders, he went down for breakfast early and then spent half an hour in the lobby talking with Eddie Dames and Neville Butler—between ten and ten-thirty. Butler talked to three or four other people, but nobody Ellis recognized.

Ellis and Dames went shopping for music equipment and returned to the hotel around two-thirty. When they asked for their keys at the front desk, the police swooped in and told Dames he would have to go with them to the station. At this point, the two men saw Butler standing on the sidewalk outside the hotel. Dames and Butler had a brief conversation, but Ellis was off to one side and did not hear what they were saying. Dames and Ellis went to the police station together. After they had given their statements, Butler picked them up and told them what had happened. They insisted that he should talk with Buhrmaster, but Butler said that he wanted to go home to change his clothes before meeting the detective.

A hotel employee, Arlene Rivero, is next to take the stand. She testifies that a person matching the description of Kris Maharaj booked room 1215 in Eddie Dames's name. She diverges slightly from the story Kastrenakes told in his opening statement—she says the man gave his name as "Derrick Jaghroo." She does not know how to spell the last name, but it is something like that.

She identifies a photograph of Krishna Maharaj as the person who booked the room. "I want to say positive," she says, rather oddly. "It looked familiar to me, so that is why I ID'd it."

Inez Vargas, a clerk at the hotel, backs her up, confirming that a man from India had booked the room.

José Aparicio, a security guard at the DuPont Plaza who was on duty on October 16, testifies that he knocked on the door of room 1215 after someone noticed blood seeping into the hall, and a voice said nothing was wrong.

"The voice was 'clear' English," he tells the jury. "Not American, not Black, not Latin."

Eric Hendon makes one of his few dramatic interventions here: Aparicio gave an earlier statement to Detective Buhrmaster, saying that he had actually heard a South American accent. But where does this lead? There are no South Americans involved. Hendon made passing mention of a man named Mejia who was staying across the hall, but the jury has heard nothing since. Perhaps this thread will be pursued as the case continues?

The prosecution rests its case. Its side of the story is now explained as fully as possible. There is the usual anticipation: what will the defense put forward to disprove the prosecution's case? The defendant is a successful businessman, so he has no need of a court-appointed attorney. Various lawyers vied for the job, like sharks churning up the water at feeding time. But Maharaj had not become wealthy by wasting money, and he had settled on Hendon because his offer was the most competitive. He had proposed a fixed fee of $20,000. That might sound like a lot of money, but it was well below market rates for a complex criminal case. Other lawyers had insisted on much more—twice Hendon's fee—and refused a cap. Hendon told Maharaj that he had defended half a dozen capital cases before and won them all. Kris Maharaj had every reason to believe his lawyer would present a full defense.

So what will Hendon do to dent the prosecutor's case? There are the alibi witnesses mentioned by Tino Geddes—will they come forward? The defendant himself has some explaining to do—will he testify first or last, for surely he must take the stand? This will be the highest drama of the case, as the prosecutors will try to attack him and tear his testimony apart. Then there are hints of other suspects: for starters, the Colombian, Jaime Vallejo Mejia. Hendon suggested on cross-examination that Butler was in league with Geddes in some way. How will he show this? And what of the scientific evidence? What experts will the defense present to call the ballistics proof into question, or to explain what really happened that morning in room 1215?

The jury is sent out of the room while the lawyers argue some legal issues. Eric Hendon makes much of his motion for a directed verdict. He insists that there is not enough evidence for a reasonable jury to convict Krishna Maharaj of capital murder. Judge Solomon dismisses this argument out of hand. The jury files back in, and the judge turns to Hendon and asks him to proceed.

"The defense rests," Hendon intones.

The defense rests? Without a single witness? Hendon will not try to rebut anything the prosecution said?

Ron Petrillo, the investigator hired by Hendon, was sitting next to Kris Maharaj at counsel table and later described the scene.

"Eric Hendon stands up to begin the defense portion of the trial," said Petrillo. "He simply says, 'The defense rests.' The prosecutors' jaws drop, their mouths fall open . . . I think they are going to fall off their chairs. Kris is holding my arm so tight I thought he was going to draw blood."[2]

There is a plummeting sense of anticlimax in the courtroom, made all the more pronounced because it is the end of the day. The jurors are sent home with instructions that they should bring suitcases packed the next morning. They may be out deliberating for several days, and during that time they will not be allowed to separate and will have to stay the nights in a local motel.

The next morning, a Wednesday, one year and five days after the murders, the lawyers make their closing arguments. The prosecution takes a line similar to its opening statement. The defense focuses on a cryptic definition of reasonable doubt. Hendon disparages Neville Butler's testimony as unworthy of belief. He speculates about Eslee Carberry's motives—what was the scandal-monger editor of the *Caribbean Echo* up to? He argues that Tino Geddes's story of assassination plots and trial runs at the DuPont Plaza is not credible. Hendon does not mention the word *alibi*—rather, he insists that the burden of proof rests with the prosecution, and that his client is not obliged to do anything. He is a cook without any ingredients.

Judge Solomon reads a lengthy recitation of the law, taking a little over an hour. Then comes the moment—at 10:23 a.m.—when the jury is sent out to consider its verdict.

As always, waiting on the jury is agony. What is the defendant meant to do, alone in the holding cell behind the courtroom? Marita, his wife, remains in the courtroom, not allowed to be near her husband. He has always been certain of an acquittal, but she cannot be so sure, despite her faith in him. Members of the Moo Young family are sitting in the audience, behind the prosecutors, and they are tense as well, waiting for justice for Derrick and Duane. Eric Hendon leafs nervously through the papers at his table and goes out to make some telephone calls. The prosecutors go back to their nearby office, as they can return within minutes of the judge's call. This waiting can go on for hours, for days.

But this time the jurors' discussion is brief. They barely have time to eat the sandwiches that are brought in for their lunch. They return at eight minutes past two with a verdict.

The twelve jurors and an alternate file back into the courtroom, taking up the same seats they have occupied throughout the trial. They do not look at anyone. Guessing the outcome is like reading tea leaves, but a quick verdict is rarely good news for the defense. It tends to take more time for twelve jurors to agree to acquit someone than it does to convict.

The tension rises as the verdict is passed to Judge Solomon, who looks at it impassively, conscious that every eye in the courtroom is on him. He then hands it to the clerk to be read out.

"As to count one, the murder of Derrick Moo Young. Guilty.

"As to count two, the murder of Duane Moo Young. Guilty.

"As to count three, the armed kidnapping of Derrick Moo Young. Guilty.

"As to count four, the armed kidnapping of Duane Moo Young. Guilty.

"As to count five, the unlawful possession of a firearm. Guilty."[3]

They are unanimous. Krishna Maharaj is guilty beyond a reasonable doubt on all charges.

The prosecution and defense teams had all stood for the verdict to be read, but Maharaj has now slumped down into his chair. He appears to have fainted.

2

The Sentence

Once it has presented its verdict, the jury in a capital trial is asked to make a recommendation as to whether the defendant will live or die. Technically, the jury's vote will not be binding on Judge Solomon, who will make the final decision. But the jury's decision is entitled to significant weight, and few elected judges in Florida will override a death sentence, reducing it to life.

This second, distinct trial follows shortly on the heels of the first. When the guilty verdict comes in, Judge Solomon gives the parties two weeks to prepare. Eric Hendon needs the extra time, as he had not expected this outcome. Over the course of those two weeks, the jurors are allowed to get on with their lives. Now they are back, seated in the jury box.

This time the prosecutors are very brief. They call only the pathologist, Charles Wetli, a doctor who conducted the autopsies on both Derrick and Duane. The prosecution wants the jury to consider what the victims went through as they were being killed. Wetli testifies that Derrick could have been conscious for a minute or two after being shot as many times as he was. With Duane, the doctor agrees that "execution style" was an apt description of that murder.

What will Eric Hendon do to save Krishna Maharaj's life? The defendant is a successful businessman. There must be someone who can speak as a character witness. Sometimes the penalty phase of the trial can last longer than the trial itself. But not so in this case. The presentation is short. Some impressive people are marshaled in to ask for mercy, but their pleas seem to cut both ways.

Mervyn Dymally, a U.S. congressman from California, comes to vouch for Krishna Maharaj's good character. He is never quite clear as to how he came to know the man on trial, so the jury is left with the sense that Maharaj must have been a campaign contributor—or maybe, since it is obvious that Dymally is originally from either Jamaica or Trinidad, it is simply a matter of ethnic loyalty. Dymally proffers the opinion that Maharaj is a trustworthy person. A judge and a surgeon, both from Trinidad, have also flown up at Maharaj's expense to describe how much they respect the man on trial. They tell a few anecdotes to attest to his generosity. Few people convicted in capital cases are in a position to muster such witnesses, as most penalty phase presentations focus on the unfortunate background of the person on trial, and the seeming inevitability of his descent into crime. For this very reason the jurors may hold Kris Maharaj's witnesses against him—unlike so many people, he has had every chance in life, and he has blown it.

Eric Hendon also calls Levi England, the attorney in the civil case Maharaj brought against the Moo Youngs, who testifies that Kris was on the point of winning his suit for the money the Moo Youngs had allegedly stolen—so why would he want to kill them? But the jurors have already made up their minds, beyond a reasonable doubt, that he did kill them. It is too little, too late. Why didn't England testify at the first phase of the trial, when it might have made a difference?

Next Krishna Maharaj finally takes the witness stand himself to insist on his innocence. In an emotional speech, with frequent digressions, he expresses his belief that he will ultimately be vindicated. He says he wants to set the record straight and explain his relationship with his old business partner. He tells the jury that he first met Derrick Moo Young in 1965 in London, though nothing came of their discussions at the time. Fifteen years later they went into business together and bought property in South Florida. Kris put up the money, and Derrick rented out the houses. Later Derrick started embezzling the funds. "But I say, praise God," Kris testifies, "what he took from me I could afford. It wasn't important; money was not that important to me, never has been."

None of the articles in Carberry's paper bothered him, he says. He certainly did not kill the Moo Youngs. "As true as Jesus Christ was cruci-fied on Friday, I had nothing to do with the murders," he swears. Then he turns to the jury to make his case.

"Ladies and gentlemen of the jury, I have been convicted, I know, for Derrick and Duane Moo Young's deaths. I had, as I said, absolutely nothing to do with it. I feel very badly that those people were killed, but I do not know anything about it. All my life I have been helping my fel-low man, regardless of the race, the color, creed, religion. That has been my life since I was nineteen. It's not how much money I give to charity, but in 1963 I donated ten thousand dollars to build a church in the east-ern region of Nigeria. I donated every year five thousand pounds to the Cox Fund, a program for famine relief.

"I will not go into the first part of the trial because it is not important now, but all along I believe that the police know in their hearts I have nothing to do with it. I am hoping that time will tell that I am innocent of these murders.

"When you spend three hundred and eighty-four days as I have spent in jail . . . every day I expected at the trial to be released and found not guilty. I was found guilty. I know I fainted. I apologize for fainting, but the reason I fainted was because I was shocked that I could have been found guilty, and I am hoping and praying that with the grace of God I'll be able to be vindicated as soon as possible.

"You know I'm in—" He hesitates, perhaps wondering where he should go with this. "In 1967 I donated thirty thousand dollars to the British Cameroons for polio. In 1968 I donated fifty thousand dollars to cancer research. I have donated, it's in black and white, I have donated several thousand dollars. Money has never been a goal. I helped Derrick Moo Young. I didn't hurt him, and I did not kill him, and the people who are responsible for it will eventually be brought to justice.

"I hope," he says, finally drawing to a close, croaking out a faint whisper as he almost loses his voice. "I can't help it."

Judge Solomon offers the defendant a glass of cold water. Maharaj has shown feeling, but he has rambled. Eric Hendon let him testify with-out guiding him, without once breaking in to ask him questions. He has described how he made and spent money. This is not necessarily something that will endear him to a South Florida jury.

"Any cross-examination?" the judge asks Kastrenakes.

"Yes," comes the slightly fevered reply. The prosecutor has been waiting for this moment for months. He expected to get the chance to question Maharaj at the first part of the trial, but the defendant did not take the stand. Now, at last, is his chance. "Take a minute, judge?"

"Thank you," says Krishna Maharaj. "I'm ready, sir."

"Since October 16 of 1986," Kastrenakes begins, "until November 6, 1987, I have wanted to ask you one question. One question."

"Yes, sir."

"What did you do with the murder weapon? That's the only question that's left, the only one. What did you do with it?"

"Well, I can answer your question, Mr.—" Maharaj seems to have forgotten the name of the man who is seeking his execution. "Ladies and gentlemen of the jury, Detective Buhrmaster, when he arrested me that night, told me that he had found the murder weapon, the gun. He said that the fingerprints . . . that the fingerprints of that gun would have been matched with mine. I have his identical words written on a yellow piece of paper I just handed to Mr. Hendon, when I was arrested. . . . But the jury was never told."

"Did you hear my question?" Kastrenakes asks impatiently. "What did you do with your Model 39 Smith and Wesson semiautomatic pistol? Where is it today?"

"Right. I told Detective Buhrmaster . . ." he begins, but Kastrenakes moves again as if to cut him off. The question has nothing to do with the policeman—where is the gun? Maharaj holds his hand up. "Are you going to let me answer your question, please, sir? I told Detective Buhrmaster that particular night I bought a gun from Detective Bernie Buzzo of the Miramar police station, Miramar police, and the last time I saw that gun was when it was—when I was stopped by the state trooper.

"Hold on!" Maharaj holds his hand up once more, as the prosecutor gets set to interrupt. "The state did not believe me. Mr. Hendon's private investigator spent thirty-two hours, sir, on the turnpike. We supplied, we supplied the state. . . we supplied you all, sir, with respect, the address and the name of the state trooper who stopped me. I told—"

"You are telling us that the trooper stole—"

"Counsel, counsel!" interrupts Judge Solomon.

"—that the trooper stole the murder weapon?"

"I never said that."

"Your Honor," intervenes Eric Hendon. "I am going to object. My client said nothing—"

"Hold it!" Judge Solomon is holding his hand up now. "Sustained. Sustained."

"I never said that." Krishna Maharaj continues anyway.

"Mr. Maharaj, don't answer it until I tell you to," Judge Solomon admonishes him. He turns back to the prosecutor. "The court does not believe at this time that we should go into matters that would have come out on cross-examination at trial. A decision has been made by this jury as to guilt or innocence."

Kastrenakes asks to be heard with the jury out of the room. He argues strenuously that since Krishna Maharaj has asserted his innocence, he should be allowed to cross-examine the defendant on all facets of the crime. Hendon says that they cannot retry the case, and yet it was his client who brought up the whole issue of his putative innocence, long after the jury decided he was guilty. The debate oscillates for several minutes, tempers flaring. For a while, Judge Solomon sticks to his ruling. Then he caves. Kastrenakes can ask the questions and even call Detective Buhrmaster to disagree with what Krishna Maharaj says.

Maharaj explains that the trooper who stopped him on the highway, a few months before the murder, supposedly put the gun back in the trunk of his rental car, but it was missing that evening. He says it was with twelve army and navy surplus jackets, six pairs of boots, twelve crossbows, and twelve cutlasses, or machetes. "And there was nothing like no Chinese throwing gear," he says. "I have forty-nine percent in a farm in Costa Rica that grows tropical plants. I went to get those machetes and so forth for the Costa Rican farm."

Now it is Kastrenakes's turn to object. He protests that the defendant is telling more of the story than the question called for. Judge Solomon overrules him, and Kastrenakes moves on to his next line of questioning. He runs through Maharaj's career and tries to get him to agree that he has been a good salesman. He could sell anything to anybody.

"October 16, 1986—you remember that day?"

"Yes, sir, I do."

"You told Detective Buhrmaster you were never in room 1215."

"I did not say that to Detective Buhrmaster," he corrects. "I said to Detective Buhrmaster that I was in room 1215 earlier on." Then, for the first time, he gives his version of events. He explains that Neville Butler had invited him to the hotel to meet with Eddie Dames, to discuss the potential for distributing his new paper, the *Caribbean Times*, in the Bahamas. Dames never showed up, so after an hour he left and went about his business.

"Was Detective Buhrmaster being truthful when he said to this jury that you told him on the night of the murder that you'd never been in 1215 that day?" the prosecutor asks incredulously.

"No." Maharaj is emphatic. If the defendant is telling the truth, this means that the lead homicide detective has committed perjury. In a capital trial, it is an offense that could carry many years in prison. "He was not being truthful when he said that because I told him I was there on Wednesday. . . . I told him I was there on Thursday," he corrected himself. "I am probably the only one in this court who told the truth from the very beginning to Detective Buhrmaster."

"All right," Judge Solomon interrupts. Perhaps he has a glimmer of sympathy for the defendant, seeing him dig his own grave even deeper. Or perhaps he feels this is going nowhere. He turns to Kastrenakes. "Go on to the next question."

"Nobody else in this case told the truth except for you?" The prosecutor cannot resist shaking the bone, despite the judge's order.

"I didn't say nobody else. I said probably one of the few who told the truth, sir."

"Go on to the next question," Judge Solomon says impatiently.

"Who else did not tell the truth in this case?" demands the prosecutor.

"Mr. Butler certainly didn't tell the truth," says the man on trial.

"Who else?"

"Mr. Butler, Mr. Geddes . . ."

"Mr. Carberry?"

"Mr. Carberry, well, I don't think he knows the difference. With all due respect to him."

"With all due respect to *him*." Kastrenakes's sarcasm is heavy.

The prosecutor confronts Maharaj directly. Where was he on the day of the murder, after he allegedly left the DuPont Plaza at ten that morning? The man on the witness stand enters into a long and rambling account of everything that happened that day, throwing in various things that he told Buhrmaster and that the detective ignored.

Finally, the judge interrupts him. "Counsel. Counsel for the state. I don't know how to bring an end to this. You are going to have to help me, state."

Judge Solomon sends the jury out and finally tells the prosecutor he can go no further.

Krishna Maharaj is not through talking. "I didn't finish the last question he asked me," he says.

The judge shakes his head. He has heard enough.

There is one other thing the defendant wants his lawyer to do: to offer into evidence the fact that he has taken a lie detector test and passed.

"Who passed the polygraph?" asks Judge Solomon, confused.

"Krishna Maharaj took a polygraph and passed," says Hendon. It is true. George Slattery, a highly respected local expert, administered the test. Maharaj insisted he was innocent, and Slattery found that he was telling the truth.

"And Mr. Butler took a polygraph and passed," throws in Paul Ridge, the other prosecutor on the case.

So what does this prove? That Butler is telling the truth as well? Recognizing that the tests are not accepted as reliable, Judge Solomon excludes any evidence about the polygraphs, so the jury will never know that the defendant has passed a polygraph test insisting on his innocence.

There is one additional surprise just before closing arguments, and before the case goes to the jury. Judge Solomon discloses that the mother of one of the jurors, Ms. Taylor, died in the middle of the trial. Nobody says anything. It seems rather unfair. It is impossible to tell how the shock of her mother's death might affect her judgment.

It is time for the prosecution to argue that Krishna Maharaj should die. John Kastrenakes begins the penalty phase; Paul Ridge will finish it. Ridge is the senior of the two lawyers. They have shared duties throughout the trial, but the closing argument often goes to the more experienced member of the team. Ridge does not have long to make the case for death; the judge allows each side only half an hour.

"May it please the court and counsel," he begins. "Today the defendant sits before you a murderer, a man who has killed two human beings. Yet he's had the opportunity to come before you and present evidence in mitigation on his part, evidence in mitigation to convince you that his life should be spared, that he should not be punished with the imposition of the death penalty for the deeds he has committed. You are about to go back in a few moments and make a decision. I would submit to you that under the law and under the facts of this case, this decision is not a tough one.

"We started out approximately a month ago in front of a different judge, in a different courtroom, but the one unifying thread throughout this trial has been you, the ladies and gentlemen of this jury, and it is now that the court is going to ask you to make a recommendation. You are the people who make this system work. You are the unifying thread, people from all walks of life, clerks, people from the military, pilots, Realtors, construction workers, manufacturers, living in different parts of Miami.

"Does this man deserve life for what he did, or does he deserve the death penalty? And that is a recommendation that you must make to this court. The court will remind you today, as it has already, that the final decision as to what punishment shall be imposed rests solely with the judge of this court. Remember, ladies and gentlemen, it is only a recommendation.

"You may say to yourself, 'If I vote that the defendant is guilty of first-degree murder, I may be responsible for placing a man in Florida's electric chair? That is not a matter to be taken lightly, but it is also not your responsibility. You are not putting the defendant in the electric chair. You did not put this defendant in the chair here in the courtroom either. The only person in this courtroom who put the defendant in the chair in which he now sits is the defendant himself. It was his actions, and his actions alone, that brought him to the chair in which he sits today.

"He was the one motivated by hatred, who lured Derrick Moo Young and his son to the DuPont Plaza on October 16. He was the one who took justice into his own hands on that day and decided he was going to be the prosecutor, he was going to be the jury, and he was going to be the judge.

"If you recommend the death sentence and the judge imposes it, it is not you, it is not the judge who is responsible. It is the defendant who is responsible. He will be sentenced to death only because he deserves to be, because he put himself there by not following the law. And you, the ladies and gentlemen of this community, and the judge, recommend and impose such a sentence because you are following the law.

"And I would submit to you that under the law in this particular case, and under the facts of this particular case, as much as you may not want to do it to another human being, the law and the facts compel the imposition of the death penalty.

"It is simply that clear.

"Even though you as jurors may not like the law, even though you may not believe that it should be the law, nevertheless you all stood up, you all raised your hands, you all took an oath to follow the law, and you must do that now, when you go back to deliberate on this case.

"You must recommend that the appropriate sentence be imposed. When you stop and you take a look at what has transpired in this courtroom over the past month, the facts that you have heard, the evidence that you have heard, and the law that you are about to hear, there can be only one recommendation as to what is the appropriate sentence under the law.

"You will hear that there are several mitigating factors that you are to weigh against the aggravating factors. You heard a congressman come all the way from California or Washington, D.C., to testify on this defendant's behalf. A politician who admittedly had received campaign contributions from the defendant came here and testified that the defendant, in his opinion, was truthful and honest.

"But you, the ladies and gentlemen of the jury, know better. You know the defendant is not truthful. You know he is not honest. You also know he is a violent person, because you convicted him.

"The only thing Congressman Dymally has demonstrated to you today is what a poor judge of character he is. There is a letter for your consideration that you can take back into the jury room and read, a letter from this defendant, asking this congressman to take official action with government agencies on behalf of this defendant, not only asking him, but if you read the letter he's telling the congressman, 'I want you to do this, I want you to do that.' He's not asking that congressman. He's telling a United States congressman, 'I want some things done, and I want you to do them for me.'

"You also heard from Levi England, the defendant's attorney in his civil matters against the Moo Youngs, a man employed by the defendant, a man who has been paid by the defendant, a man who is still paid by the defendant.

"Krishna Maharaj was candid enough to tell you in his testimony that money doesn't mean much to him. What did mean much to Krishna Maharaj was this hatred generated by the court battles, by the articles, and by Derrick Moo Young, and it was this hatred that compelled him, that drove him to lure Derrick to the DuPont Plaza.

"If you look at the testimony of the people you heard today, you look at all the advantages that Krishna Maharaj has had throughout his life, this is not a person who is deprived, who didn't have the benefit of a good education, who didn't have the benefit of growing up in a comfortable environment. This is a defendant who at every step along the way of his life has exercised free will. He's had money. He's had status. He's been a successful businessman.

"Look at the people who this defendant had come before you to testify in his behalf: a congressman—" Ridge lets the word hang. Not many capital defendants get to call elected officials as witnesses. "A congressman. A judge from Trinidad. A neurosurgeon. An attorney. This man has had the benefits of everything that society has to offer.

"And what does he do? He has no excuse. He has no excuse for what he's done. He is simply a man motivated by hatred for Derrick Moo Young.

"These mitigating factors should be considered in light of the aggravating factors in this case. You'll hear five of them.

"Number one, you can consider that the defendant has been convicted at the same time for other capital felonies, and also other violent crimes. In other words, what that means is that under the law, you as jurors can consider the number of murders that the defendant committed or the number of violent crimes. And I would submit to you that an individual who is committing other violent crimes—not one but two first-degree murders, within the space of minutes, certainly deserves special consideration, deserves a greater punishment.

"The great punishment in this case is the death penalty.

"Number two, you will also consider that the defendant committed the first-degree murder in the commission of a felony. The felony in this case, the felony that you have found by your vote, is kidnapping. So the law allows you to consider as an aggravating circumstance the fact that he was actually committing another felony when he killed Derrick and Duane Moo Young, a second aggravating factor.

"And I'd like you to focus when you go back, in addition to that, on three other ones, and these are as follows: Three, preventing a lawful arrest—the defendant prevented or attempted to prevent his own arrest. Four, that the homicide, the murder, was especially wicked, evil, atrocious, and cruel. And five, that in addition to that, the murder was cold, calculated, and premeditated.

"What is it about these murders that sets them apart? You know from the testimony of Mr. Geddes that the defendant had been planning the death of Derrick Moo Young for months. I'm not going to go into that. I'm sure you all remember that. The coldness, the calculating nature, the extended premeditation, certainly is deserving of the death penalty in this case. If you remember, Tino Geddes testified that the first time he was at the DuPont Plaza with the defendant, the defendant says to him, as he's holding his model thirty-nine in his right hand, with his glove on in his right hand, 'You know, Tino, do you have the guts to see two guys laid out?'

"Tino says, 'What do you mean?'

" 'You know, dead. Do you have the guts?'

"Elimination of witnesses to prevent his arrest. He's already thinking about that. Not on October 16, but way back several weeks and months before. He's already made up his mind that whoever comes with Derrick, whether it be his son, whether it be his daughters, whether it be his wife, is going to be eliminated as a witness in this case. And that's exactly what he did to Duane Moo Young in Suite 1215.

"This defendant had no compassion, no compassion whatsoever. Yet he's going to ask you for compassion. A man who to this day walks in front of you, and insults you, and tells you, as the members of this jury, that you have convicted an innocent man. The audacity of that individual! The sheer audacity of that individual! He's going to ask you for compassion. He showed no compassion to Derrick Moo Young, and Duane Moo Young, and he deserves none from you.

"He put that gun to the back of Derrick Moo Young, and he killed him. And then what did he do? He turned his attention to the surviving witness. A boy who had just seen his father murdered in front of him, helpless to do anything for him, helpless . . . and himself then executed.

"That's exactly what the defendant did in this case, executed him. He forced that boy to watch the murder and execution of his own father, and then he took him upstairs.

"What must have been going through Duane Moo Young's mind at that time we can only imagine. But I think you as the members of this jury certainly understand and know that Duane Moo Young knew he was going to die. If that is not wicked, if that is not atrocious, if that is not cruel, then nothing is.

"So when you go back to vote, when you go back to make your recommendation, think about that stairway, and Duane Moo Young's walk up that stairway, and being told to kneel down and put your hands behind your back, and seeing that gun put in his face.

"Because you know it was right in his face.

"Think about what he thought about. And how he felt. And whether you think that is wicked, atrocious and cruel; and whether that is deserving of the death penalty. When you vote in this case, think of a young man aware of his own death. He looked death right in the face, and he saw the trigger pulled.

"The type of man who would do that deserves but one sentence. I ask you to follow the law, ladies and gentlemen. Follow the law and recommend to this court that it impose the sentence of death for the murders of Derrick Moo Young and Duane Moo Young.

"Thank you."

With that, Paul Ridge walks slowly back over to his chair. Judge Solomon sends the jury out for ten minutes while Eric Hendon, the defense counsel, prepares for his own summation. Hendon is brief. He does not beg for compassion. He tells the jury that they are wrong, that Krishna Maharaj is innocent. He says that they have "disregarded" the evidence and "paid no attention" to the facts. That they need to give his client the chance to prove his innocence.

This is Maharaj's last chance, and Hendon does not present any evidence of innocence, save for his client's self-serving assertions and the opinion of a few prominent friends that he is an honest man. It's a risky strategy, telling the jury they are wrong. Telling them this with only a few whispers, mere hints of evidence that might have been but were never presented at trial.

Hendon resumes his seat.

Judge Solomon reads a few pages of jury instructions: incomprehensible even to most lawyers, numbing to any juror.

It is thirty-two minutes after five in the afternoon. The clerk of court records every detail. The jury is sent out to deliberate. In the courtroom, there is nothing for anyone to do. The slightest effort to show an interest in anything else seems to undervalue the importance of the moment. Yet as before, this deliberation could last for many hours, even days.

Again, Krishna Maharaj is not allowed to stay with his wife. He must go back to the holding cell, where he waits alone.

It is twenty minutes past six. There is an announcement.

"Got a question from the jury," Judge Solomon says. "As to the definition of the word *contemporaneously*. I couldn't find it in Black's Law Dictionary, but we have *contemporaneously* in Webster's Dictionary: 'originating, existing or happening during the same period of time.' "

"Fine," says Paul Ridge.

"Yes," says Eric Hendon.

"Acceptable," says John Kastrenakes.

Another twenty-seven minutes pass. It seems an age. Yet it seems nothing.

There is another announcement. The jurors have a verdict. Again it is fast. But the computation is not the same as at the first phase of the trial—quick does not necessarily mean bad for the defense. Sometimes with the death penalty, the jurors can decide quite quickly that they do not want to do it.

The jury files back into the courtroom. In most states it takes a unanimous verdict to impose a death sentence. Not so Florida. The vote can be split any number of ways. So there is no way to read the looks on the jurors' faces. Half could vote one way, half the other.

Again the tension rises as the verdict is passed to Judge Solomon.

"All right," says the judge. "I have the advisory sentence, as to Derrick Moo Young, the jury advises and recommends the court that it impose a sentence of life imprisonment on Krishna Maharaj without the possibility of parole for twenty-five years. [What counts as] the majority of the jury, by a vote of six to six. Mr. Udell has signed it. I'm going to date it today's date. Today is the fifth."

"The sixth, judge," intones the clerk.

"The sixth. As to the advisory sentence for the capital crime of first-degree murder as to Duane Moo Young, the majority of the jury by a vote of seven to five advise and recommend the court that it impose the death penalty upon Krishna Maharaj. Signed by Mr. Udell. Dated today.

"The defendant will be sentenced on November the twentieth at eleven o'clock in the morning. Take the defendant out of here please."

The judge turns back to the jurors. "I've got certificates of appreciation for everybody here. Please when you come out, one by one, take it from me and turn in your little red badge to Mr. Shapiro. We thank you again for your attendance and your being good American citizens."

The prosecutors turn to congratulate each other and shake hands. It has been a job well done.

Behind them, Marita Maharaj is crying.

The judge's official sentencing is delayed a few days. It comes nearly a month later, on December 1, 1986. Thanksgiving has passed, and it is the Christmas season. It is tropical outside the Miami courthouse, but inside the incongruous holly motifs abound.

It is time for Judge Solomon to pass a final sentence. He has options. He can accept the jury's verdict, or he can override it. He can impose a death sentence, rather than life, for the murder of Derrick Moo Young; or he can reduce the death sentence to life in the case of Duane. But there are judicial elections coming up, and Krishna Maharaj cannot expect any mercy here. It is going to be death for the murder of Duane Moo Young. And life for the murder of Derrick. Life each on counts three and four, the kidnapping charges, and fifteen years for the illegal use of a weapon.

Three life sentences and an additional fifteen years consecutive to the death sentence, whatever that is meant to mean. So Krishna Maharaj will have to spend several incarnations in the custody of the Florida Department of Corrections.

A capital case would not be complete without the reading of the dreadful words out loud: "It is further ordered," Judge Solomon intones, "that you, Krishna Maharaj, be taken by the proper authority to the Florida State Prison and there be kept under close confinement until the date of your execution.

"MAY GOD HAVE MERCY ON YOUR SOUL."

3

The Defendant

My first meeting with Kris Maharaj at the state penitentiary in Starke, Florida's maximum security prison, came in August 1994, when he had been facing execution for seven years. I have a British passport as well as being American, and I'd received a call from the British consulate in Atlanta asking me if there was anything I could do to help this fellow British citizen on death row in Florida. I was working on another case in Florida at the time, so I promised to look in on him the next time I was down that way. I've never been very good at saying no.

Before setting off, I did a quick check on the case. I discovered he had already lost his first appeal to the Florida Supreme Court. "We conclude that the evidence is sufficient to sustain the convictions of each of the convictions for which Maharaj was found guilty," the court opined. "We affirm the convictions and sentences, including the sentence of death for the murder of Duane Moo Young."[1] Reading the seventeen-page judgment, I did not see much to undermine their confidence. The justices devoted more than half of the opinion to a recitation of the crime: they cited the dual motive for the murder (the disputes with Derrick Moo Young, and the hostile exposés in Eslee Carberry's newspaper), the fact that his fingerprints were all over the room, Neville Butler's eyewitness testimony, and the expert testimony suggesting that a Smith & Wesson nine-millimeter gun exactly like the one he had owned had been used to kill the two men. The court noted in passing that Maharaj "did not present any witnesses in the guilt phase of the trial"—the use of the term *guilt* reflecting their view that there was little question as to who had committed the crime.

The Florida Supreme Court did not identify any serious legal issues that might call the conviction into question. There was something strange about the fact that the original trial judge had been taken off the case in the middle—I'd never heard of that happening before—but the justices underlined that Maharaj's lawyer had waived any claim on that score; he had agreed that the case should go forward. It was also odd that Maharaj had waited until the penalty phase to insist on his innocence. By then, the jury had found him guilty. Why had he not testified at the first stage of the trial?

"It is clear from the record that the initiator and perpetrator of the two murders was Krishna Maharaj," the court concluded. So far, I could see no concrete reason to question this verdict. But there would be little point in having an appeals process if trials invariably reached the correct result, so I determined to keep my mind open—at least ajar.

I was thirty-four years old and had been representing prisoners in capital cases in a small nonprofit in Atlanta for nine years. At eighteen, I'd turned down a place at Cambridge University to go to UNC Chapel Hill, to my parents' surprise and despair. I'd had the naïve idea that I could write the seminal book about the death penalty in America and everyone would see the light. Although I did eventually produce a manuscript while on a six-month externship in Georgia from college—I called it *Life on Death Row*—it wasn't going to win a Pulitzer (indeed, I didn't even try to publish it). By then I'd realized that I had very little experience, and even less credibility. I figured I'd better begin by getting a law degree, so I went to Columbia Law School before returning to Atlanta to work with the Southern Center for Human Rights from 1984 to 1993. Then I moved to New Orleans to set up a new charity of my own, focused on capital trials. I still had a lot to learn, but my inexperience was outweighed by the confidence of youth. I'd already been involved in several dozen cases. So far I'd lost three prisoners to the executioner—two in Mississippi's gas chamber, one to Georgia's electric chair—but the vast majority of my clients had survived, either because of, or in spite of, my efforts.

Over the years, I've won about half of what are called "direct" appeals, the initial review that goes straight from the trial court to the state supreme court. If all goes well, you secure a new trial; failing that, you get a new sentencing hearing. That first appeal is by far the best chance you have of reversing the verdict. A procession of courts follows, but the prospect of relief is ever more distant.

Kris Maharaj had already lost his direct appeal and petitioned the U.S. Supreme Court. The chances of prevailing there are roughly one in a thousand, and his application had been turned down without comment. Then the case had moved into the state habeas corpus proceedings. This often goes before the same judge who imposed the death sentence in the first place, or one of his close colleagues, and success is rare. At the time, I had never won any case at that stage. The odds would get a little better when we reached federal district court, but in the real-life game of hangman, by the time you get to federal court, the gallows are drawn, the prisoner's torso is dangling, and the final body parts are being drawn in.

The small town of Starke is a succession of fast-food signs not far from the Georgia border, southwest of Jacksonville. I stayed the night in one of the cheap motels and then made the short drive to the Florida State Prison. Along the side of the road, the dry, sandy soil supported little but pine trees. Set back among the trees was an occasional one-story wooden house with a mandatory pickup truck in the driveway and a yard strewn with pinecones.

At the sign announcing the prison, the woodland cleared into a large open space, with a visitor parking lot to the right and, to the left, more vehicles in front of the imposing prison facade.

I made my way past the usual identification inspection and metal detectors and was led to the death row "family visitation room" to await my new prospective client. Kris Maharaj shuffled in with a chain between his ankles. I was struck by how much older he appeared than his age on file, fifty-five. Pictures from the trial portrayed him as stocky, with a thick wave of dark black hair. Now what little hair remained was gray. He was still fairly thick around the waist, but his dark skin seemed pallid, as if someone had dusted him with talcum powder. He was in a prison jumpsuit. He greeted me and then sat down awkwardly across the table, the shackles hampering his movement.[2]

Generally, when I meet a prisoner for the first time, I never ask him whether he committed the crime. He does not know me and has no reason to trust me—his opening gambit in our relationship is not likely to be an admission of murder. Most prisoners want you to like them: they are human beings, after all. So if you ask them straight up whether they "did it," they will doubtless lie if they did. And later on, when you have established a rapport and really need to know what happened, they will be loath to admit that your relationship began with a falsehood. So I find it best to steer clear of such topics on a first date.

I asked Kris Maharaj how he was being treated in prison. He told me the monotony was really getting to him. It didn't take much prodding for him to describe his daily routine on death row. He spoke dispassionately, with the precision of a scientist reporting on an experiment.

"Around five a.m. I awaken, brush my teeth, use the toilet, have a sink bath, then make a cup of instant coffee and wait for breakfast," he began. His accent was English, but he retained a Trinidadian lilt. "At six, a guard passes breakfast through the feeding hole on a plastic tray. It is something like scrambled eggs, grits, two slices of bread, two slabs butter, two packets jelly, and half a pint of milk. The eggs are made from powder," he added quickly, lest I should think it sounded wholesome.

"At seven, I take my medications." The good health he carried into prison had given way to diabetes, high blood pressure, high cholesterol, and the residual daily pain from a broken arm. He described how he had slipped one day on return from the shower; the metal shackles had prevented him from breaking the fall. He immediately knew his arm was broken, but prison administrators refused to believe him for days. When he finally got to the hospital, his arm was going gangrenous. The civilian doctor who saw him told him if his visit had been delayed any longer, he would have lost it. His eyes softened briefly as he recalled her kindness.

"She saved my life," he said without elaboration.

"After my medications, I listen to the news and kneel down to say my prayers. At seven-thirty, I start walking up and down my cell, from the back wall to the bars at the front. Some days are faster than others, according to the level of pain in my spine, which I also injured falling in the shower. At ten, after walking, I do thirty minutes of leg raises, lying on my back on the bed—to try and keep the strength in my right leg.

"At ten-thirty, I take a sink bath and clean the cell." He could not take a shower when he needed to, he said, so he would swab himself down at the stainless-steel toilet-sink combination in the corner of the cell.

"I read until lunch. Lunch is served at midday, on a plastic tray. It's something like shredded cold turkey, baked beans, two slices of bread, and fruit cocktail. I eat lunch and listen to the news on the radio. At one, I start walking for two hours. At three-thirty, I have a sink bath—it's extremely hot in the cell," he explained, "over one hundred degrees." The Department of Corrections is eager for taxpayers to know that prisoners on death row are not benefiting from air conditioning.[3] "At five, dinner is served on a plastic tray. Normally something like hamburger casserole, green beans, squash, two slices of bread, canned pear slices." Kris said he was only given a spoon to eat. A knife or fork—even a plastic one—could be used as a weapon.

"I am reliably informed that the cost of all three meals per day per prisoner is less than a dollar fifty," he said matter of factly. Then bitterness crept in. "Our animals in England are fed better.

"At six, I listen to the local news, then the world news. At seven, if it is shower day, I get a shower; I am allowed three a week. I am handcuffed and taken for an eight-minute shower by two guards, and then handcuffed and brought back to my cell. At seven-thirty, I read any mail I've received and write some letters. At ten-thirty, the guards come to collect the letters I've written. At eleven, I brush my teeth, say my prayers, and go to bed.

"The only time I leave this cell is either for a shower on shower days, to see the doctor, to see my attorneys whenever they call, or to see my wife on her regular visits. With these exceptions, I am in this cell twenty-four hours a day, seven days a week."

I asked him why he didn't go outside for "recreation." It's not much, a few hours a week in a small courtyard, but Kris would have none of it. For one thing, it was even hotter outside, he said, with no shade from the Florida sun. But more significant was his fear. Kris Maharaj was the first prisoner I had ever met on death row who was afraid of those around him. He was worried that someone would pull out a homemade shank and stab him, so he never went out to "the yard," as it is called—a small paved square fenced in with wire. I pressed him: no, nothing had ever happened to justify his concerns. It was simply the media-induced paranoia that he had carried with him into prison.

It was not long before he asked me whether I would agree to help with his case. By now, the former millionaire had no money, so he could not actually pay anything. But he was desperate for help. As I never take on cases of people who can afford to pay, this was hardly relevant. I knew myself well enough to know that I'd never be able to say no. So I said yes, I'd take on his case.

This gave me an opening to ask him about himself. I urged him to tell me more about his life before the crime.

Kris Maharaj was born in 1939 just south of Port-of-Spain, before Trinidad gained independence—hence his British nationality and passport. His family was middle class by local standards. He fought with his father and at twenty-one left home to seek his fortune in Britain. He arrived in London in 1960, with no family or friends to help him find his way. His first job was driving a truck, but he always wanted to be in business, and it wasn't long before he persuaded his bank manager to lend him £1,500. He began by exporting beef to Nigeria and soon found his niche importing exotic fruits from the Caribbean and Africa. Even bananas were exotic back then. He was one of the first to bring mangoes and plantains into England.

"All my life, money has never been important to me," he told me on that first visit. "Whenever I needed, God gave me ten times more than I could have spent and a hundred times more than I deserved." He said it was the battle that is business that motivated him. One of the few moments when his eyes lit up was when I asked him to tell me how he'd made his first million. Wheeling and dealing could be ugly. His competitors had planned to call a strike to prevent his fruit from leaving Africa. A friendly docker warned him about the plot. Kris decided to turn the strike against his rivals and paid the dock men extra to put his fruit on board first, then refuse to load anyone else's. His bananas and plantains reached Liverpool days before anyone else's, and he was paid top price for his cargo.

His flamboyance grew along with his bank account. By the mid-1960s he was in a position to buy his first Rolls-Royce with cash. He went on to own twenty-four in succession, never fewer than four at any one time. He personalized the registration plate on one Corniche—KNM1, for Krishna Nanan Maharaj—and it caught the eye of an Arab sheikh who had the same initials.

"Name your price," the man said.

Kris politely told him that money was not the object.

He started dabbling in racehorses in the late 1960s, when his accountant told him it would save him in taxes, and rapidly came to love the racing world. By the mid-1970s he was the second-biggest racehorse owner in Britain after the queen mother, with more than one hundred thoroughbreds to his name. He was only thirty-five when one of his horses, King Levenstall, beat the queen's at Royal Ascot. It was the Queen Alexandra Stakes in 1974, one of the longest endurance tests of the year, traditionally the final race of the June meeting. Nearly twenty years later, he could not conceal his pride as he told the story.

While he frittered away money on horses and cars, he lived in a modest home not far from his company warehouses in Peckham, in south London. One night at a party in Oxford he met a young Portuguese woman, working for Banco de Brazil, named Marita Sabino. Five months after they met, they were married. Marita's father and uncle had been senior government officials in Portugal before the coup that overthrew the military dictatorship in 1974. She was beautiful, probably the best-dressed banker of her day, able to converse in multiple languages, and was very much in love with her husband.

By now, Kris was wealthy and his life was sometimes complicated. Powerful interests were unhappy that an upstart from Trinidad was eating into their market share. Britain's largest banana importers—Fyffes Group, Geest Industries, and Jamaica Producers—were eager to squeeze him out and muttered in their London clubs that they should clip his wings. A word to the British authorities, and in November 1982 his company, Chris International, was denied a license to bring in the fruit he needed if he were to expand. He would not give in and took the government to court to challenge the state-sanctioned monopoly. Kris loved to tell his tale of battling the British government. The big three were granted 90 percent of import licenses, while 120 smaller businesses had to divide up the remaining 10 percent.

When they met to try to resolve the issue, Lord Cockfield, minister for imports, sneered at his temerity. "It's Co-field!" he exclaimed haughtily, correcting the pronunciation of his name. "And you can't win against the British government."

The interests of the major corporations were represented by ranks of pin-striped government lawyers. The case dragged on, costing £180,000 in legal fees, an enormous sum at the time. The interference with his business, and the litigation itself, put Kris under a huge financial strain, but on March 4, 1983, in what had come to be called the Green Bananas Trade Battle, Justice Hodgson ruled that Lord Cockfield had violated the law in denying Chris International Foods, of Kings Grove, Peckham, a license.[4]

"Cock-field," Kris said with a smile, mocking the disappointed minister, "why don't you appeal it?"

"This is a victory for the small importer," he told the *Daily Telegraph*.[5] His import quota rose more than one-hundredfold, from 220 tons a year to 26,000.

When he finished telling me this story, Kris turned to another victory, this time over the Nigerian government, in the London courts. "It may not be perfect," he said in speaking of the British system of justice, "but it's the best in the world." The high opinion he had developed for the judicial process may have contributed to his downfall in the United States, where he trusted the court implicitly to reach the correct judgment, however seemingly strong the evidence against him.

The 1970s were a difficult time for most people in Britain. Inflation ran at over 10 percent for the entire decade, peaking at 24 percent in 1975. The three-day week was a lot of fun for those of us still in school, but businesses suffered. Kris had won his legal battle with the fruit importers, but the war continued, and he was severely outgunned. Britain joined the European Community in 1973 and voted to remain a member in a contentious referendum in 1975. Europe promised new regulations that would favor small businesses, but it would be some years before these were in place. Kris decided to wait before expanding any further. He thought he would invest in property in Florida, which was a magnet for British tourism and business.[6]

When he started looking into investment opportunities, he was contacted by a Jamaican he had met some years before, who was now living in Florida. Derrick Moo Young had visited England in the 1960s, and the two men had briefly discussed doing business together then. Kris had been importing foods into Britain and, perhaps, Derrick had suggested, he would need some help with fruit from the Caribbean? But Kris had been happy with his contacts in West Africa and had declined the offer. Now Derrick proposed to act as his manager in Florida. Kris would buy property and rent it out; Derrick would ensure that the rent was collected and would generally tend to the buildings. It seemed a good match, as Kris planned to be in England for much of the year. In 1985 he set up a business, KDM International, taking the first initial of his name, Derrick's, and Marita's. Derrick would be his business partner, and both men would have access to the company's bank accounts.

Kris and Marita liked what they saw in Florida. For a couple from Trinidad and Portugal, the climate was a pleasant change from London. The same year they bought a large house in a suburb of Fort Lauderdale, on South West 193rd Lane. Derrick had recommended the place; his family lived just across the same street. Kris and Marita settled in for an interlude in the sunshine, while waiting for new European rules to make business easier back in London. But the relationship with Derrick rapidly ran afoul.

We were getting close to the time of the crime, and I did not want to get into that until I had had a chance to go through his whole file. So I cut him off and suggested we talk a little about legal strategy. I outlined the options available to him and explained where we could go next, and how we might get back in for a hearing in the state trial court.

"I didn't do it," he said, interrupting me and looking at me straight in the eye. "You know that, I suppose."

"I understand," I said noncommittally. "So who did, do you reckon?"

"I don't know," he said. "I wasn't there."

After that one meeting, I already had an advantage over most people involved in Kris Maharaj's trial—the prosecutors, the judge, and the jury. I had met Kris and spent time with him. I could listen to him and ask him anything I wanted. So I could assess whether I believed him. On the face of it, the evidence presented at trial had been compelling. Nonetheless, he said he didn't do it, and whatever I thought, I knew I had to approach the case as if he were innocent. If not, there wasn't much point in agreeing to represent him.

The stereotype that every guilty prisoner insists on his innocence is just not true. A guilty prisoner may not mention the crime at all, or he may say something ambiguous. But I can think of only one occasion when someone insisted he was innocent on a first meeting—despite my efforts to avoid the subject—and I later came to think he almost certainly did commit the crime.[7] So Kris Maharaj's insistence concerned me.

I don't actually like representing people who are innocent. It's partly the pressure; if you screw up and send someone to death row who had nothing to do with the crime, that is as bad as it gets. But I have also convinced myself over the years that often the *why* is more interesting than the *whether*: it is easy to condemn the terrible acts of others but much harder to understand them.

Innocent defendants are often useless as clients. It's not just that they don't know who did it; they are also (reasonably enough) impatient and generally don't allow the time for a proper investigation. Indeed, the first unwritten rule of criminal law is that an innocent defendant is predisposed to being convicted. Most of us have a rather touching faith in the justice system, perhaps because it's so positively advertised in endless television programs: despite a few bad apples who threaten to derail the process, by the end of every show justice of some kind is generally served. If he is anything like the rest of us, the innocent defendant is likely to believe that the system works, and he will have little doubt that he will be acquitted. That's understandable—he is 100 percent certain he did not commit the crime, so why would he believe that any sensible person, let alone twelve of them, could be convinced, beyond a reasonable doubt, that he did?

If he is paying for his defense—as Kris did in the early days, before his legal bills bankrupted him—he is likely not to want to spend too much on a defense attorney, as he will consider it a waste of money. No matter how intelligent he may be, he is likely to see little need for an investigation because the ultimate fact is so clear—he did not do it. When asked to pay large sums for defense experts to refute evidence presented by the prosecution, he is likely to demur.

If he has no money—and this is much more likely in a world where "capital punishment" generally means that those without the capital get the punishment—he will have a court-appointed lawyer. Though the public defender will not be spending his money, the prisoner will not press for public funds to prove that which seems so obvious: it would only delay the trial and his eventual release.

Occasionally, the innocent defendant can provide his lawyer with critical evidence. He may have an alibi. But a provable alibi has various preconditions: the time of the crime must be precisely known (often it is not), and the defendant must know where he was and have been with someone he can identify who can vouch for him. By the time of the arrest, the time in question may be days or weeks away. How many of us could prove their whereabouts for a complete twenty-four-hour period yesterday, let alone last month?

Some defense lawyers share the common prejudice that an alibi is dangerous.[8] In theory, the alibi only needs to raise a doubt of guilt in the minds of the jury, but the moment the defendant pits his version of where he was against the prosecution's, the jury has a tendency to pin him to the same burden of proof. In other words, they may expect the defendant to prove his innocent whereabouts beyond a reasonable doubt, and if he cannot do so, they will conclude he's likely guilty.

Strong alibis are vanishingly rare in contested trials. If the defendant has a solid alibi, the case is not likely to go to trial.[9] But we all spend a lot of time alone or in a crowd of strangers. That doesn't make us murderers.

This brings us back to one of the fundamental problems that the innocent person faces: he is generally of little assistance to his lawyer, since he does not know what took place and cannot prove what did not happen.[10]

"So who did it?" you ask.

"I don't know," he answers. "I wasn't there." Exactly what Kris Maharaj told me.

As I walked down the prison corridors after that first visit, I asked myself why an astute businessman would do so little to marshal his defense when he found himself charged with capital murder. Was it because he did not see the need for a strong defense? When he was convicted, he fainted. Was this a guilty person turning amateur thespian, or genuine shock?

I had not paid much attention to the prison guards as I came in. But as a sequence of chaperones escorted me back to the front gate, I engaged them on the subject of my new client. These were hardened men who had watched the electric chair in action many times and invariably came away feeling justice had been done. But they clearly thought something was amiss in the case of Kris Maharaj.

I spoke to James Guthrie, a sergeant on duty that day—I would encounter him several times on subsequent visits. He told me that he had been in corrections since 1977. His father was a policeman, and he had been around law enforcement his entire life.[11] "I've always believed in the death penalty," he confided. "There are certain things that shouldn't be done—there are some crimes committed in ways that are so different from the way ordinary people think."

He told me that between 1978 and 1992, he had had something to do with every execution in Florida. Later, I looked up the department Web site to see what this meant:[12] by his account, he had been involved in the deaths of twenty-nine men, including that of David Raulerson, who I had briefly helped represent, and Jesse Tafaro, whose mother used to ride up with Marita Maharaj from Fort Lauderdale for visits. "Some of the time I was working in the clothing room, we'd measure the death row prisoners for their uniforms before execution," he said. "I actually witnessed two executions by electric chair. I reckon everyone who's been executed since then has been in the category of person I'd consider appropriate to execute."

Sergeant Guthrie said he had been struck by Kris Maharaj the first time he met him. "I opened the cell door, Kris stepped out immediately and across the hall as the rules require, and he said, 'Thank you.' It was such an unusual thing for a prisoner to do. I asked other members of staff about him, and I heard that it was just his way."

He veered into a long digression on how different Kris was from other prisoners, explaining how good his hygiene was, how he kept his cell clean and tidy, how he didn't let the misbehavior of his neighbors rub off on him. "Other than being behind bars, I don't think he behaves any different than he would if he was outside," he said.

"There's been only one time I've ever had to have words with Kris," he continued. "It was when I'd just started running the Visiting Park. Visitors are allowed a kiss and a hug on entry and again on leaving. His wife Marita was here, and one day he tried to have two kisses on leaving. I took it up with Kris. He apologized and said it would not happen again. He was polite and respectful on this occasion."

Normally, prison staff are reticent when it comes to discussing prisoners. They are warned not to get too close to the people in their custody, and in most instances they don't have to be told twice. The last thing they want is a subpoena from a criminal defense lawyer forcing them to come to testify. But every guard I ran into had a kind word for Kris. I'd never experienced anything like it.

It didn't seem to fit with the kind of man who would commit two murders in cold blood. To be sure, I could be wrong: Kris Maharaj might have hidden his true character from me during one brief legal visit. But he would have found it much harder to fool these guards for seven years. I left the prison grounds worried that I might have just got myself into a terrible mess.

4

The Witness

I drove straight down to Miami to see Ben Kuehne, a criminal defense lawyer whom Kris had recently retained for his next appeal. I'd checked him out with some lawyers I already knew in the area, and even in 1994 he was well respected by members of the Miami bar. Most of his clients were wealthy, accused of white-collar or drug crimes, but periodically he felt a moral obligation to help someone who could not pay his expensive fees. He had agreed to work on Kris's case for a greatly reduced rate, but even this had taken the last of money the former millionaire had in the bank.

Ben's office was right downtown. My first challenge was to find a parking space that would come in under twenty dollars. I parked the Dodge Neon I'd picked up on a cheap weekly deal, then found his office—on the thirty-fifth floor of a high-rise, with a spectacular view of the Miami harbor area. Thick blue carpet muffled the sound, and the receptionist spoke quietly into the phone when I gave her my name.

Ben was a few years older than me, dressed in a dapper blue suit, with a bow tie and horn-rimmed glasses. He was very well connected in Florida and quickly impressed me.[1] He had little experience in capital cases, he said, but he welcomed me warmly—the sign of a good lawyer who is not threatened by someone else offering help. Capital litigation was my area, so I thought we would make a good team. He let me have a copy of the trial transcript, along with all the pretrial statements and depositions. There were twenty-one volumes in all, each one bound in brown cardboard. I loaded them into my rental car for the long drive home to New Orleans.

As I settled into the tedium of I-95, I have to confess I was a little annoyed. I had just signed myself up for an enormous amount of work at a
time when I could ill afford it. After nine years working on civil rights
and death penalty cases at the Southern Center for Human Rights in Atlanta, I had recently relocated to New Orleans. I'd always wanted to live
there—I loved the spirit of the city, as well as its architecture. But the
move was a huge upheaval. David Utter, a colleague from the Southern
Center, had moved to the Big Easy a few months before me to follow his
wife, who was about to start law school at Tulane. When he'd suggested
that we set up a new nonprofit law center there, it seemed like a good
idea. We hashed around plans and decided we would establish Louisiana's first full-time capital trial office. There were, at that time, very few
lawyers devoted to defending people facing capital punishment, particularly in the South. From Texas to Georgia, there was no law firm dedicated to providing a top-level trial defense for people who could not
afford to pay. If you were rich and lived in California or New York, you
could expect a Perry Mason–style defense or better. If you were poor
and on trial for your life in Louisiana, your lot was very different. So David and I had set about launching the Louisiana Crisis Assistance Center, which we quickly took to calling LCAC, to try to fill the breach.

I had already done a couple of capital cases in Louisiana, and I'd
made some friends there. One, Tom Lorenzi, was head of the indigent
defender board in Lake Charles, on the Texas border. Tom was enthusi-
astic about our plan and drowning in work. He suggested that his
office contract out three cases with us—that would help solve their crisis
and would give us enough in the bank to tide us over for the first few
months. His offer came at a steep price: one of the Lake Charles cases
promised to be the most complex trial I'd ever faced. Despite this, somehow I had just allowed myself to be roped into a new capital appeal in
Miami, 862 miles away. The uncle of one of my Louisiana clients had recently given me a radar detector, but it was still twelve hours each way
on a good run.

Ah well, I thought, when I made it home: I'd better dive in and get
ahead of the game before other crises piled up in Louisiana. I flipped to
the back page of the transcript, ready to depress myself: 4,550 pages. It

was Saturday morning, and I'd much rather have been working on my garden, but I settled down on the back porch to read through the case.

It didn't take me long to realize that Neville Butler was the key to the case. Butler was a jobbing journalist with the *Caribbean Echo* who had just started part time with the *Caribbean Times*. He was the "eyewitness" to the crimes for which Kris Maharaj had been sent to death row. If Butler was telling the truth, then Kris was in room 1215 of the DuPont Plaza Hotel at noon on October 16, 1986, killing Derrick and Duane Moo Young. No doubt about it. Butler had told the jury that he had watched as his boss had killed the two men.

I ruffled through the binders until I found Butler's original statement to Detective Buhrmaster, given on the night of the crime. According to his original story, Butler had scheduled a business meeting with Derrick Moo Young at the DuPont Plaza, in a room he had rented for Eddie Dames. To his great surprise, and wholly unheralded, Kris Maharaj had appeared right when the meeting was supposed to take place. Derrick was not yet there, and Kris sat down for a chat. A few minutes later Derrick and his son Duane called from the hotel lobby. Butler vaguely noticed that Kris stepped into the bathroom as they came in the door. Once they were in the suite, Kris emerged with a gun, which he pointed variously at all three of them. He was demanding large sums of money from Derrick, and he handed Butler two immersion heaters (I remembered them from my college dorm at UNC, a length of electric cord with a heating element for boiling water for tea or coffee). He ordered Butler to tie up Derrick and Duane. Butler complied, fearing for his life, but left the knots very loose. An argument ensued, which ended when Kris shot Derrick once in the knee and then, when Derrick lunged at him, several more times in the torso. Then he shot the son.

At this point, Kris instructed Butler to follow him. He led him down the elevator to his car at gunpoint, where the two men waited for two or three hours while ambulances and the homicide police arrived. Eventually they left, parting until that evening, when Butler led the police to Denny's restaurant, where Kris was having dinner.

If all this was true, then Kris was guilty on two counts of capital murder, as well as the forcible kidnapping of Butler.

Kris's story—to his lawyer and, at the penalty phase of the trial, to the jury—was very different. He described how Butler had told him that a man called Eddie Dames was interested in distributing the *Caribbean Times* in the Bahamas. Kris was eager to expand his readership and felt there would be an appetite for the goings-on in Miami among Bahamians, since the city was such a short distance away. Dames would be flying in from the Bahamas, and the two men were to meet at the DuPont Plaza Hotel on the morning of October 15. Kris went to the hotel that morning, but when he got there, he discovered that Dames had rescheduled for the next day, so he left. On October 16, a Thursday, Butler ushered Kris up to Dames's room, but no one was there. He sat down and read the paper. Kris was very familiar with the DuPont, as he had used it many times. He knew the room had no coffee maker, so he had bought two immersion heaters at the hotel store to make drinks for himself, Butler, and Dames. After waiting in room 1215 for over an hour, he left, rather irritated. He had other things to do that morning and didn't appreciate having his time wasted.

He drove back to Fort Lauderdale, where half a dozen witnesses would confirm that he spent the rest of the morning sorting out issues at the paper—it was payday—before lunching at Tarks with a friend from Trinidad. Kris's story accounted for all the physical evidence, such as the fingerprints in the room. Butler's testimony was—starkly—the only direct "proof" that the various items at the scene were incriminating.

At this stage, all I had in front of me was the transcript of the trial. Very often I find the first run-through the most revealing. I can approach the case as the jury would have heard it presented. Later, it's easy to get caught up in the minutiae. As I padded into the kitchen and pulled a beer out of the refrigerator, Butler's tale struck me as implausible: Would a man who intended to kill someone really show up on the off chance of a meeting, expecting two other people to be there, and then indulge in idle chatter until his victim showed up? If Kris had carefully planned a murder, why would he bring two immersion heaters with eighteen-inch electrical cords to tie up three people (Derrick, Butler, and Dames) instead of rope or handcuffs? Besides, it made no sense that he would wait outside the hotel for hours after killing two people while the police investigated it—what could he possibly hope to achieve? And if he had really kidnapped Butler, why would he have let him live? Would he really have wanted a witness to a double homicide floating around? It seemed to me far more likely that Butler would have died in the room.

Butler stuck with this initial story for five months, from his sworn interview with Detective Buhrmaster on the night of the crime through a number of meetings with the prosecutors, and into his first sworn deposition. Thereafter his testimony changed quite radically. At the trial, he claimed his conscience had pricked him and he had come forward voluntarily to set the record straight. He had a new story: Kris Maharaj had confronted him, saying that his name had surfaced as part of an extortion plot in which Kris and various friends and associates had been ripped off. Kris wanted to set up a meeting with the true extortionist (Derrick Moo Young) to get him to sign checks reimbursing the money that had been stolen. He told Butler this would give him a chance to clear his name. He asked Butler to set up the meeting because he thought Derrick would never knowingly agree to meet with him—their relationship had deteriorated to such an extent that they were no longer on speaking terms. Kris told Butler he should tell Derrick that the meeting was with Eddie Dames, a Bahamian restaurateur who wanted to do business with him.

This still made no sense. For starters, this "plan" assumed that Derrick would bring his checkbook to the meeting. Even if he did, the sums involved were very large—hundreds of thousands of dollars—and what chance was there that a bank would certify a check for that kind of sum for a man whose annual income—as the prosecutors told the jury—was no more than $24,000? And why would Butler agree to kidnap a man, a crime punishable by life in prison in Florida, for someone he barely knew? According to his own statement, he had only just started working part time for the *Caribbean Times*.

The story began to break down the moment Butler painted in the details, under oath in a second pretrial deposition. "He told me he believed I may have been involved in this extortion based on articles that were in the *Echo,* and he knew I had been contributing to the articles," Butler explained. If this was true, why had Kris hired Butler to work on his paper? By the time the trial came around some months later, Butler claimed that he did not actually have anything to clear up.[2] If this was true, what motive did he have to be involved at all? The prosecutors did their best to coach him in the right direction.

"He convinced you that your name was being used in Trinidad in connection with this extortion?" suggested John Kastrenakes, attempting to clean up the problem.

"Yes," Butler said, perhaps only now remembering the details of his complex story. Kris's plan, he then insisted, was to get a confession from the person behind the extortion—Eslee Carberry.[3] But here again he had gone off script. A moment before, the theory had been that Derrick Moo Young was the extortionist, and that the meeting had been set up in the hope of coercing Derrick into admitting what he was doing and getting the money back.

"What did he say that the benefit would be to you of setting up this meeting with Derrick Moo Young?" Kastrenakes asked next. The prosecutor had taken the role of a director prompting his lead actor. Butler had just said the meeting was to be with Carberry; Kastrenakes neatly substituted Derrick's name to get the story back on track.[4]

"Very simply," Butler continued, as if oblivious to the name change. "He said he would have my name cleared. I would get a statement from him, and once we sit down and talk, it would all be clarified, and he would see to it that my name would be cleared and not be associated with this sort of thing."

This basic issue—why Butler would have had anything to do with the crime—was all very confusing, even under the revised version he provided at trial. A second patent problem with Butler's story was the location of the murder, a room in a very public hotel that had been registered to the elusive Eddie Dames. Not only was Kris Maharaj committing a crime with someone he barely knew—Butler—but he was doing it in a room rented by a man he had never met who might turn up at any moment to claim his key.

"What is Mr. Dames's occupation?" queried Kastrenakes.

"He is a flight controller, and he also had a business in Nassau, a restaurant, discotheque business," Butler replied.[5]

The jury may have had some questions surrounding this preliminary part of Butler's testimony, but as I plowed on, I found that Judge Gross had interrupted the prosecutor in midflow.

"Excuse me, sir," growled the judge to a member of the audience. "Let me have that beeper, please. There's a sign outside that you cannot bring those into my courtroom. That is the direct purpose of that. Give that beeper to my bailiff, and you have now lost the beeper. You no longer own that beeper. It will be turned over to the county."

The miscreant, blushing, passed the offending item across the bar to a suited official.

"Please put that in my office, Casey," the judge said to the bailiff. He turned back to assistant state attorney John Kastrenakes. "Continue on, sorry."

Judge Gross's intervention cut into my thoughts, and I paused from reading the trial transcript to ponder the alternatives. I could not understand why Eddie Dames had come into the plan at all. If you were going to set up a meeting with someone whom Derrick Moo Young would never actually meet, why use a real person? This would merely create another witness to your crime. Why not just reserve the room in the name of a fake person? And what was Butler's real relationship to Dames? He told the jury that they were close friends, but the prosecution did not call up Dames to testify, although his account would have shed light on some of the stranger aspects of Butler's story. Then I remembered something I had seen earlier in the police files: Detective Buhrmaster had spoken with Shaula Nagel, Derrick Moo Young's daughter. She had told him that a man called Dames had repeatedly called her father before the murders, but he had ignored the calls because he did not know who Dames was.[6] How, then, could Butler's testimony be true? These calls meant that Dames was the one trying to set up a meeting with the Moo Youngs—not Butler, and not Kris Maharaj.

As I pressed on through the transcript, I saw that Butler's story at trial hung together relatively well, passing without serious challenge from Eric Hendon, the defense lawyer. But I had reviewed dozens of records like this, and as I read further over the course of that afternoon and evening, a pattern began to emerge. I gradually came to see how a silk purse had been manufactured out of a sow's ear.

The two assistant state attorneys, Paul Ridge and John Kastrenakes, knew they would have to rely on Butler's testimony if they wanted the case to go to trial. They must have recognized that Butler's evidence presented them with problems, but they were conscientious, and they understood that their job was to put the case together as best they could. So each time they came up against evidence that jarred with Butler's story, they tried to reengineer his testimony to make it work. In a way, I had to respect the thoroughness of their preparation. But I was depressed at how little Eric Hendon had seen through it, and how little he had pointed out to the jury.

Arlene Rivero, a sales representative for the DuPont Plaza Hotel, had given a sworn statement to Detective Buhrmaster saying she was 100 percent certain that Kris Maharaj was the person who had reserved Suite 1215 for Eddie Dames around nine in the morning on October 15, the day before the murders.[7] This was crucial evidence: an independent witness who had Maharaj playing an integral role in the conspiracy. At trial, her evidence was not quite so solid as it had been in her original statement to the police. "I have already forgotten about it," she said in an Hispanic accent and a scramble of tenses. She blamed her uncertainty on the two-month delay between the crime and the time when the police asked her to make an identification.

"Were you positive about the identification?" the prosecutor asked her, trying to shore up her memory.

"I want to say positive, but it looked familiar to me, so that is why I identified it," she replied as helpfully as she could. She had to admit, though, that she had been shown only one picture of the person who might have booked the room—and that was a picture of Kris Maharaj.[8]

Her testimony was not as strong as the prosecution might have hoped, but it was still vital. Yet in his early statements, Butler had repeatedly asserted that he'd booked the room himself on the morning of October 15.[9] The prosecutors noticed this inconsistency and found a clever way to resolve it: Kris must have reserved room 1215, and Butler must have then paid for it. But when he was under oath at his second deposition, Butler forgot his lines and said again that he had done the original booking.

"Well, I went to pay for it," Butler was explaining. "I said I want a reservation for Eddie Dames, and the lady promptly pulled out a card and said all right, whatever it was, and $55 a day I think it was, and she pulled out the card, had me fill out something, and she said room 1215."

Paul Ridge interrupted. "My proffer," the senior prosecutor said, simply butting in and testifying for his witness, "was that he did not make the reservation, but he signed in and paid for it on the day before the shooting." Ridge didn't merely tell Butler what to say; he spoke for his witness. A gaping inconsistency was well on the way to becoming a *fact* corroborated by an independent eyewitness.[10]

There was another similar—telling—example of Butler changing his story to fit the evidence. He had originally said that he and Dames secured a rental car when his friend arrived from Nassau. But the prosecution checked out the rental agreement—it showed that the car was taken much later in the day. So Butler's story duly changed to fit the "corroborating" proof.

Unfortunately, these maneuvers passed by Eric Hendon like ships in the night. As I continued to make my way through the file, I was increasingly struck by how much he had missed.

"Do you remember receiving a phone call from the defendant at approximately 7:19 in the morning?" Kastrenakes asked Butler at trial. 7:19? Why so precise? Butler was testifying a year after the events in question and would not have remembered the exact minute of the call. Once more this seemed designed to "corroborate" his testimony, since telephone records showed that a call had been made to Butler's home number at precisely nineteen minutes past the hour.

"Yes," Butler said carefully. "I believe I received his call."

To be sure, there was documentary proof of this call. But the timing fit with Kris's story, too. He said he expected to meet Dames at the hotel at eight a.m. It was a forty-minute drive from his home near Fort Lauderdale, so he would have been leaving just then to make an eight a.m. appointment. A thought struck me, though: this did not fit with the timing of the murders, which happened at noon. Why would a killer go to the scene and hang around for a rendezvous scheduled for four hours later?

Kastrenakes moved on swiftly to other independent evidence to buttress his witness. "You had indicated . . . you had called the Moo Youngs," he said. "Did you write the numbers down?"

"Yes, I, at that time I couldn't remember the number . . . all the numbers . . . so I wrote a number down," Butler began. If he did not know the number, I wondered, who had given it to him to write it down on a complimentary copy of *USA Today* provided by the hotel? "Because I remember I wanted to call him to assure him that Dames was there, for me to put Dames on the phone and he would know—to let him know that Dames was here. And we were waiting to—"

What was this about putting Dames on the line with Derrick Moo Young? That would imply that Dames was in the room at 9:47 a.m., when the call was made. This was *after* Kris said he had left to go about his business, irritated by Dames's second no-show in as many days.

"Was there another number that you called Mr. Moo Young at?" Kastrenakes interrupted, eager to move along. He had to have known about Derrick's daughter's statement: Dames had constantly been calling her father in the week before the murder. Hendon had missed this.

"Yes."

"What was the number that you called?" Kastrenakes would have wanted the jury to think that only Butler had called Derrick, and that the mention of Dames was a slip of the tongue. If Dames had been on the phone as well, it would suggest that he was involved in the conspiracy.

"The one I remember was, I think, 434-5074, I think that is the other number," Butler testified, opaquely. If he did not remember Derrick's number in October 1986, how could he possibly remember it at trial a year later? There was only one explanation: he had been carefully prepped: his memory had been supplemented to match the records.

Not every amendment to Butler's story came from the prosecutors. When the narrative needed drama, Butler would overegg it himself. At trial, he claimed that Kris had gone into the bathroom to the left of the main entrance to the suite around 11:30 a.m., just before Derrick and Duane entered the room. Butler greeted them.

"Did Mr. Derrick Moo Young make any comments to you concerning Eddie Dames?" Kastrenakes asked.

"Yes, he did," Butler replied, describing the Moo Youngs' entrance. "He said, 'Where's Dames?' Immediately after, he said, 'Where's Dames?' . . . Immediately after that . . . he recognized me then. He said, 'You are the fellow Carberry or was that from—' He said, 'Where's Dames?' I told him to have a seat."[11]

"Tell the ladies and gentlemen of the jury *exactly* what happened next," Kastrenakes said. I recognized the prosecutor's stratagem: the stress on the word was designed to make it clear that this was the *precise* truth.

"As he repeated, 'Where's Eddie Dames?'" Butler said, "I think I mentioned to him, 'Well, Dames is not here, and I think you need to sort something out about extortion.' Before I was able to get the word out, Maharaj came out of the closet and said, 'You know, you have to deal with me . . .' He had in his right hand a gun, and his left hand there was a small pillow or cushion. I think I remember crying out to him, 'Krishna, what is this? What is this?' Because I was as surprised as Moo Young was to see a gun, and I think I did cry out, 'What is this?'"

Butler's feigned surprise at Maharaj wielding a gun was new to the tale at trial, and it was hardly credible. Surely he would have expected a weapon to be involved. Even if the plan really was to make Derrick sign a check in compensation, this could hardly have been achieved by artful persuasion alone.

I had long since retreated inside, safe from the evening mosquitoes that are so much a part of life in New Orleans. I was intrigued by what I was reading. None of it spoke, ultimately, to Kris Maharaj's innocence: it is, after all, possible for a witness to lie even about his own name and still tell the truth about what he saw. Later, I would often wonder whether Mark Fuhrman—clearly a liar who was later convicted of perjury—had simply tried to frame a guilty man when he'd put together the case against O. J. Simpson.

A description of the murder weapon is central to almost any prosecution, so I kept an eye on the details as they surfaced. On the night of the crime, Detective Buhrmaster had asked for a description of the pistol that Kris was supposedly waving about.

"Can you tell me what color the gun was?" Buhrmaster had asked.

"It was white," Butler replied.

"Meaning shiny color?" Buhrmaster asked. He was obviously confused. A white gun would be unique, like the trademark Colt revolver brandished by General George S. Patton as his tanks swept through Europe in 1944.[12]

"No," Butler insisted. "One color, white." He was specific and emphatic. He had allegedly spent three or four hours earlier that day with the gun in question pointing at him. Surely his description would be rock solid.

Not so. To fit the prosecution's theory, the murder weapon had to be a nine-millimeter Smith & Wesson—later they would present evidence that Kris Maharaj had bought such a handgun from a police officer a year before the crime. The officer who sold his Smith & Wesson to Kris said his gun had been silver—he described it at trial as "shiny." There was nothing white about it. So by the time of trial, Butler's description had to change.

"Please describe the gun, as you saw it, to the jury," Kastrenakes told Butler, in front of the jury.

"It was a flat gun, sort of flat in his hand," said Butler.

'Was it dark or a light color?"

"It appeared to be a light color," said Butler.

"How would you call the color as it appeared to you?"

"Whitish or silver, it was a light color, off-white, bone, could have been silver," Butler fudged as best he could. The murder weapon had just undergone a subtle and strategic transmutation. This was hugely significant, as Kris had only ever owned one handgun. Butler's mistake, saying the gun was white, would have been strong evidence that he was confecting the whole story. Yet now he had redrawn his description to match the gun Kris had bought. Another yawning discrepancy had vanished, and his testimony was again "corroborated" by physical evidence.

Once more Kris's lawyer, Eric Hendon, failed to confront Butler with the metamorphosis at trial.[13]

According to Butler's story, Kris had argued with Derrick for several minutes over money.[14] Then he'd shot him in the knee, apparently to show that he meant business. As it became increasingly apparent that he might not get out of this alive, Derrick made a desperate lunge at his assailant, whereupon Kris allegedly pumped several more shots into him. As Kris turned to question Duane, he somehow failed to notice Derrick crawling to the door and throwing himself out into the corridor. When he saw what was happening, he dragged Derrick back in and administered the coup de grâce, a bullet to the head.

BOOM! BOOM! BOOM! BOOM! BOOM! The heavy-caliber handgun was firing repeatedly in the enclosed space, followed by a final shot in the public hallway. But as I read on, it appeared that none of the hotel staff had heard anything. In his original story, Butler had told Detective Buhrmaster that there was no silencer on the gun. The detective seemed to find this improbable and probed the issue. Butler retreated, saying that Maharaj had brought a pillow with him to the room in a brown bag to muffle the shots.[15]

Again, this was a fact that could be readily checked. On a copy of Butler's first statement, I noticed that one of the prosecutors had written, "Is that a hotel pillow?" It did not take much of an investigation to figure it out. There were photographs in the case record of the pillow with a bullet hole, as well as pictures of the rest of the crime scene; one glance showed that the perforated pillow matched the other green cushions on the hotel sofa.

In other words, Butler appeared to be lying. He said Kris had brought a pillow with him to use as a makeshift silencer—a relatively silly story, since there would obviously have been plenty of pillows in a hotel room. But the pillow had patently not been brought to room 1215 in a brown bag—it was one of a number of identical ones already there.

Instead of facing up to the fact that their witness was not telling the truth, the prosecutors worked out a way to clean up his testimony. They decided that there must have been two pillows—one brought in and later taken away, and one from the scene—and this is what they suggested at Butler's deposition. However at trial, rather than presenting this tenuous theory, the prosecution avoided the issue altogether. Kastrenakes pointedly did not ask Butler about any pillow, and Eric Hendon did not notice.[16]

There was another aspect to Butler's story that I found particularly difficult to believe. Butler said that Maharaj had a glove only on his right hand when he fired the gun. Once again this did not pass the common-sense test. Only golfers buy a single glove, and as far as I knew, Kris did not play the game; even Detective Buhrmaster expressed incredulity when Butler first told him this was what had happened. I mentally dubbed the problem "Michael Jackson's glove."

If it was untrue, what made Butler latch onto this story? Had he worried that the police would do a gunshot residue test on Kris and discover no evidence that he had fired a gun? If so, Butler was giving them too much credit, as nobody testified that such an examination had ever been performed.

When the fingerprint report came in, the prosecution might have viewed it as physical proof of Butler's dishonesty. After all, there were six fingerprints identified as coming from Kris Maharaj's right hand—so he could not have been wearing a glove, at least not all the time. Instead, the prosecution constructed a complicated story for the jury that "corroborated" the single-glove theory. All the right-handed prints could have been left by Maharaj as he was waiting in the room, they suggested, and before he put a glove on to commit the murder—on a soda can, a newspaper, and so forth. So this physical evidence now supported Butler's previously implausible story.[17]

It was getting very late. I was one part intrigued, one part frustrated. Kris's transcript was in some ways better than a novel. Who would commit a murder in a famous hotel in downtown Miami with a coconspirator who had no reason to want to protect him and think he could get away with it? Butler struck me as a particularly fishy witness. But the rest of what I had found that day was all too familiar. Whatever else I had learned in my first day's reading, one thing seemed clear: Kris had not hired a very zealous defense attorney. So far, Eric Hendon had been a wallflower. He had done little or nothing on his client's behalf.

I had a choice: continue into the small hours, or get a good night's rest and pick up a new volume first thing in the morning. I opted for bed.

I began the next day with a full pot of coffee and with Derrick's inert body lying on the carpet of the DuPont Plaza Hotel. Now, according to Butler, it was time for Duane to die. Room 1215 was a split-level suite, with the bedroom up a set of stairs, around a corner at the top.

"I remember just before he took him upstairs, I was pleading with him to let the boy go," Butler testified. "I said, 'Leave him alone.' Even before, I said to him, 'It's not too late, you might be able to get the father to the hospital, the boy has nothing to do with this, leave him alone, leave him alone . . .' He kept talking, 'What did your father do with it?'" Presumably Maharaj was talking about the money. "And finally the kid said to him, 'I don't know. I think my sister would know. He doesn't trust me. I think my sister knows about it.' He finally said—the last thing he said to him was, 'All right, why didn't you tell me that before, you are a good boy. I wouldn't kill you.' Then I heard a shot."

BOOM!

"The last words you heard from him, 'I wouldn't kill you'?" Kastrenakes underlined.

"Yes."

Duane, who was twenty-three years old, was dead, one execution-style bullet through the head. It was a point of high drama in the trial. And suddenly Butler's testimony was interrupted. Eric Hendon had been quietly seated throughout the entire performance to date, but now he was on his feet asking for a sidebar with the judge.

"Your Honor," the defense lawyer began, "for the record, I would like to note that during Mr. Kastrenakes's direct examination of Mr. Butler, one of the victims' family members, who is in the court, stormed out of the court and commenced screaming or wailing in the hall." Finally, Hendon was representing his client's legal rights. If the victims' family— or any spectator—made an emotional outburst in court, that could provoke a later reversal. The appellate courts might decide that it had prejudiced the jury.

"Let the record reflect that defense counsel is incorrect," said Judge Gross with some sarcasm, protecting the case from the years of anticipated appeals. "The victim walked out of the courtroom, did not scream, did not wail, did not utter a word and that was the end of it and that took precisely four seconds."

He frowned at Hendon, daring a contradiction. None came. Hendon was cowed by the aggressive judge.

The interruption gave me a moment to reflect. All this while, as Kris Maharaj was supposed to have been marching Duane up to his death, Butler said he was standing at the bottom of the stairs. Had Hendon simply looked at the photographs of the crime scene, he would have seen at least three things: that Butler could not have seen what was going on upstairs[18] and therefore could not have described it; that Kris Maharaj would not have been able to see Butler if he had been intent on shooting Duane; and that Butler was within two feet of the door to the hallway and could easily have escaped.

"I was sure I was going to get shot," Butler told the jury dramatically. "I was sure my turn was next." But he made no effort to flee[19]—which would have meant simply opening the door and running down the hall. Kris was gone for at least ten seconds, he said. In that time, Usain Bolt could have run more than one hundred meters. Butler was no Bolt, but if he was scared for his life, he could certainly have made it to the elevator or to either of two sets of emergency stairs. Instead, Kris allegedly came downstairs from the bedroom loft, his brown holdall with him, and the two men walked out of room 1215 together. "I saw the gun in his hands, and I think he took it in his hands as we were walking out of the room going to the elevator."

One question must have been reverberating in the mind of any inquiring juror, as it was in mine: why was Butler still alive? If Kris had committed two murders—one when the situation perhaps got out of control, and the second in very cold blood—then it is difficult to understand why he would not have shot Butler, too. Here is a man who had no real connection to the defendant and therefore no loyalty, who claimed he had vociferously opposed shooting either man, and who was now the only witness to the crime. Once again Hendon never confronted Butler with this question at trial.

According to Butler, the two men rode the elevator down together and walked out of the DuPont Plaza. Most killers—relieved to have escaped the scene of a double murder—would have been on the next plane to a country with no extradition treaty. But Butler told the jury that he and Kris sat in the car in front of the hotel for three hours with the engine running and the air conditioning on. Police cars were screeching to a halt around them, blue lights flashing. Why were they waiting? Butler suggested that it was to meet the elusive Eddie Dames. But Kris said he did not know Dames, and there was no suggestion that Dames knew him. Why would Kris want to hang around to make his acquaintance? The only person Dames could finger to the police would be Butler—all the more reason for the killer to give Butler a pair of cement shoes and drop him in the Everglades for an alligator's dinner.

Butler's tale was almost complete at this point. He described how Dames appeared outside the hotel, whereupon Butler leaped out of Kris's car and drove off in Dames's rental. Kris followed but then lost him on Biscayne Boulevard. Butler then told the jury about a telephone conversation he had with his employer later in the day.

"Maharaj said, 'I want you to meet me at the Denny's—'" Butler testified. "I said, 'Which Denny's?' 'The Denny's at the airport.' I further said to him, I said, 'You know, the police know that I was there and they are looking for me.' He said, 'It doesn't matter. I want to see you so we can get all our stories.'"

"He wanted to get your story straight together?" Kastrenakes clarified.

"Yes."

Here the prosecutor seemed to have glided around another worrying segment of Butler's story—a long, and potentially crucial, time had passed. The phone call supposedly took place that evening—seven or eight hours after Derrick and Duane had been killed. What had happened in the meantime? Butler wasn't saying. He led the police to the Denny's, where Detective Buhrmaster arrested Kris on two counts of first-degree murder.

It seemed to me, reading all this, that Butler had been jiggled along like a marionette on the end of a string. Each time he said something that was provably false, the prosecutor not only ignored the possibility that it might prove Kris Maharaj to be innocent, but refashioned Butler's testimony so that the physical evidence, or an independent witness, "corroborated" Butler rather than impeached him. But who exactly was manipulating whom?

In almost every case I have ever been involved with, the main prosecution witness, if he is wrapped up in the crime, has got some kind of sweetheart deal from the state. Even assuming that Butler was telling the truth at trial, he was now admitting that he had conspired with Kris Maharaj to bring the Moo Youngs to the room where they were to be held (kidnapped) until they signed a check (extortion) turning over money. Also, because Butler was involved in a felony that ultimately resulted in death, under Florida law he was guilty of murder at least as an accomplice—notwithstanding his protestation that he had never intended the Moo Youngs harm. Thus, at the very least, he faced life in prison. He had also admitted to committing perjury in his earlier statements. Yet he never spent a single night in jail.

All an effective defense lawyer would have had to do was to start asking Butler what lengths he would go to in order to avoid life in prison: Would he lie? (Of course.) Would he sell his own mother? (Probably.) Prosecutors don't like to watch that kind of butchering of their witness. John Kastrenakes tried to pull the sting out of the expected cross-examination.

"Has anybody from the state attorney's office or the police department promised you anything to make you say anything of that nature?" the prosecutor asked.

"Nobody promised me anything," Butler insisted.

"Have you been promised any immunity whatsoever for your own involvement in this case?"

"Absolutely none."[20]

Butler knew very well that he needed to toe the prosecution line or he would face decades in prison. For the prosecutors to pretend that there was no deal—overt or covert—was a charade. Indeed, the proof of the pudding was there before me: I was reading the transcript eight years after the trial, and Butler had remained at liberty the whole time. That is a mighty incentive for a witness to "cooperate"; it is a power that no defense lawyer has at his disposal to secure helpful evidence. The prosecutors might have thought that they benefited from Butler's testimony, but who was getting the better deal? Whose strings were really being pulled?

If Kris was telling the truth, the prosecutors were rewarding Butler twice: once by not prosecuting him for his complicity in two murders, and a second time for taking no action as he committed perjury against an innocent man.

Sunday was slipping by. Normally, I would have been out in the garden or trying to implement my grandiose plans to fix up my new house. When I first arrived in New Orleans, I had set about finding a home and rapidly located a two-story Greek revival in the Lower Garden District. The Realtor was dubious; she thought the neighborhood was dangerous. She had never, she said, lost a client, and she did not want to start with me. But there was nothing she could do to dissuade me: it was love at first sight.

The house was on Euterpe Street, named improbably after the muse of music and elegiac poetry. Built in 1803, it had what must have been a ballroom on the left of the main door, where I found a plaque proclaiming that Abraham Lincoln's nephew had been one of a long line of owners. Looking around the place, I thought he might have been the last one to paint the house or do anything much in the realm of maintenance. The roof leaned rather precariously at the front, and a couple of the columns were missing. Judging from the syringes I found in the kitchen cabinets, the previous occupant had quite a drug habit; I later learned that he had chipped off many of the plaster ceiling centerpieces around the chandeliers when high on something or other. The farther back into the house I went, the more floorboards gave way under my feet. The house was huge, far bigger than anything I could possibly need, but as I walked around it, I saw only history and potential—all for just $40,000.

I remember coming close to tears after the closing—the potential had suddenly transformed into the prospect of hard labor ahead. I had little time in the early months for home repairs. Trying to put out the fires in various Louisiana capital cases kept me busy seven days a week and part of most nights. None of this helped the relationship I was unsuccessfully trying to maintain back in Atlanta. I tried to patch it together with a 469-mile drive as often as I could manage, but it wasn't enough to make up for my sudden disappearance to New Orleans.

So I was wholly single again, and my only affair was with this creaky and demanding old house. I generally resented it when work kept me from fixing it up on weekends. But I was hooked on Kris's case and wanted to read on. So I got another cup of coffee, went out onto the balcony that sloped rather precipitously between the Corinthian columns at the front of the house, put my feet up on the railing, and made myself comfortable.

It had been up to Eric Hendon, as the defense attorney, to rake Butler over the coals. He had plenty of materials from Butler's earlier statements.[21] Presumably I would get some insight into what Hendon thought had happened when he took on the state's star witness. Butler had answered Kastrenakes's questions for over three hours; Hendon began his own interrogation as lunchtime approached. Before he had made any headway, he stopped short and turned to the judge.

"Your Honor," he said, "I have several other legal pads full of information with reference to my cross-examination of Mr. Butler, and I must have left those matters at my desk at home."

Hendon was permitted the lunch break to collect his papers and give more thought to his theory. As they ate their court-supplied sandwiches, the jurors must have been wondering what Hendon would present after lunch. Logic dictated that dismantling Butler's testimony would have to be a primary focus of the defense; Butler had to be lying for Kris to be innocent. Who else had a motive to kill the Moo Youngs? Kris had told Hendon that he thought the Moo Youngs had something to do with drugs, though he could point to nothing more than rumor. Still, there was something questionable about the man in the room across the hall from the murder scene: Jaime Vallejo Mejia, the "export-import" businessman from Colombia.

And who was this Eddie Dames? The fact that the murder room was booked in his name was hugely suspicious, as was the evidence that he had been calling Derrick from the Bahamas. Dames was an air traffic controller in Nassau. If Hendon simply read the newspapers, he must have known that Nassau was a major transit point in the drug trade. The planes that ferry cocaine have to avoid detection. What better ally could a drug courier have than the man whose radar kept track of each flight?

Hendon needed to explain what Kris had been doing in the room that morning. If he was not guilty, there had to be an explanation, and the jury would be waiting to hear it. Perhaps someone had planned to frame him. Or was he meant to end up dead as well? Did the actual killer mean to shoot him too and try to make it look like a murder-suicide—the furious British businessman kills his mortal enemy, then takes his own life in horror at his act?

It did not take long for my sense of anticipation to be deflated. If cross-examination is meant to be the "greatest engine ever invented for the discovery of the truth," then Hendon was *The Little Engine That Couldn't*. He had spent twelve months preparing for trial. He should have come up with a theory that was far superior to my off-the-cuff musings—after all, I had only been pondering the alternatives, without investigating the case. But Hendon's feeble theory involved Carberry and his tabloid paper, the *Caribbean Echo*. Butler had worked for Carberry for some months before his recent move to Kris's paper. Perhaps, he suggested, there was a dastardly plot between them to kill the Moo Youngs to provide a scoop for Carberry's paper.

"As a matter of fact, knowing Carberry's zest for sensationalism, you and he devised this particular plot which would provide the best sensational type of news that could have been put together and put in Mr. Carberry's paper," Hendon said, his voice rising with his accusation. "Isn't that correct?"

I was only reading the black and white page in front of me, but I imagined that Butler must have blinked. What on earth was this lawyer trying to say? That he and Carberry had killed two people in order to sell a few more copies of the *Caribbean Echo*?

"That's very incorrect," Butler said emphatically. This was one of the few things that Butler said with which we might all agree. Hendon had seriously let his client down. The prosecutors must have felt rather smug as they listened. What they feared would be a tough battle was turning out to be a cakewalk.

I threw the transcript onto the wooden deck. The boards were rotten in places; continuing the task of replacing them was one of the jobs I'd put off that day. Hendon's performance had been simply hopeless. Butler's testimony was an archetype of something I had seen many times: the prosecutors had sculpted the evidence to fit their view of the truth—doing it so cleverly that the jurors would barely have glimpsed their handiwork.

Witnesses are prepared for their time on the stand every day in courtrooms across America. Not only is it considered permissible, but a lawyer might be deemed ineffective for failing to do it. Yet it is rarely discussed, perhaps because there is a thin line between effective adversarial lawyering and what amounts to suborning perjury.[22] I have been unable to find any cases in which a prosecutor has been sanctioned for "preparing" his witness overzealously.[23] One of the few that comes close involves President Bill Clinton, who was held in contempt of court for committing perjury in a deposition he gave under oath about his relationship with Monica Lewinsky. Notably, though, the lawyers who vigorously prepared him (and other witnesses) for this deposition were not punished—although even at the time they must have known that their client was on shaky ground.[24] More to the point, once Clinton made inconsistent statements to the grand jury, to Congress, and in the media, they should have known to correct his earlier testimony. They did not, but nothing happened to them.

But here, right in front of me, Butler's evidence had undergone a methodical metamorphosis. At every step he had edged closer to the story the prosecution wanted to tell. I did not think the prosecutors were guilty of malicious misrepresentation; one could even argue that their work fell within the broad limits of normal U.S. practice. Indeed, when the jury came back with a guilty verdict and a death sentence, Ridge and Kastrenakes no doubt celebrated with their peers. They had taken a difficult case and put it together with great care.

But Kris Maharaj had received no kind of defense. Of course, this did not mean he was innocent. Plenty of guilty people on death row have useless lawyers. In truth, few people facing execution have the kind of legal assistance that can hope to match the prosecution. But my doubts spread deeper. It is hard to feel much confidence in the outcome of an adversarial system in which one of the combatants seems to have dozed his way through most of the trial.

5

The Prosecutor

My life was already pretty full when I first went to see Kris Maharaj, and it took some drastic turns after that. David Utter and I had set up the LCAC, operating on a very tenuous budget. A grant from the Public Welfare Foundation helped get us off the ground. But then my Realtor's fears were realized. I was walking home along St. Charles Avenue, the main street that traces the Mississippi River through New Orleans. It was late at night, but there were plenty of streetlights. I was approaching Lee Circle when suddenly someone grabbed me from behind. Taken by surprise, I instinctively jabbed him with my right elbow. I turned to find three young men—in their late teens or early twenties—all armed. I knew there was no point resisting and put my hands up, asking them just to say what they wanted. Unfortunately I had already provoked one of them, and while I held my hands up in surrender, they beat me to the ground. One was waving a knife, which glinted under the streetlamp as I was forced onto my hands and knees. I had a terrible sense that my back was exposed. For primordial and perhaps irrational reasons, exacerbated when I once accidentally stepped on a rusty nail that came through my foot, I have always been more afraid of knives than guns, and I had a vision of the sharp point plunging in between my shoulder blades.

They took my wallet, rifled through my pockets, and then kicked me a few times for good measure. One boot connected with my jaw with an ugly crack. None of the three said a word—at least nothing more than the occasional, staccato "motherfucker"—and I was only semiconscious as I heard them trampling away.

This had not been the welcome I had hoped for in New Orleans. There were no police around. Somehow I got myself to a hospital—I barely remember getting there, or how—and the next day a dentist wired my broken jaw shut for a couple of months. I half-wondered whether Smoothie King had put my assailants up to it, as blended peanut butter drinks were all that I could get through my clamped teeth. Meanwhile I was on a vile painkiller—liquid Demerol. I tried to distract myself by doing some much-needed plumbing work on the house. Whether I should have been soldering copper pipes under the influence of narcotic pain medication is an open question. In any event, I hooked up all the connections backward, so hot water filled the toilet cistern every time it was flushed—providing a warm feeling for the winter but damaging my utility bill until I switched it over.

With all this, Kris Maharaj's case was not at the top of my priorities. A few months went by before I could really do anything. Only as I managed to stabilize both my health and my obligations to all the prisoners in Louisiana whom we'd agreed to help did I finally make time for an investigative trip to Miami.

Any investigation in a capital case must be exhaustive; a single piece of paper may be the key that unlocks it. This proposition is not as simple as it may seem. Florida has an extraordinary rule, duplicated in most American states, that the defendant in a criminal case can have access to the prosecution and police files only *after he is convicted.*[1] In Florida, the freedom of information law is called the Sunshine Law. Sunshine is a great disinfectant, and shining light on a process should exorcise the evils that might hide or distort the truth. But for some reason, at the time of trial, the rules of discovery limit defense access to the evidence. In some states, I have tried capital cases where the prosecution gave us only a witness list, with no indication of what anyone might say. None of this makes any sense: surely there would have to be a compelling reason to deny an accused man information related to his case. To keep him in the dark turns the trial into a crapshoot.

Florida is actually one of the better jurisdictions, as it gives the defense the right to depose each witness under oath before trial. Additionally, the prosecution is obliged to reveal any evidence they plan to use at trial, along with anything "exculpatory"—although the definition of that term is hotly debated. There are two dangers: first, that the prosecution will not comply with its discovery obligations; and second, that the defense lawyer will come to rely too heavily on the prosecutors and will fail to conduct an independent investigation. One way to test how candid the state has been at trial is to submit a Sunshine request afterward and peruse the prosecution file. I don't generally hold out much hope of finding useful information, as inconvenient documents have a bad habit of disappearing. But I had made an appointment with the Office of the State Attorney in Miami to check through its files on Maharaj's case. When I turned up, a secretary took me into a windowless room, where a dozen boxes of materials had been stacked on the table.

As I sat leafing through the documents, I soon came across an original letter from someone called Dudley Dickson, a polygraph expert from Tampa. He had written to the prosecutor, John Kastrenakes, about a test he had administered to Neville Butler. I flipped to his conclusion on page three. "Based on the subject's polygraph responses," Dickson wrote, "it is the examiner's opinion he was untruthful and was withholding and falsifying information as indicated above."

I sat back in my chair, totally surprised. Until that moment I had assumed—as Eric Hendon would have done—that Paul Ridge had been telling the truth when he said that Butler had passed a polygraph test. But Dickson had obviously thought certain parts of Butler's story were not credible, including the notion that Kris had waited for three hours outside the murder scene, with flashing police lights all around. He tried to force Butler to tell the truth by labeling him a liar on that question. And yet, notwithstanding the fact that Butler had failed several questions—all of which were "facts" subsequently presented as truth to the jury—Dickson passed him with respect to central aspects of his examination. I compared these questions with similar queries that the polygraph administrator George Slattery had put to Kris Maharaj.

"On or about October 16, 1986, did you actually see Kris Maharaj shoot Derrick Moo Young?"

Butler replied, "Yes." Dickson called this a Pass.

Kris Maharaj had been asked a similar question. "Regarding the shooting deaths of Derrick and Duane Moo Young," Slattery had asked him. "Did you kill them?"

Maharaj replied, "No." Slattery called this a Pass.

There was an irreconcilable conflict. They could not both be telling the truth.

Soon afterward I came across a copy of Butler's first deposition. One of the prosecutors had annotated each statement as "TRUE," "FALSE," or "UNCLEAR." For a moment I wondered how he had come to such objective clarity, but then I noticed that he had simply cross-referenced the statement against the lie detector report. Apparently the polygrapher, Dudley Dickson, was to be the ultimate arbiter of the veracity of the central government witness. In every instance where Dickson had passed Butler, the prosecutors were convinced he was telling the truth. They now viewed their task in a new focus: they just had to prove Dickson right. If that meant reshaping Butler's testimony, then that must be the right thing to do. Butler had to tell the truth, and they now knew what the truth was.

All this brought me up short. On one level, I was excited. The polygraph results gave me great hope for Kris's appeal. The results would not, perhaps, be admissible at a trial, but various facts that sprang out of this document were highly relevant to the state's star witness.

Butler told the jury—at least six times, under oath—that he had voluntarily come forward to change his story. This was patently false. The prosecutors, who had come to doubt aspects of his story, had summoned him in to explain himself. In particular they had questioned Butler's claim that he had not known that Kris Maharaj would come to the room, and his portrayal of himself as a victim, kidnapped at gunpoint by the killer. Only under an aggressive interrogation by Dickson did he back off this story—one he had repeated several times, often under oath, in the five months since the murder. By the end of the afternoon he had spent hooked up to a polygraph machine, Butler was telling quite a different tale, much closer to the one he told at trial.

Other telling statements emerged in the polygrapher's report. Butler told Dickson that while waiting outside the hotel for Dames's return, he got out of the car to feed the meter. This might seem like a minor point, but he had given the jury the impression that he was held at gunpoint the entire time. On cross-examination, an attentive defense lawyer would have posed an obvious question: If you got out of the car to feed the meter, why didn't you escape?

Perhaps the greatest contribution this document made to my understanding of the case was the insight it gave me into the mind-set of the two prosecutors, John Kastrenakes and Paul Ridge. I had already seen, from a quick perusal of the transcript, how they had cajoled and coached Neville Butler to ensure that his story hung together. Now I began to see what had provoked them to take this course. They had spent a lot of time with their star witness and knew that without him Kris Maharaj would walk free. They believed Kris to be guilty, and Dudley Dickson had confirmed for them that their essential instinct was correct. In Dickson they felt they had an authority on the truth, and their job was simply to ensure that Butler told it in a compelling way.

It did not matter to them that an equally respected expert had come to the opposite conclusion. They were only seeking to have their own preexisting views corroborated. To me, Kris's polygraph result was significant. I don't believe in such machines myself, but I knew that Kris did—he was a lie detector acolyte, he thought the expert could see into his soul, and so the result told me something about his state of mind: he would not have taken it (let alone passed) if he had worried that he might fail. His willingness to take the test, and his faith in its outcome, injected further questions in my mind as to his guilt. It was by no means dispositive, just another factor to place on the scale and consider. Butler, on the other hand, had not volunteered for the examination—he had been required to submit to it.

I found the prosecutors' uncritical acceptance of Dickson's report absurd. If they believed it, why did they let Butler testify to things that Dickson had said were false—like the silly *Waiting for Godot* story that had him and Kris sitting in the car outside the hotel for three hours after the murder, surrounded by police, hoping to run into Eddie Dames? If they thought he was lying about that, then they were knowingly presenting perjured testimony.

I spent many hours plowing through the boxes, tabbing each relevant page. At the end of the day, I stood in front of the Xerox machine and copied the pile of papers on the table beside me, then handed the secretary what I owed—it was ten cents a copy. I'd got several hundred pages that I'd study in closer detail when I got home. I already had a sense I'd found enough to get Kris a new trial.

As I drove the 862 miles back to New Orleans, I considered what I had learned. My anger and frustration were simmering. I recognized a trait in myself that I have criticized in others: the liberal defense lawyer who immediately condemns a prosecutor. It is a bad habit. We are willing to defend people who have committed terrible crimes; indeed, we view it as a badge of honor to do so. But we'd sometimes like to see those who prosecute our clients in the dock instead. It's better, by far, to try to understand what motivates the "other side." In this regard, Kastrenakes and Ridge were in no way unique—they were archetypes of their kind, as I had come to understand in the dozen years I'd spent litigating criminal cases across the South.

One major flaw in the American legal system has to do with the Darwinian selection process for state prosecutors.[2] There are more than 2,300 local prosecutor's offices in the United States, handling more than 2.3 million felony cases each year. While a minority of state prosecutor's offices have experimented with different practices, all but Connecticut, New Jersey, and the District of Columbia "share one common trait: the job of chief prosecutor, or district attorney, is . . . an elected position."[3] As a result, politics enters into every decision they make.

As one academic put it, "The political pressure on prosecutors has been said to lead to a subtle shift away from the prosecutor's goal of 'doing justice' and an increased focus on conviction rates."[4] The understatement makes me chuckle. It is a very rare prosecutor or district attorney who runs for election on a platform of "doing justice"; candidates generally boast about how they will convict more criminals, or send more prisoners to death row.[5]

Prosecutors or district attorneys must run for election, but what of the assistants, who more often actually prosecute the cases? One might hope that they would come, straight out of law school, urgently seeking to do justice. Unfortunately, as a general matter, this is not the nature of the beast.

American prosecutors are chosen (or self-select) from a very specific pool. Logic suggests, and practice confirms, that those who choose to become prosecutors usually believe that people who commit crimes should go to prison for long terms, and that the system generally finds and convicts the right person. Prosecutors, according to those who have studied them, tend to share a perception that the police arrest only guilty people in the first place, so they are generally quite comfortable that they have charged and convicted the right person. Indeed, more than half of all prosecutors in one survey thought the presumption of innocence was bunk, since the police and prosecutorial screening procedures determined guilt before the trial. They look over the available evidence and decide whether to go to trial; if there is not enough evidence to find the accused guilty beyond a reasonable doubt, they won't go forward. So if they proceed to trial, then obviously they think the accused is the one who committed the crime.

Whatever aspirations prosecutors may initially bring to the job, plenty of evidence shows that they gradually learn to emphasize convictions as the overriding goal, without asking too many questions about whether they are convicting the right people.[6]

In my own experience, I have found that many prosecutors believe *all* people who make it as far as the defendant's table at trial are guilty. Soon after my arrival in New Orleans, I called a prosecutor as a witness in a pretrial hearing and asked him whether he ever had doubts about the guilt of those he was seeking to send to prison. (If asked the same question, I would have to concede that while I have defended a fair number of guilty people, I have also defended many who I am convinced did not commit the crime.)[7]

"How many innocent people, or people you think maybe might have been innocent, do you think you've ever prosecuted?" I put this question to Roger Jordan, an assistant district attorney in New Orleans, who was prosecuting Clarence "Smitty" Smith for murder. Smith had been on death row for twelve years, and we had secured him a new trial. I thought he was innocent, and the jury later agreed.

I expected a pause, some reflection. But Jordan's response was instantaneous and emphatic.

"None. Never."

In retrospect, I suppose this reply was inevitable. First, had he said anything else, I would have then asked him to identify the cases about which he had qualms, and would then have set about investigating them. If the prosecutor has any doubt at all, then the defendant is very probably innocent. Second, had he tried to put someone in prison whom he thought might not have committed the crime, he would have been admitting to an ethical violation: in theory, a prosecutor is supposed to do justice, not merely to convict. But I do not believe that Roger Jordan's response was strategic or self-serving. I think he said it because he believed it. He subscribed to the creed that the criminal justice system is essentially faultless insofar as it places people in jail—and is flawed only in allowing the guilty to escape through the machinations of defense lawyers. That belief is shared by a remarkable number of his peers.

As a matter of human nature, it is probably inexorable that those who spend their lives locking up people hold this notion of prosecutorial infallibility. It would be difficult to drive to work each morning wondering how many innocent people you were going to deprive of liberty that day. The second self-selection procedure sets in as those who harbor doubts tend to move on from the prosecutor's office quite rapidly. The remainder confirm one another's biases around the coffee machine.

In Kris's case, human factors contributed to the prosecutors' tendency not to question their star witness. Because John Kastrenakes and Paul Ridge came to know Neville Butler personally, spending many hours

with him, they no doubt came to see him as a human being and appreci-
ated his effort to work with them. In contrast, they had no interaction at
all with Krishna Maharaj, beyond his undoubtedly hostile stares across
the courtroom. Indeed, the lawyer seeking to condemn a defendant
never actually talks to him, unless it is to cross-examine him and try to
"break" him at trial. This is another unique aspect of the justice system:
most participants, including the prosecutors, judge, and jurors, are
asked to reach a decision about the person on trial without ever having
met him.

There may be some company managers out there who hire employees based on a written résumé of the candidates' experience without the
benefit of a personal interview, but they are probably few and far between and I suspect their success rate is low. I've made my share of mistakes hiring people even after a lengthy interview; overwhelmingly, I
have made my best decisions when the applicants have worked with us
as volunteers or temporary staff and we have come to know them. Few
choose to assess someone solely on the say-so of others, particularly
when those others have their own hidden agendas.

So the justice system might be more likely to work if the participants
knew one another better. I have sometimes made attempts to bring
prosecutors and defendants together. The first person I represented at
trial—in 1985, when I was a year out of law school and should not have
been allowed into a courtroom in any role but spectator—was John
Pope. John was a rather hapless forty-two-year-old armed robber who
had held up a pharmacy in a small town west of Atlanta, by the Alabama
border, to feed his drug habit. The pharmacist grabbed the gun, the assistant hit John over the head with a broomstick, and during the struggle the gun went off, killing the innocent pharmacist. John, deeply
remorseful for what he had done, was facing capital punishment in that
small Georgia town.

I spent a lot of time with him, and it was clear to me that even though
he had committed the crime, and would go to prison for life no matter
what I did, he never meant to kill anyone. It occurred to me that the
prosecutor, Bill Foster, might be more understanding if he got to know
John himself. Bill was a potent adversary—an experienced lawyer who

was respected by jurors and who connected with them. He was also very likable, and I knew he would get along with John. So I told Bill that he could sit down with John—without my being there—and ask him whatever he liked. I admitted that I was fairly confident that if he met John, he would end his campaign to send him to the electric chair. But I said that if it did not change his mind, he would be free to use anything John said at the upcoming trial. It was a calculated risk, but we did not have a lot to lose.

Bill would have none of it. He didn't want to talk to John. It was apparent to me that he feared what it would do to his resolve.[8] Since then, from time to time, I have tried to get prosecutors to do that same thing, without success.[9]

By the time I set up shop in Louisiana, I thought I had identified three flaws in the prosecutorial design: the mind-set of those who take the job, the reinforcing nature of the prosecutorial club, and the way the system discourages any contact between prosecutors and the person on trial. These factors conspire to make it very unlikely that a prosecutor will accept that he has sent an innocent person to prison. Few people are very good at admitting their mistakes; fewer still, when those mistakes are more serious. Meanwhile, the more entrenched one's position becomes, the less chance one has of beating an honest retreat.

If the average American prosecutor enters the fray with prejudices firmly intact,[10] what legal framework is in place to steer him or her in the direction of doing justice? Bizarrely, lawyers have come up with a regime that achieves precisely the opposite: insulating prosecutors from any chance of being held responsible for their actions. Not long after I arrived in New Orleans, I was lying in on a Sunday morning, the sun streaming through the slats of the bedroom shutters. The phone rang. The caller was a local lawyer with whom I had been consulting in a vague way. He and two colleagues had been representing Shareef Cousin, a sixteen-year-old facing the death penalty for a shooting outside the Port of Call restaurant, on the eastern edge of the French Quarter. They had been confident of an acquittal, but the previous evening, the lawyer said with an edge of panic, the jury had come back with a verdict of guilty. Judge Raymond Bigelow wanted to move forward immediately into the penalty phase, to decide whether the young defendant would spend the rest of his life in prison or be put to death. This lawyer asked if I could help.

I went down to court in shorts that morning, and we persuaded the judge to give us a couple of days. David and I helped the lawyers pull together a rough and ready case to argue for Shareef's life. But it was a catastrophe—the only available witnesses were his family, and they were furious at the jury for convicting Shareef. It did not take long for the twelve jurors to teach Shareef and his family who was boss: they imposed death.

When the LCAC took over the appeal, it became a case study in how the legal system encourages prosecutors to perpetuate their mistakes.

Michael Gerardi had taken Connie Babin to the Port of Call on a first date. As the white couple emerged from the restaurant at the end of the evening, three young African American men confronted them and demanded money. A gun was fired, and Gerardi fell to the ground, fatally wounded. The prosecutor was Roger Jordan, the same assistant district attorney who'd been responsible for Smitty's case. Roger was a couple of years younger than me and the same height—well over six feet—but in other ways we differed. He was good-looking in a classic American blond way. He had spent almost his entire career as a prosecutor. His brief stint in a private law practice (defending criminals who could afford to pay) had convinced him he wanted to get back on the right side, so he returned to the Orleans Parish district attorney's office, then run by Harry Connick, Sr.

Connick was a colorful career prosecutor in New Orleans. His son was by then a famous balladeer, and Harry Sr. had parlayed this into his own Tuesday gig at a local bar, where he would shake his hips on stage, crooning some 1950s songs. The staff in his office, meanwhile, had a repertoire of prosecutorial misconduct, all directed at rebalancing their sense that New Orleans jurors, who were predominantly African American, let off far too many guilty criminals.

Detective Anthony Small, who led the investigation on Shareef's case, told his colleagues early on that he had "some problems" with one of his witnesses. One "problem" that he and Jordan faced was Shareef's alibi. At the precise time of the murder, Shareef insisted that he had been some distance away playing basketball—ironically, in an official program intended to keep young people off the streets and away from committing crime. One of the parents at the game came forward with a timed and dated videotape that showed Shareef taking shots with an orange ball at the very moment when someone else was shooting Gerardi outside the Port of Call restaurant. But Roger Jordan, who hailed from the same prosecutorial school as John Kastrenakes and Paul Ridge, meticulously challenged the accuracy of the time shown on the tape. The time was only as reliable as the setting of the camera and—he contended—could be shown to be true or false only insofar as the witnesses could remember—and tell the jury—when the game had taken place. At trial, he twisted up several alibi witnesses on their timing, and the defense evidence began to look fallible.

This led to a new maxim in Orleans Parish about the criminal trial process: a picture may be worth a thousand words, a videotape a million, but with many jurors the testimony of a weeping white woman will count for more than either. The star eyewitness against Shareef Cousin was Connie Babin, who had seen her dinner date gunned down in the street. She insisted she was 100 percent certain that the young man on trial had killed Michael Gerardi. Shareef was convicted and sentenced to death.[11]

Shareef's lawyers had been confident of victory, certain of their videotaped alibi. Now, as we began the investigation that should have been done in the first place, Shareef was already on death row. Detective Small and Roger Jordan had obscured a second big "problem": Connie Babin had made various earlier statements that cast great doubt on the vehement identification of Shareef she made in court. "Ms. Babin stated she did not get a good look at the perpetrators and probably could not identify them," wrote the officer who first interviewed her at the scene of the murder. "Ms. Babin was visibly shaken up."

"It was dark and I did not have my contacts nor my glasses so I'm coming at this at a disadvantage," Babin had told the next person who interviewed her that night, Detective Pete Bowen. Some days later, in the calm setting of her own home, she had repeated her uncertainty to Detective Small on tape. "I saw a movement, my . . . left eye perforated vision," she said hesitantly, struggling to come up with the word *peripheral.* "And I knew it was a movement."

In other words, all she really saw was a blur. If Shareef's trial lawyers had known about these statements, Shareef could not have been convicted for truancy, let alone sentenced to death for murder. But the prosecutor had elected to keep these statements from the jury.[12] Indeed, Jordan had made various similar decisions. He failed to turn over information that Babin had identified another person who had no link to Shareef as one of the perpetrators. We tracked down a local bird-watcher who had actually witnessed the crime through his binoculars, writing down a license plate that might lead to the real killers. Jordan had known of this witness but had kept the information to himself. And in a separate, anonymous Crime Stoppers tip, someone had called in identifying the same people as the bird-watcher.[13] None of this was disclosed to the defense.

The prosecutor was so convinced that the police had the right man that he willfully withheld evidence and distorted the key witnesses' testimony. When we located the various statements indicating that Babin had bad eyesight, the prosecution provided us with her driver's license physical exam. This reflected that her right eye was 20/20 and her left was 20/40, with her full vision being 20/20 *without* corrective lenses. The document made no sense. I have worn glasses since the age of six, when I was unable to read the hymn numbers on Sunday. My mother hauled me off to the optician and made me wear the kind of glasses that only became fashionable forty years later—a fate that I have held against the Anglican Church for almost half a century. Connie Babin would hardly have needed corrective lenses if her eyesight were perfect. So we requested a subpoena for the original result of the eye test, and it reflected that her eyes were actually 20/40 *with* corrective lenses—the doctor's record had been doctored.

The shenanigans did not end there. When the original trial had been in full flow, four boys who had been playing in the basketball game at the time of the murder showed up at the courthouse. They had read in the paper that the prosecution was casting doubt on Shareef's alibi, and they wanted to testify to his innocence. But one of the prosecutors intercepted them and instructed them to leave the courthouse and to report to the DA's office for the duration of the trial. Effectively, they were held against their will—kidnapped. As a result, Shareef's lawyers were unable to locate them, and they never testified.

Shareef's conviction and death sentence were ultimately reversed on the basis of a technical legal issue, rather than this litany of misconduct. One of the chief prosecution witnesses, a friend of Shareef's called James Rowell, had recanted an earlier statement that Shareef had boasted about the murder. Jordan had nevertheless presented Rowell's original assertions as "evidence." The full story was far more alarming than the term *legal technicality* might suggest. Rowell described how the prosecutor had coerced him into lying about his friend.

Rowell, then just sixteen himself, had been charged with a number of other robberies. "My lawyer came to me and told me I was looking at eight hundred years unless I had something for them on Shareef committing the murder," he said. "Then I'd get fifteen years, otherwise life. I argued about taking fifteen years and being able to tell them nothing since I did not know anything." But the lawyer insisted that he needed to give up Shareef to get the lower sentence.[14]

Rowell described two meetings with the prosecutor. "Jordan provided me with the questions I would be asked in court, and the answers, always telling me 'the main thing is just to emphasize how Shareef was bragging to you all about doing the murder,'" he reported. Rowell told the jury that he had an agreement with the prosecution. If he helped out, he would get the lesser sentence—harsh enough for armed robbery, given that Rowell was a juvenile, but infinitely preferable to life in prison.[15]

"Jordan told me to lie about whether I had a deal with the State," he said. "But I knew that the reason my sentencing date kept getting moved back was to make sure that it would occur after the trial date, so they could hold that over me."

As he sat in the Orleans Parish jail, waiting to testify at his friend's trial, Rowell's conscience caught up with him. When Jordan called him as a witness, Rowell admitted that his earlier statements had been false, and he denied that he knew anything that might link Shareef to the murder of Michael Gerardi. Nevertheless, Jordan went through the statement Rowell had recanted and argued to the jury that it was true. He knew he was not allowed to do this—once recanted, a statement is not "evidence"—and Shareef's conviction was reversed for this reason.[16] Jordan's other transgressions received virtually no mention by the Supreme Court of Louisiana.

When a conviction is reversed, the prisoner may be prosecuted again—and again and again, if necessary. We prepared for Shareef's retrial, but on the Friday before it would have started, the district attorney dismissed the charges, having concluded that they could not win the case. Shareef and I discussed suing the prosecutors and the police for what had happened to him. He was eager to do it but said he did not care whether he received compensation: he would settle for a simple apology, and proof from Harry Connick's office that it had introduced rules that would prevent anyone else from suffering the same fate. Perhaps we could also force them to adopt open-file discovery, where the defense would see everything in the possession of the prosecution in advance of trial.

Far from issuing an apology, Roger Jordan continued to insist publicly that Shareef was guilty. So we sued everyone who had been involved in placing Shareef on death row, police and prosecutors alike, laying out in our complaint the full spectrum of Jordan's misconduct: his team had kidnapped witnesses, falsified evidence, and covered up the proof of Shareef's innocence.

One might suggest that Jordan was simply corrupt, but pure corruption is an aberration, and for the most part Jordan's behavior was more common than one would like to think.[17] He no doubt began his career with a law enforcement bias, and his intentions were most likely heartfelt: the defendant's clamor for constitutional rights was drowning out the voice of the victim's family. He doubtless believed that people who came to his attention, arrested by the police, were almost always guilty. His ally was the police officer; his enemy, the opposing advocate. More and more his bias would have drawn him to expect defendants' lawyers to employ underhanded tricks to get their guilty clients off the hook, such as using a video recording that reflected an inaccurate time setting.

In Shareef's case, Jordan would have talked to Connie Babin, the eyewitness, and then seen the video alibi. He knew Babin as a person and a victim but regarded the video only as a defense plot to weasel Shareef out of the frame. When he managed to undermine the alibi, far from thinking that he was condemning an innocent person, he would have congratulated himself for cracking a fraud on the court. When he promised to take several decades off James Rowell's sentence if James identified Shareef, Jordan would have viewed this as a necessary price to pay for the truth; later, he would have deemed the recantation a lie. He very likely did not even notice some of the exculpatory evidence in the file: Shareef was guilty, so how could this detritus genuinely absolve him? Later, by the time we piled up new evidence that undermined the prosecution case, Jordan was so firmly committed to his version of the truth that he would have been unable to believe anything else: the wish had become the father of the thought.

So if I found myself on a jury trying Roger Jordan for *purposefully* attempting to convict an innocent person, I would be bound to acquit him. I don't think he did it intentionally. I suspect he genuinely believed that what he was doing was just and right, and that he still thinks—years later—that Shareef Cousin was the killer. In this sense, he is like most prosecutors I have encountered over the years. This mind-set is far more dangerous than that of a venal man. The problem posed by corruption is recognized, and everyone agrees that it should be rooted out; but the profound imbalance created by the hiring patterns and work environment of virtually every district attorney's office in America is not even acknowledged. So nobody is on the lookout for a cure.

Jordan faced no meaningful punishment for what he had done: we lost our lawsuit against him, and even the bar association imposed nothing more than a slap on the wrist. A sensible legal system would be structured to identify prosecutorial misconduct, should it put an innocent person on death row. It would then provide a strong disincentive against this ever happening again. Sadly, that is not the system we have in place.

America is famous for its compensation culture, but Shareef never received a cent in recompense for the three years he spent growing up on death row for a crime he did not commit. I have worked on the cases of half a dozen innocent people who were sentenced to death in Louisiana, and the most that any of them received when they were set free was ten bucks—the putative bus fare home. I still have the check on my wall that the State of Louisiana issued to Dan Bright, dated June 14, 2004. I bought it off him for twenty dollars.

The lack of compensation is slowly changing. Even Louisiana has now enacted rules governing what a prisoner may be paid for a wrongful conviction, although it remains very low—roughly $15,000 for every year spent in prison.[18] The average income for those outside prison is double that figure, so it is a derisory amount—what would you want to be paid for each year stolen from your life, if you found yourself thrown into a cell and threatened with execution? Yet other countries have even more insulting rules: in Britain, a sum for board and lodging is deducated from any compensation an exonerated prisoner receives. Even when someone has been freed, he has to live with his neighbors' sneaking sense that he was probably guilty anyway and should feel fortunate that he has been released at all.

Prejudice compounds itself. When society adopts the position that prisoners are less than fully human, rules that reinforce that notion become acceptable. After all, the prosecutors are the good guys, and they should be allowed free rein to protect us from criminals. There are many examples of this creeping devolution—the denial of the vote to prisoners, for example, removing any last vestige of power from the powerless. But none perhaps is as insidious as the rule that prosecutors should have absolute immunity from being sued by prisoners, no matter how blatant the professional malfeasance. This rule—grandly called the "doctrine of the prosecutor's sovereign immunity"—was invoked in the federal court of appeals' verdict in Shareef Cousin's case. The court assumed that all the allegations against Roger Jordan were true but dismissed the claims on the grounds that Jordan enjoyed immunity for anything he might have done.

The "doctrine of prosecutorial sovereign immunity" is not codified in American federal law.[19] It is a rule made up by lawyers to protect members of their club. It is very difficult to see its justification. There is no proof that those proven to be innocent would bring more frivolous lawsuits than do those who claim to have slipped on the wet floor of a supermarket aisle. And yet because we despise "criminals," we have allowed the creation of a system that makes it impossible to sue a prosecutor who frames an innocent person for capital murder.

There is a second way in which a prosecutor might be brought to account and encouraged to do the right thing: discipline by the bar association. Shareef's outspoken sister, Tonya Cropper, was outraged at Roger Jordan's single-minded efforts to put her kid brother on death row, and she insisted on reporting him to the bar. The Louisiana Bar Disciplinary Board refused to sanction Jordan at all, but eventually his case percolated up to the Louisiana Supreme Court. The court found that he had violated his ethical duties in suppressing the evidence favorable to Shareef. In its decision, it emphasized that there are few ways of holding a prosecutor to account. "Prosecutors are in a unique position from other members of the bar as they are immune from civil liability," the court noted. Bar disciplinary sanctions are therefore all the more important to ensure the integrity of the process.

The court canvassed the various states. The harshest punishment they could find that had been meted out to a prosecutor for hiding exculpatory evidence was a suspension with the possibility of reinstatement after three months; in only half a dozen cases nationwide had there been any punishment at all, and normally the worst a prosecutor could expect was a "public reprimand," a mild slap on the wrist. In Jordan's case, the court voted for what it believed to be the second harshest punishment ever imposed: a three-month suspension from the practice of law. However, the suspension was itself suspended. In other words, Jordan would not miss a paycheck.

The court's entire discussion showed a remarkably cavalier attitude to the seriousness of the offenses: withholding exculpatory evidence, effectively kidnapping witnesses (forcing them to stay in the DA's office against their will), and putting a minor on death row for a crime he did not commit. A footnote in the history of the Jordan family serves to illustrate the value that the profession places on integrity when it comes to prosecuting "criminals." When I was browsing the bar reports one evening, I came across mention of Roger W. Jordan, Jr.'s, father. Jordan *père* had been referred for a disciplinary violation some years before. He had apparently received $3,000 for the settlement of India Matlock's personal injury case. After deducting his third—the contingency fee— he should have passed the remaining $2,000 on to Matlock, but he apparently failed to do so. While at one point the older Jordan had offered to repay the money in installments, the Supreme Court ruled this was insufficient—he should be permanently disbarred.

"The conversion of a client's funds is one of the most serious violations of an attorney's obligations," wrote the court. "For the protection of the courts and the public, we have concluded that [Roger Jordan, Sr.] must be disbarred."[20] So for pinching $2,000 from a client—which could readily have been reimbursed—Roger Jordan Sr. lost the right to practice law forever. But for committing acts that the Fifth Circuit Court of Appeals assumed were criminal, that put a sixteen-year-old on death row for a crime he did not commit, Roger Jordan, Jr., received only the mildest rebuke.

If we took seriously the goal of protecting the innocent from being framed, there is a third alternative we might consider: prosecuting those who kidnap witnesses or pervert the course of justice. But that is not going to happen either: prosecutors don't prosecute prosecutors for sending an innocent person to prison. They are rarely even held in contempt for a direct violation of a judge's order that favorable evidence should be turned over to the defense.[21]

The field on which justice plays out slopes steeply in one direction. Perhaps the greatest indicator of this is the fact that prosecutors can actually charge defense lawyers with crimes. To take two examples close to home, both of the lawyers representing Kris Maharaj—Ben Kuehne and myself—have faced charges brought by aggressive prosecutors. Ben had to deal with highly publicized criminal charges brought against him by U.S. attorneys who assumed that criminal defendants were paying legal fees with the proceeds of drug dealing—an allegation that presumed them guilty before they had been tried. The prosecutors charged him with offenses that could carry fifty years in prison. A federal judge eventually tossed the case out, vindicating Ben, but not before it caused him immense damage.[22]

Similarly, I have been put on trial for contempt of court and faced prison for nothing more than advising my client that he could assert his right to remain silent under the U.S. Constitution when the prosecution tried to force him to take part in an illegal mental health evaluation. The prosecutor charged me with criminal contempt of court simply because he was angry at me. He had the power to do so without any input from a judge or a grand jury, and I had to go through a full trial to prove that the charge was nonsense.[23]

For both Ben and me (and our families), such experiences have been intimidating, and they run a brightly colored highlighter over the imbalance between defense lawyers and prosecutors. Again, this speaks to the justice system's priorities: our interest in securing convictions far outweighs our desire to ensure that we prosecute the correct person.

But none of this theorizing would get Kris any closer to a new trial. My immediate problem was how to find a way to do the investigation we needed to prove his case—without the money to do it.

As I drove yet again from Miami to New Orleans, I took a difficult decision: because we had no funds for a proper investigation, and because Kris was British, I contacted a friend who worked for British television. European political opinion is solidly against the death penalty, and I needed to rustle up some support for Kris. A roving television camera could operate in Kris's favor in various ways: the British government might decide to support him, both with funds and with expert assistance from Scotland Yard. Certainly it might flush out some of his old friends, who could become witnesses for us, or help to pay some of the expenses. And a journalist might do some of the investigating that we could not afford to do—going to various Caribbean countries, locating witnesses. I recognized that it was a dangerous game to play, and I would never have taken this path if we had been able to properly fund the defense. But the LCAC was a brand-new nonprofit. We were paid court-appointed rates to do capital trials, but that money had to be spent on the relevant Louisiana cases. With no clients who could contribute a dime to their own defense, we were not in a position to finance the kind of investigation that Kris deserved.

In the end, journalists from Channel Four in Britain carried their cameras around South Florida and the Caribbean and made a documentary, *Murder in Room 1215*, that aired in 1996. The team ended up presenting something close to my own emerging view—that there were serious reasons to question whether Kris had committed the crime. One of the people they interviewed was John Kastrenakes. The interview offered up fascinating insights that I would otherwise never have heard.

"John, what was the real fascination of this case for you?" the reporter asked.

"Breaking, or having Mr. Butler tell the truth of exactly what his role was in the case," Kastrenakes replied.

"You said you broke Neville Butler," the journalist queried. "Why use the word *broke*?"

"That's a term of art," Kastrenakes corrected himself. "What, in fact, he did was, he changed his testimony to a truthful version of what really happened."

"Why did he change his version of events?"

"Well," began Kastrenakes, "we, over the course of several months, Paul Ridge and I, were able to obtain telephone records, the evidence of other people, that showed that he, in fact, was in touch constantly with Krishna Maharaj, and that as he would call the Moo Youngs to arrange for this meeting, the next phone call would be made to Krishna Maharaj. So it didn't take a rocket scientist to figure out that his role was much more than he had let on to be. We had confronted him with that, and we offered him a chance to take a polygraph examination, because we doubted that aspect of his testimony. And, in fact, he flunked the polygraph examination and, over the course of several hours, admitted all these other things that he eventually testified to."

"Was he offered a deal?"

"He was never offered a deal. He was never offered—uh . . . by Paul

Ridge or myself... uh... immunity from prosecution," Kastrenakes said cautiously. "But... uh... he testified under the fear of being prosecuted for being involved and for perjury... uh... in his initial sworn statements."

"A general question about the judicial system here. It's expensive, it's lengthy. What are the general worries you perceive?"

"I think that in a country such as ours and such as yours," Kastrenakes began, "where the philosophy is that it's better to let nine hundred people... nine hundred and ninety-nine guilty people go free than to convict one innocent man, and that the burden is on the government to prove an accused citizen's guilt beyond and to the exclusion of every reasonable doubt, that it's necessarily going to be long, and it's necessarily going to be expensive, and it should be tough on the government to prove a person's guilt.

"I've always felt that being up front, telling the defense every bit of the evidence that you have, is always the right way to go," Kastrenakes continued. "Because... uh... if you try to hide something, if you try to... uh... create your own web of deceit, then things come around to haunt you in the end. And certainly... there was never one bit of deceit by us. The deceit that was spun in this case was... was spun by Krishna Maharaj, not by the prosecutors."

Reading the transcript the journalist gave me, I was irritated that Kastrenakes had said this. After all, I had found the polygraph test in his file, and he had not shared it with the defense. I used to think that some prosecutors were wicked, that they intentionally hid material that could be used to destroy their case. By and large, I have come to believe I was wrong. I suspect it never occurred either to Kastrenakes or to Ridge that they were withholding evidence that could help prove Kris innocent— for the simple reason that neither thought Kris was innocent, so how could such evidence exist? They would have rationalized their failure to turn over the lie detector result the same way they justified the case they presented to the jury: the polygrapher had passed Butler on the ultimate issue, whether he saw Kris Maharaj shoot the Moo Youngs. So everything else was incidental to the ultimate truth: the defendant's guilt.[24]

"Now Krishna Maharaj still claims he's been denied justice, and he still claims he's innocent to the charges for which he was convicted—" the journalist said next.

"So do ninety-nine percent of criminals in America who are imprisoned for their crimes . . . say that they did not commit a crime," Kastrenakes cut in before the journalist could finish his question. "Uh . . . it's the rare, it's the unique case where you find a prisoner either on death row or incarcerated for a crime they committed that owns up to their commission of the crime and says that they did the crime that they are charged with. I dare say that there is not a single person on Florida's death row who will come forward to anybody and say, 'I committed the crime that I am being convicted of and sentenced to death for.' "

Kastrenakes was entirely wrong on this point. That was hardly surprising—he would never have represented a prisoner on death row, so how could he know? Most of the people I have represented who did commit the crime have been forthright with me about what happened and rather scathing about those who claim innocence whom the other prisoners believe to be guilty. But convicts tend to be very protective of those among them they believe to be truly innocent.

"So you have no doubts?" the journalist asked.

"I have no doubts about Krishna Maharaj's guilt, involvement in the murders of a"—he started—"of a father and a son, a child who . . . uh . . . he got the death penalty for killing a boy who had no grudge with Krishna Maharaj, called him uncle, looked up to him as a family member."

The stumbling choice of words revealed some of Kastrenakes's self-justification. I have sometimes wondered whether it is fair for me to call my clients "kids" when they are fifteen or sixteen—but I don't like the term "juvenile," which dehumanizes the person on trial. But Duane Moo Young was twenty-three. He was neither a "kid" nor a "boy," and by most definitions no longer a child. Kastrenakes chose the word "boy" to make the crime seem worse.

"That's what he got the death penalty for," Kastrenakes said. "And that's what he deserves the death penalty for."

But would he, John Kastrenakes, ever consider the possibility that he might have made a mistake? "Could it be said that the system is intrinsically flawed, that there have been hundreds of cases of miscarriage of justice this century in capital cases?"

"I . . . I have no comment on that," Kastrenakes stuttered. "Because I . . . I have not been privy to the facts or information in those kinds of cases."

"What does it mean to you to win a capital case of this kind?" the reporter asked, shifting gears.

"Personally? I was—I was very satisfied that, in fact, that I . . . the jury came to the same conclusion that I did about the evidence in the case and that it was overwhelming. That he deserved the death penalty for the crime that he committed and . . . uh . . . there was the satisfaction that I had done, I hadn't fumbled the ball, I hadn't blown the kick, you know . . . so to speak, and that I'd done the best possible job that I could in presenting the case."

In theory, the prosecutor is a bulwark between the innocent defendant and the electric chair. According to the U.S. Supreme Court, the prosecution is "the representative not of an ordinary party to a controversy, but of a sovereignty whose obligation to govern impartially is as compelling as its obligation to govern at all; and whose interest, therefore, in a criminal prosecution is not that it shall win a case, but that justice shall be done."[25]

It's a nice idea, but if we took it seriously, we would not hire and foster prosecutors in the way we do. I had seen the two prosecutors at work on the problems presented to them by Neville Butler. They were not trying to convict an innocent person; they were striving very hard for justice, as they saw it. But I was now pretty sure they were very wrong.

6

The Police

Kastrenakes and Ridge had inherited the case against Krishna Maharaj from the Miami-Dade Police Department and—in common with most prosecutors—seemed to think that the most important evaluation of Kris's culpability had been completed, first by the police's pronouncement that he should be charged, and subsequently by their own office's decision to go forward with the case. The jury verdict was simply a way to ratify these assessments. Any bias on the part of the prosecutors, then, comes on top of the predisposition of the police—and one is likely to compound the other.

In 1978 I got a scholarship to study as an undergraduate at the University of North Carolina, and every year I was offered a summer of work experience. The first opportunity was meant to inculcate students in the value of public service, and I spent ten weeks with the Los Angeles Sheriff's Department (LASD). It was not a great time to be in L.A. A city full of people accustomed to traveling everywhere by car was facing a gas shortage, with mile-long lines at the pumps. Violence was rampant—I was with some officers on patrol when they shot a man who had a knife in his hand, which was quite a shock for someone from the quiet world of Cambridge, England, where no policeman carried a gun.

Nonetheless the LASD officers were welcoming, and amused at my naïve view of the world. One lesson they taught me was how to cheat on a lie detector test. An LASD sergeant put me through a sample examination. The way it works is this: you are hooked up to the monitor, with various sensors that are meant to detect your emotional state. At the beginning, the examiner asks you some anodyne questions, based on true answers that you have already provided, in order to set your baseline—in my case, "Is your mother's name Jean?" was one query; "Are we in the month of July?" another.

The sergeant advised me that when he asked these calibrating questions, I should think the wildest sexual thoughts possible. While it was a little difficult to do that when being asked about my mother, I did my best. Then we got to the real test. Here, as he interrogated me, he told me to think the same wild thoughts and answer yes or no at random, regardless of the truth. That way, he said, the physiological response that had been set for a true answer would be replicated for the subsequent lies. I am a very bad liar, but I followed the sergeant's instructions and beat the test.[1]

The sergeant told me how he used the machine. To be sure, he wanted the subject to feel its tentacles latching onto his skin, and reaching into his soul. But the key part of the lie detector equipment was, he said, the policeman. The officer would size up both the suspect and his story, ask questions, peer ominously at the jagged graphs that spat out of the instrument, and then pronounce his own verdict: as the truth diviner, he would simply identify those aspects of the story that he did not believe. As likely as not, the witness would begin squirming, and the story would start to change.

Ultimately, he said, out came the truth.

Or at least—I thought—*what the sergeant deemed to be the truth.*

In the twenty-eight years I've spent representing defendants in criminal cases, I've slowly come to the conclusion that the law enforcement system is not structured to select officers who are likely to bring the wrong person to trial. This is not meant as a personal criticism of those who join the police force—they are not bad people, but they are often predisposed to certainty and indisposed to recognize or correct their mistakes.

It starts at the very beginning, with the people who apply for the job, and it is reinforced by police training and further cemented by their experience on the job. Police officers have been sued so often for discrimination in hiring, or misuse of power, that they have undergone a battery of psychological tests. Using well-worn testing techniques, law enforcement agencies seek to hire people with "police oriented" attitudes. If you are inclined to question authority, you are probably not going to make it. If you tend to think it possible that the wrong people get banged up on occasion, you will not be considered the right person for the job.[2]

The studies demonstrate the existence of a police "subculture," bolstered by a set of implicit value judgments, that has remained relatively unchanged over many years. Descriptive terms applied by psychologists to the policeman's character profile include *conservative, suspicious, cynical,* and sometimes *authoritarian.* Unfortunately, *suspicious* does not imply self-doubt so much as a predilection to doubt other people and to believe the worst about a suspect. *Cynical* often translates into a refusal to accept a plausible explanation if it is made by the "wrong" person. *Authoritarian* speaks for itself.[3]

Social scientists cannot say conclusively whether these characteristics merely reflect the type of people attracted to police work, or whether the environment in which police find themselves operating nurtures these attitudes. From the perspective of the criminal defendant, it does not much matter, as the result is the same: the officer who arrests them is predisposed to disbelieve their claim of innocence and to do whatever he feels he has to do to prove their guilt. There seems to be little recognition of the problem and still less effort to turn the tide. Remarkably, advertisements for jobs in the world of law enforcement generally omit *all* reference to the possibility of doing justice and focus solely on apprehending criminals.

David and I had founded the LCAC in Louisiana in late 1993 with three clients from Lake Charles, on the Texas border, but we were soon sucked into a number of capital cases in New Orleans. Our finances were shaky, and we were in an office on the thirteenth floor of a downtown building: it was called the fourteenth floor, but the elevator skipped from twelve to fourteen. Rents were lower because of superstitions. In the early months we struggled to keep the doors open, but gradually we were appointed to more capital cases. They paid little, but so did we—our salaries were only $16,000 a year in those early days, and we paid ourselves only when the going was good.

The landlord wouldn't let me bring Vesta, my Labrador, into work. It seemed cruel to leave her at the house for our long workdays, and I liked to have her sitting under the desk. The landlord said that other tenants were afraid of dogs in the elevator; I said I would take the stairs. He said that wouldn't do, so I said we'd move out. Looking around for a different space, we found a building for sale four blocks away. For what seemed like the ridiculous sum of $150,000—the mortgage payments would be less than our rent—we got three stories and 12,000 square feet. We grandiloquently named the building the Justice Center and painted it my idea of New Orleans Mardi Gras colors—puce, gold and green. It was generally agreed that the result was appalling. Suddenly the organization was on a slightly more permanent footing: we were even able to lure a few more staff to work with us. First Shannon Wight joined us, volunteering to be an investigator for no pay. Gradually, we had the money to hire other young people, including Rachel Chmiel, who had just graduated from law school.

Shareef Cousin, the sixteen-year-old who had been put on death row by Roger Jordan for the French Quarter shooting, was one of our first local clients. Jordan had built up his case on foundations supplied by Detective Anthony Small. And my experience with Small led me to coin a new rule for our office: If you want to expose police malfeasance, search out the lead detective's soon-to-be-ex-spouse.

I knew there was something fishy about Anthony Small's testimony from the very beginning. The evidence of Shareef's innocence seemed compelling, and Small had constructed much of the case against him. I decided we needed to know everything we could about Small. Rachel sought out his wife, Regina. The couple were in the midst of a messy divorce. She agreed to talk to us.

When Rachel and I went to her apartment, Regina welcomed us in without fuss, offering us iced tea. She was an attractive woman, gripped by an extraordinary anger at her husband. She seemed happy to hold forth to any ear that would listen to his perfidy. As we sat down on her sofa, she described a man who was drunk on the power of his police badge. Anthony Small, she said, would play for any side that paid him. She said she often saw him bring his police reports home to doctor them, to help those willing to buy their way out of serving time. He had fixed a drug offense for a resident of St. Croix for a fee of several thousand dollars, altering his report to bolster the suspect's case. He sold confidential information that he obtained in the police department. He stole jewelry from crime scenes whenever he could get his hands on it.

If I ever got him on the witness stand, under oath, Regina said I was to ask him where he got the Rolex watch that he always wore. It had come from a homicide victim, she said—the man who was later put on trial for the murder had also been convicted of robbery for taking the watch. Regina told me that her husband had a particular fondness for tropical fish. Once when he'd carried out a search on the home of a fellow enthusiast, he'd netted some of the rarer specimens and brought them home to his own tank.

Detective Small was proud of his win-loss record. He boasted that he had never failed to convict someone charged with murder. He told Regina he was going to make sure that he did not start losing with the case against Shareef Cousin. He was going to make sure that Connie Babin, his eyewitness, did not let down the prosecution at trial.

It took me a while to get a word in, but I finally brought up a subject that had been puzzling me: the Crime Stoppers tip against Shareef did not match the Shareef Cousin I knew. He was six feet tall and solidly built. On March 24, 1995, at 10:05 p.m., Detective Small wrote a report saying he had received Crime Stoppers tip number 3519 from someone who had overheard Shareef boasting that he had shot and killed a white man coming out of the Port of Call restaurant. The caller added that Shareef lived in the basement of 3811 Marais and described him as "dark complexion, skinny, short."

We had collected some police files on Shareef, and I had noticed that the only document that gave a physical description of him before the murder involved his arrest for truancy four years before, when he was only twelve. The description of twelve-year-old Shareef was consistent with the Crime Stoppers tip. So I had wondered how the Crime Stoppers description could have matched a four-year-old police profile from when Shareef was not yet a teenager.

Regina seemed surprised, as if I had stumbled onto a dark secret that she thought well hidden. She said her husband used to call in tips himself. This was another scheme he used to supplement his police income. He'd done it in Shareef's case, which was particularly high profile, so he could collect the $10,500 reward.

I had not considered it before, but Crime Stoppers is a very dangerous tool in the wrong hands. It takes anonymous tips from citizens and passes them on to the police. When you call in with information, you don't have to leave your name; you are given a code number, and when the subject of your tip is arrested, you call back and give your number to collect your reward. Across America the system varies, but in essence you identify the dark alley where you would like to collect your cash in a brown paper bag. You pay no taxes on the reward. Nowadays encryption systems ensure that the tipster remains even more securely anonymous.

Regina Small told me that her husband had phoned in the tip on Shareef, relying on the description in the police file, then arrested him and had a friend—she knew the name but would not tell me who it was—collect the cash.

There is pure corruption, where the goal is simply to line one's own pockets; and then there is corruption of a different form, where the officer's motive is not personal gain but to convict a man who he believes to be patently guilty but who might be set free by a worthless judicial system. Both "corrupt" the system, in the sense that they hinder justice. Detective Small was an extreme case, but it is a sad fact that policemen often lie to get the result they want, thinking they are acting for the greater good.

By the end of Shareef's case, the LCAC had developed a fair amount of experience with the New Orleans Police Department. Off-duty officers would have too much to drink in the local bars and boast that they had been down to court to "testi-lie" rather than testify, in order to ensure a conviction. We caught police committing perjury in eight consecutive capital cases. Each confection was not just a passing recharacterization of a disputed fact, but a full-on falsification of evidence that could have sent the wrong person to his death.

As we continued to catch officers lying, I met with New Orleans police authorities and tried to persuade them to take action. I cornered local politicians. I met with federal prosecutors to exhort them to bring cases against proven perjurers: after all, actively lying in a capital case should theoretically send you to prison for life. But nobody was interested.

As my Realtor had suggested, my own neighborhood in New Orleans was not the most salubrious. I lived a few blocks away from the St. Thomas Projects, where sixteen of the sixteen hundred residents were murdered in 1996 alone—one in one hundred, roughly the same death rate suffered by American soldiers in the Vietnam War.[4] The police were meant to be the last line of defense between the people of St. Thomas and a tsunami of crime, and the authorities did not want to be heard admitting that officers manning the thin blue line were too lazy or venal to seek out the true perpetrators.[5]

Our slowly expanding band of lawyers and investigators would hold brainstorming sessions once a week. We threw around all kinds of ideas on how to confront the officers' testi-lying, but we could not get the authorities to take the issue seriously. We decided our only recourse was to turn to the court of public opinion. We set up a watchdog called Stop the P.I.G. (Perjury In Government). Each month we would make a very public award to an officer whom we had caught lying in court. At the same time, to ensure balance, we would give a *Serpico* award to the officer who had been fair to a criminal defendant[6]—but we kept this award secret to avoid getting the officer into trouble. Our whole campaign had minimal impact. Achieving fairness for a person accused of a capital crime was a long way down on the public's list of priorities, and the press wasn't really interested in covering the problem. The murders themselves made much better copy—and almost every day there was another killing somewhere in the city. Each one would be another potential capital trial in the Orleans Parish Criminal Court.

In New Orleans I was involved in a number of capital trials and the first time I had to go through the process of picking a jury was in the capital case of Clarence "Smitty" Smith. In other places in the South, I had habitually asked prospective jurors how much weight they would place on the testimony of policemen. In some parts of rural Mississippi, people will tell you they will believe an officer over a defense witness no matter what the facts might be. Given some policemen's predilection to doctor the facts, that could be dangerous for any chance of a fair trial.

"Who here would believe everything a police officer says no matter what it is?" I asked the panel of Orleans Parish jurors, trying to get a sense of my new community.

A loud guffaw came from the back row. I looked up. It was a black man in his mid-thirties. "Believe everything?" he asked, visibly incredulous. "You gotta be kidding me! I'd disbelieve pretty much anything a cop might say in this town!"

A number of other jurors chimed in. Nobody stood up for the New Orleans Police Department.

This was all very well for me as the defense lawyer—my client was acquitted in short order, as he should have been—but as a citizen it made me very sad. When people lose all faith in the police, we are well into a vicious cycle that is difficult to circumvent: the police, knowing they have no allies among the people, reach for their guns more often; the people, in turn, don't trust the police, so they have a tendency to either shoot first or return fire. The net result is that nobody is safe.

Unlike most police across the country, certain members of the New Orleans Police Department have worked especially hard to earn this unhappy reputation. Indeed, two officers are now on death row for their own crimes—Antoinette Frank and Len Davis—and four others were convicted in what was originally a capital trial in 2011 for killing unarmed citizens during the aftermath of Hurricane Katrina.[7] Yet the broader problem is not the overt corruption of a small group of officers but the bias that permeates most police forces, from Los Angeles to Miami.

When I took on Kris Maharaj's case, I had made a freedom of information request for the prosecutors' files. Before my next trip to Florida, I did the same for the Miami-Dade Police Department. The evidence custodian showed me into another airless and windowless room and brought in box after box of materials. He pointed out the copy machine, and told me to Xerox anything I wanted—I just had to keep a running tally. He kindly pointed to the coffee machine. It was free, it was dark (vintage from early that morning), and it was very welcome. I had not expected quite so many boxes. I was going to be in that room for a while.

I marveled at my good fortune. Here were files of material, thick reams of potential evidence that should help explain some of the inconsistencies in the case. The folders were even tabbed.

The lead policeman on the case, Detective John Buhrmaster, had testified to various things that Kris had supposedly said and not said on the day of the murder, and Kris had thrown some of those statements into question when he finally took the stand to offer up his own version of events. Buhrmaster did not claim to have recorded these statements in any way—he produced no tape, no signed statement, no notes of the conversation. Yet his testimony was central to the prosecution's case. If Kris had really denied being in room 1215 that day, as the detective had testified, then how could he explain the fingerprints found all over the suite?

When I asked him, Kris insisted that he had told Buhrmaster the whole story—how Neville Butler had invited him into the room to meet a man by the name of Eddie Dames who was supposedly interested in distributing the *Caribbean Times* in the Bahamas. He said he had arrived around eight in the morning, waited an hour, read the paper, made some instant coffee, and finally got impatient and left shortly after nine—three hours before the murders.

In the file I pulled together back in New Orleans, I had already found evidence indicating that Buhrmaster's trial testimony might be false on

one score: in a deposition, Eric Hendon had asked Buhrmaster's partner, Officer David Romero, whether, on the night of his arrest, Maharaj
had told Buhrmaster that he had been in room 1215 on October 16, 1986,
before the Moo Youngs died.

"He had been there," Romero replied, "prior to the homicides, that's
correct."[8] If Hendon had called Romero to testify, the officer would have
contradicted his colleague on this key point: since Kris had told Buhrmaster that he had been in room 1215, there was an innocent explanation for all the supposedly incriminating fingerprints.

But at trial, Eric Hendon simply (and amazingly) failed to call
Romero as a witness to show Buhrmaster up as a liar. Hendon could
also have taken another step as well: If a statement by a defendant appears to be inculpatory, any defense lawyer worth his salt will generally
consider whether it might be excluded from the trial. The famous *Miranda* rule requires police to read a suspect his rights and permits
them to interview him only if he agrees; certainly, police cannot question him if he asks to speak with an attorney. Kris had told me that,
over the course of Buhrmaster's interrogation late on the night of
the Moo Youngs' murder, it had quickly become evident to him that
the detective thought he was guilty, so he had demanded access to a
lawyer.

I was shocked when one of the first pieces of paper I found in Buhrmaster's file was a note: "Buhrmaster and Amato go to jail at 12:18am
with Maharaj. (D invokes his right to attorney.) FORGET THIS. * BE
CAREFUL ABOUT THIS." Someone had written a script for his testimony. *D* meant the defendant; the detective knew that if he conceded
that Kris had asserted his rights, anything said afterward would be inad-
missible at trial.[9]

By now, I was very excited. I knew that this note alone provided a strong
legal claim to raise in Kris's appeal. But my review of the boxes had
hardly begun. One box was labeled "contents of Moo Young briefcase." I
vaguely recalled a note I had read in the defense lawyer's file: Ron
Petrillo, the defense investigator, had gone to Buhrmaster's office and

asked whether he could see the briefcase that Derrick and Duane Moo Young had brought to their appointment at the DuPont Plaza Hotel. Buhrmaster had told Petrillo that it had been returned to the Moo Young family. But the detective had clearly misled him, because here were its contents, laid out before me.

When we later confronted him with this contradiction, Buhrmaster said he had given the briefcase back to the family but, after Petrillo's request, he had retrieved it. If this was true—and it seemed to me highly improbable—then Buhrmaster's behavior would have reflected a remarkably irresponsible attitude to the evidence. After all, it meant he had handed over a treasure trove without making a copy. Moreover, he would have been under a clear duty to correct his statement to the defense investigator, who had no reason either to predict the relevance of the material in the briefcase or to think that it might later become available.

The briefcase contained hundreds of pages, including all kinds of corporate documents, all of which were copied in the police files. Maybe these would cast light on the Moo Young business dealings. On my trip from New Orleans to Miami, I had stopped off to see Kris—the Florida State Prison, in Starke, was not far off my route—and Kris had told me some details about the civil case he had brought against Derrick to try to recoup the money he had embezzled. Derrick had been running Kris's Florida investments when some $14,000 in rent went missing. Then entire properties seemed to have changed hands, and Kris soon discovered that Marita's car had been registered in Derrick's name. When he looked more closely into the accounts, he discovered that Derrick had misappropriated more than $400,000.

He had confronted Derrick and his son Duane about the missing money, and they promised that they would make good on it. Duane wrote Kris checks for $200,000 and $243,000—but both bounced. At this point, Kris sued them; it was a simple case, and he was confident of an easy victory. After all, had he not taken on the establishment in Britain and won a major court victory against Lord Cockfield? He hired Levi England as his attorney and went to court.

When I discussed the civil case with him—by now, eight years later—Kris still did not fully understand how the Moo Youngs had ripped him off. The briefcase began to supply answers. Kris had named his Florida holding company KDM International—taking the initials from his name, Derrick's, and Marita's. KDM International was originally registered to the Moo Young home address in Fort Lauderdale, and Derrick was a signatory on all the KDM International accounts. Here in front of me were documents showing how Derrick and Duane had created a company with a very similar name, KDM Distributors, listed at the same address. They had commingled the bank accounts, transferring money and buildings from one to the other. On March 3, 1986, they had gone one better: Duane filed papers removing Kris and Marita as officers of KDM International and substituting himself. In this way, he concluded a stealthy takeover of the entire company. When Kris sued, Derrick fought back by planting defamatory stories in the *Caribbean Echo*. He hoped to shame Kris into dropping the case in the interest of preserving his good name.

Kris did understand, of course, that the Moo Youngs had used the *Caribbean Echo* to smear him with all kinds of defamatory allegations, but he had no sense of the degree to which the Moo Youngs and Carberry (editor of the *Echo*) had been acting hand in glove. In the police file, I came across a copy of KDM International's articles of incorporation, which Derrick had apparently given to Carberry for use as the prototype for his own new corporation. Derrick, it seems, was sharing his newfound expertise in setting up a business.[10]

Indeed, the Moo Youngs' next move was equally subtle. Kris told me that his response to the defamatory articles in the *Caribbean Echo* was not, as the prosecution suggested, to ride around Florida hatching bizarre murder plots. Rather, relishing a new game of business chess, Kris had established a rival paper, the *Caribbean Times*. Nothing about the Moo Youngs or the *Echo* ever appeared on the pages of the *Times*; Kris simply planned to drive the *Echo* out of business by publishing a better alternative for the Caribbean community in South Florida.

Here, in the briefcase file, I found the Moo Youngs' countergambit. Apparently, Kris had not completed the technical documents establishing his new paper, so on July 11, 1986, Derrick and Duane registered a company with a similar name, the *Caribbean Times International,* to initiate another surreptitious takeover. On August 12, 1986, just two months before they died, Derrick started writing to the Barnett Bank demanding all the financial records for Kris's paper. Derrick said he was president of the *Caribbean Times International* and demanded to know what accounts had been opened in the company's name, hinting darkly at financial impropriety.

I was thrilled with what I was finding and I was making copies of everything, oblivious to the mounting charges. The air conditioning was running, it was hot outside, and I had no interest in taking a break. I skipped lunch and concentrated on a new pot of coffee and a snack machine that dispensed small packets of salted peanuts. As I continued, the briefcase gradually unlocked even more convoluted secrets.

Next up were deeds of another Moo Young company, Cargil International SA. The name *Cargil* was vaguely familiar to me. If memory served, it was a huge multinational corporation, maybe from Canada. When I looked it up later that evening, I learned it was based in the American Midwest. *Cargill* (its name had an extra *l*) was a multibillion-dollar food and agriculture business. The Moo Youngs lived in South Florida, but the main office of their *Cargil* was registered in Panama. There was also a branch of *Cargil* in the Bahamas.

I noticed copies of Derrick's and Duane's passports, along with various credit card records. I only glanced at the pages as I was copying them—a close analysis would come later—but I saw immediately where some of the money they had embezzled had gone. In the nine months leading up to their murder, the Moo Youngs had taken at least thirteen international flights, staying in expensive hotels wherever they went. They went to Europe (for two weeks on two occasions), the Cayman Islands, Mexico, Panama (a total of six times), Puerto Rico (twice), and Trinidad, and they took multiple flights all over the United States.

I came across a letter dated June 6, 1986, purporting to be from someone called Richard Solomon, addressed to Derrick Moo Young at an address in Panama, discussing some gems. Not just "some" gems—stones worth over $130 *million.*[11] I had no idea what to make of it. Notes in what I now recognized as Duane Moo Young's spidery handwriting suggested that the gems were being held in the Bank of Tonga. Given that the other Bank of Tonga documents in the briefcase were clearly fakes—I could see one original, and a copy where the names had been whited out and retyped—this seemed to be some kind of fraud. But precisely what kind, I was not sure.

The file contained various other drafts of letters in Duane's handwriting. They were extraordinary. They purported to offer loans of vast amounts of money to various governments around the Caribbean. The Moo Youngs, writing to someone called Dr. Enrique Van Brown, offered to provide $100 million to the governments of Paraguay and Venezuela. Another letter proposed $250 million to Trinidad; notes suggested other offerings to Panama and Costa Rica.

How, I asked myself, were the Moo Youngs in a position to offer this kind of money? My emotions were mixed. None of these materials had been turned over to Kris Maharaj's defense—they clearly should have been. But they ought to be enough to get Kris off death row. Already they promised to reshape the entire case against him: no longer were the Moo Youngs to be regarded as subsistence businessmen; they had been conducting shady deals worth hundreds of millions of dollars. If the prosecution at trial had suggested that $441,000 was Kris's motive for killing them, here was evidence of other deals that dwarfed any complaint Kris might have had. With every new page, I felt my pulse racing. Rather than wait to Xerox everything the next day, I made sure that I copied each document I had flagged before I left that afternoon. I had the sense that at any moment someone might come in and put a stop to my research. I was doing nothing wrong, of course—indeed, the prosecution should have turned all this over to Eric Hendon before the trial. But I was afraid that these gifts might be snatched from Kris.

I did not go back to the police department the next day—that would have to wait another twenty-four hours—as I had made an appointment elsewhere. In the police file, I had found various insurance policies taken out by the Moo Youngs. On January 26, 1986, Derrick had applied for $1 million in "key man" life insurance, naming the beneficiary as

NEC International, a Panamanian corporation. Why Panama? In 1986, Panama was the fiefdom of the notorious General Manuel Noriega. Although the prosecution described Derrick at trial as disabled and effectively retired, he claimed in his insurance application to have been employed by NEC for a year. I had no idea what NEC was, or why Derrick would take out a huge life insurance policy on himself. But I had a general sense of what key man insurance was—it had something to do with reimbursing a company for the loss of an important employee.[12]

As I had leafed through the pages, I found copies of more policies. On August 7, 1986, Duane Moo Young had taken out half a million dollars in insurance on himself. That same day Paul Moo Young and Shaula and Kerry Lee Nagel (all family) had applied for a total of $1.3 million in insurance through a corporation called DMY International, another company named after either Derrick or Duane Moo Young— presumably Duane, as he had signed each application as president. On October 13, 1986, Alan Stuart Carr and Andrew Wong, also members of the family, had applied for a total of $800,000 of insurance with DMY International. I rapidly totted it up: in the ten months before the murder, more than $3 million worth of life insurance was taken out on family members, some just three days before Derrick and Duane were killed. Why? Did they know that disaster was looming? Had someone threatened Derrick and told him that his children might be targets? These policies were even more helpful to Kris's case than the earlier materials had been. The evidence did not yet point at another suspect, but who, or what, had the Moo Youngs feared?

Before making this trip to Florida, I already knew that after Derrick and Duane were killed, the surviving Moo Youngs had had litigation with the William Penn Life Insurance Company, suing to recover on the insurance. Indeed, not long after his trial, a lawyer for the insurance company had contacted Kris, seeking the answers to some questions. Kris had told me about it and given me the lawyer's name—Brenton Ver Ploeg. I had called him before I left New Orleans and made an appointment. But only when I came across the papers in Detective Buhrmaster's file did I get an idea of the full scale of the issues here. Meanwhile, Ver Ploeg had obtained permission from his client to share any materials with me that would not betray legal privilege. We had agreed to meet the next morning.

Ver Ploeg's law practice was located in a high-rise in downtown Miami, similar to Ben Kuehne's. The panorama from the reception window was breathtaking—the blue harbor stretched between the city and Miami Beach, with cruise ships calmly sailing in from the Atlantic. It was a very different world from our scruffy office in New Orleans. The woman behind the main desk politely asked me to wait, and a few minutes later Ver Ploeg appeared to usher me into his own office.

He was around fifty, hair graying and receding, the image of a courteous Dutchman. We discussed the case briefly. He referred to Kris by his first name and had clearly liked him when he had met him up at the prison. In a capital trial, the defense rarely has the resources to investigate the case as thoroughly as it should. Civil lawyers who are arguing over money tend to be much better funded. Ver Ploeg described how he had hired John Healey, a gumshoe out of New York to investigate the case. The lawyer was appropriately coy about confidential issues, but he implied that William Penn had spent hundreds of thousands of dollars defending the suit, although it was finally settled and a payment of some description had been made to the Moo Youngs.

Detective Buhrmaster had turned over a copy of the Moo Young briefcase documents to Healey years before, giving the insurance investigator the evidence he had withheld from the defense in the criminal trial. The investigator then trawled around the Caribbean trying to decrypt some of the notes. Ver Ploeg told me that, on the basis of what he and Healey had learned, he was concerned that Kris Maharaj had not received a fair trial. He set me in front of another pile of boxes, this time with a window and a view. This room was decidedly tonier than the police department; the copy machine was faster and free, and the coffee rather better. My level of excitement remained the same.

Healey had been very thorough. He had uncovered documents that revealed that the Moo Youngs were negotiating to buy a bank in Panama for $600 million. He'd located the original letters that the Moo Youngs had sent, typed up from the drafts in the briefcase, offering loans around the Caribbean. With $100 million here, and $250 million there, the letters escalated to an offer made to the country of Trinidad for a loan of $2 *billion*.

Later, I came across documents suggesting that the Moo Youngs had access to $5 billion in Japanese yen bonds. In 1986 there were thirty-two countries with a gross national product under $5 billion a year. How could the Moo Youngs, a Jamaican family of modest means, have had access to enough money to buy various countries?

Ver Ploeg had copies of the bank statements from the Moo Youngs' legitimate private account, doubtless the one the tax man might have been allowed to see. It hit a February low of $6.85 on Valentine's Day 1986 and went into deficit, minus $14.65, on April 7. By and large, the account reflected very modest balances.[13] During the same period, Derrick and his son had been offering several nation-states billions of dollars in loans.

What on earth was going on?

Again I trembled with excitement and frustration. These documents would have been dynamite in the hands of the defense lawyer at trial, but would I be able to get a jury to listen now? Kris was on death row. Before anything could come of this, we would have to persuade a judge to grant him a new trial.

On my third day in Miami, I went back to the police department to complete my review of Detective Buhrmaster's files. By the end of another long morning fueled by terrible coffee, I had copied several hundred pages that I would take back to New Orleans to study more closely. As I leafed through one folder and then the next, I periodically paused to consider what these documents said about the detective who had chosen to suppress them. The meticulous files suggested that he was organized, which meant that their significance could not wholly have escaped him. Was he corrupt, a tool of larger forces behind the case? Or was he, like so many prosecutors, simply focused on convicting a man whom he believed to be the killer, a determination that had led him either to cover up or disregard anything that did not fit with his theory? I was a long way from having firm answers.

As I started the long drive back to New Orleans the next day, I wondered whether we would ever have the necessary resources to do this case properly. It was 1995, and we'd got our salaries up to $24,000 a year—not what lawyers think they should be paid, perhaps, but survivable, at least in New Orleans. The grant money we had obtained in the early days to set up the office had mostly expired. With almost all of our funding coming now from the state for court appointments, we had to be vigilant, ensuring that none of that income went toward other, extracurricular cases.

That meant I'd be making long drives along I-10 to see Kris, and down I-95 to Miami—rather than flying. It meant that I'd stay with Marita Maharaj when I got there, rather than in a motel. I had earned a bad reputation at the office for encouraging everyone to stop for a coffee and a large bag of peanuts on the interstate, rather than pay for proper meals. We had no money for the full investigation into Detective Buhrmaster and his police colleagues, let alone for what Brenton Ver Ploeg had done: sending an investigator around the Caribbean to gather up all the evidence Kris would need. As I'd hoped, the British journalists had tracked down some of the witnesses in Florida and the Caribbean. None of this approached the sort of inquiry that a man on death row deserved. But I hoped it would be enough to crack open the door and get us another shot at a trial.

7

The Expert

"Is it your conclusion that this man is a malingerer?" the judge demanded of the expert.

"I wouldn't be testifying if I didn't think so," testified Dr. Herbert Randolph Unsworth, "unless I was on the other side. Then it would be a post-traumatic condition."

—*Ladner v. Higgins*, 71 So.2d 242, 244 (La. App. 1954)[1]

With respect to the gun used in the murder of the Moo Youngs, the prosecution had put together a compelling case against Kris. No murder weapon was produced at trial, but that was not so unusual. Any killer with half a brain would dump the pistol after killing two people, and Miami had plenty of waterways where a gun could vanish for all time. But there was one blip in the presentation—in his first statement, Neville Butler had said that the gun was white. (The one Kris had owned was silver.) Hendon had taken Butler up on this in his pre-trial deposition, but he forgot to do the same at trial, which meant that the jury knew nothing about the discrepancy.

Once again Detective Buhrmaster provided the key evidence: he testified that the defendant had denied ever owning a handgun. That lie made Kris look like he had something to hide. As with all of Buhrmaster's assertions, there was no tape, no signed statement, no notes. The jury depended on the policeman's say-so. But then, Hendon gave them no reason to doubt him.

The prosecution labored over its presentation in this respect, dotting every *i*, and crossing every *t*. Their motive was obvious: the point about the gun was central to their case, and they wanted to spend plenty of time on it, to underline its significance for any juror who might be dozing. They began by demonstrating that Kris had bought a Smith & Wesson pistol some months earlier. He had obtained it through a friend who was a police officer, Lieutenant Bernie Buzzo. Detective Bellrose of the Miramar Police Department told the jury that he had wanted to sell his gun and that Buzzo told him he had a buyer. Bellrose did not know who it was until much later, when he "found out" that it was Krishna Maharaj.

Next, officer Gregory Jansen, of the Plantation Police Department, was called as a witness to describe how Kris Maharaj had been stopped for speeding on the Florida Turnpike on July 2, 1986, three and a half months before the homicides. Jansen responded to the call at 2:40 in the morning. He searched Kris's rental car, and his report reflected that there was a Smith & Wesson nine-millimeter handgun in the trunk, with the serial number A235464. More than a year later, having briefly seen him in the dark, Jansen said he could identify Kris as the driver of the car.

Finally, the prosecutors summoned Thomas Quirk, an expert firearms examiner from the Metro-Dade Crime Laboratory, to discuss ballistics. Various bullets had been removed from the bodies of the two victims, Derrick and Duane Moo Young, and the shell casings that had been ejected in the room had been gathered up. Quirk's task was to determine whether it was possible to say which type of gun had fired them. He went into such excruciating detail that the judge finally interrupted.

"I don't think it's necessary for someone to tell how a weapon works," said Judge Solomon, trying to move the case along. "Believe me, when those jurors go in there, men with experience in weapons will tell the ladies how a weapon works, if people don't know. But if you insist on telling how a weapon works without objection from defense we will listen to this gentleman."

In the end, Thomas Quirk did far more than explain how a weapon works. He essentially told the jurors that the bullets found at the scene had come from the type of gun owned by Kris Maharaj—a Smith & Wesson. Quirk opined that it was immediately clear to him that the bullets had been fired from one of six brands of guns, all nine-millimeter semiautomatics—Browning, Leyte, Llama, Sig Sauer, Smith & Wesson, or Star. He had then test-fired all six types of guns, recovered the slugs, and decided that the Smith & Wesson was the most likely, since the striations on the bullets (the marks made as the bullet went down the weapon's rifled barrel) were the closest match. After discussing the slugs, he moved on to the bullet casings.

"The only fired standard that I have in the lab," Quirk testified, "that matches the same type of morphology on the casings from the scene is a model thirty-nine Smith and Wesson." In other words, he was saying that the casings found at the scene were likely shot from a Smith & Wesson gun. All in all, he concluded that all these bullets were probably fired through just such a gun as Kris Maharaj had owned.

Next, the prosecutor marked a photograph of a semiautomatic Smith & Wesson pistol for Quirk to show the jury. At last, Eric Hendon objected. What was the possible relevance of this? It could not be the actual gun.

"Overruled," snapped Judge Solomon. "This is demonstrative. Go ahead." He nodded the case on.

Here, the prosecutors were playing with a psychological phenomenon known as Wigmore's Horse: if a horse is brought into the courtroom where the man on trial is accused of horse theft, the jurors will automatically—albeit unconsciously and irrationally—leap to the conclusion that it is *the* horse he stole, and he must therefore be guilty. The same was true of the photograph of the gun. On cross-examination, Hendon did point out that perhaps 270,000 Smith & Wesson handguns were produced from 1954 to 1986, any of which could have been the murder weapon. But by now the damage had been done, and Hendon's focus on the number of such weapons would have left the impression that everyone agreed that a Smith & Wesson had been used to kill Derrick and Duane Moo Young.

Quirk had focused the jury's sights directly on Kris Maharaj.

To understand the extraordinary influence of the expert in a court-room, we needn't go much beyond the intimidation that many people feel in the presence of people in white coats. We defer to science for deep-rooted cultural reasons: in an earlier era of experimentation, sci-entists studied the world, they asked questions, they discoursed in the Royal Society or in the coffeehouse, and they proposed the rules that governed the confusing universe around us. They were viewed as the unbiased intellectual cream of society. In 1673 an unknown Dutchman called Antonie van Leeuwenhoek advanced a novel theory of biology that involved the first microscopic study of how a bee might sting. Since nobody had studied this phenomenon before, the Royal Society simply asked him for character references from the ministers and lawyers of Delft.[2] It was a matter of honor: if he came from the right social class, his conclusions should be accepted on trust. Only more recently, when some scientists began working for corporations, has their credibility come into question. But few lawyers—and fewer jurors—feel inclined to challenge witnesses in their field of expertise, so their testimony still carries overwhelming weight.

The scientific method, developed over many hundreds of years, is designed to test whether a particular hypothesis truly reflects the opera-tions of nature: whether the observer has happened upon a theory that can honestly be replicated, or whether it is just an alluring but random happenstance.

The true scientist comes up with a hypothesis, then tests it: for ex-ample, does a particular medication actually help cure an illness? The scientist does randomized, controlled, double-blind studies to see whether the results of administering a new pill are significantly better than the benefits of the currently available medication, of a placebo, or of no treatment at all. The scientist then publishes both the methods and data, so that others can attempt to reproduce the result, direct criticism, and help establish the truth.

But in order for the scientific method to operate, there must be oth-ers in the field who have an incentive to cast a critical eye over this work;

otherwise it cannot truly be deemed reliable. If these other experts come from within the company that manufactures the medicine at issue, they may be eager to ensure that a hefty investment in the development of a particular medicine will not go to waste. That is one form of bias. Those from a rival company may have a different bias, hoping to demonstrate that the new pill is an expensive fraud. Ideally, then, the peer review comes from an independent body, whose only motive is to establish the efficacy of a medication before another thalidomide is unleashed on the market. But while such a scientific watchdog may be impartial, who is going to fund it?

The central problem with forensic science—where science is applied to solve crimes—is that there is no scientist with an incentive to question the proposed hypothesis. Take forensic hair analysis, for example. Every day a "trace evidence expert" looks down his binary microscope (a microscope with two lenses) so that he can see two hairs at the same time, side by side. He compares a hair found at the crime scene with one belonging to the suspect. He runs his eye along the two hairs until he comes to the point where the two look most similar, and then he starts identifying an intimidating array of characteristics—the hair's color, its buckling, its cortex, medulla, and so forth. He may opine on the racial class of the hair, often—remarkably—still describing it in arcane terms such as Caucasian, Negroid, or Mongoloid. He then reaches an opinion as to whether the two are microscopically similar, sometimes loosely referred to as a "match."[3]

The forensic hair analyst then appears in court and takes the oath. The prosecutor has him list his qualifications, and the hundreds of cases where his view has been deemed important, before turning to the judge to ask that he should be respected as something more than a mere witness—he is an *expert* witness.

"In light of his years of training and practice," the robed eminence on the bench will intone, "I recognize this witness as an expert. He may state his opinions to the jury."

There are many flaws in this "science," some obvious on a cursory evaluation. What, for example, is meant by "Negroid" hair? Years ago I worked with a Mississippi lawyer who would officially change race as he crossed the border into Louisiana. His blood was, he told me, one-sixteenth African American. In Louisiana, he was deemed to be white, as a mixed-race person was classified as "Negroid" only if he had at least one-eighth African American blood (one great-grandparent). But when he drove back into Mississippi, he reverted to "Negroid," defined there as one-sixteenth black (one great-great-grandparent). However fatuous and offensive such racial grouping might be, for a forensic science category of "Negroid" to mean anything, there has to be a definition—in order to distinguish commingled genes. But at no point have I ever persuaded a hair expert to tell the jury what he or she meant when using the term.

But forensic science has a far deeper problem: nobody who spends his days looking down a binary microscope does it while thinking he is wasting his time. In other words, nobody questions whether what a supposed expert sees down the microscope actually tells us anything about who shed the hair. Everyone trained as a forensic hair analyst believes that his work is valid, and no independent study has ever meaningfully validated it.[4]

For me, the case of James Raulerson,[5] who was on death row in Mississippi, brought this problem into sharp focus. Raulerson had been granted a new trial, again to face the death penalty, and I was representing him along with Jackson Brown—not the singer, but a loud and opinionated attorney from Starkeville. Jack was a colorful and successful criminal defense lawyer who insisted on carrying his automatic pistol wherever he went. To keep costs down, since we were not being paid for the case, we shared a motel room when preparing for trial. Nothing I could do would persuade Jack to remove the gun from under his pillow. He insisted he would whip it out and take care of any prosecutor who might decide to burst into the room to take us out. When I got up in the middle of the night to use the bathroom, it was always with great trepidation.

James Raulerson had originally been charged with the rape and murder of Annie Martin in Tupelo, Mississippi, in 1986. Jack and I were doing the retrial several years later, and a central focus of the case was the hair analysis by a technician from the Mississippi Crime Laboratory.

The crime scene was searched for physical evidence that might identify the perpetrator. The victim's clothing was combed for hairs. Nearby, on the ground, there was a bloody white T-shirt. That was combed as well. Later, known samples of scalp, pubic, and chest hairs were taken from James when he was arrested.

The Mississippi Crime Lab technician, Joe Amos, compared the hundreds of hairs from the scene with those taken from James and found ten "matches" between James's chest hairs and hairs found on the white T-shirt and on the victim's clothes. He also found two pubic hair "matches" to James, one in the victim's pubic combing and one on her clothes. Since James denied committing the crime or having anything to do with Annie Martin, the hair evidence took on huge significance: if it was to be believed, it proved that James was a liar and that he had been with the victim.

Two key questions arose: First, did any scientific evidence show that a "match" between hairs meant anything at all? And second, how likely was a false match?

Forensic hair analysis has been used in criminal trials since the 1850s. According to the Mississippi Supreme Court in James's original appeal, hair analysis is a "very useful tool in criminology." It has been used as the basis for innumerable death sentences, right up to recent times. Indeed, in at least fifteen cases in the past ten years[6] hair analysis has made a significant contribution to a capital conviction, later upheld through the entire state and federal system; many other death sentences have not yet completed this legal journey; and hundreds, if not thousands, more people are serving criminal sentences based in part on this "very useful" forensic tool.

Astoundingly, in the 140 years during which forensic hair analysis had been used prior to James Raulerson's second trial, only two studies had been completed in an effort to determine what a "match" might mean. Both had been done by the same person, Barry Gaudette, a Canadian trace evidence expert.[7] Gaudette made his living at the time as a forensic hair expert and was therefore hardly impartial: if he were to conclude that his expertise meant nothing, not only would he put himself out of a job, but he would also be saddled with a Himalayan sense of guilt for all the Canadians he had sent to prison over the years on the basis of his "expertise."

Gaudette argued that his study confirmed the validity of forensic hair analysis. According to his published article, the probability of a false match with respect to pubic hair was 1 in 800. In other words, according to him, there was a 99.875 percent chance that a single pubic hair found at Annie Martin's murder scene matched the sample removed from James Raulerson. As there was no innocent explanation for James's hair being at the scene, the prosecution might argue that this evidence alone was proof beyond a reasonable doubt.

The Mississippi analyst, Joe Amos, took the matches he had found and had the bright idea of multiplying them: surely, if the odds of one false match are 1 in 800, then the odds of two hairs matching by chance would be 800 times 800, or 1 in 640,000, at which point we could be 99.9999 percent sure James was guilty. And so forth. Amos decided that with eight chest hairs and two pubic hairs matching, there was only one chance in several trillion trillion that James Raulerson was innocent.[8]

Mark Twain once commented on the dangers of statistical extrapolation. He had been told that the changes in the course of the Mississippi River had resulted in its shortening by 242 miles in 176 years, a change of just over a mile a year. "Therefore," suggested Twain, "any calm person, who is not blind or idiotic, can see that during the Old Oolitic Period, just a million years ago next November, the Lower Mississippi River was upward of one million three hundred thousand miles long, and stuck out over the Gulf of Mexico like a fishing rod. And by the same token any person can see that seven hundred years from now, the Lower Mississippi will be only a mile and three quarters long, and Cairo and New Orleans will have joined their streets together, and be plodding comfortably along under a single mayor and a mutual board of aldermen. There is something fascinating about science. One gets such wholesale returns out of such a trifling investment of fact."

Twain was right. Amos's analysis merely illustrated that he had forgotten what little arithmetic he had learned in grade school. If all of my hairs are similar, and if one somehow matches someone else's hair, then the chances are presumably good that all of them will.

But there was a much deeper problem with Gaudette's study: it was thoroughly unscientific. When I was preparing for James's trial, I telephoned him to ask to see his raw data. He wanted to know my motives. I candidly explained that I doubted Joe Amos's testimony and was trying to ascertain whether his analysis was correct. Because I was a defense lawyer questioning his "science," Gaudette refused to share his data with me. So much for scientific impartiality: he was willing to share data only with those who were committed to upholding his technique.[9]

I was reduced to using the figures he had published, which were incomplete but sufficient for my purposes. Gaudette had made various assumptions that might be suited to a clean laboratory but not to a grubby crime scene; he had also used an erroneous statistical method. By plugging into Gaudette's equations the actual number of hairs collected in the Annie Martin murder, the odds dropped dramatically. Many hairs were found at the scene, and many were taken from James Raulerson. Joe Amos found two pubic hair "matches" in a sample size where, under a correct analysis, we would expect to find 1.4 *false* matches. In other words, assuming that he did his work studiously, Amos found roughly what we would expect to see if the evidence meant nothing.

It is bad enough for lawyers and jurors to be blinded by true science, but in the case of hair analysis, they are misled by something masquerading as science, a technique that has never passed the most basic test of validity. But who is going to challenge the experts? The courts are unlikely to, in part due to the fact that many lawyers chose their profession because they were hopeless at the scientific subjects that might have taken them into medicine.

Presenting any challenge to this kind of evidence before a jury highlights the next problem of forensic science. The judge in James Raulerson's case was an amiable man, the Honorable Frank Richardson. He had a distaste for Johnny Oldam, the local district attorney. Oldam's dedication to securing a conviction was never quite matched by his ability to present a case, and Judge Richardson had not fully recovered from an earlier encounter with him in a criminal trial where there was insufficient evidence to allow the decision to go to a jury. Richardson had directed a verdict against Oldam. Oldam had thrown a fit in the courtroom and then stalked out toward the back of the courthouse, where he proceeded to urinate all over the carpet of the judge's chambers.

Judge Richardson was far from biased in our favor, but he was at least willing to listen. Nonetheless his attention appeared to wander fairly soon after the first mention of statistics. He did bar Joe Amos from sallying forth with his more outlandish numbers at the retrial: the state's expert could call his findings a "match" but could not say what that meant. Unfortunately the only way we could show that his findings were meaningless was to get into a lengthy battle over numbers. But if we tried, we would lose the jurors' attention faster than we had lost Judge Richardson's.

In the end, I was reduced to playing a card trick on Joe Amos. He said that when he looked down the microscope, he saw two hairs that matched in every respect. I had him go through various playing cards that I had glued onto polystyrene board, and explain that he would call a match between two queens of hearts only if they were similar in every respect. He agreed that a certain pair of queens on one piece of board were similar in every respect—a match. At that point, I asked him to remove the two cards. He smelled a rat and resisted my request to take the cards off, but Judge Richardson ordered him to do as he was asked. The seemingly identical queens of hearts, it turned out, came from two different packs, one blue and one red. This made the point that he had called as a match two "hairs" that came from different "heads." It was a simplistic way to illustrate the blind faith with which he approached his profession, but an expert witness will fall for such a ploy only once, and it does not solve the problem of phony science in the courtroom.[10]

Once the legal system has accepted a potentially bogus science, it is difficult to challenge it. In the decade after James's trial, I toured the country giving presentations about the unreliability of evidence gleaned from hair analysis. But I could find no experts to testify to my view. Of course: the only people who qualify as experts in the field are those who believe in it. There is no such person as an Anti-Forensic Hair Expert, someone who trains in hair analysis and then spends his entire life testifying that it is a sham. Indeed, on one occasion, a colleague in Atlanta was so desperate for an expert to challenge hair analysis in a capital trial that he called me as a witness, simply because I had written an article on it. It was absurd that I should be considered an expert, and it happened only because there was nobody else.

Crime author John Grisham waded into the debate with his first nonfiction book, *The Innocent Man*, in which he described what had happened to Ron Williamson, a minor league baseball batter for the Oakland Athletics. A shoulder injury and an unhealthy appetite for alcohol cut short his career, but his life soon got far worse. In 1988 he found himself facing a capital charge for the rape and murder of Debra Sue Carter. At his trial, a forensic expert, Melvin Hett, testified that thirteen hairs found at the scene were consistent with either Williamson or his codefendant, Dennis Fritz. Hett testified that he found two pubic hairs on the victim's bed, where Williamson had supposedly raped the victim.

"They were consistent microscopically and could have the same source as Ron Williamson's known pubic hair," Hett concluded.

The prosecutor asked what he meant.

"When a hair matches, if you will, it is consistent microscopically to a known source," Hett explained. "The hairs either did originate from that source, or there could be or might be another individual in the world somewhere that might have the same microscopic characteristics."

This, along with the testimony of an informant, Glen Gore, constituted most of the evidence against Williamson, who was dispatched to death row. Fritz's wife had passed away some years earlier, and he had been raising their daughter alone when he was arrested. He was sent away for life.

"I'm innocent! I'm innocent! I'm innocent!" Williamson screamed repetitively from his death row cell. He lost his appeals through the state courts and came within five days of dying in the chamber. By then he was well along the path to losing his sanity as well.

In 1994 Federal Judge Frank Seay stayed his execution. Judge Seay, from the old school, was shocked at the way Williamson's trial had gone. He penned a long, 176-page opinion tearing the prosecution case apart. In particular, he shredded the use of forensic hair analysis. Philosophically conservative, he struggled with his duty, but ordered a new trial,[11] writing an unusual epilogue to his opinion.

"While considering my decision in this case I told a friend, a layman, I believed the facts and law dictated that I must grant a new trial to a defendant who had been convicted and sentenced to death.

"My friend asked, 'Is he a murderer?'

"I replied simply, 'We won't know until he receives a fair trial.'

"God help us," he concluded, "if ever in this great country we turn our heads while people who have not had fair trials are executed. That almost happened in this case."

Williamson's trial had not been fair, but that did not mean he was deemed innocent. His exoneration did not come until much later. In 1999 DNA evidence proved that the "inculpatory" pubic hair had not come from Williamson at all but from the victim herself. In other words, the strongest "scientific" evidence offered to show both that he had been at the crime scene, and that he had raped the victim, turned out to be evidence that at some point Debra Carter had been in her own bed.

Another round of DNA helped prove that Glen Gore, called by the prosecution to testify against Williamson, had himself committed the murder. The police had taken samples from him at the time of the crime, since he had been the last person seen with the victim. Because they thought Williamson was guilty, they never bothered to test them.[12] In short, the "forensic science" had been bunk, and in Ron Williamson's case it was—belatedly—debunked by DNA.

After such a catastrophe, how can anyone still use "forensic science" today? Five years after the Williamson case, Max Houck, an FBI "physical scientist," compiled a bibliography of articles about forensic hair analysis. Emphasizing that forensic hair analysis has been used for sixty years, he referenced many articles supporting its use. He ignored the articles and legal decisions that had found the procedure wanting, such as Ron Williamson's case, and he explicitly omitted DNA studies that disproved hair testimony. Instead he quoted from an article published five years before Williamson was exonerated: "Hair is extremely important as physical evidence. It must be collected in every case in which it occurs, and subjected to thorough study . . . [and] it is dangerous to depend on any but expert study of hair found in evidence."

"It is hoped," Houck concluded, "that this listing will provide some assistance to forensic hair examiners who are seeking information and support for courtroom forensic challenges." Translated into plain English, Houck meant that experts must stick together to defend themselves against defense lawyers who are challenging their livelihood. [13]

Is Houck a conscious charlatan? Not at all. It simply reflects the pervasive human bias that allows junk science to continue long past its sell-by date. Houck has devoted his professional life to this "science," and both his job and his reputation depend on its being valid. How likely is it that he would agree that the reports he issued in eight hundred cases for the FBI, and hundreds more in Texas—the hub of capital punishment—that had helped consign so many to prison or the death chamber, were bogus?

It is important to be clear about what is meant by "bogus" here: the DNA result in *Williamson* showed that the hair evidence was wholly false. However, a purported science is also bogus if it is unproven yet is presented as proven. This is ultimately the flaw in hair analysis—whether there is anything to the process or not, it has not been validated. [14]

If only hair analysis were the solitary example of this phenomenon. Unfortunately, in "forensic science" it is as much the rule as the exception. Recently a number of established forensic sciences have come under fire, including fiber analysis, ballistics, bullet content analysis, neutron activation analysis, bite marks, handwriting, and shoe print identification. All suffer from the same profile: they are techniques masquerading as science that essentially serve only one purpose, which is to assist in the prosecution of those accused of committing a crime. [15]

Even fingerprinting has not been immune to criticism. Brandon Mayfield, a lawyer in Oregon, was arrested for his alleged involvement in the Madrid train bombing in 2004. The terrorist attack killed 191 people and injured as many as 2,000. A fingerprint was found at the scene that the FBI matched to Mayfield. No doubt the decision to arrest him was partly prompted by his recent conversion to Islam. The Spanish authorities, skeptical that someone 5,403 miles away could have left a fingerprint, ultimately convinced the FBI that its method was flawed and the print was not Mayfield's. The U.S. government paid Mayfield $2 million to settle his claims against them.[16]

Some apologists point to DNA as the silver bullet that will solve all the problems of our flawed forensic science: why do we have to worry about forensic hair analysis, for example, when we can use DNA? This optimism is again misplaced. One reason is the limited relevance of DNA to criminal cases. At best, only perhaps 2 percent of cases involve DNA testing. DNA may be left at many rape scenes, but if you commit an armed robbery the chances are that you will leave none, the police will fail to collect it, or it will not prove much. For example, nothing was found to test at the scene of the Moo Young murders.

A rather higher proportion of exonerations from death row—fifteen of the first 124, or 12 percent—involved DNA.[17] Again, this reflects not the prevalence of DNA material but the fact that courts tend only to accept DNA results as definitive proof of innocence. In other words, a statistician would expect that because DNA evidence is often not available to prove innocence, the legal system has perpetrated miscarriages of justice in many more cases where there is no DNA to test.

I was struck by our own experience in New Orleans between 1999 and 2002. By then, the LCAC was on more stable footing, and we were able to deploy a small team of young lawyers and investigators to tackle the enormous number of capital prosecutions each year in Orleans Parish alone—perhaps as many as fifty. The moment we heard that a homicide had taken place, one of our team would be on the case, investigating the facts before the trail ran cold. We would then turn over our work to the prosecution, to try to reach a sensible resolution before trial. Ultimately (and this is a true indictment of the Orleans Parish system) we resolved a total of 171 cases and persuaded the prosecution to dismiss 126 cases—based on powerful evidence that the police had arrested the wrong person. Of this total, DNA was relevant to none—not a single solitary case.

But the most important danger with DNA comes with the technician who does the work. Indeed, while DNA testing is an entirely valid area of science, *forensic* "DNA fingerprinting" is something else altogether. The very use of the term *fingerprinting* indicates an unscientific bias. When forensic DNA was novel, its promoters sought to benefit from a public perception that the fingerprint technique was infallible. But a careful and well-trained scientist performing the work in a pristine laboratory is a far cry from an overworked and underpaid technician who labors under pressure on a jumble of soiled samples found at the crime scene. The theoretical probability of a false match between two DNA profiles might be one in a billion; the odds that a crime lab employee using contaminated samples will make a mistake may be closer to fifty-fifty.[18]

The testimony of Thomas Quirk, the firearms expert in Kris Maharaj's trial, stretched out over seventy-nine pages of transcript and had the imprimatur of "science." But what did it really prove?

Since the mid-1980s, Florida has been at the forefront of the pro-gun movement. The passage of a series of gun-friendly laws has made it incrementally a "shall-issue, concealed-carry, stand-your-ground, take-your-gun-to-work" state. This means that the state has no discretion to refuse a gun license; citizens are allowed to carry concealed weapons—indeed, concealment is encouraged, while carrying guns openly is generally forbidden. It is illegal for an employer to discriminate in any way against someone who wants to come to work fully armed.[19]

All this is a roundabout way of saying that owning a gun, on its own, is not viewed as suspicious either in Florida or in the nation as a whole. There are an estimated 200 million guns in private hands in the United States. Of them, perhaps 65 million are handguns, and 26 million are semiautomatics.[20] It seems highly likely that the Moo Youngs were killed by one of these 65 million American handguns. The challenge for Thomas Quirk and his "science" should have been to meaningfully narrow the pool of possible murder weapons. He thought it could. Indeed, his testimony left the jurors with the clear impression that only one of these guns—the one belonging to Krishna Maharaj—was likely to have been used to commit the crime.

Was Quirk's evidence reliable?

Like forensic hair analysis, efforts to identify the bullet used to commit a crime began in the nineteenth century. The first expert to testify in court is said to have been Oliver Wendell Holmes Jr., later a justice on the U.S. Supreme Court. In 1902 he is supposed to have fired a bullet into some cotton wool and then used a magnifying glass to compare the markings on that bullet with those on the bullet retrieved from the victim at autopsy. This story seems apocryphal, since Holmes was elevated to the Supreme Court that year, and he had previously been chief justice on the Massachusetts Supreme Judicial Court. However, if the tale is true, then not very much changed between 1902 and Kris Maharaj's trial nearly a century later. Ballistics testimony went unchallenged for decades. Indeed, some purveyors of the trade took to calling it "ballistics fingerprinting," again hoping to piggyback on the perceived reliability of fingerprinting.

Not until recently have lawyers begun to ask whether the testimony that had been used to put so many people in prison had any scientific basis. Sure enough, the "science" had never been verified: no independent, unbiased studies had ever been done to prove that the bullets fired from one gun could be distinguished from the millions of others. In 2008 Jed Rakoff, a respected federal judge in New York, finally held a series of full hearings on whether ballistics qualified as scientific, provable expert testimony. Judge Rakoff was clearly nonplussed by the fact that ballistics had been accepted in the courts for more than a century. He speculated that the process might once have been more reliable, when firearms were effectively handmade and therefore more distinct one from the next. This notion, if it was ever true, had long since evaporated with the mass production of identical weapons. Ballistics experts purport to match bullets under a microscope, but when their own practice was put under close scrutiny, Judge Rakoff could find no evidence that they were capable of making the distinctions they claimed.

"Whatever else ballistics could be called," Judge Rakoff concluded, "it could not fairly be called 'science.'" Seen from Judge Rakoff's point of views, Thomas Quirk should not have been allowed to limit the possible murder weapon to 225,000 of a particular type of Smith & Wesson. He would have been forced to concede at least that several million Brownings, and similarly large numbers of Sig Sauer pistols, were candidates.[21]

Back in New Orleans, I started looking into Quirk's track record. I soon discovered that he had grossly overstated his conclusions in several other capital cases. Of the small number of capital trials in which Quirk has testified, the most worrying was that of Dieter Riechmann, a German national charged with a capital murder that took place in Miami on October 27, 1987, six days after Kris Maharaj was found guilty in a nearby courtroom. At Riechmann's trial, Quirk testified that the only weapons that could have fired the fatal bullet were an Astra revolver, a Taurus revolver, and an FIE Derringer. Riechmann had two such guns in his hotel room at the time of his arrest. The relevance of Quirk's testimony was dubious since he had tested both of Riechmann's guns and concluded that neither was the murder weapon. The best that might be said was that Riechmann had two such guns, so perhaps he had previously had a third. However, the confusing power of expert testimony is illustrated by the decision upholding Riechmann's capital conviction: the Supreme Court of Florida blindly believed the evidence to be significant to the outcome of the trial.[22]

Almost ten years later, new lawyers representing Riechmann did their ballistics homework. At an evidentiary hearing, Quirk conceded that any of numerous other guns could have fired the fatal bullet—guns that he had failed to mention in his trial testimony. The database he had used to make his ironclad assertions at trial included only the guns that had passed through the Metro-Dade Crime Lab—essentially covering just Miami—as opposed to the FBI database, which included tens of thousands of weapons.[23]

In other words, Quirk's ballistics testimony was unscientific in the extreme. Yet Riechmann's challenge was rejected, and he remains on death row today.

There was another, even more important, element to Quirk's ballistics analysis of the gun evidence in Kris's case. Under the best of circumstances, scientific conclusions are only as good as the information that is fed into the formula that is being applied. If garbage goes in, then garbage comes out. For Quirk's testimony against Kris Maharaj to have any meaning, Kris had to have owned the relevant type of gun at the time of the homicides.

I'd already come across good reason to doubt Detective Buhrmaster's "recall" of Kris's statements on the night of his arrest—regarding whether Kris said he was in room 1215 on the day of the murders. If he had an innocent reason to be there, the fingerprint evidence was meaningless. Likewise, Kris claimed to have told Buhrmaster that he had lost his handgun three months before the crime, after being pulled over by a traffic cop. Buhrmaster told the jury something quite different: that Kris had denied ever owning a handgun. Again, Buhrmaster denied having any record of this "interrogation." If Kris could be shown to have told the truth, then all of Quirk's ballistics testimony would become irrelevant. Indeed, the fact that Quirk seemed to be stretching his evidence to suit the prosecution's needs would be significant proof that the entire case was a house of cards.

I carefully scoured the hundreds of pages I had Xeroxed at the Miami-Dade Police Department, looking for some trace of what Kris had actually said on the night of the crime. And I found it—Buhrmaster had apparently scrawled what Kris actually told him: "Approx. six months—$150 for protection. F.H.P. took gun Orlando, Fla. $1,000.00-$700.00 & gun." The first line was readily understood, and it fit with what Kris had told me. Around March or April 1986, six months before the murders, he had bought the gun through Police Lieutenant Bernie Buzzo—a friend—for $150, as he was concerned about his safety while he delivered copies of his newspaper to distributors late at night. This alone proved that Buhrmaster's testimony was false—Kris had not only admitted to owning a gun but had said when he got it.

The second line of the note was also easily interpreted: Kris had apparently reported to Buhrmaster that sometime later, when he was driving back from Orlando on the Florida Turnpike, the Florida Highway Patrol ("F.H.P.") had pulled him over. He described how they had taken a large portion of the cash ($700) that he had in the car, as well as his gun. Again, this was precisely what Kris had told me, and this notation was direct evidence that Kris had told Buhrmaster the complete story. Buhrmaster might have thought that Kris made it up, but that would not excuse his misleading the jury. What exactly was the detective up to?

I wrote to Kris and asked whether there was any way that we could substantiate his version of events. He wrote back telling me to track down a Greek man called Manuelos Stavros—Marita would probably have an address. Sure enough, Stavros told me that in July 1986 Kris had generously offered to loan him $1,000 to travel home to Crete for a family emergency. However, when he went to see Kris to pick up the money, Kris was "emotionally upset." He told Stavros that the police had stopped him and had taken some of the money and "a gun" from his car. Stavros remembered the incident clearly. Though he was several hundred dollars the poorer, Kris had retrieved more cash from the bank to lend to Stavros.

Finally, there was a third line to Buhrmaster's note: "Subsequent to arrest, 'Don't you remember. I told you in July that the gun was stolen.'" Kris said he made this statement to Buzzo, in Buhrmaster's presence. Buzzo had confirmed that he did indeed remember Kris saying this back in July. Small wonder that Buzzo was one police officer whom the prosecution did not call as a witness at trial. Sadly, Eric Hendon never spoke with him, and by the time I took over the case, Buzzo had died.

Here was independent proof that Kris was telling the truth.

While Buhrmaster appeared to be completely compromised at this point, none of this reflected well on the prosecution either. They were clearly aware of the exchange. I found another note, this time in the prosecution file. Paul Ridge had written to Buhrmaster to "speak with FHP liaison about money and gun." In other words, Ridge wanted the detective to talk with the Florida Highway Patrol to see whether Kris

Maharaj's story checked out. This was clearly how they came to call Officer Jansen to identify the gun that he had seen in Kris's car.

I could hardly fault the prosecutors for presenting Jansen's evidence, though I vaguely wondered why the prosecution had called him rather than the other troopers who had stopped Kris. Because something just did not seem right, I issued a demand for the personnel files of the officers involved, and soon got part of the answer. Another officer, Jeri Nuzzo, had resigned effective November 18, 1987—in the middle of Kris's trial. He "chose to resign rather than face a disciplinary review." The allegations included falsifying a police report when he assaulted an unarmed citizen with his service weapon. He apparently lied when he accused her of aggravated assault, trying to come up with an excuse for using his gun. Prior to that, a report dated June 13, 1986—right around the time he stopped Kris Maharaj—suggested that he was "having great difficulties with report writing . . . with the English language." What could a competent defense lawyer have done with this information if Nuzzo had appeared as a witness!

That the prosecution chose strategically to skip over a problematic witness was understandable, but that they let Buhrmaster lie under oath was a different matter. Buhrmaster's claim that Kris had denied ever owning a handgun was proven false by the very note that the prosecutors had relied upon to instruct the policeman to check into Kris's story.

So what did this all add up to? Kris had owned a Smith & Wesson gun and had apparently been forthright about it with the detective; by Kris's account, someone had stolen it and taken money from him when the highway patrol stopped him. Quirk went to great lengths to convince the jury that only the gun that Kris Maharaj had owned could be the one that had fired the fatal bullets. But what would it mean if Kris had lost that gun three months before the crime?

8

The Defense Lawyer

When Kris Maharaj was thrust into the maelstrom of a capital prosecution, one of the first things he did was ask to be allowed to contact a lawyer. That should, of course, have been the end of any interrogation by the police. For reasons that only Detective Buhrmaster knows, it was not, but eventually Kris was able to call an attorney he knew—Robert Trachman. Trachman suggested that the case would cost around $50,000 but admitted candidly that he knew nothing about death penalty trials. Nonetheless he immediately hired three investigators, led by Ron Petrillo, to look into Kris's alibi, asking them to take statements from witnesses. Then he told Kris that he needed to find a real capital defense lawyer.

That was when Kris hired Eric Hendon. Kris did not think that his lawyer's task would be very complicated. He had a cast-iron alibi, with six sworn statements taken from independent witnesses. He insisted that his own word—which, he felt, had been good enough in his business dealings for many years—could be corroborated by a lie detector. All in all, he felt the case should be open and shut.

Kris was, first and last, a businessman. While he could be generous to others, he had not become rich by paying more than he had to for services rendered, even if he did have a weakness for race horses and expensive cars. Fifty grand seemed far too steep a price, so he interviewed other lawyers for the job. Soon he settled on Hendon. The attorney had recently left the Office of the Public Defender, hoping to build a successful private practice. He said he would do the case for $20,000 and reassured Kris with his résumé: he said, according to Kris, that he had previously handled seven death penalty cases, and won them all.

Hendon failed to take a number of steps that would have been basic for any defense lawyer in a capital case. There should have been—at a minimum—two lawyers, so one could concentrate on any possible penalty phase. But that would have meant splitting his fee with someone else, and Hendon was confident that the case against Kris was weak. While he kept Ron Petrillo on as the defense investigator, he watched the fees closely and assigned Petrillo little to investigate. The only expert Hendon consulted was the polygrapher.

When it came time to present the case for the defense, Hendon could have told the jury that at noon on October 16, 1986, when everyone agreed that the murders took place, Kris was miles away from the DuPont Plaza Hotel. Actually Hendon never mentioned an alibi from the start to finish of the trial. Kris did tell the jury, when he took the stand at the penalty phase of the trial, that he had been in Fort Lauderdale at the time of the crimes, but that begged a rather obvious question: why had he not taken the stand at the first phase of the trial, when this testimony could have made a difference? Kris told me that his lawyer had advised him against it, saying he did not need to testify to win the case. So who was this defense lawyer who had given his client such bad advice?

I did not need to file a freedom of information request to see the defense files. By law, the file belonged to Kris, not to Eric Hendon. So I had in my office in New Orleans a copy of everything that Hendon had had on hand as he prepared for trial.

I found statements from the six alibi witnesses interviewed by Trachman's investigators, all of which backed up Kris's story. The first and in some ways most important was that of Tino Geddes, who was put under oath and tape-recorded by Ron Petrillo just a week after the murders. Geddes told Petrillo that around eleven a.m. on Thursday, October 16, he was leaving the Kenyan Press (where Kris's paper was printed), on West Sunrise Boulevard in Fort Lauderdale, when he saw Kris driving up in his wife Marita's blue car. The two men got along well, and Kris asked Tino where he was heading. Tino said he was going for a quick drink with his friend Clifton Segree, and Kris invited himself along. They went to the Disco Lounge, where Tino asked for a rum, but the man behind the bar said they were not serving strong drinks at that time of day.

"Well," Kris interjected, "one beer won't hurt." So they each had a beer, downing it quickly. Geddes remembered that Kris was wearing what he referred to as a "bush jacket" at the time, which he said was white.

"Kris paid for the beer," Geddes said. He remembered that it was a ten-dollar bill. Then he added with a laugh, "Kris always pays the bill, uh, whenever we go out."

Kris left in his car, while Geddes and Segree went to the office to work on the paper.

"Have you given this statement of your own free will and voluntarily?" Petrillo asked.

"Voluntarily and of my own free will and it is the truth," Geddes replied.

At trial, Geddes changed his story and became a witness for the prosecution. He claimed he had received a call from Kris asking him to confect an alibi. He explained that he had persuaded each of the other five witnesses to tell the same story. It had not been difficult, he said, because they were describing events that had happened the day before— on October 15, a Wednesday. He merely confused them into saying that it had all happened on the Thursday, when the murders took place. Geddes's testimony fatally undermined Kris's alibi and made Kris look doubly guilty, as he was ostensibly creating false evidence, suborning perjury to avoid his just deserts.

The defense needed to pursue several obvious avenues of inquiry. First, why had Geddes changed his mind and testified in such a devastating way? I talked to Marita on the phone. She and Geddes had always got along well, she said, and she had been sitting in court when he testified against her husband. As he left the stand to walk out at the end of his testimony, he had mouthed "sorry" to her. She told me that she had heard rumors that he had been paid a large amount to change his story.

I filed that thought away to consider, but for now we had no proof to back it up.

Perhaps Geddes's change of heart could be explained by the prosecutors' trip to Jamaica, when they testified on his behalf to get him out of a gun charge. It might not sound like a huge favor, but nobody should ever underestimate the effect of the Damoclean sword of imprisonment hanging over a witness's head: how many people would not tell a lie to avoid a stint in jail? Geddes could have readily rationalized his betrayal— he had only just started writing for the *Caribbean Times*. His testimony about assassination plots involving camouflage uniforms and Chinese throwing stars truly had been outlandish, and he might have thought that Kris was unlikely to get convicted on such tall stories.

But something told me that this explanation fell short. Either Geddes was telling the truth (and Kris was guilty) or there was another reason. Only a proper investigation would tell.

A second point that stood out for me was Geddes's claim that he confabulated the entire alibi, by persuading the other five men to ascribe to Thursday an event that had taken place on Wednesday. There was a relatively simple way to assess the truth of this: check with the other witnesses.

And finally I would need to talk to Eric Hendon to understand why he had not presented Kris's alibi to the jury at trial, or called up any of the other witnesses. It seemed an extraordinary lapse, all the more so after Geddes had testified: that redoubled the need to impeach Geddes by proving the alibi.

Before finding Eric Hendon, I decided I'd make another trip to Florida to speak to some of the alibi witnesses myself. My absences from the New Orleans office were putting all kinds of pressure on others at the LCAC, since we had expanded mainly by hiring young, eager people with limited experience, willing to work long hours for minimal pay. A wry joke was circulating among the staff, on occasions when I abandoned them for another adventure on Kris's case: LCAC stood for Lead Counsel Always Clive, and the only person who had ever actually tried one of our death penalty cases had gone off to Miami again.

Nevertheless, I piled back into a cheap rental car and took off for

South Florida. First, I needed to find Arthur McKenzie, the bartender who had refused to give Kris and Tino a stiff drink. I tracked him down, on a broiling afternoon, at his garage.

McKenzie was a diminutive man from the West Indies who appeared shriveled by a long life in the sun. He fixed cars next to the Disco Lounge in Fort Lauderdale, and as a favor to the owner, he would open up the lounge in the mornings. He said he knew Tino Geddes and had seen him sometime before noon on Thursday, October 16, accompanied by one or two other people—he could not be sure how many. One was an Indian man who was a little taller than himself, wearing some kind of "bush jacket."[1] McKenzie seemed certain of his story. I asked him whether Geddes had put him up to saying this, and he said no. I found him convincing, but he gave no firm reason as to why he could be so clear that this had happened on a Thursday.

George Bell, a heavyset sixty-year-old accountant from Jamaica, had also given a statement soon after the murders took place.[2] I found him easily, since Marita had an address for him. One of Bell's clients had been the *Caribbean Times*, Kris's paper. Bell told me he had been in his office on Thursday, October 16, working on some documents, when Kris walked in at ten minutes before noon—in other words, ten minutes before the murders took place miles to the south. Douglas Scott, who worked with Bell, was also there.

"Let's go," Kris said, in his typically matter-of-fact way. He scooped George up, and they went to the 420 Club, to rendezvous with a friend who went by the name "Gang." From there, they drove in Kris's car to the Margate Shopping Center on Southwest Seventh Street, where Kris wanted to look at a building that he was thinking of renting, as his newspaper business expanded. They left the shopping center around half past twelve and went to Tarks Restaurant for lunch, arriving around one p.m.

At Tarks someone George did not know, a slim man with a beard, greeted them. George had chicken wings and corn on the cob, and Kris ordered oysters. As ever, Kris paid. After lunch, they drove around the Margate area again for a while as Kris wanted to see what kind of neighborhood it was. Around 2:45 p.m. they dropped Gang off at the 420 Club, and Kris took George back to his office around 3:20 p.m.

"I'll see you later, at about seven o'clock," Kris said as he left. They were going to have dinner that evening, along with Marita.[3]

Again, Bell was convincing and denied having had any conversations with Tino Geddes about his testimony. However, like McKenzie, he could give no particular reason why he was so certain that these events had happened on the Thursday, rather than the Wednesday.

Douglas Scott had also given a statement, which I found in Hendon's file.[4] He said he worked for a real estate company but had recently done some work on the side for the *Caribbean Times*. On Thursday, October 16, he said, he had been in George Bell's office in the Romark Building in Fort Lauderdale shortly before noon, when Kris had walked in, wearing a cream safari-style jacket. Scott said that he had just received his pay packet, and that Kris had left with George Bell soon afterward.

As with all the other alibi witnesses, the jury never heard from Douglas Scott, but he repeated his earlier statement to me when I located him at his house. He added only that George Bell was his brother-in-law.

"And do you recall roughly what time that was?" I asked him.

"It was—it was before noon," he replied.

"When you say before noon, was it way before noon, or close to noon?" I tried to narrow him down. "Roughly when."

"It was close to noon," he said.

Scott was particularly important for two reasons. First, he firmly denied that he had ever talked to Tino Geddes about the alibi. "I have never spoken to him about any of the issues," he said.

Second, he said he was absolutely sure it was Thursday rather than Wednesday. It had been payday, he said, which is why he would make no mistake. He was always paid on a Thursday.

I was unable to talk to Gangabissoon "Gang" Ramkissoon—sadly, he had died. But I found the statement that he had given to one of the defense investigators in the file. He said he had known Kris for thirty years.

On October 16, shortly before noon, Kris had picked him up in the parking lot of Club 420, a local bar. Gang remembered the date and time—he had been interviewed soon after the murders, on November 5, and the day was clear to him because that morning he had purchased a radio. He described going to see some property before heading for lunch at Tarks around one o'clock.

Gang remembered someone at Tarks asking, "Kris, how come no more 'stash?" Apparently Kris had shaved off his mustache that day. Kris explained that he had made a mistake shaving, then decided he might as well get rid of the whole thing.

Gang's memory was consistent with George Bell's—he said that they went by the property again before Kris dropped him off back at Club 420. Kris seemed totally normal to him—certainly not like someone who had just killed two people.[5]

The last alibi witness in the file was Ronald Kisch, the "slim man with the beard" whom George Bell had not recognized. He was twenty-seven and had been the manager at Tarks Restaurant for more than two years. Kisch knew Kris well, as Tarks was one of Kris's favorite places to eat. He told the investigator under oath that Kris had arrived for lunch on October 16 and was there from sometime around noon until two, with two friends.

Again, Kisch was sure of the particular day—Thursday—as he normally worked evenings, but he had come in early that morning at eleven o'clock. When first interviewed, he had had records of his work schedule, so he could prove it was Thursday, not Wednesday. He remarked on the fact that Kris did not have his normal mustache that day. This was another incidental, but important, fact: the prosecution had tried to make something of Kris shaving, portraying it as evidence that he was trying to change his appearance to make an identification by a witness to the crime more difficult. It was therefore significant that two witnesses remembered that he had taken it off that morning, before the crime occurred. So if Geddes had been telling the truth when he said these events had taken place the day before, on Wednesday—and this seemed increasingly unlikely—that would also have fatally compromised the prosecution's theory, since he would then have shaved the day before the crime.

These six statements had been taken by three separate investigators at the behest of Robert Trachman, the civil lawyer whom Kris had called from the police station. Each investigator was a notary public, licensed to place the witness under a formal oath, and each witness was simply asked to give a statement into a tape recorder about what he knew. It could hardly be suggested that the three investigators were creating a consistent story.

One witness tends to lead to another: I found a seventh person who corroborated the alibi. This was Dr. Marianne Cook, a psychologist who rented office space to the *Caribbean Times*. She said she had talked to Kris on October 16. On the next day, Friday the seventeenth, she had heard that Kris had been arrested, and she had been shocked: she had seen him just the day before.[6]

These people seemed convincing and solid to me. I later learned that they had seemed pretty convincing to the prosecution, too. The British TV journalist who had been roaming around Florida and the Caribbean had interviewed John Kastrenakes and confirmed that the prosecution team had done its homework. Someone from his office had talked to each of the alibi witnesses.

"They, in fact, confirmed Tino Geddes's original story," he said. "The prosecution was presented with evidence of fingerprints, a motive, identification by disinterested people at the scene which pointed one hundred percent to guilt and, on the other hand, this seeming air-tight alibi that Krishna Maharaj had on the day in question."

As they prepared for trial, the prosecutors faced a real dilemma: what to do about this evidence that pointed to innocence?

It turned out they didn't have to do anything. Geddes told his revised version of the story. Then, fortunately for Kastrenakes and much to his surprise, Eric Hendon chose not to call any of the alibi witnesses at trial. The next question was, why?

———

The time had come to speak to Hendon. I went to see the other lawyer on the case, Ben Kuehne, to map out our strategy. We had both made a few inquiries. Hendon had begun his career as an assistant state attorney in the office that later prosecuted Kris. He transferred over to become an assistant public defender because he felt more suited to defense. Not long before he took on Kris's case, he had set out on his own, trying to make a go in solo private practice. A few years after the trial, Hendon went back to being a public defender, where the paycheck was less than he might have hoped for in private practice but was more regular. He was described by his former and current colleagues as being a congenial man, not known for burning the midnight oil on his cases.

Ben and I were slated to speak with him at the public defender's office. I was glad to have Ben there. I had the advantage of having tried a number of capital cases—Ben had not, at that point—so I could sympathize with the experience Hendon had of losing. I felt that Ben could appeal more directly to Hendon as a fellow member of the local bar and a respected representative of the Miami establishment.

Ben drove us to the Dade County Courthouse—an unattractive edifice in an ocean of parking lots. The public defender's office was housed in an ugly modern building nearby. We went in and found Hendon behind his desk. He regarded us both rather owlishly. From the start, it was obvious he cared about Kris's predicament but was reluctant to give anything away. I could see the push-pull going on in his mind: he wanted to do the right thing by his former client, but he did not want to admit that Kris was on death row because of his own failings.

After a few sympathetic pleasantries, Ben observed that Hendon had received only $20,000 for a complex capital case, well below what he would have needed to carry out a full investigation. Hendon nodded and said that Kris had seen little need to spend money on building a defense—he'd insisted on his innocence and felt there was no way twelve jurors could possibly find him guilty. So it wasn't really the lawyer's fault that things hadn't gone well; his client had not given him the resources to do the job right. Hendon would not accept that he had done anything wrong.

I tried another tack: I said I thought the defense lawyer's last, and often most difficult, duty to the client was to admit to his mistakes. I told him I'd had to do it myself, but Hendon wasn't biting. He refused to concede that he had made any mistakes at all, not even his failure to present the alibi.

"I advised Mr. Maharaj that in my opinion he really did not need to call these alibi witnesses," Hendon said.[7] If the prosecution had had no evidence against Kris this might have been true, but nobody could sensibly suggest that the prosecution's presentation had been weak. Neville Butler had told the jury that he had watched while Kris had killed both Derrick and Duane, and there was powerful proof that Kris had a motive to do so. The prosecution's case was substantial, so why did Hendon advise his client to do nothing?

"At the time the only witness listed by the state was Neville Butler and the police-related witnesses. My review of the information from those witnesses suggested that the state's case was a very weak case," Hendon said. "Mr. Butler's testimony was beyond belief, and if that was all the state had, my advice to Mr. Maharaj was to proceed without supplying the state any additional information."

Neville Butler's testimony did seem problematic on close scrutiny, but at the time of the trial Hendon barely touched him on cross-examination. What had he done to prove Butler a liar? He had advanced the ridiculous notion that Butler was conspiring with the tabloid publisher Eslee Carberry to commit a double homicide and pin it on Krishna Maharaj in order to improve the circulation figures of the *Caribbean Echo*. If he felt that Butler's testimony was so weak, he did very little to make his point to the jurors.

So Hendon retreated to another position.

"I advised him that I was not completely satisfied with the affidavits that had been prepared by his investigator and that I did not believe he would gain by filing this alibi list," Hendon said. "Mr. Maharaj advised me that he wanted the list filed, those were his witnesses. So I filed the list. Shortly after I filed it I believe the state attorney adopted the list and indicated they would call them as state witnesses."

Hendon betrayed himself again when he said he had merely filed the list. Why would a defense attorney give a list of his own potential witnesses to the prosecution without talking to each one in person? And then he said the prosecution told him they intended to call all the alibi witnesses to prove their testimony to be false. This was true with respect to just one of the six—there was never a suggestion that any of the others was going to change his story. While Tino Geddes's testimony was not proof of guilt, the notion that Kris had asked Geddes to provide a false alibi would have weighed heavily against him. This made it even more important for Hendon to present the other five alibi witnesses. Any lawyer would have deemed it crucial—if it were possible—to undermine Geddes's testimony and throw his veracity into question. Had Hendon taken the time to speak to any one of the five other witnesses, he would have learned that they were firmly sticking to their account of October 16, and contradicting Geddes.

Each time Hendon took a position, Ben tried to persuade him back around. It was vital that Hendon admit his mistakes. If he blamed the decision on Kris, or claimed it had been a "strategy" not to call the witnesses, in all probability the reviewing court would uphold Kris's conviction. In the parlance of any appellate court that reviews a conviction, if it was the defense lawyer's "strategic decision," rather than his mistake, the case could not be revisited. Getting Hendon to come clean was therefore potentially a matter of life or death for Kris.

Ultimately, falling back from one position to the next, Hendon reached his final line in the sand: he just did not like alibis. He considered the very idea of an alibi to be dangerous. He felt that this was illustrated by Kris's case—look what had happened, a witness had recanted. But this was the refuge of the scoundrel: Hendon had not done anything meaningful to meet with the alibi witnesses and assess their stories.

There are, in truth, traps for the unwary lawyer in presenting alibis to a jury. When a defendant tries to show that he could not have committed the crime because he was elsewhere at the time, the jury may allow the burden of proof to shift to him: if he says he was somewhere else and cannot prove it, then he must be guilty. It is important to recognize the problem, but that does not mean that a good defense lawyer will throw out all alibis. The jury has to be reminded over and over again that the prosecution bears the burden of proof.[8] If Kris said he was in Fort

Lauderdale at noon on the day of the murders, then the prosecution would have had to show *beyond a reasonable doubt* that he was in the DuPont Plaza at that time. Obviously, if there was a question as to whether Kris was at the crime scene at noon on October 16, there must be a doubt as to his guilt.

Hendon expressed concern that the witnesses might not have held up to cross-examination. Again, putting any witness on the stand is not easy—it is far easier, even for the marginally competent lawyer, to attack the case presented by the other side. But this cannot be a reason to forgo putting on a defense at all.

Hendon initially said that he had not spoken to any of the alibi witnesses and had relied solely on what Ron Petrillo, the investigator hired by Trachman, had reported. But perhaps he realized how inept this sounded. So he later fudged and said that he had spoken to "a couple" of the alibi witnesses.

"I can't tell you specifically what names these witnesses had," he said when we later called him as a witness in a hearing in Miami, challenging Kris's conviction, "but the ones I spoke to really wanted nothing to do with any further involvement with this case." None of the witnesses I talked to remembered speaking with him, and none expressed qualms about testifying. But whether we believe his first statement or the self-serving version he told later in court, there is no suggestion that Hendon spoke to all of the alibi witnesses or sought out anyone else who might have been missed in the initial investigation.

"Well, what I can tell you, counsel, is when I reviewed the affidavits, the affidavits did not meet the standard that I would have required," Hendon told Ben Kuehne when pressed on the issue. "The affidavits were affidavits that I thought would cause Mr. Maharaj more harm than good. It appeared to me as if these were alibi witnesses who had been sought out, trying to account for every half hour of the entire time surrounding the incident and it seemed all too convenient and I just felt that going forward with these alibis would not be in Mr. Maharaj's best interest."

In other words, Hendon thought the alibi was too good—not a complaint that many lawyers would be heard to make. The witnesses had been sought out, but seeking out witnesses is the essence of investigation! Rarely do they come forward on their own. Hendon said he was not satisfied with the "affidavits" of the witnesses, but he was again demonstrably mistaken: They had not given affidavits, but rather had recorded complete sworn oral statements, without prompting. This was not a case where someone had carefully crafted a written statement. Nor had one person gone around, located each witness and prodded them to say the same thing: here, three separate licensed investigators had talked to six people who had no apparent knowledge beforehand of what the others had said. In other words, on the face of it, Kris's was one of the most convincing alibis I had ever seen.

If Kris Maharaj was not at the DuPont Plaza Hotel at the time of the murders, he was palpably innocent. And yet over the entire course of the trial, no juror ever heard the witnesses who would have strongly supported his claim that he was not there.

What was the real reason for Eric Hendon's failure to present this all-important evidence?

Hendon would not admit it, but the reason seemed relatively clear to Ben and me. When he persuaded Kris to hire him, Hendon had apparently assured him that he had won all seven capital cases he had taken. This was not quite accurate. At the time—in 1986—Hendon was only eight years out of law school, and he had never actually conducted a capital trial in front of a jury at all. Rather, he had taken on the defense of some murder cases and either settled them on a plea or gone to trial on a noncapital charge. So Hendon had inflated his résumé—hardly unique in the legal profession.

Ben and I knew that Kris was partly the cause of his own downfall. Hendon had agreed to a flat fee of $20,000. Anyone familiar with complex capital litigation would know that that amount was far too low. Moreover, the flat fee worked as a powerful disincentive to mount a full defense. Hendon should have hired someone to help him, but that would have cut his own remuneration in half.[9] Every hour that Hendon worked cut back on his profit. If he had settled the case with the prosecutor in just sixty minutes of negotiation, his rate would have been $20,000 an hour; if he'd taken two hours, it would have gone down to

$10,000, and so on. A set fee establishes a structural disincentive for lawyers to work. Indeed, while Hendon might deny it, this consideration must have played a role in some of his advice. When it came time to depose the witnesses, Hendon wanted only fifteen minutes per person; the prosecutors had to urge him to take longer. Why the rush?[10]

The way the judicial system values the tasks lawyers perform makes little sense. Most people would agree that nothing is more significant than a death penalty case, when a human life is at stake; litigation between corporations over contractual disputes pales by comparison. We might expect someone on trial for his life to receive the very best defense available, paid at the highest rates. If we wanted to avoid convicting the innocent at all costs, we would ensure that the defense was provided with all the resources and tools necessary to do the job well.

Unfortunately, what actually happens is an inverse reflection of such values. Corporate lawyers straight out of law school often have starting salaries of over $150,000; partners make far more, often in the $2 million-a-year range. The median rate for New York lawyers of all stripes is $252 per hour, but some demand $1,000, or $16.67 for each minute they work. The cup of coffee you have with your lawyer may cost $5 to buy, but by the time you have finished drinking it, it will cost you the better part of $300, even if you scald your tongue slurping it down quickly.[11]

At his capital trial in El Paso, Texas, Frederico Martinez-Macias was represented by a court-appointed attorney who was paid only $11.84 per hour. A federal court later reviewing his death sentence noted caustically that you get what you pay for: the lawyer failed to present an available alibi witness and failed to interview and present witnesses who could have rebutted the prosecutor's case. On appeal, Martinez-Macias had volunteer lawyers who did everything that his trial lawyer should have done. He was granted a new trial, whereupon the grand jury refused an indictment and he was released. By that point he had spent nine years on death row for a crime he didn't commit.[12]

That court seemed to think that $11.84 was an extraordinarily low hourly wage for a trial where a man's life was at stake. It is far from the lowest I have seen. When I began trying capital cases, several states paid a maximum of $1,000 for the entire process—including not only the attorney's costs and expenses but investigation and experts. I average more than one thousand hours for a complicated capital case, so the hourly rate would fall below one dollar per hour. Indeed, we once sued the State of Mississippi when we found out that the hourly fee for four capital trial lawyers varied from $1.28 to a high of $2.22 per hour. We demanded that they be paid at least the federal minimum wage—then about four dollars. We won, and the rate eventually rose to $25 an hour, but that is still well below what it costs to keep a law office functioning. For every hour a lawyer works on a death penalty trial in Mississippi, he loses money.[13]

Criminal defendants themselves are divided between the well heeled and the downtrodden. O. J. Simpson is reputed to have paid around $10 million for his acquittal for two murders.[14] In 1995 America was transfixed by Johnnie Cochran's clever rhymes ("If the glove don't fit, you must acquit"). At that time, as I was periodically driving to Miami to investigate into Kris's case, the LCAC was helping out in a parish in the middle of Louisiana, where eight people were facing the death penalty. The total budget for the defense of everyone in the parish for the entire year—all trials, capital and not—was $16,000, less than O.J. was paying a single expert per day. Our budget for defending Kris was even less—zero funding from the state, and only the occasional donation from well-wishers to help with gas money and photocopies.

Lawyers can still make a reasonable living by doing court-appointed cases, but only if they ignore the needs of their clients and simply trawl for money. Linda Carty, a British woman on death row in Texas, was another case I worked on. At trial, she was represented by the infamous Jerry Guerinot, an ambulatory violation of the right to effective assistance of counsel. Counting Linda's case, Guerinot managed to lose twenty capital trials—sending more people to death row than are currently condemned in twenty-six states. Thankfully, he retired from capital "defense" in 2003—but thereafter he still managed to pull in $100,000 a year on felony cases. He achieved this feat by taking on as many as two thousand felony cases in two years. To set this number in perspective, most people only know about three hundred people; Guerinot was supposedly representing seven times that number, each of whom was relying on him to achieve a fair verdict and sentence. But since he would have had to resolve several cases every working day, the prisoners would be lucky if he spent more than an hour with each one of them.[15]

Guerinot is not unique. Other lawyers take on similar caseloads without venal motives. The LCAC handled a number of cases in Lake Charles, in Calcasieu Parish, close to where I-10 crosses the Texas border. Since the funding situation there was so dire, we decided to mount a challenge to it. We surveyed the parish jail to assess the quality of defense that the prisoners were getting. We had the full cooperation of the sheriff, who was tired of fielding the prisoners' complaints—complaints that he felt were entirely reasonable.[16]

The results of our study were horrifying. Each year in Calcasieu Parish, the court assigned the public defender's office roughly 2,400 new felony cases. Each lawyer there had on average 587 open cases; one had 3,395 misdemeanor clients, many of whom could face several months in jail. Because the system was so overloaded, a prisoner would not be charged for six months and would not generally appear in court for the first time until he had spent nearly a year in jail. We checked the visitation logs at the jail: each month, fewer than one prisoner in a hundred received a visit from a lawyer. Prisoners who were able to pay for a private attorney were visited more than forty times as often as those with court-appointed lawyers. We found, in hundreds of indigent client files, only two brief investigative reports. Only twice in three years (out of perhaps twenty thousand cases in total) did the public defender's office use an independent expert to challenge the state's case.

In one year, while the prosecution filed 6,950 criminal cases, there were only ten jury trials. This meant that 99.86 percent of those in prison did not receive a full trial—and therefore ended up pleading guilty (often simply to get out of jail) or, after months, having the charges dismissed against them for want of any evidence. The volunteers who did the survey for us found forty-two prisoners in jail who had no case pending in the courthouse—in other words, they should never have been locked up in the first place. At least thirteen people were languishing there whose sentences had long since expired. Eddie James should have served six months, but he had been in jail for two years; Jeremiah

Rodriguez had been sentenced to sixty days but was still in prison fifteen months later. Mark Celestine had been given thirty days, but he had not been released eighteen months later.

Thirty people had not gone to trial, though they had already been held in the jail for longer than the maximum possible sentence for their offense. Another man had been incarcerated for three months on a charge of trespassing, although even if he were guilty he was not subject to jail time, only a fine. One man had been in jail for six months, even though the charges against him had been dismissed three months earlier—the district attorney had decided that there was not enough evidence to support the case but failed to tell the jail. In all, eighty-five of the prisoners should not have been in jail at all under any interpretation of the facts.

Calcasieu Parish was a shambles, but it was not unique. Thanks to an enormous amount of work by various volunteers, we were able to conduct similar evaluations of the indigent defense systems in other parishes—including Caddo, Orleans, and Rapides. The results were similar. Indeed, compared to Orleans Parish, Calcasieu was rather well organized. After Hurricane Katrina hit New Orleans in 2005, it took months for the LCAC and others to work out who had been in jail, and much longer than that to resolve who should have been there. The story told by these figures is depressing: if capital defense is hopelessly underfunded, then the plight of those facing felony criminal cases (carrying the potential for years in prison, or even life without parole) is even worse.

Systemically, the United States does not take seriously its obligation to avoid convicting the innocent. At $110 per case, each Calcasieu Parish prisoner would receive less than half an hour of a typical corporate lawyer's time. Nationwide, the accused cannot expect much more. Meanwhile, a businessman will spend many times more than that each time he shares a café latte with his lawyer to get an update on a contract dispute. Such is the value our society places upon life and liberty.

While there will always be zealots who choose to become lawyers for reasons other than money, it is the nature of the capitalist system that price affects quality. Those with effective counsel tend not to get sentenced to death.

My own career rather painfully reflects this fact. I graduated from law school in 1984 and tried two capital cases in 1985 and 1986, when I barely knew the way to the courthouse; both men—John Pope and Willie Gamble—were sentenced to death. Those outcomes were not surprising, and I should never have been allowed to represent them. I was totally incompetent. The only saving grace was that their death sentences were later reversed, and they avoided going back to death row.[17] Thereafter I stuck mainly to doing appeals and avoided representing anyone else in a capital trial until 1993, when I had accumulated a great deal more experience. I then tried nineteen cases, and the jury voted for the death penalty in only one—which I am grateful to say was also reversed on appeal.

The structural problems with the system make it inevitable that people who face the death penalty are represented by the worst lawyers available. More than one hundred condemned prisoners have been exonerated from death row in the United States in recent years, and the State of Illinois enjoys the dubious distinction of having exonerated more condemned prisoners (thirteen) than it has executed (twelve).[18]

The stories of incompetent lawyering make for depressing reading.[19] In George Dungee's case, the defense lawyers begged to be relieved from the appointment, as they feared that they would receive bad publicity in their local community for representing someone accused of a terrible crime. "This is the worst thing that's ever happened to me professionally," complained one man assigned to Dungee's defense. Said another, apologetically, "I only stayed on the case because to refuse would be a contempt of court." These lawyers referred to Dungee as a "nigger" during trial.[20]

In Talladega County, Alabama, we did a study of how much time each lawyer spent with the client before trial. It ranged from fifteen minutes to a couple of hours. One local attorney turned up drunk to represent a capital defendant. At least the judge recognized it and jailed him for contempt; sadly, that spell in a cell was the only time he seems to have spent with his client preparing for trial. Of course, the prisoner ended up on death row.[21]

In more than one case, the defense lawyer has slept through parts of the trial. In Texas, Joe Frank Cannon was the court-appointed lawyer assigned to defend Calvin Burdine at trial. Cannon said he became bored and was finding it hard to remain awake. On appeal, Burdine complained that his lawyer had slept through his trial, but the state judge gave him short shrift: "The Constitution does not say that the lawyer has to be awake," he opined. Indeed, even the first panel of the federal court reviewing the case found no error, since Burdine had failed to prove that the lawyer had slept through the parts of the trial that really mattered. I was at the argument in the appellate court where these issues were discussed. It was surreal: at one point, a judge asked whether there was a constitutional distinction between an attorney sleeping during a death penalty trial and one who only dozed.

In the event, Burdine might have been better off if his lawyer had slept through the entire trial rather than occasionally clambering to his feet to speak. With a defense lawyer like Joe Frank Cannon, Burdine hardly needed a prosecutor. Cannon referred to his client as a "queer" and a "fairy," and when the district attorney told the jurors that "sending a homosexual to the penitentiary certainly isn't a very bad punishment," he made no objection.[22]

I can never make up my mind which anecdote of defense advocate ineptitude is my grim favorite. One contender would have to be the Mississippi trial of Alfred Dale "Woodrow" Leatherwood. This mentally disabled young black man was accused of raping a young girl (a capital offense at the time). He was represented at trial by a third-year student from Ole Miss law school, doing her clinical work experience.

"Excuse me, Your Honor, can I have a moment to compose myself?" she said at the start of the trial. "I've never been in a courtroom before."

I ended up doing the appeal. The justices were aghast during oral argument, but in their opinion (which reversed Leatherwood's conviction), the Mississippi Supreme Court did not even mention that a student had been involved in the trial, as it would have fueled criticism of Mississippi justice. Since the problem was not publicly acknowledged, little effort was made to avert its recurrence.[23]

Court-appointed lawyers are not the only ones who are pressured financially and psychologically to underperform. Sometimes retained lawyers are even worse. A person facing a death sentence will hear that court-appointed lawyers are hopeless and search for a lawyer to hire himself. But if a proper capital defense costs hundreds of thousands of dollars and the typical prisoner is impoverished, who is he (or his desperate mother) going to find to do the job? For the kind of fee that the family can afford, only a bottom-feeder will take the case. When I was living in New Orleans in the late 1990s, the public defenders were underfunded and ineffective, but many of the retained lawyers were even worse, pacing the halls of the Orleans Parish court building, cornering the weeping families of prisoners charged with serious crimes. For $500 or even $5,000, they could *really* mess up the case.

Every courthouse has this breed. Some wear sharp suits and slick their hair, giving off a smooth air of financial success to lure their prey. Some cannot afford the costume and spin a line to account for their threadbare suits—they are the true defenders, they say, dedicated to preserving the rights of their clients, intent on keeping their fees as low as humanly possible.

The defendant plays a little-recognized role in this judicial train wreck. While this trial may be the lawyer's hundredth, it is often the prisoner's first. He may suspect that the lawyer is no Perry Mason but he is unlikely to know what to do about it. It's no surprise, then, that he rarely stands up to complain that his lawyer—his only ally in the courtroom—is not living up to expectations.

Even those who try to help themselves have a steep mountain to climb. Soon after he was arrested for murder in New Orleans, Calvin Duncan—still a teenager, barely literate, but showing more initiative than most—filed a hand-scrawled request with the trial judge: "Motion for a Law Book." Accused of a crime he had not committed, he realized he needed to figure out what to do about his problem with the law. He could see that his public defender was going to be of little help. But Duncan was convicted. While he taught himself a lot about the law in the ensuing years, he had to wait twenty-three years in prison before he got his day in court. He could not investigate his own case from behind bars. Only when Innocence Project New Orleans took his case were the facts finally revealed that enabled him to go home. Duncan now dedicates himself to helping the scores of other victims of Orleans Parish justice whom he left behind at the state penitentiary.

So perhaps what Eric Hendon did—or did not do—in Kris's case was not so shocking after all, just another example of a defense lawyer doing an inept job.

Or perhaps not.

When I went to see Ron Petrillo, the defense investigator at trial, I asked him why Hendon had not instructed him to spend more time on Kris's case. There was, after all, so much he could have dug up to shape a proper defense. Petrillo's reply cast a whole different light on what may have transpired.

"A few weeks before the trial, Hendon called me early one morning," Petrillo recalled. "He told me someone had called him at home and threatened him." The caller apparently said that if it looked like Hendon was doing too much to get Kris Maharaj off, something might happen to Hendon's son. Petrillo said that from then on his job was mainly to keep an eye on the boy to make sure nothing happened to him.

When we interviewed Hendon, Ben Kuehne confronted him with Petrillo's story. He denied that he had ever been subjected to intimidation. But he would, wouldn't he? If he had really been threatened, admitting it would place his family in jeopardy, as well as raise questions concerning his own actions at trial. I wondered what motive Ron Petrillo might have for making up such a story. I could not think of one.

If it had in fact happened, what did it mean? Who could have placed that phone call? Who wanted Kris Maharaj convicted of capital murder badly enough to threaten the defense lawyer and his family?

9

The Other Suspects

The popular stereotype of the death row prisoner is a man seeking to avoid punishment at all costs by constantly filing frivolous appeals. "Never put off until tomorrow that which can be put off indefinitely," as the saying goes. But in reality many condemned prisoners want to move their cases forward as quickly as possible. When he was first convicted, Kris could still pay for his own attorney. He immediately fired Hendon, hired Ken Cohen as his new lawyer, and pressed him to seek a new trial as quickly as possible.

I met Cohen briefly on a trip to Miami. He was the picture of the establishment, a solidly conservative kind of person. He handed over his case files, and he was perfectly amiable—but he had no expertise in death penalty litigation—indeed, he did not have much of a background in criminal law at all. After law school he had briefly worked for a judge and then tried his hand as a prosecutor of white-collar crimes. Later, he specialized in civil cases—personal injury and wrongful death litigation as well as insurance policy claims. Kris told me he hired him because he felt he was serious, a businessman's kind of advocate. But this case wasn't about challenging Britain's banana import rules. Kris's life was at stake. I could not understand how he had taken on another lawyer with virtually no capital experience.

Cohen filed a limited brief with the state supreme court. He also asked for a remand for a hearing on the evidence of the Moo Youngs' life insurance policies. Kris had learned about them from Brenton Ver Ploeg, when the William Penn Life Insurance lawyer had contacted him on death row. The Florida court sent the case back for a hearing, to be held within ninety days, but Cohen declined to represent Kris (he felt this was not included in his fee arrangement), and Kris was in his death row prison cell. So no hearing was held, and Kris missed a significant opportunity to challenge his conviction.

Kris had arrived at the Florida State Prison in December 1987. Every other weekend Marita traveled more than seven hundred miles to see him. She soon figured out that Katherine Tafero, the mother of another death row prisoner, Jesse, lived near her in Miami, so the two would often travel up to Starke to the prison together. But on May 4, 1990, Jesse was executed. It went spectacularly badly—flames flickered around the skull cap that delivered the electricity to his brain, a gruesome reminder of what Florida had in store for Kris. Jesse's death shook Marita. Up to now she had kept very much in the background and hadn't gotten involved in the details of the case. Kris had been so sure he would be freed, and she didn't think she should challenge his optimism. Even now he expected to be exonerated at the next roll of the judicial dice. Marita felt it was her role to buoy his spirits, not to question his judgment.

Three other men were put to death in Florida's electric chair that year, followed by two more in 1991. Six of Kris's neighbors were dead by the time the Florida Supreme Court handed down an opinion on his direct appeal, four years after the trial. The justices unanimously affirmed Kris's conviction. They stated as uncontroverted fact that "these murders occurred as a result of an ongoing dispute between Derrick Moo Young and Krishna Maharaj."

Cohen had argued that the gossip in Carberry's newspaper, the *Caribbean Echo*, should not have been introduced as evidence against Kris. But the appeals court ruled that even though Hendon had asked prior to the trial that the stories be excluded from the case, he had failed to object when they were actually presented, so the issue was barred from review.[1] Various other concerns that Cohen raised were likewise "procedurally barred" because Hendon had failed to object at the time of trial. With respect to every other challenge, the court airily dismissed them in one sentence: "We find that the remaining claims are without merit and need no further discussion.

"Furthermore," the court unanimously concluded, "the evidence is sufficient to sustain the convictions of each of the offenses for which Maharaj was found guilty."

With respect to the death sentence, the review was even more cursory. A legal mistake had been made in allowing the jurors to find the crime to be "especially heinous, atrocious or cruel." Under the proper standard, the case did not qualify, but the error was harmless, the court said. Two of the seven justices did not agree with their colleagues' analysis here, and a third, Justice McDonald, thought the sentence should be reversed, but none of them bothered to explain why. "Accordingly, for the reasons expressed," they summed up, "we affirm the convictions and sentences, including the sentence of death for the murder of Duane Moo Young."

Kris then sought review from the U.S. Supreme Court in Washington. He was unsuccessful. His case then came back to the Florida courts, to begin the next round of proceedings: state habeas corpus. At this point new lawyers can reinvestigate a case and present evidence showing that the original trial was not fair. (In referring to the next round of appeals as habeas corpus, I am using shorthand. Each state uses a different nomenclature: Florida actually calls these proceedings a 3.850 writ, named for the section of the code that sets out the process. But the term habeas corpus is used in most states and in the federal courts, and I shall use it here.)

At this stage Ben Kuehne and I assumed responsibility for Kris's appeals. After losing his direct appeal, Kris had filed a state habeas petition; it had been summarily dismissed. So our initial problem was to persuade the Florida Supreme Court to send the case back for a proper hearing. In those first six months, I had reviewed the cold trial record, pulled together other public records from the police and the prosecutors, met with the alibi witnesses, and talked with Hendon. But I had hardly begun to look into the facts properly, and there were already strong indicators that this investigation was going to be much more complicated and costly than the average capital case.

Ben had been paid $10,000 for this stage in the process, with the last of Kris's money. It may sound like a lot, but it was not going to go very far, with everything that had to be done—and even with me and others in the New Orleans office working for nothing. Ben and I decided the best way forward would be to divvy up the work. He would take care of the legal filings in Florida, while I took responsibility for the investigation. We would first have to persuade the courts that we had enough evidence to warrant a hearing.

We knew we had to look into every angle: Could we prove that Kris was innocent? Could we show that he should not have been sentenced to death? Could we show that Hendon had failed to act competently? Should Hendon have presented the alibi witnesses? Had the prosecutors done something to undermine the validity of the verdict? What had happened when Judge Gross was removed from the case? What could we learn about Judge Solomon—why had he decided to impose the ultimate sentence on Kris? Had anything else happened that might call into question the fairness of the trial result? The scope of what we had to do was unlimited. Effectively, we would be completely retrying the facts, albeit without the benefit of a jury or the chance of an acquittal; we would have to investigate all the players in the case, including the defense lawyer, the police, the prosecutors, and the judge. Nonetheless the best we could hope for was that the judge would rule that Kris deserved a new trial—the chance to start the whole process all over again.

Those unfamiliar with the legal process are often flummoxed by the notion that the state ever stops bearing the burden of proving guilt. But once the original trial is concluded, the burden of proof shifts to the prisoner in every sense, and he must come up with a compelling reason why the original verdict should be reversed. In Kris's case, this was not going to be easy. The real killer wasn't going to burst through the double doors at the back of the courtroom to make a confession. The prosecution had done a thorough job establishing a motive and coaching Neville Butler, its star witness. The jury had never heard the testimony of the other alibi witnesses that Tino Geddes's claim to have tricked them into providing an alibi was false. Persuading a court that both Butler and Geddes had been lying would take some doing. We would have to come up with a compelling counterstory, a more persuasive explanation than the one the prosecutors had offered of who had actually killed the Moo Youngs and why.

Early on in our investigation, as I've explained, I came across the contents of Derrick Moo Young's briefcase, withheld from Hendon at the time of trial. It gave us plenty of hints as to where we might begin to look for the actual killer. Another clue came from Hendon's original files, where I found a copy of a letter written by U.S. congressman Mervyn Dymally to a certain Adam Hosein. Dymally had been one of just four witnesses called by Hendon as character witnesses for Kris. This letter suggested to me that Dymally might have information that could be relevant to the crime. He had asked to know whether the Cargil International of which Hosein was a director related in any way to the Cargil International in the Bahamas. And he asked whether the address on a letter Dymally had received from Derrick Moo Young was correct: Frederick House, P.O. Box 4839, Frederick Street, Nassau, Bahamas?

Nothing in Hendon's file explained Dymally's letter. Hendon had apparently cast it aside as Kris's case had headed for trial. When Ben and I asked Hendon about it, he said he could recall nothing about this Cargil International.

Kris was of no more help. He did tell me who Adam Hosein was: a Trinidadian acquaintance who, like many others, had been attracted to Kris's wealth and success in England. Kris thought him a mildly irritating but harmless poser, though in time I would learn that there was more to his story. Hosein bore a close resemblance to Kris, and in Kris's horse-racing heyday Hosein had apparently passed himself off as the millionaire to get into the better stands at the track. He later made his home in Florida and set up a business running a garage. Hosein knew the Moo Youngs and might have had something to do with them, but Kris did not know him well enough to be sure.

I'd found a number of documents concerning Cargil in the Moo Youngs' briefcase. It seemed to be the main front that they had set up for whatever it was that they were involved in. Clearly whatever Dymally was alluding to in his letter merited a follow-up.

———

I called the former congressman to see what he could tell me and found him at home in California. He picked up the phone at once and sounded like just the courteous Caribbean gentleman Kris had described. He was in his eighties, and the events I was asking him to recall had taken place ten years before, but he was convinced that Kris was innocent. He told me that he had received a letter from the Moo Youngs with an address in the Bahamas and Adam Hosein's name on the letterhead. Something had made him think that the corporation on the letterhead had to be dodgy. He couldn't recall the contents of the letter—they'd wanted some favor from him. He promised to look for it but called back the next day to say that his records from that year had been destroyed. He could tell me nothing more.

This was frustrating. I had already planned a trip to the Bahamas, as I had various leads to chase there, so I decided to add this to my list of things to investigate. Early one morning in November 1996, I took a cheap twenty-minute flight from Fort Lauderdale to Nassau. I'd managed to persuade my friend and fellow lawyer Bart Stapert to come along with me. Bart was a towering Dutchman who had come to the United States after university and studied law. He had set up the St. Thomas Community Law Center in New Orleans, providing legal aid to people in the projects near my house. Partly, I wanted him to be a witness in case we found anything useful, but there was also something unsavory about this case, and I was glad to have him as backup. I am six foot three and Bart is four inches taller than me.

We knocked first on the door of Eddie Dames, the man in whose name room 1215 had been reserved. According to his pretrial deposition, Dames had traveled to Miami the day before the murders with his friend Prince Ellis to buy equipment for his disco and restaurant. He had not been called as a witness at the trial, and I had my suspicions as to why. His role in the prosecution's story did not make sense: Why would Kris have booked a room in Dames's name if his sole purpose was to convince Derrick Moo Young that the meeting was with someone other than himself? Why, if this was all a ruse, would Derrick's daughter recall a series of calls from Dames to her father in the days running up to the murders? For Butler's tale to be true, surely Dames would have had to have nothing to do with Derrick before the meeting.

I'd done some background checks and discovered that "Fast Eddie" Dames was a flamboyant character in the Bahamas, front and center in the Carnival season. Since Bart and I were both looking forward to our next Mardi Gras in New Orleans, that was not something I would hold against Dames. But he was a Bahamian government air traffic controller by day who ran discos and restaurants on the side. Was he living beyond the means of a salaried civil servant? Was there any truth to the rumors I had been hearing about the involvement of Bahamian air traffic controllers in drug running?

When I told Eddie Dames who we were and why we were there, he was immediately and vehemently hostile. Before he threw us off his porch, I warned him that the investigation was going to go on regardless, until we learned the truth.

"Mr. Dames," I said, "you obviously know more than you're currently willing to tell me. But you and your friends need to understand that you have only two choices: Either you refuse to help me, in which case I'm going to be investigating you for the next twenty years. Or you do the right thing and tell me what's going on. I'm not the police—I'm a defense lawyer—and I'm not out to get you. I'm just trying to do the right thing by Kris Maharaj, because I think he got a rough deal from the American justice system."

The door slammed in my face. Bart and I backed away, rather grateful to be getting out of there in one piece.

Despite this inauspicious beginning, our approach may have borne fruit. Later that day I received a call from Prince Ellis, who had testified against Kris at trial. He wanted to meet us. When he showed up, he told us he was wracked with guilt and wanted to give a statement concerning the case. Bart took notes. Later we filmed Ellis—I'd invited along a camera crew from British television, and they set up to film him in a corner of the hotel lobby. (This was another of my cost-saving measures, since I knew we'd never have the money to do a formal deposition, though in this instance it would ultimately backfire quite spectacularly.) Since

Bart's notes were obviously not verbatim, I'm quoting here from the transcript of his statement on film.

"I always believe that there could be somebody . . . oh, it's probably happened before, where someone was sent to the electric chair or was hanged and could have been totally innocent," Ellis began, after agreeing to have his interview recorded on camera. "And I am a firm believer that before one is sent to the electric chair or sent to the gallows that all avenues should be explored and all possible opportunities should be given. . . . I was very much concerned about Kris's guilt because after learning about the character of the individual I found out that he was not . . . don't appear to be the person he was made out to be. And it concerned me because it seems as if there could be a possibility of an innocent man being sent to the electric chair."

This was a good start. Ellis then said he was concerned that Eddie Dames had been telling lies about him. "I just thought that maybe I was used at that time for Eddie's alibi, because of his reaction at Ace Music Studio," he said. He explained that when they got to Ace, Dames was not very interested in buying the music equipment that was meant to be the purpose their trip to Miami. Later, after the murders, when Ellis and Dames met up with Neville Butler, Dames seemed to be controlling the discussion, making plans for what Butler would tell the police. "There is no doubt in my mind that Eddie was involved with the meeting and what went on in the room," he said.

"I got very frightened when I found out that Neville's watch was broken off and his shirt was torn," Ellis said. "That told me one thing—he had been in a scuffle. So he had to be close enough for that to happen." None of this had been in the version of the story that Butler had presented at trial.

"Neville was saying something to the effect that they just went crazy and bullets were flying all over the place. They just started shooting," Ellis continued. Over and over again, without being prompted, Ellis emphasized that Butler used the word *they*. What did he mean? Kris Maharaj could not have been *they*. Who had actually been in the room?

Ellis went on to describe a time when he had gone on a boat ride with Dames. Unbeknownst to him, he said, it turned out to be a drug run. He said he had been deeply shocked. That would certainly link up Fast Eddie's lifestyle with his job as an air traffic controller. "I am here," he said in closing, "because I feel like this chap who I never met, who I do not know, never had any affiliation with, could very well be innocent. During my conversation about the entire scenario I have never heard them say this gentleman . . . pulled the trigger."

I was not sure what to make of Prince Ellis. He seemed to be open and sincere, but his sudden phone call to me came right after my conversation with Eddie Dames. I suspected that he was the small fry trying to buy us off with a few tastes of the truth, in the hope that we would leave the bigger fish alone. After all, Ellis could help us, even perhaps come to Miami to testify later, but there was nothing we could do to force Dames to do anything. Only the U.S. government could seek Dames's extradition, and then only for a crime. And while it was all useful for Kris, nothing Ellis had said so far would be sufficient to convict Dames of any crime against the United States.

I pondered this dilemma as Bart and I made our way to Frederick House, the ostensible home of Cargil International Bahamas, the address Dymally had mentioned in his letter. It was, I discovered, the law office of Bowe & McKay. The first member of this partnership was none other than the lawyer F. Nigel Bowe, a man with interesting associations, to say the least.

By the late 1970s, the Bahamas were a major conduit of drugs into the United States. Of its seven hundred islands, Bimini was the closest to the United States, just fifty-three miles due east of Miami, and thus ideally suited to transit the cocaine and marijuana that was then flooding in from Colombia. It helped that the prime minister from 1969 to 1992, Sir Lynden Oscar Pindling, was a crook himself, perennially on the take from almost anyone willing to pay. He had been knighted in 1983—the queen apparently chose to overlook an NBC television report that same year entitled "The Bahamas: A Nation for Sale," which made a strong case that Pindling was facilitating the massive drug shipments of Carlos Lehder, a major figure in the Medellín cartel.[2]

If Pindling was the political facilitator of Bahamian narco-traffickers, then F. Nigel Bowe was their chief advocate, and the biggest name on

Bowe's dance card was none other than Carlos Lehder. According to U.S. Attorney Robert Merckle, who would later prosecute him, Lehder "was to cocaine transportation as Henry Ford was to automobiles." Lehder's innovation was to build a heavily protected thousand-meter runway on Norman's Cay, an island he bought to create a way station for the mass transit of cocaine. By 1982, 300 kilograms of cocaine, worth perhaps $10 million, would arrive on the island with every flight. It would then be divided into smaller shipments that were essentially fired at the U.S. coastline in small planes and high-speed boats. The U.S. Coast Guard was overwhelmed and was lucky to intercept one shipment in fifty.[3]

Lehder's personal wealth mounted into the billions. He used some of his money to keep the locals on his side. On July 10, 1982, the ninth anniversary of Bahamian independence, a large crowd gathered to celebrate at Clifford Park in Nassau. Lehder dropped leaflets into the crowd from a light aircraft with the message "DEA GO HOME." He did not like the attention he was receiving from the U.S. Drug Enforcement Agency, which was beginning to close in on him. To help bring the Bahamians around to his point of view, he attached hundred-dollar bills to his promotional material.

The Bahamian government was by then beginning to buckle under intense American pressure. Lehder needed local agents to keep his Bahamian estate secure. He hired Nigel Bowe and paid him to "persuade" the Bahamian authorities to stop causing him trouble at Norman's Cay. Lehder set up a front company to give a semblance of legitimacy to his accumulating wealth. That company, International Dutch Resources Ltd., was incorporated by Bowe.[4]

Notwithstanding his retainer, Bowe proved unable to keep the Americans off Lehder's back. "I know Nigel is ripping me off," Lehder complained to another Bahamian fixer, Everette Bannister. "And, when I get proof, I'm going to have him removed from the population count." Bowe got into further trouble with Lehder when the drug king sent a $250,000 necklace to Lady Pindling as part of his ongoing effort to keep the prime minister sweet. When she rejected the present, Lehder found he could not retrieve it. Bowe denied that he was responsible for its loss.

Eventually, Lehder was evicted from Norman's Cay—it was just too close to the U.S. mainland and had become too hot even for Pindling to shield. But this did not slow down Bowe. He served other members of the Colombian cartels by introducing them to smugglers, and he continued to facilitate transit through the Bahamas. In one instance that would later come to haunt him, Bowe accompanied smuggler Jack Devoe to Cartagena, Colombia, and hooked up Devoe with José "Pepi" Cabrera Sarmiento, who was considered a pioneer in the cocaine trade for his imaginative ways of evading law enforcement. Devoe flew Cabrera Sarmiento's cocaine into the Bahamas and subsequently to the United States, earning about $10 million over just nine months. He kicked back 10 percent to Bowe, who was also being paid by Cabrera Sarmiento.[5]

Soon the U.S. authorities were heavily focused on Bowe. In 1985 the United States began to seek his extradition, but Pindling's government blocked it. Seven days after the Moo Youngs were killed, on October 23, 1986, a new indictment was published in Miami accusing Bowe and Cabrera Sarmiento of importing 7,304 pounds of cocaine into the United States, with a street value of $100 million. Soon afterward the same Miami grand jury released indictments against Pablo Escobar and Carlos Lehder. Lehder was extradited in February 1987 and was convicted the following year. He complained bitterly on appeal that "the district court erroneously admitted evidence of his views on Hitler . . . and impermissibly allowed comparison between Lehder's organization and the Third Reich."[6]

Bowe remained a free man in the Bahamas, thanks to Pindling's patronage. But the prime minister's winning streak ended with the 1992 election when, based largely on the recurrent stories of narco-corruption, his party lost for the first time in a quarter century. He'd had a good run and took his defeat well. "The people of this great little democracy have spoken in a most dignified and eloquent manner," he said in his concession speech, "and the voice of the people is the voice of God." His retirement plan was, of course, well funded.

Bowe was finally extradited in 1991, but the Bahamian government struck an agreement with the United States eliminating some of the more serious charges against him. The next year he went to trial in

Miami federal district court with Devoe as a prosecution witness. He was without his retained lawyer, David Markus, who had just been arrested on narcotics charges. Bowe was convicted and sentenced to fifteen years in federal prison.[7]

When Bart and I flew back to Miami, we went to the federal courthouse to look for the record of Bowe's trial. It was stashed away in storage somewhere, and it took some months before I was able to get my hands on a copy. The transcript was ripe with accounts of his drug dealings, from the early days at Norman's Cay to his subsequent visits to Colombia. Given the fact that Cargil International, Derrick Moo Young's company, had a branch office at Bowe's address in the Bahamas, I tried to trace Bowe through the U.S. prison system. After several months of being stonewalled and redirected, I was finally told that he was no longer in U.S. custody. He had apparently received remission on his sentence and had been sent back to the Bahamas.

We didn't have the resources to keep flying back and forth between Nassau and New Orleans, so it was a long time before we had a chance to chase down Bowe. Finally Joe Hingston, a Brit who had joined our New Orleans office as an investigator, offered to take a run at the Bahamian lawyer, and he went back there with another journalist, Tim Samuels, who was making a news piece for the BBC. Again, Tim's presence meant we would get a proper recording of what happened, as well as an independent witness.

The two of them knocked on Bowe's door unannounced, and the lawyer was expansive in his welcome. But he very quickly became cagey.

"I wanted to ask you about Derrick Moo Young . . . ," Joe began.

"Who?" Bowe asked. "Don't know the man." His denial was emphatic and rapid.

"What about the company Cargil International?" Joe asked next. "Can you tell me anything about them?"

"Cargil?" Bowe repeated. He said he knew nothing about it.

Joe explained that Derrick Moo Young had sent a letter from Bowe's address in Nassau to Congressman Dymally's office in Washington. The letterhead gave Bowe's address as Cargil's headquarters in the Bahamas. Then he said that Adam Hosein was a director of the company.

"That is impossible. That's simply not true!" Bowe said.

While Joe failed to extract any information about Cargil, Bowe spoke openly about his close friendship with Adam Hosein. When Joe pressed him on their business associations, Bowe said it was strictly a social relationship, and that they did no business together. Joe left feeling that his visit had been a failure; Bowe was not going to risk going to prison again so soon after getting out.

Joe checked back with Prince Ellis, but he could provide us with no new information. Indeed, after that foray, we made no further headway in the Bahamas for some time. We had not even been able to corroborate Congressman Dymally's recollection that the Moo Young company, Cargil International, had been registered to Bowe's address. But then a colleague who had developed a deep interest in Kris's case was dabbling one evening with an online research tool that could track corporations around the world. And there it was: *Cargil International Corporation SA (Bahamas)*. Sure enough, just as Dymally had recalled, the records showed that its registered office was at Bowe & MacKay Attorneys, Frederick House, P.O. Box 4839, Frederick Street, Nassau, Bahamas.

So Nigel Bowe was lying when he denied having any link to Cargil International or knowing the Moo Youngs. Had he also been less than truthful about his relationship to Adam Hosein?

In Hendon's file, I had found another significant piece of information: a sworn statement from one George Abchal, who had worked at Hosein's garage at the time of the murders. Ron Petrillo, the defense investigator, had spoken to him two months after the crimes and had taken a sworn statement that was full of allegations about the Moo Youngs' being mixed up in drugs. When I spoke to Petrillo on the phone, he said he had run into Abchal ten years later and, even though he was no longer on the case, he felt he owed it to Kris to do what he could to help. Petrillo interviewed Abchal again, and this time he filled in a few more crucial details, speaking more freely now that he was no longer working for Hosein.

"Abchal said Hosein kept a gun and a silencer in the drawer of his desk, and on the morning of the murders, he said, Hosein took the gun and left," Petrillo said. Abchal claimed that the gun was a nine-millimeter Smith & Wesson. Petrillo thought a silencer could explain how seven or eight shots could have been fired in the DuPont Plaza Hotel without alerting security.

"Ask yourself," Petrillo said, "why is it that nobody heard anything?'"

Abchal also said that when Hosein came back to the office later in the day, he was clearly nervous. This reminded me of another piece of evidence linking Hosein to the crime scene. I went back and located it among the reams of pages I had copied from Detective Buhrmaster's file: a message had been left for room 1215 on the day of the murders, and the call had come from Hosein's number. Yet the police had never investigated Hosein in the murders of the Moo Youngs. He hadn't even been questioned. He apparently went back to Trinidad shortly afterward, though he later returned to the United States.

Hosein seemed to be a key figure, and I decided to go to Trinidad to find him, but first I wanted to catch up with Petrillo's witness, George Abchal. I flew to Fort Lauderdale on a cheap Southwest flight and met Abchal at a fast-food restaurant. He recapitulated his story, adding still more important facts. A few days before the Moo Youngs were killed, he said, Hosein had tried to buy six kilos of cocaine from them on credit. They kicked him out because he allegedly owed them too much money. On the day of the murders, Hosein had returned to the garage, obviously nervous, and told Abchal not to mention to anyone that he had gone out, or where he had been.[8]

Before leaving for Trinidad, I poked around and discovered that Hosein's brother Arthur had been convicted in one of the most high-profile murder cases in British legal history. He had allegedly conspired to kidnap Rupert Murdoch's wife, Anna, but got the wrong woman (Muriel McKay, the wife of a senior Murdoch executive, who had borrowed the Murdochs' car). Mrs. McKay's body was never found, and a rumor persisted that the Hosein brothers had chopped her up and fed her to their pigs, though that was never proven. Adam testified on his brother's behalf, and suggestions were made (not substantiated) that he had been involved in the crime himself. This had perhaps been one reason for his abrupt move to Miami.

When Hosein had returned to Trinidad in 1986, he had apparently been in legal trouble there. I was eager to find physical evidence—fingerprints or DNA that might link him to the crime scene. Many prints had been taken from the scene that had never been matched to anyone, and I wondered whether we would get lucky and find physical proof that would be difficult to discount.

My main contact in Trinidad was Ramesh Maharaj, Kris's younger brother. Family members described to me how Kris had paid for Ramesh to fly to London to complete his legal studies and had covered all his expenses while he was there. After qualifying for the bar in 1967, Ramesh had returned home and made a name for himself as a human rights advocate. His cases often made the front pages of the local Trinidad papers. In 1975 he was jailed for contempt of court in a case that went all the way—successfully—to the British Privy Council in London, making him something of a folk hero in Port-of-Spain, the capital. Later he achieved further notoriety representing members of Jamaat Al Muslimeen, a Muslim group charged with an attempted coup in July 1990.

In 1995, shortly before my trip, Ramesh had risen to become attorney general of Trinidad and Tobago. I had heard rumors that in his new position he'd abandoned his commitment to human rights. While his older brother languished on death row in Florida, Ramesh was fighting to bring the death penalty back into effect in Trinidad. He would later—in 1999—authorize nine hangings over a four-day period, ignoring an eleventh-hour plea for clemency from one prisoner who appeared to be innocent.[9]

I checked into a small hotel in Port-of-Spain, switched on the television, and found, to my enormous pleasure, that the stations were blanketed in cricket. I had played cricket with more devotion than talent in school and had even found a team to join in Atlanta. The captain there had been Conrad Hunte, once the vice-captain of the West Indies international team, and I was way out of my league. Since moving to New Orleans, I'd had a hard time finding other cricket enthusiasts. I wanted to stay in and watch a match, but I dutifully phoned Ramesh.

After waiting in vain for some time for Ramesh to return my call, I went to check Adam Hosein's court files. You can imagine how taken aback I was to discover that the defense lawyer he'd hired for his recent criminal travails had been none other than Ramesh Maharaj. Obviously, this made it all the more urgent for me to talk to Kris's brother.

I left Ramesh several messages over the course of the day, explaining that I was trying to follow leads that might exonerate Kris. He never called back. Eventually I got through to his home number and spoke to his wife. By now I was thoroughly annoyed, so I told her I'd be dialing the local newspaper in half an hour if I didn't get a call back from her husband. I felt sure it would be interested to hear that the attorney general was unwilling to help his innocent brother, even while campaigning aggressively for more executions.

Ramesh called back moments later and suggested I come by his office to see him. We met up briefly later that day. He was a handsome man who had clearly done well for himself: gold chains flashed distractingly around his neck and wrists.

"I just could never imagine that Kris could kill anyone," he told me, leaning forward. He clearly believed what he was saying. "I just can't accept that." I told him I thought Kris had too much faith in the legal system, and that this was in part responsible for his current predicament. Kris was a savvy businessman, but when it came to the law, he was naïve. I hoped I could appeal to Ramesh as the lawyer in the family to help.

"When all this happened," Ramesh said, "Kris remained so confident. He felt that because he was innocent, he had nothing to worry about. He didn't realize how fallible the legal system can be. I followed the case as carefully as I could. I traveled to Miami and met with his lawyer. I wasn't impressed with Mr. Hendon. I felt he was not competent. However, Kris was totally confident that the truth would prevail."

Ramesh said all the right things in person, but he was unwilling to follow through with any useful action, such as procuring the fingerprints of his erstwhile client to compare to the nineteen found in room 1215 that had yet to be matched to anyone. He was obviously concerned about the impact publicity about his brother on death row could have on his political career. He palmed me off to an aged retainer in his law firm, who lectured me on the superiority of British law and the importance of barristers' wigs, and he was of little help with my mission to learn more about Adam Hosein—even though I shared everything I knew, and suspected, about the man. Ramesh kept making promises but did nothing to facilitate a meeting with his former criminal client. I was rather horrified by his attitude—then and in the months that followed—and hoped that under similar circumstances my own brother would take my predicament more seriously.

Overall, while I nibbled at the edges of Kris's case and learned more about some of the scams that the Moo Youngs had been onto—embezzling the U.S. savings of a number of wealthy Trinidadians—my trip was a failure. I tried going to Hosein's last known address but found nobody. I suspected that word had long since got to Hosein, and he did not want to be located.

Again, it was some time before we could afford another trip, but after his meeting with Bowe in the Bahamas, Joe Hingston went with Tim Samuels for another try at tracking down Hosein. They finally caught up with him at the airport, but Hosein refused to talk and grew hostile. Joe did some real James Bond stuff: he picked up a soda can he'd seen Hosein drinking from in the airport and bagged it, in the hope that we could lift some usable fingerprints (we couldn't). In their few snatched moments of interaction, Hosein denied having anything to do with the Moo Youngs, business or otherwise. He knew nothing about them. He cursed and threatened Joe, then stormed off with Joe's questions hanging unanswered in the widening gap between them.

The evidence, of course, strongly suggested that he knew quite a lot about the Moo Youngs. He was listed as a director of Cargil, a company established by Derrick Moo Young. He was close friends with Nigel Bowe, whose office address was listed on Cargil's letterhead. And the documents the Moo Youngs were carrying with them on the day of the murder showed that they had incorporated a company in Panama called Amer Enterprises. It took me a while to crack this code; eventually I worked out that Hosein's full name was Adam Amer Hosein.

So I knew Hosein was more involved than he was letting on. I wished he would sit down and tell me all kinds of things. Among the various glaring questions was: why were most of these businesses registered in Panama?

I doubted we would have the resources to get to the bottom of the Panamanian links to the case. We were already very lucky that William Penn had paid Brenton Ver Ploeg to investigate the case so thoroughly and to take the investigation all the way to Panama. Ver Ploeg had enjoyed several advantages: he had funding, he had hired an investigator who could find his way around the country, and he had been searching for records that were then very recent. Now, ten years later, the waters were considerably muddied—in 1988 the United States had launched a full-scale invasion of the country (Operation Just Cause) to oust Noriega, and since then Panama had been purged of most of its drug links.

As the Bahamas became ever less hospitable to the drug trade, the Bahamian drug connection had not simply closed down. Plenty of people like Nigel Bowe had no other way to make up for their lost earnings. By now they were experts in the field, so they simply branched out, using other countries to run their narco-business. Panama had been a favorite new venue, largely because it had a convenient border with Colombia, not too far from Medellín. Manuel Noriega was then in power, and he did nothing to discourage this new trend.

For a while, the United States had considered Noriega an ally in the "War on Drugs." He used to show visitors to Panama the letters of appreciation he had received from American legislators, praising his efforts. Gradually, though, the United States came to appreciate that he was a key supporter of the Medellín cartel. By the 1980s, staggering sums, amounting to several billion dollars, were being laundered each year in Panama, and Noriega was insisting on his percentage.[10]

The first record I could find of Derrick and Duane visiting Panama City was on June 13, 1985. Between them, they returned seven times in 1986.[11] The Moo Youngs' entire reported annual income would have been consumed by their travels to Panama alone. Documents in their briefcase revealed the existence of three companies set up in Panama—Cargil, Amer Enterprises, and NEC International. The Moo Youngs were also negotiating to purchase a Panamanian bank for $600 million. A contemporaneous Senate report suggested that roughly half of the banks in Panama—more than fifty—were owned by Colombians.

We were a long way from solving the case, but as I ushered in a rather raucous New Year with David Utter and my other New Orleans friends in the early hours of January 1, 1997, the work on the case had come a long way. It seemed clear to me now that the Moo Youngs had been mixed up in the drug trade—maybe trading in drugs themselves, maybe laundering money for the cartels. Whatever the ultimate nature of their involvement, the profile of the crime had changed entirely from the case presented to the jury.

10

The Money Trail

Our efforts to find out what had really happened that morning at the DuPont Plaza Hotel were taking us into dangerous territory. As I pursued the possible relationship between the Moo Youngs and the drug cartels, my first instinct was to go to Colombia myself, but a colleague who had done human rights work there told me I was being ridiculous. She said I should get serious and buy a program to encrypt office e-mails instead, as the cartels had a far greater capacity for snooping than the CIA. If they felt that our investigation might harm their interests, there would be few corners of the Earth where we could hide. If the real killers were involved with the cartels, the last thing any sane person would want to do was to walk into the lion's den.

I didn't know much about Colombia, beyond the occasional headlines that would sometimes appear in the newspapers. I didn't even know much about the drug business. The closest I'd come was a case involving the Outlaw bikers, but they were minor league compared to the Medellín and Cali. It did not take much research to figure out that the cartels had few scruples. They had the money to get things done— whether it was kill an errant dealer, frame an innocent man, intimidate witnesses, or buy off the police. At the time of the Moo Youngs' murders, three of the five richest men in the world were members of Colombian cartels: only the sultan of Brunei and King Fahd of Saudi Arabia were richer. In 1986 General Motors ranked in the top-ten traded companies in the world, with more than 200,000 employees; the Cali Cartel's profit that year, at around $7 billion, was three times that of GM.

This was hardly surprising given the high demand for cocaine. According to a report prepared for the U.S. Congress, the American market for drugs produced annual revenues of well over $100 billion at retail prices, twice what U.S. consumers spent each year on oil.[1]

The man in charge of the Cali cartel, Gilberto Rodríguez-Orejuela, was nicknamed the "Chess Player" and tended to bribe everyone in government to achieve his goals. By contrast, Pablo Escobar, the head of the much larger Medellín cartel, preferred killing officials to buying them off. "Escobar never forgot an insult," wrote Guy Gugliotta, in *Kings of Cocaine*. "He held grudges. He took revenge."[2] Anyone who ripped him off could expect to pay the price. "The Medellín people . . . are operating in the Stone Age, killing whoever gets in their way," said one Colombian expert at the time. "The Cali people are much more elegant. They buy people, they buy into the system, they do not offend. They buy police, politicians, whole towns."[3]

To be sure, Escobar was not above buying up the police. When he was arrested one time, it was generally accepted that the police officers had done so by mistake.[4] He was quickly released, but for good measure the policemen involved ended up dead. The drug lords raised private armies, and in the 1980s as many as seventy *thousand* well-equipped thugs roamed Colombia, enforcing the will of their employers.[5] Since these people were given weapons and used them, the national murder rate was inordinately high.

One weak point in the cartels' import-export business was getting drugs *into* the United States with the help of a middleman who was not working for, or compromised by, U.S. law enforcement. Cali's solution (starting in the early 1980s) was increasingly to use Mexico as a conduit, selling to Mexican narco-traffickers, who were then left to assume the risk of distribution into the United States. Nevertheless, a great deal of traffic was still going directly from Colombia to the United States.

Getting drugs into the United States, although not easy, was not the riskiest part of the operation. The point of maximum exposure came when the cartel wanted to move their profits out of the United States. It is a maxim of American law enforcement to "follow the money." After all, Al Capone went down on tax evasion charges rather than murder. The DEA knew that tracing money leaving the United States was a lot easier than tracking drugs coming in. Ensconced in Colombia, the drug lords agonized over how to bring the money home to fund the exotic elephants penned up at their ranches, and to pay off the politicians and police.[6] As one journalist put it at the time, the half-trillion dollar bills that they needed to launder each year would "weigh more than the entire population of Washington DC."[7]

In the early days, Colombians were notoriously ethnocentric, refusing to trust anyone but a fellow Colombian to handle their drugs or money. But their operations soon became too large for their compatriots to handle. "Because of the staggering sums generated daily by street sales in the United States," wrote a journalist in the 1980s, "the normally nationalistic Colombian traffickers are willing to step outside the Hispanic community to find professionals who can launder their money quickly and efficiently. They want service from U.S. residents with expertise in accounting and a high comfort level around big bucks—'respectable type people from the suburbs,' as one DEA agent puts it."[8]

Around the time the Moo Youngs seem to have got into the game, the cartel had been suffering an unusually high number of seizures by the authorities, as well as rip-offs by some middlemen. Carlos Madrid Palacios, a former Venezuelan naval officer who helped recruit for Medellín, went to Miami to sort out operations. He put out a profile of the kind of "employee" he was hoping to hire; it read like a portrait of Derrick and Duane. The laundryman must have his own house—the "operating center 'par excellence.'" He must try to "imitate an American in all . . . habits, like mow the lawn, wash the car, etc. He must not have any extravagant social events, *but may have an occasional barbecue, inviting trusted relatives.*" (The emphasis on permissible barbecues came directly from the Cartel HQ in Colombia.) The "minimum standards" for the employee's house must include a "residential location, lots of green space, garage for two cars, garage hopefully not within the neighbors' sight, swimming pool (arguable)." He must always have "a trusted lawyer" and a "vehicle ready for escaping."[9]

By now we had gathered all kinds of interesting material from the Moo Youngs' briefcase, supplemented by several thousand pages of documents from Brenton Ver Ploeg, the lawyer for the William Penn Life Insurance Company. The documents suggested that the Moo Youngs were offering millions—if not billions—of dollars in loans to various Caribbean countries. It was clear that they did not have that kind of money themselves. From where I was sitting, it seemed to me that there were only two possible explanations. Either the money did not actually exist, and the Moo Youngs were pretending to have money on hand and persuading cash-strapped governments to pay up front for the promise of loans; or they had access to these enormous sums and were laundering the money. I was leaning strongly toward the latter theory, because of the many other drug links that had emerged over the course of our investigation. It seemed unlikely to me at this point that there was no drug connection, given the fact that their front companies were based in two centers of the drug trade (Panama and the Bahamas), and that various of their associates—Eddie Dames, Adam Hosein, and F. Nigel Bowe, to name but three—were allegedly in the business. And then there was Jaime Vallejo Mejia, the Colombian who was staying in the room across the hall at the DuPont Plaza Hotel when the murders had taken place— Mejia had to be significant, though I had not yet worked out what his role might be.

I would need more than my own hunch to file a persuasive legal brief. With billions of dollars involved, I was way out of my zone of competence. So I checked around and was grateful when Laura Snook, a forensic accountant with Ernst & Young in London, agreed to do a close analysis of the documents we'd pulled together without charging us a fee, so that we could try to prove what the Moo Youngs were up to. After analyzing the documents, she rapidly confirmed my amateur analysis on one point: "The Moo Youngs were involved in potential arrangements to launder illegal money." That the money was headed to various Caribbean destinations was one factor in her reasoning. "I understand that back in 1986 there were far fewer regulations concerning the laundering of illegal (particularly drug) money than exist today. Additionally, the Caribbean and Panama were among the regions of the world that delayed enacting tough banking legislation to prevent the laundering of these illegal monies."

The forensic accountant then made a hugely important observation that I had missed. "Furthermore, it appears that the Moo Youngs were trying to include secret arrangements in the details that would allow them to receive part of the interest payments directly," Snook wrote. "There are specific admonitions not to tell certain parties to the negotiations about these arrangements. For example, while some loans initially provided for a commission of five percent, and an interest rate of six percent, the documents reflect Derrick Moo Young's attempt to raise the commission to six percent, and the interest rate to seven percent, with the additional commission and interest payable to Mr. Moo Young's business interests. This would, of course, represent a very substantial amount of money. A one percent commission on $1 billion would be $10 million. The vehicle that the Moo Youngs planned to use for these arrangements was, apparently, St. Jude Investment Co. Ltd."

In other words, the Moo Youngs had decided to skim 1 percent off the top. Snook agreed that in 1986 the only people who would have had this kind of money floating around were the cartels. St. Jude is the patron saint of desperate causes. If the cartel got wind of the Moo Youngs' plan to rip them off, Derrick and Duane would very quickly have found themselves devotees of St. Jude. The cartels thought nothing of killing people just for looking at them askance; if the Moo Youngs had given them reason to suspect they were trying to steal millions of cartel dollars, they would effectively have signed their own death warrants.

Money laundering and high finance were not my areas of expertise. I had represented around three hundred people on death row, but every one of them had been poor—including Kris, by the time I met him. I'd been paid an attorney's fee by only one client in my life, and that was a friend who I helped with a traffic ticket in Atlanta. She bought me two six-packs of Newcastle Brown ale as payment, which I put in the trunk of my car and forgot. When I visited Parchman prison in Mississippi, the guards found the bottles and told me I would have to take the alcohol off the penitentiary grounds. It was pretty silly (I was not going to carry a six-pack into the legal visitation room), but I obeyed and hid the beer in a ditch just beyond the prison sign. When I went back to get it at the end of the day, it had vanished. I suspect the guards watched me as I stashed it and decided it would be a nice supplement to their weekend plans.

I began reading up on the cartels' business practices and found it all rather interesting. There are plenty of ways to launder money. One technique is to buy a business, preferably in the service industry, and create a false record of the amount you are making. You have to choose the right front: the manufacture and sale of televisions, for example, leaves a trail of component parts and a traceable number of TV sets sold. With a laundry service, by contrast, the only barometer of how many shirts you've actually cleaned is your soap consumption, and that is easy enough to fudge. You are not required to keep the contact details of clients who bring their clothes in, so you can make up receipts, and nobody will be any the wiser. The problem, of course, is that however extortionate dry cleaners' bills may appear to be when you're on the receiving end, they don't bring in nearly enough money to resolve the cartels' dilemma. If you owned every Laundromat across the globe, you would still have a hard time papering over billions of dollars in profits.

Another strategy is to deal in goods that are extremely valuable. Here, the problem is the identity of the goods in question. If you buy the *Mona Lisa*, it is unique, and you'll leave a paper trail between your purchase and the source of your money. If, on the other hand, you buy a gold bar, it may be uniquely identifiable—it may have a stamp on it— but that can be removed without destroying its value if you melt the gold bar down. In this sense, all gold is fungible. But gold is heavy and doesn't easily pass through metal detectors. If you were to be caught at the airport carrying a couple of ingots, you would have some explaining to do.

There is a way around this problem, and an imaginative money launderer figured it out long before I did: you buy a small number of legitimate ingots in America, ensuring that they have no serial number or other form of unique identification. You put them in a safe-deposit box at a respectable bank with all the proper paperwork. Nobody knows whether the ingots are there at any given time, as you can take them out without giving notice. So you immediately remove them and hold them elsewhere. Meanwhile you convert your illegal money into gold, which you then melt down into ingots that match the legitimate ones for which you have paperwork. Each time you travel out of the country to your chosen destination, you carry another couple of ingots, along with the same paperwork. If you are stopped, you have the documentation to prove their provenance, and you can even take the authorities to the bank and show them the empty deposit box. You can repeat this process any number of times.[10]

Another popular option is jewelry or gemstones. A jeweler can fashion original pieces that are much more valuable than the constituent parts, and can create many copies of the same item. Raul Vivas had the perfect profile for a Colombian cartel: he traded jewelry in Los Angeles, was respectable on the surface, and was greedy. In two years, Vivas laundered $1.2 billion for the Medellín cartel before the feds caught up with him.

In the briefcase from the scene of the crime, I had found evidence that the Moo Youngs were negotiating the acquisition of hundreds of millions of dollars' worth of jewels. It was long past time to try and work out what was going on there.

William Caswell "W.C." Bryant, who died on January 13, 2008, at the age of eighty-nine, was the stereotype of a Southern Baptist minister. Some would rue traveling through life with the moniker W.C., but he rose above such puerile humor. He was born in Hood County, Texas, on November 12, 1918, the day after the Great War ended. Although he always felt called, it was not until 1943 that he enrolled in Southwestern Baptist Theological Seminary. When he and his wife, Evelyn, moved to Amarillo in 1947, he did not know what God had in mind for them. When he prayed, he asked God for three things: a lot upon which to build a church, an interim meeting house, and a place to live with Evelyn. His prayers were answered in abundance. He began his new church with just thirteen charter members, but within three years he had almost a thousand parishioners a week in Sunday school.

W.C. had planned to live in Amarillo, but he soon discovered that God had other plans for him. After a stint establishing Baptist churches in Colorado, he and Evelyn moved to California in 1959. During his twenty-one years as pastor of the First Baptist Church of Norwalk (a suburb of Los Angeles), one of his roles was as western director of the Baptist Church Loan Corporation, an entirely legitimate organization that helped foster the establishment of Baptist churches around the world.[11] Less obviously licit was the Los Angeles Church Loan Corporation (LACLC), founded in 1963, which he later described as a nonprofit, tax-exempt religious institution.[12] It was to do business with the LACLC that Derrick Moo Young went to visit Bryant in 1986. When the Moo Young family later tried to collect on Derrick's life insurance policies, William Penn sent their lawyer, Brenton Ver Ploeg, to the west coast to try to figure out how the LACLC was involved in the Moo Youngs' business. Ver Ploeg gave me a copy of the deposition he took of W.C. Bryant.[13]

What was the purpose of this Los Angeles Church Loan Corporation? Ver Ploeg asked.

"To furnish loans to churches, primarily buildings and ground land, and to help to promote and institute senior citizens, and whatever—world hunger needs, and that sort of thing," Bryant said, rather vaguely. The nebulousness did not seem to have deterred donors. Bryant talked—again without any great precision—about staggering sums of money that had supposedly flowed into the coffers of the company. The LACLC owned some gemstones worth, he estimated, around $500 million. Later, Bryant mentioned Japanese yen bonds that, he said, were held in trust for the church.

"And what was the total amount of the Japanese yen bonds?" Ver Ploeg asked.

"About twenty billion dollars," Bryant replied calmly, as if this were the normal endowment of a church, as opposed to a nation. As I read over the deposition one evening at home, it brought to mind the Reverend Creflo Dollar, the televangelist whose billboards exhorted me for tithes as I regularly drove from New Orleans to Baton Rouge. Reverend

Dollar advertised his paltry endowment of $69 million; he was clearly minor league.

As hard as Ver Ploeg pressed, it was difficult for him (and later me) to divine exactly what Bryant and the LACLC did with all this money. Whatever it was, Derrick Moo Young clearly wanted in on the action. For their first meeting, Bryant would have us believe that Derrick just walked in, uninvited, to his office in Norwalk and asked a lot of questions about the gems.

"He told me that he was connected with the banking institutions in South America and the Virgin Islands, the Bahamas, Panama, Mexico, Costa Rica," Bryant recalled. "He gave me the idea that he was in a commodities business, and he had a way of using the bonds back through the commodities business that he had and through the banking institutions."

"He represented his main place of business to be Mexico?" Ver Ploeg asked.

"That's what I understood, yes." This was curious. We had not located any Moo Young company in Mexico. I jotted a note: here was another country we'd need to investigate, though I doubted we'd ever find the resources to do so.

Derrick's initial interest was in the church's gemstones. Bryant told Ver Ploeg they were worth $500 million, but the lawyer then pulled out a letter Bryant had written on May 1, 1986, in which he claimed they were valued at $94 million. I found another valuation close to $150 million. Did this mean that there were different valuations? Different gems? Or was it all some kind of scam?[14]

Bryant identified three men who had made significant bequests to the church: a Steve Bailey, a Mr. Janovich, and a Mr. Kazangian. Bryant had written to Derrick that the church's gem collection included the "Liberty Bell and the Star of Queensland, which are of undeterminable value." The only reference to a "Star of Queensland" that I was able to find as I scanned the Internet was the famous Black Star, which had been purchased in 1947 by a jeweler named Harry Kazanjian—the spelling slightly different, but close to matching one of the benefactors Bryant listed. When it was cut and polished, the jewel was a six-ray star of 733 carats. At first blush, perhaps it was plausible that the Anaheim-based church would have received a gift from one of the Kazanjian brothers, since their business was only thirty-five miles away, on the other side of Los Angeles. Yet upon closer consideration it seemed highly unlikely: the history of the company on the Kazanjian Web site boasted that the sale of the gem had funded a scholarship program at the Gemological Institute of America, rather than help establish Baptist churches around the world.[15]

This gem alone was worth about $50 million. But while Bryant wrote about this stone in one document, elsewhere he listed all the gems in "his collection," and none matched the description and weight of the Black Star. This other list included several uncut sapphires that, if they really existed, were far larger than the "legendary" Australian jewel. One was said to be 11,250 carats. I do not pretend to be an expert in jewels, but a quick search on the Internet suggested this was as large as some of the most famous sapphires ever found.

It was difficult to know what to make of all of this.

Then there were the yen bonds. Who would have been in a position to give $20 *billion* in bonds to the LACLC? Bryant was under oath when he gave his deposition to Ver Ploeg, but he could not, or would not, say. He did describe how the LACLC had wanted to convert the bonds into dollars, but when they approached potential buyers, most felt the bonds were fraudulent, and it was next to impossible for someone who was neither Japanese nor living in Japan to negotiate the instruments. The bonds were apparently issued by the Dai-Ichi Kangyo Bank Ltd. While the bank was legitimate, my cursory research threw up a scandal connected to it in the 1980s, involving shady connections with organized crime.[16] Were the bonds real but dirty? Or were they fake?

None of these questions seemed to bother Derrick Moo Young. In September 1986 he wrote to Bryant from Panama saying that he wanted to use $5 *billion* of the Japanese yen instruments as collateral for transactions in Barbados, Trinidad, Costa Rica, Panama, Venezuela, and Paraguay. They would each, he said, be loans of twenty years and one day, with interest paid biannually. He was talking huge sums. Six percent interest on $5 billion would be $300 million a year.

"There was a bank in South America that Moo Young said he had owned or he controlled or something to this effect," Bryant told Ver Ploeg. This must have been a muddled reference to the note I had found in the William Penn files, where the Moo Youngs appeared to be negotiating to buy a bank in Panama for $600 million. Bryant went on to explain that he knew some people who wanted to buy a bank or two, so he thought they might be able to do some business there as well.

What did Derrick plan to do with a few hundred million dollars' worth of gems, and $5 billion in yen? Again, though it seemed unlikely, I felt I had to consider one possible, quasi-legitimate, hypothesis: in return for helping Bryant realize the value of some dodgy donations, Derrick wanted a commission on their sale. But the Moo Youngs' lawyer solved the dilemma. He was sitting in on Ver Ploeg's deposition, hoping to collect on more than a million dollars in life insurance; to do so, he would have to prove that the Moo Youngs had been involved in legitimate business. He pressed Bryant to help his clients' case.

"Obviously, if anybody converted them to cash, they would have received some kind of commission or bonus for it. You wouldn't expect people to do that for nothing?" he asked Bryant.

But he did not get the answer he wanted.

"Most folk aren't that generous, but we weren't paying any commission—" began Bryant.

"You mean to tell me, if somebody converted these to cash—" the lawyer interjected.

"We would not pay any commissions. We never paid any commissions," he insisted. Those who dealt with the church were not expected to seek a profit. They were meant to be supporting the church's work, whatever that might actually be. "What Mr. Moo Young was—he told me he was purchasing the instruments through Cargil."

That ruled out the commission hypothesis. According to Bryant, then, Derrick wanted to *buy* the gems and the yen bonds. This fell in line with my primary theory. To purchase the gems, Derrick would have had to come up with around $100 million. Who knows how many billions he would have needed to buy the yen bonds? A question hung over the room: how was a man whose declared annual income was $24,000 going to come up with money like that?

In 1986 only one client could have supplied that kind of money: the cartels. Derrick would not have actually had to buy either the gems or the bonds. He could have used them as a kind of collateral. If his client had a huge amount of money in America that he wanted to export, one way of doing it would be to obtain documents for extremely expensive and portable items, like gemstones. If Derrick was going to carry gems through customs, he would need the right kind of documentation in case he was stopped. He could not carry documentation for gems he had actually bought, because then he would have to explain where the money had originated to make the purchase. But if he had documents that purported to show that the gems belonged to the LACLC and that he was merely taking them to a prospective buyer outside the country, he would be covered—notwithstanding that the gems he was ferrying were not the ones reflected in the documents. So long as he was not questioned too closely, he could make the same trip many times.

One matter was clear: nothing Derrick was doing was above board. Bryant stressed that the LACLC had never given Derrick authority over the gems or the yen bonds. Nonetheless, the vice-president of Cargil, one S. Scott, wrote to the ministry of finance of the government of Barbados: "Our corporation is currently holding the equivalent of one point five billion of US dollars in Japanese Yen instruments." They were AAA-rated bonds, Scott assured the minister, and Cargil had many years of experience in international banking.

I did not need to spend much time investigating the validity of this claim. I had long since figured out that "S. Scott" was an alias used by Derrick Moo Young. In her deposition in the life insurance case, Derrick's daughter Shaula had identified Shernette Scott as the name of a woman who had been the family babysitter in Jamaica years before. Presumably, this faithful family retainer was not the vice-president of Cargil with years of international banking experience.

Ver Ploeg pulled other documents out of his briefcase during Bryant's deposition. There were two letters of credit issued by the "International

Bank of the South Pacific," each for $100 million. In one, the name of the beneficiary had been whited out. The second had a name filled in; the letter of credit was made out to "Banco Continental / Amer Enterprises SA and Cargil International Corporation." Both were dated September 17, 1986, and both bore the same identifying code ODA-170986-SL5-10: in other words, they were the same document, but Derrick had whited out the real name and typed in his own company's name in an unsophisticated forgery.[17]

It seemed that Derrick intended this letter of credit to be the basis for some kind of deal with Bryant and the gems.

"This document says it's an 'irrevocable and transferable letter of one hundred million dollars of credit,'" Ver Ploeg noted, dubiously.

"It's only worth the paper it's written on, probably," replied Bryant, mangling the aphorism.

"Do you recall telling me several months ago that Mr. Brimberry had investigated the Moo Youngs and told you not to have anything further to do with them?" asked Ver Ploeg, as their interview drew to a close. Robert Brimberry was Bryant's lawyer in California.

"I know he did investigate, and that something was said between us that he was not"—Bryant hesitated, looking for an acceptable word—"that Derrick Moo Young was bad medicine.... There was something, you know, bad about the situation."

As the dates on the correspondence between the Moo Youngs and Bryant got closer to the day of the murder, the Moo Young side of the exchange seemed increasingly desperate. On September 22, 1986—just over three weeks before he would die—Derrick wrote to Bryant about "problems" that had arisen with the Bank of the South Pacific: "To have received this news so soon after the Dai-Ichi Kangyo Bank incident, with respect to the bonds, is," Derrick observed, "to say the least most disheartening, discouraging and disappointing."

Bryant testified that he could not remember what these "problems" might have been, but it took me only a moment on the Internet to figure it out. The Bank of the South Pacific was the brainchild of another man of the cloth, a Mormon called Glen Bell. He had set up the International Bank of the South Pacific, described in one article as one of "Tonga's adventures in the insta-bank trade." Reverend Bell had promised high rates of interest to fellow Mormons; he invested the money in local ventures in the United States before apparently emptying the coffers and absconding.[18]

Derrick ended his letter with the rather peremptory demand that Bryant provide him with a signed form of "irrevocable commitment" to release the gems to him. "We trust that you will provide us with this immediately," he wrote. Again, he seemed desperate—hoping, but barely expecting, that he would get what he sought. I wondered: Perhaps he or his son had made promises to some powerful people whom they didn't want to disappoint? Perhaps they were facing some angry "investors" of their own?

Bryant told Ver Ploeg that he had informed Derrick that the "church" would not give him authority over the gems.

"What happened in your relationship with Mr. Moo Young after you told him that you were not going to sign the form letter which he said he needed to deal with the bank?" Ver Ploeg asked.

"I don't remember the date of that, but I do—" He hesitated, as if there were something he wanted to add. Then he thought better of it. "I don't recall. . . . The weeks before he left he was aware of the fact that we were not going to sign it, the document, that he had sent us to sign."

Bryant was eager to give Ver Ploeg the impression that he had nothing to do with the Moo Youngs after that September 22 letter. But then Ver Ploeg pulled out another document dated later in September, when Bryant had written to Derrick again. From its content, it was apparent that it had been followed by a phone call. Then, twenty-four hours later, Bryant wrote another letter to Derrick, offering the yen securities for twenty years at 6 percent interest a year or, if he preferred, allowing him to buy them outright for 20 percent of their value—a cool billion dollars. When confronted with this evidence, Bryant initially said he did not think it was a letter that he would have written, but he had to admit that it looked like his signature.

Derrick appeared to be trying to fill an enormous financial hole in his affairs shortly before his death. Bryant must have struck him as a possible lifeline. The credit card receipts in the briefcase reveal that

Derrick and Duane left Miami for Los Angeles at eight in the morning on October 6 on Eastern Flight 533. On arrival they checked into the Hyatt Anaheim, not far from Bryant's office. They stayed for four days and twice dined out at the Chin Ting restaurant. They returned to Florida on October 10, only to be killed six days later.

What deals they struck on that visit, W.C. Bryant would not say. Ver Ploeg did not ask him. By and large Ver Ploeg's deposition had been thorough, and at the time I did not see the need to chase up on it. When I belatedly noticed the various holes in Bryant's testimony and started looking into how I might make a trip to Anaheim, I discovered that Bryant had taken his knowledge to the grave.

11

The Colombian Connection

By now, I was sure that Derrick and Duane had been laundering money for the cartels, but I'd still not forged one vital link. From the very first time I read the transcript of the trial, I was certain that Jaime Vallejo Mejia somehow held a key to the case. Mejia was the Colombian occupying the suite directly across the corridor from room 1215, where the murders took place. A reporter from the *Miami Herald* latched onto this fissure in the original police investigation and confronted Detective John Buhrmaster about it in an interview.

"I questioned him," the indignant policeman retorted. Buhrmaster said he peered inside the room, without entering, and "everything seemed fine." He explained that after chatting with Mejia in the doorway to his hotel suite, he had taken a very brief statement from him. The Colombian was ruled out as a suspect, according to Buhrmaster, because he "seemed legit." Buhrmaster never looked into Mejia's claim that he had been on a different floor of the hotel at the time of the crime; nor did he take Mejia's fingerprints to compare them with the various unmatched prints found in room 1215. He apparently felt no need to look into precisely how "legit" Mejia was: unless it had been purged from the file, at no time did he ever run a criminal background check on the man.

Kris Maharaj was no idiot. He knew that if he had not committed the crime, someone else must have done it. The fact that a Colombian was so close to the crime scene was an obvious lead. He wondered whether the Moo Youngs were involved in drugs and urged his trial lawyer to poke around and see what he could find out. But prior to the trial, Eric Hendon made only the most desultory effort to follow up on Mejia.

Ron Petrillo did locate George Abchal, who insisted that the Moo Youngs were peddling drugs to or with Adam Hosein. There was no sign in the file that Hendon followed up on this lead. He told Kris he could not find anything to confirm his suspicions.

Mejia had apparently been based in the DuPont Plaza for some years, but Derrick and Duane had hardly made it to the morgue in October 1986 before he checked out of the hotel for good. Was it not worth looking a little closer at this man? After all, the state evidence technician had found blood on the wall and door outside his room.

When I reviewed the brief statement Mejia gave to Detective Buhrmaster on the day of the crimes, I noted that he listed his address as Pereira, Colombia. I knew nothing about Pereira, but I looked it up and found that the city was twinned with Miami—I wondered whether this was some councillor's idea of a joke. Pereira may not be as well known as other drug hubs in Colombia, but it is halfway between Medellín and Cali. Carlos Lehder, cofounder of the Medellín cartel, was born close by. In the 1970s and 1980s, Pereira was one of the most important centers in the world for processing Quaaludes (methaqualone). The powder was imported from Germany and Holland and then manufactured into "jumbo" pills. Both major cartels had a strong presence in the city, as did the much smaller and more discreet Pereira cartel.[1]

Mejia had told Buhrmaster that he worked for All Leather Import and Export Inc.[2] He gave Buhrmaster two business cards; the second one listed him as *agente general* for American Protectors Life Insurance Company, based in Pereira. If you're looking for window dressing to export drug money, life insurance is almost as good as a laundry service. An insurance policy is no more than a piece of paper—nothing physical is ever bought and sold, and nothing has to be manufactured or shipped.

What role exactly did Mejia play in this "import-export" business? Did a sense of irony prompt his choice of second business—was he a life insurance agent, or did he deal more frequently in death?

It was some time before we were able to make any headway in tracking down Mejia. Back in 1986, there was no Internet to search, and the defense had no practical way to run a search for the criminal history of a witness. This was still true when I first got involved in the case in 1994. But Buhrmaster could have pulled up any record Mejia might have had by typing his name into the National Crime Information Center (NCIC) computer and clicking his finger on the return key.

As the years went by, with ever more material coming online, we finally found the lead we needed through a simple Internet search. In March 1987, seven months before Kris Maharaj's trial for the murder of the Moo Youngs, indictments and arrest warrants were issued in Oklahoma City against Mejia, along with one Francisco Javier Ocando Paz. The indictment listed a lawyer for Mejia in Miami. When I asked yet another volunteer investigator to stop in to talk to him, the lawyer said he was bound by attorney-client privilege and could not talk to us about either of the "two matters" he had handled for Mejia.

Two? The investigator queried what the second might have been.

Mejia had apparently wanted to establish another business in Miami, selling alcoholic beverages. If he was in the drug business, this was a rather bold plan, as any such license would require a full investigation of his moral and financial background, performed by the Florida Division of Alcoholic Beverages and Tobacco. Perhaps he thought they were incompetent; I leaned toward the view that enough people in law enforcement had long since been bought and paid for.

On October 15, 1986—the day before the Moo Youngs were murdered—Mejia's personal banker wrote a letter in support of the liquor licence application. "Mr. Vallejo has always handled all his accounts in a most satisfactory manner," wrote Alexis Gomez of the Florida National Bank. The account had varied from a low of $120,848 up to $524,529. As of the day of the letter, his balance was a little under half a million dollars. Mejia seemed to be a very good customer indeed. One day in June he had deposited $100,000 into his current account, where he earned very little interest. I compared this to the 1986 profit and loss statement for All Leather Import & Export, which he had attached to the application for the liquor license. The total business income for the year was $42,961.26; expenses were $82,967.02, for a net loss of $40,005.76. The telephone bill alone—$8,497.63—was almost as much as the money made from the sales of leather goods. What was going on here? Where were the hundreds of thousands of dollars coming from that flowed through his account?

Others had already done the next phase of the research for us: the Florida Department of Business Regulation had sent an investigator to analyze Mejia's latest venture. "The premises is located in a small shopping mall in the center of the downtown Miami shopping district," noted Earl Simmons, "a strange place for the receiving and distributing of alcoholic beverages." However, this criticism was minor compared with other information that came Simmons's way. He learned from the Drug Enforcement Agency that Mejia was "believed to have hand carried more than $40 million to Switzerland for deposit to Swiss bank accounts on behalf of Colombian drug smugglers."

The DEA had been watching a man called Lizardo Márquez Pérez, considered a key player in the drug trade.[3] Pérez had been involved with Pablo Escobar in the management of hotel properties in Venezuela. He had a contact for ongoing shipments of Medellín cartel cocaine: Francisco Ocando Paz, a retired military officer, who was also a Venezuelan.[4] On February 26, 1984, the Venezuelan police authorities found 136 kilos of high-purity cocaine inside a Super King 200 plane owned by Ocando Paz. It would have been worth roughly $5 million. He was arrested in Denver and sent to Oklahoma for trial.

The charges alleged that Ocando Paz, Mejia, and others had arranged for the transfer of $40 million in cash from the United States to a numbered bank account in Switzerland. They had done it in four separate flights, using a private plane, between October 1984 and August 1985. Unless the leather trade was uncharacteristically vibrant during those ten months, there was only one plausible source for this money.

Mejia was arrested in Miami on the Oklahoma warrant just as Kris Maharaj was going on trial. His bond was set at $600,000, an unusually high amount for a leather dealer teetering on the verge of bankruptcy, yet he had no problems bailing himself out. He faced up to five years in prison and a fine of up to $250,000, but he never served a day. On

May 4, 1989, Bonnie del Corral, from Coconut Grove, Florida, flew out to Oklahoma and appeared for Mejia. She was a highly regarded—and expensive—defense lawyer who had previously defended several accused drug dealers.

A deal was struck somewhere in a back room. The allegations against Mejia were suddenly scaled back dramatically. An assistant prosecutor now suggested that Mejia had "willfully" failed to file a report on the transportation of "more than five thousand dollars" from the United States to Switzerland. With the amount of money cut by a factor of eight thousand, his punishment was also drastically reduced. He was sentenced to two years' probation and a fine—with a requirement of two hundred hours of community service a year throughout his probation. All the plea proceedings were placed under seal. Ocando Paz was never even prosecuted; he was simply fined and deported back to Venezuela, where he was later murdered in prison, his eyes gouged out—normally the fate of a suspected informant.

It seemed likely that Mejia had used one of the typical Colombian responses to a criminal indictment: he bought his way out of jail. Between them, in addition to their fines, the three defendants forfeited more than $8 million to the government, ten times what they could have been fined had all three gone to trial and been convicted. State law enforcement agencies were happy to get their cut. Mejia had been allowed to leave the country while on bail, and he never even did his community service because the U.S. government declined to allow him to return to the United States.[5]

Mejia was now safely back in Colombia. If I wanted to prove beyond a doubt that Kris had nothing to do with the murder, I would have to find out more about him. I've been to all kinds of dangerous places over the course of my career to defend victims of torture—Yemen, Sudan, and most of the Middle East—along with many trips to Pakistan. The worst that has ever happened to me was a brief detention by the Jordanian secret police. Colombia is different. The cartels have an unparalleled reputation for violence and have long since intimidated most of the population. It wasn't as if I could call a fellow human rights lawyer in Bogotá and ask him to do me a quick favor—track down Mejia and invite him to confess to his role in a double murder. We had all been spending a lot of time out of New Orleans on a case that was high in expenses and wholly devoid of remuneration. Making a quick trip to Colombia was not in the cards; nor was hiring an investigator to go there.

Luckily it was possible to establish a few things by scouring the public records, with no more than a few telephone calls. We discovered that Mejia, now in his seventies, was living in his hometown of Pereira. The house was not registered in his name—according to the town hall records, nothing appeared to be. It was listed as his sister's address. His family was well known; his brother Hernán had been minister of agriculture and treasury in Misael Pastrana Borrero's government in the early 1970s and again in Belisario Betancur's government from 1982 to 1986. Mejia was still said to be a "businessman," but it was unclear what type of business he was involved in. Colombian records gave no indication that his leather company or life insurance concern had ever existed. There were, however, records of a "chemical" company, Proquim Química Industrial Ltda, which he had run in partnership with a man by the name of Ramiro Gonzalez Betancourt. Proquim operated out of a defunct factory in a dangerous part of Cali. Its stated aim was to produce and distribute cleaning products and chemicals under the brand name Bellot. The Colombian Registry of Companies contained no evidence that the firm ever distributed a single product under that name. The company had been wrapped up.

It did not take a degree in chemistry to figure out what was probably going on. The mass production of cocaine requires an enormous quantity of chemicals, ether being the main one. In the early days of the cartels, it was readily obtainable: it was a case of the capitalist selling the noose for his own hanging—or, more precisely, the drugs for his nation's addiction. Many of the chemicals were imported from the United States.[6]

Eventually, the United States started to crack down on these chemical exports. At this point, the cartels simply turned to Europe and found a more compliant source in Germany. As it needed a legitimate company to import large quantities of chemicals, the Cali cartel established

Rebaja, which became the largest drug company in Colombia. It provided the perfect front. Mejia may well have been playing the same game, using Proquim to import the necessary ingredients.

So far, what we had learned was mainly supposition. We would have to wait much longer for our theories to gel into something more concrete.

How could a member of a Colombian cartel be in the room across the hall from the scene of a double murder and yet attract no attention from the police? And how had the chief detective on the case come to the conclusion that Mejia "seemed legit" simply by standing at the door and peering into his hotel room? Was he simply inept, or was there a darker explanation? In my experience, plain bias is normally the reason the police miss key evidence, but on some occasions good old-fashioned corruption should also be considered.

If the goal of the cartels was to get their cocaine into South Florida, hundreds of balls were in play at any given moment, and the goalkeeper was a policeman wearing a blindfold who periodically turned around and kicked a few balls into his own net. Gradually, over the years, the bigger players have begun telling their stories, as some did in the extraordinary documentary *Cocaine Cowboys*, released in 2006. Drugs would come in on mules traveling on cruise ships or commercial aircraft. They would come in on high-speed powerboats that slid into the Everglades, or on light aircraft that ducked under the radars. "Hell, they even fly coke in from a ship in one of those remote-controlled toy planes and land it on a bayshore condo," said Doug Morris of the Dade County marine patrol.[7] If the DEA stopped the occasional shipment, the loss represented a very small tax on the business.

Drugs brought violence and corruption. By 1986 there was plenty of both in the Miami-Dade Police Department (MDPD). As Miami's population exploded—in 1980, 125,000 Cubans came to South Miami in one flotilla—the MDPD undertook a massive hiring spree. Miami had become the murder capital of the United States, with a higher homicide rate than New York or Washington, D.C. Training police officers takes many years and is no easy task. In late 1985 the Miami-Dade chief of police, who was reputed to be barely competent himself, was leading what one commentator described as a force of "too many ill-trained, undisciplined, anarchic and corrupt officers."[8]

A branch of the MDPD called Centac (the Central Tactical Unit) was put in charge of stemming the flow of drugs. It was made up mainly of homicide detectives, drawn from the same office as Detective John Buhrmaster. Centac burned brightly for a few months, but there were pervasive allegations of corruption against its lead officer, Raúl Díaz, who was accused of taking kickbacks from the people he was supposed to be arresting. Another MDPD officer, Aldo Suero, got stung when he went shopping on the black market for a bazooka so he could blow the doors off the U.S. Customs building in Miami and steal the seized cocaine.[9]

An even more notorious instance of corruption was dubbed the Miami River Cops case. In 1985, just as the Moo Youngs were evidently wading deeper into the narcotics business, six homicide detectives were arrested and charged with murder and drug dealing. The MDPD officers had been ripping off the drug dealers. One policeman, Rudy Arias, had banked a little over a million dollars—$1,080,000 according to his meticulous records, later found during a search. When the federal agents began closing in, the cops confected plots to eliminate six witnesses against them, either by hiring assassins or doing the work themselves. When Arias was arrested on corruption charges, he was on the point of being nominated as the department's "Officer of the Year."[10]

Corruption in the police force was pervasive. "We are literally on the ragged edge of anarchy," a federal judge told a private audience in May 1986. Miami, he said, "is now experiencing the double jeopardy of rampant, violent crime *by* the police, and on an extraordinary scale."[11]

Up to this point, I had my doubts about the work that had been done by John Buhrmaster, the lead homicide detective on the case. His file was full of material that would have been helpful to the defense—yet Kris's trial lawyer had seen none of it. And what had Buhrmaster himself made of it all? Surely he would have pondered some of the same questions that struck me when I looked through the contents of the Moo Youngs' briefcase.

Buhrmaster supplied critical testimony against Kris, making the fingerprints and the ballistics evidence appear to be incriminating—and now his version of events had been cast in grave doubt, while Kris's version had been corroborated, suggesting his innocence. How could any competent police officer investigate a crime like this, with a list of players who seemed inevitably to have links to drug crime, without digging deeper? How could he fail, for example, to run a quick computer check on Jaime Vallejo Mejia, the man from Pereira in the room across the hall?

All of this could be explained by police bias of the kind that I had often seen in New Orleans, when officers came to court to testi-lie, intent on ensuring the conviction of a defendant they had deemed to be guilty. Was that the sum of it? Or had rampant crime *by* the police somehow spilled over into Kris's case?

Unfortunately, I doubted that we had the resources to do a full investigation of the police for corruption. Indeed, unless someone were to come forward with some inside information, the best we could hope for was that one day the federal authorities of Florida would wake up and insist on such an investigation. There was clearly something very fishy about the way Kris's case had been investigated, from start to finish.

12

The Judge

Gradually, the prosecution's case was unraveling. Neville Butler, the prosecution's star witness, had not passed a polygraph test: he had failed, and the prosecutors had willfully misled the court. That act alone might be enough to get us a new trial. We could now show how Butler's version of events had metamorphosed over the course of the year leading up to trial: every time he came up with an assertion that differed from that of another witness or the physical evidence, the prosecutors would adapt his story until it was consistent, and then tell the jury that the independent proof corroborated Butler's sworn testimony. If we could get him to testify again today, in light of everything we had discovered, he would leave the stand in tatters.

Detective Buhrmaster had testified that Kris had denied being in room 1215, making all his fingerprints seem inculpatory. But the sworn statement of Officer Romero corroborated Kris's claim that he had told Buhrmaster from the start that he had gone to the DuPont Plaza for a meeting with Eddie Dames, and that he'd left when Dames had not shown up. If Kris had an innocent explanation for why he was in the room, the fingerprints proved nothing—except that Buhrmaster had conveniently misremembered what Kris had said on this crucial score. The forensic "proof" against Kris could be thrown into question by evidence that had been withheld from the jury.

Buhrmaster's claim that Kris had denied ever owning a handgun had likewise fallen apart. His notes from the night of the murder, which I had found in the police files, revealed that Kris had told him he had owned a gun and that it had disappeared right after he had been stopped by the Highway Patrol in July 1986, three months before the murders. In any case, the ballistics evidence was meaningless as Thomas Quirk, the state's expert witness, had far overstated his conclusions.

Next was the suppression of several boxes of information by the prosecution. I had never in my career seen anything like it. The contents of the Moo Youngs' briefcase alone transformed the entire case. The prosecution had painted Derrick as an innocent, semiretired business-man struggling to get by on $24,000 a year. The briefcase papers (sup-plemented by the William Penn investigation) proved him to be a money launderer for the drug cartels who had been trying to shift *bil-lions* of dollars around the Caribbean at the time of his murder. Perhaps more important, they provided a motive for a hit: the documents indi-cated that Derrick and Duane were trying to skim 1 percent off the top of these deals.

And what of Adam Amer Hosein? Records showed that he had tele-phoned room 1215 on the morning of the murder. One of his employees, George Abchal, said he owned a Smith & Wesson with a silencer and that he had gone to the DuPont Plaza Hotel that morning with the gun. Hosein was linked to the Moo Youngs' dubious businesses in Panama and the Bahamas; and he was a friend of convicted cartel lawyer Nigel Bowe, whose office served as the business address for the Moo Youngs' main company, Cargil International (Bahamas). To top it off, one of the prosecution's key witnesses, Prince Ellis, had said on camera that he thought Kris had been framed, and that Eddie Dames, the man who was used to lure both Kris and the Moo Youngs to room 1215, was involved in drug trafficking in the Bahamas.

It seemed likely that Derrick and Duane Moo Young's fate was inter-twined with the man in the room across the hall from them. We had discovered that at the time of Kris's trial Jaime Vallejo Mejia was being investigated for carrying $40 million in drug money to Switzerland. What was the probability that the Colombian from the drug hub of Pereira, with sham businesses selling leather and life insurance, had nothing to do with the crime?

The evidence pointed strongly to a complicated drug hit.

And what of Eric Hendon? One witness suggested that he had been intimidated by threats against his family. He denied it, but he did an abysmal job over the entire course of the trial, conducting no meaningful investigation, failing to present any one of five solid alibi witnesses, telling his client not to take the stand in his own defense until the penalty phase (when it was too late), and failing to cross-examine the prosecution's witnesses vigorously or to offer a coherent alternative to its theory of the case.

You might think that the mountain of evidence uncovered thus far would be enough to prove a miscarriage of justice, but convictions are reversed far more often on legal issues that have little to do with the actual evidence. Appellate courts squabble over what the trial judge told the jury, debating whether the use of the word *or* rather than *and* in the middle of a half hour of interminable legal instructions undermined the fairness of the trial. They may reverse a case based on discrimination in the selection of the foreperson of the grand jury that indicted the prisoner—notwithstanding the fact that the trial jury that subsequently heard all the evidence had delivered a guilty verdict. Kris's case would be no exception. We had to look into a plethora of legal issues that might result in the reversal of his conviction and death sentence, none of which had anything to do with whether he had committed the crime.

My obligation, in representing Kris, was to go far beyond the proof we had uncovered thus far, which threw his guilt into question, to the very heart of what it means to have a fair trial. Judge Howard Gross's abrupt removal from the case fell into this category. A parallel issue involved the advice that Eric Hendon had given Kris when Gross failed to appear on the bench on the third day of the evidence. These were the two points Ben and I chose to focus on in our appeal to the Florida courts.

Kris explained to me that, long before the trial began, flustered, he had asked Eric Hendon to come see him for a legal visit as a matter of urgency. He was in jail, as he had not been allowed bond, and was confused and concerned. (Ben and I chased this up with Hendon when we met in his office, but I'll quote from what he later said in court, since there was a full transcript of that, so it is the most accurate reflection of what he had to say.)

"What happened, one evening my client Krishna called me to the jail," Hendon explained. "He was quite . . . I don't want to say upset, but quite agitated about a conversation he indicated he had had. He had a card bearing the name of a local lawyer. He indicated that he had been approached by a lawyer in the Dade County jail and the lawyer asked him to retain her and quoted a price of $50,000 and indicated to him if she were retained, she had a relationship with Judge Gross and he would definitely be allowed to be released on bond. He advised me that this lawyer told him that she knew he was innocent and that she knew he had passed a polygraph and that she knew Judge Gross and Judge Gross knew her and if she were retained, he would definitely be released on bond."

Kris showed him the card he had been given. It had the lawyer's name on it. It seemed to him, Kris said, that she was asking for a bribe, and he had angrily sent her on her way.

"I advised my client," Hendon went on, " 'Kris, this doesn't make any sense. This person is a prosecutor. This person couldn't have approached you. But definitely, don't—this is first-degree murder. You are not going to be released on bond on a charge of first-degree murder.' And with respect to . . . I just sort of dismissed it. I told him I found it hard to believe."

Hendon vaguely knew the woman who had left her card as a lawyer who worked in the Office of the State Attorney, alongside Paul Ridge and John Kastrenakes. But a few inquiries revealed that she was leaving to set up her own practice. Hendon did not know what to make of it—to be charitable, perhaps she was just trying to poach Kris's case, making inflated promises about what she could achieve—much as Hendon had done himself when he'd told Kris that he had won seven capital cases. Trying to steal a client would be unethical, but it would hardly impinge on the fairness of the trial. Hendon passed the information on to the prosecutors and asked them to look into it. I later found reference to the episode in the prosecutors' file, but neither they nor Hendon took any further action.

Then, on the morning of October 8, 1987, as the third day of the trial was about to begin, Judge Howard Gross did not appear on the bench. Chief Judge Herbert Klein summoned the lawyers into his chambers. Gross had, Klein told them in private, been arrested that morning and would be taking no further role in the case. It was shocking news. Nobody could remember a time when a judge had been carted off in handcuffs in the middle of a capital murder trial. Judge Klein told the lawyers on both sides to consider how they wanted to respond to this news, and he said he would speak with them again soon. The jurors were not given any details about what had happened; they were told to go home for the day and await further instructions.

Judge Howard Gross was known around the courthouse as "Mousey," or "Howie the Mouse," both nicknames dating back to his childhood, when playmates had teased him about looking like a rodent. Later in life he'd embraced the epithet and even had a swimming pool constructed in the shape of a mouse. When he was married, his wedding cake was decorated with two mice holding hands. A group of attorneys once burst into his courtroom wearing Mickey Mouse costumes; Gross loved it, and the incident was written up in the *Miami Herald*.

The Florida Department of Law Enforcement (FDLE) had set a trap for its mouse, and early on the third morning of Kris's trial, the trap was sprung. Gross, who had once been hailed as a brilliant and compassionate judge, was the target of an elaborate sting operation. An agent posing as Orlando Zirio, a drug suspect, was being held in the same jail as Kris. "Zirio" had supposedly been caught with twelve kilos of cocaine, which had a street value of close to a million dollars; his bond was set at $750,000.

Another FDLE agent, Ernesto Cassal, took the part of a cartel representative and approached attorney Harvey Swickle, a longtime friend of Gross, whom the police had identified as one of his bagmen.[1] The "cartel man" explained that Zirio was his employee, and that he needed to get him out of jail, at which point he would make sure Zirio vanished and was never seen again. While the cartel needed to take care of its own, the

$750,000 bond—on top of the loss of the drug revenue—was too steep a price to pay. Cassal asked if he could get the judge to lower the bond to around $150,000.

This might be possible, Swickle said, "if my guy is on duty."

Some negotiations ensued, and Cassal suggested that his people could meet a $200,000 bond. Swickle indicated that his fee would be 10 percent up front: $20,000. Cassal brought him $10,000 in cash. Swickle was leery of accepting only 50 percent of his fee.

"This creates a problem because . . . ahm . . . my situation is that I can't, I say, I can't have somebody do something," he explained, "unless they know that, ah, I'm fully represented."

Cassal assured him that the rest of the money would be coming his way soon.

Using wiretaps, the FDLE then eavesdropped as an unwitting Swickle called Gross at home. Swickle made twelve calls in the space of just twelve minutes, which appeared to be some kind of code. Gross called him back, and the call lasted two minutes and forty-three seconds.

"Yeah, okay," Swickle began. "I've . . . ah, I've got the signed contract."

"So they did . . . this man now has a lawyer?" asked Judge Gross.

"Yes sir."

"Okay, if you are his lawyer and you tell me those are the facts, I'll reduce the bond accordingly," the judge assured him.

"Ah, what time you going to be in?" Swickle asked, wanting to meet the judge at the courthouse the next day.

"I'll be in, ah, probably . . . eight fifteen."

"Urn" was Swickle's enigmatic reply.

"I'll be there all day. I've got that murder trial," Gross said.

"That's right." Swickle remembered that the high-profile double homicide case had just started—the prosecution of Kris Maharaj.

"I am . . . I'm going to be tied up."

"How about if I meet you in the morning at the house?" Swickle asked.

"Where? Here?" Gross sounded surprised.

"Yeah."

"Well, I don't care, it doesn't matter," Gross said.

"About eight?"

"Yeah." This would be just before Gross left to go to court.

"Okay."

The next morning Swickle drove to the judge's home in Normandy Isles and handed him $6,300 in marked bills. The first $5,000 was Gross's share of the bribe for fixing the bond for "Zirio"; the additional $1,300 was a separate payment for passing a criminal case Swickle's way. Gross stashed the cash in his garage before climbing into his Camaro to drive to the Miami-Dade Courthouse for Kris Maharaj's trial. As he was about to leave his driveway, the FDLE agents arrested him. Gross would have no further involvement in Kris's trial. His challenge now was to find a judge who would grant him bail, so that he could prepare his own defense.

When Kris had initially raised the issue of bribery, Hendon had not taken him seriously. Perhaps he persuaded himself to do nothing because he was not sure what to believe. The larger reason was obvious: no lawyer who planned on making a living in Miami was going to bring up questions of judicial corruption. Yet Gross's arrest added extraordinary weight to Kris's allegations, and surely now was the time to revisit what had happened with what must be seen as an attempt to solicit a bribe.

Hendon did nothing. He advised Kris to go forward with the trial.

Years later, when Ben Kuehne and I asked him about it, Hendon said he had not put the jigsaw puzzle together at the time of the trial. Looking back, he said, after Kris had spurned the bribery demand, the defense received an increasingly hostile reception in Gross's courtroom. Now he gave it some thought, and it was obviously linked.

"Well, it appeared to me following that," he said, meaning the solicitation of a bribe from Kris, "we—we did not get any favorable treatment." He paused. "If I can explain 'favorable.' I don't mean favorable being something we are not entitled to, but simple nuances such as scheduling, consideration of scheduling difficulties; from that point on my relationship with Judge Gross in this case, nothing that would have been convenient to the defense was ever done." At the trial itself, Hendon felt that there were all sorts of incidents in which Gross seemed biased, including the judge's misrepresentation of the outburst by one of the Moo Young relatives.

When Judge Gross was arrested, Hendon had several options. First, this was strong evidence that Kris's original complaint was now corroborated: if Gross had just been arrested for taking a cut on a $20,000 bribe, there was good reason to believe that half of the $50,000 demanded by the lawyer who had visited Kris in the jail would have ended up in Gross's pocket at well. Hendon's first duty was to ask for a full investigation into the allegation of bribery.

Beyond that, Hendon could have put an immediate stop to the trial. Surely no proceeding could simply continue when the judge on the case has been arrested. The argument carried still more force in Florida, one of only three states where the judge was the ultimate sentencer in a capital case. Two days of evidence had already been completed, including half of the testimony of Neville Butler, the key witness for the prosecution. If another judge took over now, he would be asked to impose a sentence of life or death without having heard a vital part of the case.

So what did Hendon do? He advised Kris to waive his right to start the trial afresh. He did not raise the idea of investigating into whether a bribe had actually been solicited. He did not even mention that Gross's rulings had seemed biased over the preceding months, ever since Kris had declined to pay the money.

"My client asked me what my advice would be," Hendon began. "I advised him that I believed it would be in his best interest to continue and not ask for the mistrial. I was quite pleased with the jury that we had. I was quite pleased with the nature of some of the testimony that had come forward. . . . I advised my client I thought it was in his best interest to proceed and not ask for a new trial at this time, or mistrial."[2]

Looking at the cold record, Hendon's advice was ridiculous. The idea that a capital trial could continue after the judge was arrested was incredible. But who was Kris to reject his lawyer's advice? He knew he was innocent and expected to be acquitted.

Unfortunately, there was a different argument for continuing with the trial regardless: Hendon was on a set fee. If the case had begun again, he would have had to spend days picking another jury and going over the evidence again. It would have eaten into his retainer.

So after a week went by, another judge appeared in court, and the trial continued.

Judge Gross was aptly named, given that he appeared to be grotesquely venal, but sadly his replacement, Harold Solomon, was not. Early on during my investigation, when I had been looking through the prosecution's files, I had cross-checked them quickly against documents I already had from Hendon. Sitting in the Office of the State Attorney, I had not had time to study every page carefully and had copied any document that seemed incongruous, erring on the side of inclusion. I also had my notes concerning various exchanges that had taken place at trial that I did not fully understand. One had taken place on December 1, 1987, immediately before Judge Solomon had decided to give Kris a death sentence.

"I understand that there is a supplemental order that you have drafted here," remarked Judge Solomon.

"There were two packages submitted to the court," said Paul Ridge. I did not know what either "package" was, or what order the prosecutor was referring to. Hendon was no help. He said he did not know what they had been talking about either. A reasonable lawyer would have asked. I cannot imagine the prosecutor and the judge having a conversation in court in a capital trial, and letting it go by, if I did not know what they were talking about. But—as was his wont—Hendon had remained silent.

Rummaging through the prosecution's file, I had been confused by the number of copies of the sentencing order. I found a signed copy, dated December 1, 1987, but there were other unsigned and undated copies that seemed to be slightly different from one another. This was unusual, as I had never seen a sentencing order before it had been signed by a judge. My first impression was that perhaps things were done differently in Florida, and the judge had given copies to both parties beforehand so they could correct mistakes or make objections.

But then I noticed that at the bottom corner of one unsigned version there was an annotation: "JSK.smc:11/18/87." It did not take much effort to figure out what JSK meant—I had no idea what assistant state attorney John Kastrenakes's middle name was, but it was a good bet that it began with an S. So this document showed that one of the prosecutors had typed up a sentencing order on November 18, 1987, *thirteen days before* Kris was actually sentenced. This meant that Kastrenakes had given the judge a draft order sentencing Kris to death *before* the judicial sentencing hearing had taken place. Again, Hendon knew nothing about it. It had been done without any involvement from the defense.

Later, I made a few calls to other Florida attorneys I knew to figure out what was going on. It turned out that Judge Solomon was a singularly lazy adjudicator. I was pointed to the case of Dieter Riechmann, a German citizen sentenced to death a year after Kris for killing his girlfriend in Miami. I had known his lawyer, Jimmy Lohmann, for years. Judge Solomon had also been assigned to that case. Lohmann had contested the verdict and called the prosecutor to the witness stand at a hearing challenging the death sentence. The state attorney testified that he had run into Judge Solomon in the hall of the courthouse one day. They had talked briefly before continuing on their respective ways. In that time, Solomon had asked the prosecutor to write up a sentencing order.

"I don't recall the judge asking me to include any, you know, include anything specific in the—in the order," the prosecutor said.

"Well, did he tell you the contents of the order?" asked Lohmann.

"No, I don't . . . well, I don't recall him telling me the contents of the order," the prosecutor said, in acute discomfort. "I mean, all I remember from that exchange was 'Prepare an order.'" In other words, Solomon did not bother to do any judging. He simply told the prosecutor to write up an order sentencing Riechmann to death. It was not clear when this was done in Riechmann's case, but with Kris the dates were clear: the judge had asked for the order before he had finished hearing the evidence.

This was extraordinary. A sentencing order is no mere formality. The judge is the ultimate authority when it comes to sentencing in Florida, and the law specifically requires him to write his own judgment, balancing the evidence and personally determining whether death is the proper punishment. The Riechmann order was very similar to the one that was written in Kris's case: it went on for ten pages and included conclusions that should only ever be resolved by a judge.[3]

Kris had therefore been convicted and sentenced to death with one judge in shackles and the other asking the prosecutors to write his sentencing order. A batter for the Miami Marlins would be allowed a third strike before he was out; the law is more generous, and the Florida judiciary still had plenty of chances to get it right in the available appeals.

Immediately after the trial, Kris had fired Eric Hendon and hired Ken Cohen, whom he asked to file his first appeal to the Florida Supreme Court. When that was turned down, he briefly retained Geoffrey Fleck to file a habeas corpus appeal. Fleck's stationery cheerfully announced that he preferred "specializing in complex criminal litigation, buggery, sexual deviance and perversions of all kinds." I wondered how Kris had come across him.

The purpose of this habeas petition was to raise all the matters that had been left out of the trial record—whether it was evidence that the jury did not hear or proof that the judge was corrupt. Various matters always come up in such cases: under the rubric of "ineffective assistance of counsel," the new legal team will often challenge the failings of the trial lawyer. The rule of *Brady v. Maryland* states that the prosecution should have turned over exculpatory evidence to the defense—if there is proof that the prosecution covered up material that favored the person on trial, then this is another archetypal habeas issue. While all kinds of doctrines and rules may prevent the prisoner from winning, there is no limitation on what may be raised—certainly, in Kris's case, the list would include evidence that Neville Butler perjured himself when he said he voluntarily changed his story, and the shocking information that had come to light concerning Judge Gross's arrest.

Fleck had filed a petition in late 1993, before Ben Kuehne and I came on board. He did not seem to have done much investigation of his own, but he did identify plenty of points in the trial record that suggested a full hearing was in order. He pointed, in particular, to Eric Hendon's curious failure to call even one of Kris's alibi witnesses; to his advising Kris not to testify and to waive the issue of Judge Gross's arrest; and to various other technical points. It was not the most thorough piece of work, but there was enough substance there to suggest that the trial had been unfair.

At this point, Judge Leonard E. Glick was assigned to Kris's case. His role was to decide whether Kris should be allowed a hearing on the issues Fleck had put before him challenging the fairness of the initial trial. In capital cases, evidentiary hearings are common at this stage of the Florida process, but Judge Glick called for no such hearing. He affirmed the death penalty in a summary order, refusing to hear any evidence.

In the prosecution file, I found another unsigned order—again, drafted by the prosecutors—awaiting the signature of Judge Glick. It was very short, just two pages, and it went through the best argument a prosecutor could come up with for upholding the death sentence. It was the best argument a prosecutor could make because, again, it had been written by one of the prosecutors. Kris's lawyer knew nothing about it. All Judge Glick had done to the prosecutors' draft was change the date from October to November, and then he had signed it.

Was there an epidemic in Miami? Did all judges ask the prosecutors to do their judging? It was at this moment in the case that Ben and I got involved, and we immediately made a request for Glick's personnel file. Before he denied the petition, he had pointed out to Fleck that he knew the two government prosecutors, Ridge and Kastrenakes, as he had worked in the same office as them before becoming a judge. What Glick had failed to mention was that, at the time of Kris's trial, he had in fact been their supervising prosecutor: he would have personally approved their decision to seek the death penalty for Kris, and spoken with them about the case.

Few judges are quite so venal as "Howie the Mouse" Gross, and not all are quite so prosecutor-friendly as Harold Solomon and Leonard Glick. But let us consider for a moment how it is that there should be so much corruption or bias in the judiciary.

For starters, it does not help the troubled profile of the American justice system that most judges are selected at the ballot box. Forty-two of the fifty states elect them, and of the thirty-seven states with the death penalty, thirty-one elect their judges. Securing votes is an increasingly expensive exercise, and nobody has ever run a judicial campaign on "being fair to criminals." To give but one example, consider the 1994 race for chief justice of the Alabama Supreme Court, where the challenger accused the incumbent of shaking down attorneys who appeared before him for contributions to his expensive reelection campaign. The incumbent turned around and used the money he had collected to run advertisements in which the father of a murder victim accused the challenger of being an accomplice to murder because he had not been harsh enough in a capital case.[4]

I have always wondered whether judges who have to raise large sums of money to prevail in contentious elections are more subject to corruption than those who are appointed with tenure. Straight bribery is not as uncommon as one would hope, but electing judges injects a more subtle form of corruption into the process, as the candidate will avoid making an unpopular but just decision if it will haunt him the next time he goes to the polls. It is worth noting that only seven U.S. federal judges have been impeached in more than two hundred years; they are appointed with life tenure and therefore have far less "need" to seek out money and favor than their elected state counterparts.[5]

In the early 1980s, the California Supreme Court, led by Chief Justice Rose Bird, had a reputation for being liberal and for not brooking any unfairness in capital cases. Bird was chief justice for ten years, and in the sixty-one capital cases that came before her, she voted to reverse each and every one. In California the governor appoints the members of the Supreme Court, but there are retention elections after a decade, where the justices have to go to the polls on an up-or-down vote. In 1986 the Republican governor of California, George Deukmejian, announced that he would seek to unseat Chief Justice Bird that year, and he publicly warned two other justices, Cruz Reynoso and Joseph Grodin, that he would oppose them as well unless they voted to uphold more death sentences. This pressure failed to persuade the justices to change their votes, so he carried out his threat to go after them. All three lost their seats after a bitter election dominated by the death penalty, with Bird outspent two to one during the campaign. Deukmejian wasted no time in appointing conservative replacements.[6]

The other justices on the California Supreme Court got the message. Quite understandably, they wanted to keep their jobs. While the previous reversal rate had been 95 percent, over the five years that followed this power play the court switched almost diametrically, and affirmed 97 percent of all death sentences.[7] Indeed, the court rapidly became radically pro-capital punishment, to the point that by the 1990s the members of the Mississippi Supreme Court were viewed as significantly more liberal than their California counterparts. The phrase *to be Rose Birded* entered the lexicon, and Mississippi Supreme Court justice Jimmy Robertson would soon face a Birding of his own. Robertson was certainly more liberal than most. He became a victim of law-and-order electoral propaganda and was voted out of office. His opponents were very cunning and also well funded: in addition to outspending him by wide margins, they ran a candidate against him called Jimmy Roberts—a singularly unqualified individual whose name came first on the ballot. This was sufficiently confusing that some people voted for him by mistake.

The politicization of the death penalty is not the monopoly of elected judges. By 1994, shortly after Ben Kuehne and I took on Kris's case, crime had eclipsed all other political issues in the United States, such that an official of the National Governors Association suggested that the "top three issues in gubernatorial campaigns this year are crime, crime, and crime."[8] In theory, the judiciary is supposed to protect citizens, especially minorities, from being swept away in populist tides. But even when judges are appointed rather than elected, as in federal court and a minority of states, anyone who voices qualms about the death penalty these days will face fierce opposition.

The nomination of federal judges is, in theory, straightforward: "the President shall nominate, and by and with the Advice and Consent of the Senate, shall appoint . . . Judges."[9] In practice, it is more complicated. For district and appellate judges, by an unwritten convention referred to as "senatorial courtesy," the senators from the relevant state will forward the name of a proposed judge to the president. This is the first layer of the political onion: to get the nod from some of the most powerful politicians in the state, the candidate must fit a certain mold. The president will generally nominate the person the senators propose.[10]

Arriving at the U.S. Senate, the nominee then faces what may be a series of grueling confirmation hearings designed to ensure that he or she does not harbor any views that would offend the politicians in power that year. One hot-button issue is almost certain to be the death penalty. Others will include abortion and same-sex marriage. While not impossible, it is very difficult for outspoken opponents of the death penalty to be appointed as federal district judges, and if they want to advance to the court of appeals or the Supreme Court, they had better start laying a track record of upholding the death penalty in the cases before them.[11]

One of the things that most shocked me in the investigation of Kris Maharaj's case was the fact that Judge "Howie the Mouse" Gross had been on the take. Perhaps my reaction was odd: after all, the police seemed to have framed Kris, and that should have been equally horrifying. But I was (sadly) quite used to varying levels of corruption among the underpaid ranks of law enforcement, and half-expected to see it in many cases. Catching a judge with his nose in the trough was much less common. Some might ask, what does it matter? How does this have any relevance to Kris's case? He did not pay the bribe that was apparently solicited, and while Eric Hendon thought the judge had taken it out on Kris after that, the prosecution argued that Kris waived the issue, and that anyway Hendon had offered insufficient evidence that Gross was biased against him.[12]

Perhaps, as he sits lonely in his cell twenty-five years later, Kris allows himself a few moments of regret. After all, he paid Eric Hendon about $20,000 and got only a very lukewarm defense. He then had to pay Ken Cohen several thousand more to do the appeal, followed by $15,000 to Geoffrey Fleck to file his habeas, and then his very last $10,000 to Ben Kuehne. Had he gone along with the proposal to pay off Judge Gross $50,000, he would have paid less in the long run, and he might well have walked out of that court a free man.

But there is obviously a deeper issue here. All the procedures that have evolved in the law over the last eight hundred years—since the Magna Carta in 1215, when King John was forced to grant some of his citizens a fair trial—have been designed for one purpose and one purpose only: to try to ensure that we convict the right person. In other words, what is sometimes airily dismissed as a "mere technicality" is in fact a proxy designed to protect society from making mistakes. You may agree or disagree that a particular procedure makes a just outcome more likely,[13] but there are some rules that must surely achieve the stated goal: for example, having a highly competent defense lawyer would surely have made the result of Kris's trial more reliable. The same must be true of having an honest judge to oversee the proceedings.

As Ben and I considered how to shape Kris's appeal, we knew that one major focus would have to be on the judges—first the venal Judge Gross, and then Judge Solomon, who abdicated his judging to the prosecutors. An appellate court might buy the prosecution's arguments and reject one or both of these issues, but we both felt that evidence of such flagrant misconduct would set the tone of the case. Surely Florida's appellate judges would not allow a case to go by in which their colleagues had behaved so badly. Surely, we felt, they would find a reason to allow Kris a new, fair trial.

13

The Jury

By now, I'd been on the case for more than two years. I'd spent untold hours with our small team in New Orleans figuring out the flaws in the prosecution's case against Kris, tracking down witnesses, and looking for other possible culprits. By now, if it were a matter simply of raising a doubt as to Kris's guilt, any reasonable person would agree that we had done so. And yet I couldn't guarantee Kris a retrial. I was by then convinced that he was innocent, but twelve men and women had found him guilty. That counts for a lot in the American justice system, where it is very difficult to reverse a jury's verdict.

At this stage in a case, once I've gone through the police and defense file, interviewed the significant witnesses, and followed some of the more obvious leads, I generally like to talk to the jurors. In a number of ways, jurors may themselves point to error in the case. A juror may have lied during the selection process, or may have had improper contact by someone from the outside—every now and then a bailiff will exhort them to "fry the m—f—" or something similarly lurid and improper.

Jurors are also important simply as witnesses to what took place at trial. They sat through it, whereas I didn't. I could only read the words on the pages, but they could bring it all to life. In Kris's case, I wondered, for example, whether Hendon had been correct in saying that a member of the victim's family had run screaming from the courtroom during Neville Butler's testimony, and whether Judge Gross had mischaracterized the disruption in order to protect the conviction from a successful appeal.

Talking to jurors is fascinating. It is one of the best parts of the job. Over the years I've learned all kinds of things from jurors, but irritatingly,

Florida is one of the few states where you're not allowed to knock on a juror's door. They can always come forward and volunteer to talk to defense lawyers, but that presupposes that they know their rights and choose to exercise them. If, as a lawyer, you want to make the first contact, you have to have evidence of some kind of "misconduct" to start with, and then you have to go to the judge and ask for permission. In short, you have to know the answer before you start the conversation. It makes the job impossible.

When it comes to jurors' decisions in capital cases, there are three general areas of concern: how they are selected, how they are asked to consider the case, and how the system covers up the bizarre mistakes they make. In other words, the whole process is flawed. This is not to say that the alternative—abolishing trial by jury and replacing it with judges—would be better. Countries that use magistrates to decide who is guilty often have more failings. But efforts to pretend that jury trials are inevitably fair and impartial have unfortunate consequences, especially in capital cases.

In the voir dire[1] process, the selection of the twelve people who will hear the case, prospective members of the venire (the jury pool) are called into court in the presence of the defendant and the lawyers from both sides and are questioned on all kinds of issues. If you are summoned to serve as a juror in a capital trial, early in the process the judge and lawyers will ask you for your views on capital punishment. If the evidence is there, you are asked, will you promise to follow the law and vote to execute? This is not a public opinion poll or a conversation at a bar: you are under oath, seated in the same room as the person you might be asked to sentence to death. You will probably be looking at him as you answer: if he is found guilty and the prosecution makes a persuasive case for death, *will* you vote to end his life? If you reply that you are opposed to the death penalty, then you will be sent home and will have nothing more to do with the trial. Only those who swear that they could impose the death penalty can serve on the final panel of twelve.[2] Thus a large number of people are not eligible for jury service—paradoxically, the more liberal the venue for the trial, the more potential jurors will be excluded. Sometimes any hint of leniency is enough for the prosecution to choose to "strike" a prospective juror from the panel.

In Kris's case one of the prospective jurors, Ms. McKay, lived in North Dade, between Miami and Fort Lauderdale. During the jury selection process she said she did not favor the death penalty but that that would not affect her ability to decide whether the defendant was guilty. She had, she pointed out, previously sat on a jury in a drug-trafficking case where the defendant had been acquitted. Judge Gross removed her from the jury due to opposition to capital punishment. Three other potential jurors—Mrs. Antrim, Mr. Miles, and Ms. Roberts—went the same way. Miles did no more than query rhetorically whether he would be able to impose a death sentence. This weighty issue was being dropped on him out of the blue, and that he should take a moment to consider it should hardly have been surprising. Indeed, a fairer system might worry about seating a juror who does not pause when faced with the idea of voting to execute someone.

Kris's defense counsel, Eric Hendon, made only a very cursory effort to question the jurors about their views on capital punishment—perhaps because he was inexperienced, and not very familiar with the procedure—and he did not identify and exclude a single juror who would automatically impose a death sentence if Kris were found guilty, which is also grounds for dismissal. It seemed to me improbable that there were none. I have never picked a jury without coming across a number of people who believe in "an eye for an eye, and a tooth for a tooth."

In most states, a death sentence can only be imposed if the jurors are unanimously in favor of it. Florida has retreated from this unanimity requirement: it is sufficient for a simple majority of jurors to recommend death. With respect to Derrick Moo Young, the jury's vote was six to six, and because there was no majority, Kris narrowly avoided a death sentence for that murder. But for the murder of Duane Moo Young, one juror switched and, on a vote of seven to five, Kris was sent to death row. The hangman's rope was a rather thin thread.

Four people had been removed from the jury because they opposed capital punishment. Kris was sentenced to death by a single vote, the narrowest possible margin, so any one of those four could have provided a swing vote to save Kris's life; or they might have viewed the prosecution's evidence differently and had a "reasonable doubt" about the strange case that was presented against him.

When properly conducted, American jury selection is a fascinating process, much my favorite part of any trial. At its best, voir dire is a conversation with a prospective juror that takes place in a small room with just the judge, the lawyers, and the defendant present, rather than a vast courtroom with the public listening in. The purpose is partly to educate the jurors about the system and allow them to work out for themselves whether they are right for the case.

Most people would agree that it would be unfair to choose a juror who harbors a hidden bias that might affect their verdict. The theory behind the broad American right to question jurors is a good one, but in practice in most states, and in virtually all federal courts, the actual process falls far short of its advertised goals. In federal court, the judge normally does most of the questioning, and the questions tend to be ponderous. In a capital case, a judge might ask the standard question: "Do you have conscientious scruples concerning the death penalty?" Many jurors aren't even able to decipher the meaning of that question, let alone respond to it in a meaningful way.[3]

Some prosecutors and defense lawyers do little better. After a lengthy explication of some arcane aspect of the law, an attorney will ask the juror whether he can follow that law. "The difference between first-degree murder and second-degree murder involves the element of specific intent to commit the proscribed act," the lawyer drones in the patronizing tone that he inherited from his law school professor. "This is the mens rea of the crime. To have specific intent means that the accused must actively advert to the proscribed consequences. This is not the same as motive, but it does mean that he must have the subjective desire or knowledge that the prohibited act will occur. Could you follow this law as stated to you by His Honor, the judge?"

How many prospective jurors, bleary eyed by the end of the question, will say anything meaningful in response?

The Supreme Court has done little to promote clarity and candor. The court proposed that when race is at issue, the following question be asked: "The defendant is a member of the Negro race. The victim was a white Caucasian. Will these facts prejudice you against the defendant or affect your ability to render a fair and impartial verdict based solely on the evidence?"[4]

Again, how often is someone really going to say, "Hell yes, I'm a racist!" It has been known to occur: in the many cases I have tried over the years, and in the hundreds of trial records I have read, it happened once, when the judge asked the question, and a white man with a crew cut held forth on his views about the superiority of his race in a surprisingly forthright yet apologetic way. But such honesty is rare; if you want to expose people's racial prejudices, the questions must be more subtle. You never ask a direct question, since jurors will know the politically correct response. Rather, you explore topics that will expose a bias.

For example, it is often more fruitful to ask them what they think of the O. J. Simpson prosecution. Many white people will deliver a lengthy diatribe about how O.J. was guilty and how it was a scandal that he got off. Once you have them going on the subject, you can bring them gently around to a discussion of the lead detective, Mark Fuhrman. After Simpson was acquitted, Fuhrman pleaded no contest to one count of perjury: he admitted he had lied under oath about whether he had used the word *nigger*. (He told the court the word had not passed his lips in ten years, but he had been taped saying "nigger" forty-one times just months before the trial by a writer who was preparing a screenplay about the police.) One does not need to believe Simpson was innocent to think that Fuhrman's racism was important to the case. Would the fact that the detective committed perjury make you doubt other things he had said? The racist juror, unwilling to loosen his commitment to Simpson's guilt, may say no.

If you ask jurors to name their favorite verse from the Bible, you will learn far more than you will from their religious denomination. Jurors who like Matthew 5:7 are fine for the defense; most who cite any verse in

2 Timothy, particularly lines such as 3:16, are dangerous. If you ask them what book they've most enjoyed recently, you will uncover who can't or doesn't read, and who is thus more likely to be intimidated by the prosecution's pseudoscience. And so it goes. By the end of the process, you have a real sense of who each juror is, and what language each will best understand. Without this process, the lawyer is blind, relying on the kind of skin-deep judgment that gets us all in trouble, whatever the circumstances.

Prospective jurors harboring biases specific to the case must be removed for "cause" (i.e., for good reason). This is primarily thought to be because they have a strong preexisting judgment about the guilt or innocence of the defendant,[5] but there are any number of other reasons to justify a "cause" strike. For example, jurors will be excluded if they announce that they will believe anything that a police officer says, or if they have such close ties to the police that they are likely to lean in the direction of law enforcement. They will be barred if they cannot respect a defendant's right to remain silent, or if they have been victims of a similar crime. It is difficult to argue with these decisions: if someone is biased, then why should they be permitted to sit on the jury?

I have never tried a case in which we did not identify a substantial number of jurors with such biases.[6] Some countries have done away with the jury selection process (Britain included), making their trials far more of a crapshoot. In the United States, identifying the jurors' prejudices can go a long way toward ensuring that a trial is fair. But if—as happens in many cases, including Kris Maharaj's—the process is conducted only superficially, and if jurors are asked only legalistic questions, there is no telling who may end up deciding the defendant's fate.

While Florida is one of the few states to ban lawyers from initiating contact with a juror to discuss a case after the verdict, the right of free speech means that nobody can be banned from speaking out about the experience of serving on a jury in America. Indeed, jurors write books and even—more recently—tweet about what happens.[7] Most states see nothing wrong with approaching jurors when a trial is over. Over the years, I have interviewed jurors in almost all the cases in which I have been involved. It is a fascinating and humbling experience.

Even where the trial comes out as well as could reasonably be expected, there is plenty to learn.[8] I worked on the retrial of Outlaw biker Clarence Smith. "Smitty" had been sentenced to death, and we got him a new trial at which we presented a strong case for his innocence. The jurors had me twisting in terror as they deliberated for three hours, but they finally acquitted him. I later learned when I talked to a couple of the jurors that one of them had been holding out for conviction. Watching the courtroom carefully over the two weeks of trial, he had developed a kind of podiatry polygraph test: every time I stood on the sides of my shoes when I was talking, he was convinced I was not telling the truth. He correlated this theory with his observations during my closing argument and decided that whenever I said Smitty was innocent, I didn't really believe it.

His theory was—needless to say—completely unfounded, as I was completely convinced of Smitty's innocence. (The state's two informants, John Joseph "J.J." Hall and Carl "Sick Quick" Holley, had manipulated the FBI and cut a deal for themselves not only to avoid the death penalty but to get a cushy deal in the Federal Witness Protection Program. They were, I firmly believed, the ones who had wired a bomb to the brake lights of a federal witness's pickup truck—a position the jury came to share.) This bizarre irrationality taught me a lesson, and I have never stood nervously on the sides of my shoes since. But sometimes the problems are more entrenched, and harder to address.

Sam Johnson, a black man from New York, was convicted and sentenced to death for killing a white police officer in rural McComb, Mississippi, in 1981. The local sheriff, Lloyd B. "Goon" Jones, was the man who had ordered the Mississippi State Highway Patrol to open fire on the black students at Jackson State University in 1970. He also achieved some notoriety when a number of civil rights activists dared to enter Mississippi from such Communist-infested states as California. He arrested them, took them to the local jail, dry-shaved their heads with razors, and then poured moonshine over their scalps. When he identified the leader of this civil rights rabble, he went to the additional trouble of sticking a fork up the man's nose.

Things were not looking good for Sam Johnson when I started work on his appeal. I was young and very inexperienced. Early in the case, I ventured down to Pike County to talk to the jurors who had condemned Sam to death, and to see what I could learn. One of the first jurors I talked to invited me in warmly for a glass of iced tea. She loved—l-u-u-u-ved—my English accent, she said. At some point her husband, sitting with us, mentioned how much they liked the English: "Y'all helped us out during the war." He meant the War Between the States, or the War of Northern Aggression, as the Civil War is still sometimes called down South. They began regaling me with her experience as a juror at Sam's trial, a moment's excitement for the sleepy town of McComb. She told me that one old black lady on the jury had been compliant ("She knew her place"), but there had been a black man who had caused trouble, who had not wanted to vote for the death penalty.

"It weren't no problem really," she said in a cheerful singsong. "We-all jus' told him we'd send the Klan round if he didn't make good."

I thought she was joking. She was not. As the conversation progressed, her husband said he was a Klan member and mentioned that they had a meeting the following evening—would I like to come along? Again, I thought he was pulling my leg. He was not. I politely declined. Ever since, I have regretted my cowardice, but I was terrified they would discover I was some commie-pinko-liberal and that I'd end up with my own fork, or even a noose.

I spent several more days in Pike County, avoiding lonely roads late at night. There had been only one black male juror, so he had to have been the one coerced into sentencing Sam to death. I went to see him one evening. He paled when I explained why I was there; he denied ever being picked for the jury, let alone sending Sam to death row. I left his house perplexed and frustrated. I sought the support of the local chairman of the NAACP and told him that this could be life-or-death for Sam. He went to visit the juror himself and argued that it was his duty to reveal what had happened. The juror ultimately admitted that he had been on Sam's jury, but he adamantly refused to accept that he had ever voted to send him to the gas chamber, or that he had been threatened with a visitation from the Klan. Given that his entire family lived in the area, I could understand his denials.

Sam Johnson eventually got a new sentencing trial—on technical legal grounds, entirely unrelated to the coerced juror.[9] Prior to the resentencing, we held a hearing on our claim that those associated with the prosecution were racist and that therefore the process should be invalidated. Sheriff "Goon" Jones came to testify in overalls. An enormous man, he chewed tobacco throughout the hearing, spitting the juice out as he pondered each reply. I asked him whether he still called black people "niggers."

"Nope," he said, looking down at me with disdain. "Someone told me that was rude."

So what would he call black men today? I inquired.

He pondered a moment, masticating. "Colored boys," he finally said, with emphasis.

And when, I asked, would he stop doing that?

"When someone tells me it's rude," he said.

I took a deep breath and suggested that perhaps it was rude.

"Well, boy," he said, with another spit into his plastic cup. "I guess I just don' appreciate your opinion."

As he walked past me, leaving the witness stand, he suggested in turn that I not come by his county after dark.

The judge refused to bar a retrial on the grounds of pervasive racism, and at the resentencing trial Sam only narrowly avoided going back to death row when four African American jurors declined to go along with the majority viewpoint. There had been a very strong case to be made for Sam's innocence, but despite challenging his conviction for several years, he remained in the Mississippi State Penitentiary at Parchman Farm until he died from a terrible cancer that had gone untreated. His stomach had swollen to the shape of a basketball, like that of a starving child in Biafra. Though he clung to the hope of exoneration to the end, his greatest fear was that he would end up buried on the prison grounds. It was a fate he narrowly escaped, thanks to some kind friends who paid for a "free" funeral.

There is another side to the story. Jurors can sometimes show great courage when they come to suspect they made a mistake in their verdict. In 1995, on Super Bowl Sunday, Murray Barnes had been at Creola's Bar in New Orleans and won the thousand-dollar pool on the game. As he left with his winnings, Barnes was robbed and killed. Dan Bright was charged with the crime. Kathleen Hawk Norman, a successful white businesswoman, later found herself selected as foreperson of his jury. The evidence of Dan's guilt seemed strong, and she felt she had little option but to sentence him to death.

Some years later the LCAC took over Dan's appeal, and we approached Kathleen to discuss her role in the case and share new evidence with her. Most dramatic was an FBI report, generated long before Dan's trial, that we had obtained through Freedom of Information litigation. It read as follows: "The source further stated that Dan Bright, aka Pooney, is in jail for the murder committed by ▄▄▄▄▄▄." The name of the perpetrator had been redacted from the document: the FBI argued that this was necessary to "safeguard the privacy" of the real killer.

We ultimately identified the man whose name had been blacked out as Tracey Davis, and we accumulated enough evidence to prove he was the murderer. We learned that on the day in question the state's eyewitness, Freddie Thompson, had been drinking heavily. Weeks after the murder, when the police encouraged Thompson to identify Dan, he was on parole for a prior felony. We located alibi witnesses who placed Dan elsewhere at the time of the crime.

When we showed all this evidence to Kathleen Hawk Norman, she felt betrayed by the prosecution. She had been called upon to perform the hardest task of her life: voting to take another human life. But the prosecutor who had asked this of her had hidden evidence from the jurors that would certainly have changed her mind. She was furious. She began a campaign called Jurors for Justice and came to court every day Dan's case was scheduled. She became such a vocal critic of the judge that he set hearings earlier and earlier in the morning. Finally he delivered his opinion, denying Dan a new trial, before eight o'clock, in an effort to avoid the wrath of "The Angry Juror," as Kathleen had been dubbed by the local media.

Kathleen then filed a legal brief in support of Dan's appeal, describing what all this evidence would have meant to her and the other jurors.[10] Nonetheless the Louisiana Court of Appeals found that the new evidence provided "no reasonable probability that the outcome of the case would have been different." In other words, the court felt that it was better placed to decide what the jury would have done with the new evidence than was one of the actual jurors. Kathleen became even more determined to see the verdict overturned.

The Louisiana Supreme Court eventually ordered a new trial, the prosecution dismissed the charges, and Dan was set free. Kathleen felt responsible for almost taking his life and for consigning him to prison for nine years for a crime he did not commit. She dedicated herself to helping him establish a new life. She found him his first job and stood by him through the tough transition out of jail. She then went on to devote her substantial energies to working as chair of the board of the Innocence Project New Orleans. Sadly, in 2008, Kathleen suffered an unexpected and massive heart attack, depriving those seeking justice of an indefatigable advocate, and Dan Bright of a devoted mentor.

Most jurors are not covert members of the KKK, and most struggle to do their best. Very often, though, their misunderstanding of the law leaves them ill equipped even to approximate what the system expects of them. Judges read lengthy, impenetrable instructions and imagine that the jurors are then ready to apply intricate legal doctrines. Nothing could be further from the truth: many jurors don't even comprehend the basic foundations of the system. Studies show that as few as one-third of those who have actually sat through a criminal trial understood that the prosecution bears the burden of proof.[11]

Jurors in capital trials are generally asked to consider "aggravating" and "mitigating" circumstances—factors presented at the penalty phase of a capital trial to determine whether the correct punishment should be life or death. All kinds of complexities keep appellate judges entertained: What counts as a mitigating circumstance? Can there be any limit on mitigating circumstances? What is the burden of proof when considering mitigating circumstances? And so on.

But in the real world, such issues are entirely irrelevant. If a trial may be compared to a long horse race over jumps, many jurors fall at the first hurdle. In one of the cases I worked on, I discovered that not one of the twelve jurors knew what the word *mitigating* meant. One suggested it was a synonym for *aggravating*. It was difficult to believe, then, that they had properly considered the evidence before sentencing my client, Jack Davis, to death. Yet this was not the most troublesome fact that emerged from the jury interviews after the trial. I engaged one of the jurors— the foreperson, as it happened, a woman with a Ph.D. in English—on the evidence that suggested strongly that Jack was innocent of the crime. The prosecution had used outmoded serological testimony to implicate him at trial; our recent DNA test demonstrated that the original blood test result had been false. At the same time, the government's informant had recanted, admitting that he had made up the story to avoid prison himself. None of this bothered her.

Why not? I politely inquired.

In addition to her Ph.D., she said, she had the benefit of ESP (extrasensory perception), and it allowed her to know beyond a doubt that Jack was guilty not only of this murder but of four others. She therefore had no qualms about sentencing him to death.[12]

Any human enterprise, inescapably, will be beset by unpredictable outcomes. But most people would agree that appellate judges should take note when jurors inflict a sentence of death based on entrenched racism or claims to ESP. Ignoring this kind of thing would be difficult to justify. Yet it is ignored on a daily basis in courts across the United States.

When jurors speak their minds and an unpalatable truth comes out, that does not mean that the courts will take action. Florida law is archetypal in this respect, because it is incomprehensible, and because its purpose seems to be simply to uphold a conviction at all costs. "Upon an inquiry into the validity of a verdict or indictment," says the Florida statute, "a juror is not competent to testify as to any matter which essentially inheres in the verdict or indictment." If you don't understand this, you are in good company: It is the type of nonsense that lawyers speak when they are trying to set themselves apart from the population at large. What it means is that jurors are allowed to state the facts as they observably happened in the jury room, but they cannot comment in court on what the consequences might have been. They can say that a particular book was in the jury deliberation room that should not have been there, but they cannot discuss whether its content had any impact on them. Judges authorize themselves to hear what happened, but they then require themselves to guess at whether this would have caused an unfair verdict.[13]

An additional wrinkle hauls the process even further away from common sense: if an "item" was properly in the jury room in the first place, no challenge may be raised at all, no matter how it was used. The offending influence generally has to come from outside. In other words, jurors may not look up a legal term that they don't understand in a dictionary that was not supposed to be in the deliberating room; but if they want to check whether the white substance that the police got from the suspect is actually cocaine, and they crack open the evidence bag and snort a few lines, that fact can't be used to challenge the conviction: the drug was properly introduced at trial and was therefore legally in the jury room. The fact the jurors were high when they decided to vote guilty—ignoring the prisoner's defense that the drugs were planted on him—would count for nothing.[14]

This may seem far-fetched. Unfortunately, it is not. There is, the Supreme Court has noted, a "strong policy against any post-verdict inquiry into a juror's state of mind." But this is not a rational argument; it is just a statement. Why is there such a policy? Consider the case cited by the Supreme Court for this "strong policy." A man called John Dioguardi was convicted of violating the securities laws by trying to manipulate the price of some stocks. After the trial, he received a letter from Genena Rush, one of the jurors, in which she explained that she had "eyes and ears that . . . see things before [they] happen," but that unfortunately her eyes "are only partly open" because "a curse was put upon them some years ago."[15] Armed with this letter, Dioguardi's lawyers consulted seven psychiatrists, all of whom thought Rush was probably suffering from a chronic mental disorder and might well have been psychotic while she was on the jury. All the doctors suggested that she receive a mental health evaluation.

The judge refused to look into the issue, satisfied that he had, from his bench, noticed nothing strange about her behavior during the trial. Unless a juror was patently in the midst of a psychotic breakdown, the judge held, no steps should be taken to remedy the verdict, even if it later emerged that the juror in question was certifiably insane.

If this principle seems odd, the leading Supreme Court precedent on juror testimony is even stranger. In 1987 the court was presented with a demand for a new trial by Tony Tanner, who had been convicted of receiving a $30,000 kickback on a road-building contract in Florida. The case was by no means open and shut. The first trial had resulted in a hung jury, since the twelve jurors could not agree on a verdict. Only at retrial was he convicted. One of the jurors who had voted guilty, Daniel Hardy, subsequently gave a sworn statement expressing misgivings about his experience.[16]

"I felt like," he began, " . . . the jury was one big party." Seven of the jurors, including Hardy himself, drank alcohol through the trial; they split several pitchers of beer during the recesses. The foreperson, an alcoholic, downed a liter of wine at lunch. Hardy admitted that he and three other jurors had smoked marijuana quite regularly during the proceedings, although he did not join the two who used cocaine. One juror brought various drugs and paraphernalia into the jury room and sold a quarter pound of marijuana to another juror during the trial. Some of the jurors, Hardy said, were falling asleep during the witness testimony—a fact noticed by the lawyers at the time and brought to the attention of the judge, who did nothing about it. One of the jurors described himself as "flying" during much of the case.

"I felt that the people on the jury didn't have no business being on the jury," Hardy summed up, pricked by his conscience. "I felt . . . that

Mr. Tanner should have a better opportunity to get somebody that would review the facts right."

In his statement, Hardy had admitted to committing a series of crimes during the trial and accused others of serious felonies, for which they could have received far more time in prison than Tony Tanner was up for. Surely this was sufficient to require a new trial.

It was not. The Supreme Court agreed with the lower courts that there was no point in even holding a hearing. The rule against "impeaching a jurors' verdict" forbade overturning the conviction, even if everything Hardy said was true. All of this talk about intoxication touched on the jurors' mental state, and that could not be explored after the verdict. The Supreme Court went on to suggest, however, that the trial judge might have made a mistake in a complicated and arcane interpretation of a certain law. Tanner ultimately walked free on that point, and he never went to prison at all.[17] Why, one might well ask, were the courts afraid of disturbing the "finality of the jurors' verdict" when confronted with clear evidence of jurors being high and drunk throughout most of the trial, but were happy to do so on a hypertechnical interpretation of the law?

As with many curious legal rules, this one originated long ago—in 1785, to be precise. Its roots may be traced to the outdated notion that jurors can have a "frank discussion" only if their conversations are kept totally secret. That theory should have evaporated with the First Amendment four years later, which ensured that jurors could not be prevented from talking about their service—or anything else that crossed their minds.

Those who subsequently defended the idea that the validity of jurors' verdicts should be virtually beyond discussion conjured up a secondary worry: that the ability to question jurors in court would "operate to intimidate, beset and harass them." But this concern makes little sense because in most American jurisdictions nothing can stop a lawyer from talking to a juror whenever he likes. The law prevents that questioning only from taking place in court, the one venue where the juror, if genuinely harassed, would have the protection of a judge. In truth, the decree that judges will not hear a juror's testimony about the process that led to a verdict is a relic that persists because looking too closely at jurors' conduct would result in "too many" reversals.

What we are witnessing here is an effort by the criminal justice system to achieve "finality"—a euphemism for ensuring that there is a conviction, without worrying whether it is the appropriate one. To be sure, allowing jurors to speak out, and lifting the veil on the kind of bizarre issues discussed in some jury rooms, would result in the reversal of a small number of convictions. But simply to conclude a trial, and then defend the result at all costs, is not justice.

The doomsayers who claim that transparency would spell the end of the jury system after eight hundred years might well bear in mind that between 1973, when capital punishment was effectively reinstituted in America, and 1995, 40 percent of capital cases were thrown out on their first state appeal for "serious error." Of the 599 cases that made it through to federal court, a further two out of five were invalidated for "serious error." In other words, the overall error rate was 68 percent. The process took an average of nine or ten years to complete in each case.[18]

So American courts found mistakes in two-thirds of all capital cases, for a variety of reasons. A thorough investigation of jurors would be unlikely to result in two-thirds of all death sentences being thrown out for misconduct, yet we are willing to accept such a reversal rate for other, often more arcane issues. Indeed, critics would say that many of the "errors" that were identified were mere technicalities.

Since 1995 we have had no comprehensive figures on reversals in capital cases, but my experience is that the rate has declined substantially. This has been occasioned not by any correction of the faults in the system.[19] Rather, legislation has been passed to make sure that fewer cases can be reversed. As ever, the government has attempted to address a problem by wishing it away rather than by addressing root causes.

Proponents of the jury system proudly point to the fact that twelve people must unanimously find the person on trial guilty "beyond a reasonable doubt" before they are permitted to convict him. This sounds very meticulous and grand, but what does it really mean? We know that it

falls far short of eliminating any possible mistake. Since the reintroduction of capital punishment in 1976, more than 120 prisoners have been
exonerated from death row—and these are only the people whose innocence has been established with sufficient certainty to convince conservative appeal courts bound by strict rules of procedure. Yet in each of
these 120 cases, all twelve jurors were convinced beyond a reasonable
doubt that the individual was guilty and deserved to die; in every case
they were wrong.

In Kris's case, at voir dire Eric Hendon failed to ask the questions
that would have secured a truly impartial jury. But had he decided to
explore the jurors' understanding of "the burden of proof," Judge Gross
would have pulled him up: a defense lawyer is not allowed to ask a juror
what they mean by "beyond a reasonable doubt." Why not? I have conducted a fairly unscientific survey over the years, asking audiences at
conferences to try to place some kind of definition on the term, to quan-
tify it as best they can with statistical probabilities: What degree of certainty would they demand before voting guilty? In a civil case, the
plaintiff must prove the case "by a preponderance of the evidence"—just
50.1 percent against the defendant's 49.9 percent. So what does it mean
to be convinced "beyond a reasonable doubt"?

Lawyers and judges tend to respond that the concept cannot be
quantified, but this evasion is another refuge of the scoundrel. We cannot loudly proclaim that the burden of proof is central to the system,
then assert that we cannot begin to define it. People who wish to avoid
public debate tend to be insecure as to their position. Indeed, the refusal
to define "reasonable doubt" tells us that the answer to the question is a
Pandora's box that they would like to keep sealed.

The jurors who convicted Kris Maharaj were specifically told by the
judge that they should not eliminate all doubt. "Whenever the words
'reasonable doubt' are used," they were told, "you must consider the following: A reasonable doubt is not a mere possible doubt, a speculative,
imaginary or forced doubt. Such a doubt must not influence you to
return a verdict of not guilty if you have an abiding conviction of
guilt." But at what level is the elimination of doubt sufficient to justify incarceration, let alone execution? Would the jurors have to be 75 percent

sure Kris Maharaj really did it? Ninety percent sure? Ninety-nine per-cent sure? In my unscientific study, I drew up a form for members of my audiences to fill out whenever I gave a presentation on the subject. I passed my forms out at a Louisiana judges' conference to see what they would say—and was taken aback at the results. One federal judge put the goal at 75 percent; no judge wrote more than 95 percent. So everyone was *aiming* to get it wrong at least one time in twenty. Roughly seven million people are either behind bars, on probation, or on parole in the United States.[20] If we were to *aim* to make a mistake once in every twenty cases, the U.S. judicial system would be *aiming* to have a total of 350,000 innocent people in prison—and if you aim low, you will probably miss your target.

Only a tiny percentage of people plead guilty to a capital offense, un-less they have an agreement that death will not be imposed; the large majority go to trial. Thus, of the 3,200 people on death row, aiming to be 95 percent sure we get it right means we hope to execute just 160 inno-cent people; shooting for 75 percent, the goal would be 800 innocents. It is difficult to believe that jurors would take a much more careful view of their responsibilities than judges. By insisting that nobody discuss the most central point in the decision-making process—what degree of doubt should lead to an acquittal—we are making it absolutely certain that mistakes will be commonplace.

I am very sad that the law has forbidden me from speaking with any of the jurors in Kris's case. It is a huge hole in my understanding of it. Prob-ably by now some of the jurors have died. Kris is not angry that the ju-rors put him where he is today. He thinks they were duped, and he holds out a dual hope: that perhaps they will come in contact with this book and hear the evidence that was kept from them in 1987; and that his own experience may induce others to be more skeptical before sending someone to prison in the future.

Meanwhile, we had to move forward with the appeal without any input from the jurors—without their description of how the trial had been conducted, and without any information that one juror might have concerning misconduct committed by another. Despite this, I hoped that we had enough to persuade any sane person that Kris's trial had been unfair. Hopefully, one day, an appellate court would rule that we should be allowed to present the new evidence we had developed to another jury, who would receive the kind of information that anyone should expect when faced with the awesome responsibility of sending someone to prison, or to death row.

14

The Road to Nowhere

At the point that Judge Glick denied the habeas petition Geoffrey Fleck had filed out of hand, Kris had been in prison for eight years. In early 1995 Ben Kuehne and I took over and we appealed Glick's order to the Florida Supreme Court. We asked that a judge be instructed to at least take a look at the new material we had uncovered. Fearful that the importance of the appeal might be overlooked, I corralled several dozen British members of Parliament to file a brief on Kris's behalf, to highlight the fact that his case was a matter of international interest. A British barrister, Geoffrey Robertson Q.C., came to Florida to argue as a "friend of the court." I begged him to wear his wig and gown, as I thought the more he looked like he was in *Rumpole of the Bailey,* the more the justices were likely to be impressed. He declined, and wore a suit.

Our request was a modest one: let Kris have his day in court. The prosecution, now represented by the state attorney general, argued that Kris had not objected in a timely manner to the fact that Judge Glick had supervised Paul Ridge and John Kastrenakes at the time of trial, or to the fact that the prosecutors had written Judge Glick's order. This position was fairly absurd: we had not known about it for the simple reason that they had failed to tell us. I was confident that we would win.

Not until two years later—on September 19, 1996—did the Florida Supreme Court issue its opinion. It was half defeat, half victory. The justices went out of their way to note that a number of the claims we had put forward ought not to be considered because Kris's lawyer should have raised them at the original trial. They were thus "procedurally barred." By now, Kris was depressingly familiar with the concept of a "procedural bar," a rule that says that if a lawyer fails to object to something during the original trial, that objection cannot be raised later. The idea is that at trial the defendant should be forced to raise every issue on the spot. He should not be allowed to keep claims in his back pocket so that, if the trial should come out the wrong way, he can sandbag the system by bringing them up later.

Superficially, the rule makes sense if your goal is for the legal process to come to as speedy a conclusion as possible; in practice, is entirely counterproductive if you wish to ensure that a trial reaches the right result. It is not the defendant who raises or waives claims that might be important to his case, but his lawyer. An effective lawyer will not sit back and plan to sandbag anyone; rather, he or she will raise every conceivable issue as it arises, forcing the trial judge to rule on each one, because any mistake by the judge might later secure the client a new trial. The effective lawyer will also present a powerful case for the defense, maximizing the client's chances of being acquitted. The ineffective lawyer, by contrast, will raise no issues before or during the trial and will muddle through the case, ensuring that his client is convicted.

Eric Hendon did not raise the vast majority of legal issues available to Kris before the trial. He did not challenge the admissibility of Kris's statements to Detective Buhrmaster, although they were taken in violation of the *Miranda* rule. He did not challenge the unreliable (and ultimately false) eyewitness evidence that linked Kris to the hotel reservation. He did not challenge Buhrmaster's assertion that Kris had not been in room 1215 before the murders, or his statement that Kris had claimed never to have owned a gun, or seek to compel the discovery of Butler's polygraph results (though he knew Butler had taken one). He did very little in preparation for the trial.

In a trial by jury, if you have a diligent lawyer, your chances of getting a fair verdict are relatively high. Even if you are convicted and sentenced to death, you are more likely to win on appeal, because your lawyer will have objected to mistakes made along the way. If, however, you have an inept lawyer, you have little chance of getting a fair trial, and virtually no chance of winning a new trial on appeal: your lawyer will have ostensibly "waived" all manner of claims by failing to raise them during the original trial, so you are "procedurally barred" from bringing them up later as a basis for appeal. The net result is that capital punishment is a penalty reserved for the defendants with the worst lawyers, rather than for those who commit the worst crimes.[1]

While the Florida Supreme Court suggested that many of the claims in the petition we filed on Kris's behalf should be dismissed because Hendon had failed to raise them at trial, the court did rule that a hearing should be allowed on some of the issues—mainly involving whether Hendon had been ineffective in the representation he provided. One month shy of Kris's tenth anniversary in prison, the court remanded the case to a new judge, Jerald Bagley. Kris was glad to hear that a deadline of ninety days was set for Judge Bagley to rule on his case; he expected to be free shortly before Christmas 1996.

I was mildly panicked—we had a great deal to do in three short months. We had filed an enormous petition, running to more than three hundred pages, detailing the mistakes that had been made by the defense lawyer, prosecutors, and judges, and presenting the new evidence we had amassed to date, all of which pointed strongly to Kris's innocence. The LCAC had done this work with virtually no funds. I had been driving back and forth to South Florida to save money and I'd managed to get journalists to fund some of our investigation and to tape witnesses. I had found witnesses in England when I was home visiting my mother and corralled others into contributing their expertise for free. It was a patchwork of facts and suppositions. We had done a great deal, but our effort to assemble the case was far from complete.

Christmas 1996 came and went. Two more men died in Florida's electric chair, and Kris had still not received a hearing. The problem basically boiled down to money. Kris had none, and the investigation had already cost us far more than our small nonprofit could afford to spend. Adding up the flights, the hotel rooms, the rental cars, the gas, and even just the photocopying, we were many thousands of dollars in the hole. I had spent weeks in Florida, combing through the prosecutor's files, the records of the Miami-Dade police, and the federal court records of cartel lawyer F. Nigel Bowe, as well as interviewing witnesses. We'd leaned on the help of volunteers. But the hearing was going to cost far more than what we'd spent to date, and the money was going to have to come from somewhere.

I even tried to raise some funds through Kris's old associates in England. When he had been wealthy, he had been generous. Now that both he and his wife, Marita, were destitute, I felt it was time to call in some of those favors. Kris was proud, and did not want me to do this, though he was more willing to bow to Marita's need than his own. One person from the old days volunteered, anonymously, to help Marita pay her rent and keep the electricity on, but many seemed to have been fair-weather friends.

We would have to pay the travel costs of as many as thirty witnesses so that they could testify in court—coming from several different countries. Some important people still had to be investigated and, where possible, interviewed, beginning with Jaime Vallejo Mejia, who was safely ensconced in Colombia, and Adam Hosein in Trinidad. Prince Ellis was willing to testify that Kris had been framed and that Eddie Dames was a drug dealer, but Ellis was in the Bahamas, and we didn't have the money to fly him to Miami and put him up in a hotel. We needed to prove that the scurrilous articles Eslee Carberry had published in the *Caribbean Echo* were completely unfounded, but he had since been deported to the Turks and Caicos Islands. Tino Geddes, whose story about concocting an alibi was contradicted by five witnesses, was in Jamaica.

Large holes remained in our ability to prove what the Moo Youngs were up to with their various corporations. The forensic accountant, Laura Snook, had given us very helpful pro bono assistance interpreting the documents, and she had pointed out that Derrick and Duane Moo Young were trying to skim millions off the top—but she would have to fly from England to testify. Who would pay for her flight? We should have been chasing up several other leads across the United States—including W.C. Bryant, with his gems and the billions of dollars he claimed to have in Japanese yen bonds.

Beyond the facts of the case, we would have to prove that at the original trial there had been judicial corruption. Judge Gross's greed was a matter of record, but demonstrating the link to Kris's case would take much more work. We needed disclosures from the Florida Department of Law Enforcement (FDLE), who had done the investigation. How had they come to suspect Judge Gross in the first place? He must have done something to bring attention on himself. What other evidence did they have? For our shoestring budget, it was enough of a strain that I'd have to get to Miami and stay in a motel for two weeks during the hearing.

It might seem on the surface that we had managed to blow the prosecution case out of the water with the number of irregularities we had discovered. Unfortunately, when it comes to arguing a case in court, one cannot simply state something as fact—a witness must prove it. One cannot wave a polygraph test result at the judge—it must be introduced by the expert who administered it and wrote up the results. We might have a videotape of Prince Ellis telling us that he thought Eddie Dames was involved in drugs and in the crime, but we would have to "authenticate" it—which meant that Ellis would either have to fly to Florida to say it was all true, or we would have to bring the British cameraman to court to testify to how he had pressed the record button. All of this cost money, and that was the one thing we didn't have.

By the time Kris had paid his retainer to Ben Kuehne, he was bankrupt. He could do nothing for Marita, whose situation was increasingly dire, and whose well-being was his main concern. She had lost their house to the mortgage company and had gradually sold off her possessions to remain afloat. Her only companion, their Alsatian dog, had died. So we turned to Judge Bagley and asked him how we were meant to represent Kris effectively without funds. Under Florida law, prisoners have the right to receive funding from the state to cover the costs of their appeal; the question was where in the Florida budget we would find the money.

I had high hopes of Jerald Bagley. He was a young African American who had been appointed to the bench just one year earlier by Governor Lawton Chiles—a liberal Democrat known as "Walkin' Lawton" for the number of miles he had covered in his election campaign. Bagley was therefore unsullied by the corruption that had provoked Operation Court Broom, the full-scale investigation of local judges that had followed Judge Gross's arrest.

Kris did not trust the new judge, partly because Bagley had been elevated to the bench directly from the same Miami-Dade prosecutors' office that had put him on death row. I felt I had a rather broader experience of judges and that Kris's view was colored by his bad experiences to date. Bagley seemed decent to me, and from what little I could tell, and what others reported, he appeared not to be a fan of the death penalty. Whether he would have the courage to do what was right was open to question, but then, which elected judge in Dade County could be relied upon for that?

Sometimes, unfortunately, the client is much wiser than his lawyer.

Paying for the defense of inmates on death row ranks very close to the bottom on the list of priorities of Florida legislators, who generally think state money is better spent cranking up Old Sparky and disposing of the problem on a more permanent basis. The Office of the Capital Collateral Representative (CCR) had recently been created to help provide a lawyer and investigators for death row prisoners unable to afford the costs of the defense. When we applied to the CCR for assistance, we were told that it was out of funds and could provide neither a lawyer nor help with expenses. More than three hundred people were then on death row in the state of Florida, and the office had enough money to represent perhaps a dozen of them effectively. Provisions had been made in a separate budget for cases that could not be funded or taken on by the CCR. The total amount available for 1997 was $236,084 (perhaps enough to pay to do one case thoroughly). When, in January, we asked for funds, we were told that other lawyers had already submitted bills for $360,584. Time and time again we asked for resources, and Judge Bagley turned us down, saying no money was available. In the end, twelve months went by while we beat the bushes for some source of funding.

Meanwhile Pedro Medina became the twenty-second person electrocuted by the state since Kris had been sent to death row. Medina was a Cuban refugee who had fled Castro in the Mariel boatlift of 1980, but his welcome to America had not been all that he had anticipated. By 1982 he was on death row for an ugly crime: stabbing an elementary school gym teacher. He went to his death fifteen years later insisting he had not done it. "I am still innocent!" he exclaimed in his thick Spanish accent just before he was strapped into the chair. When the electric current came, fire burst from his head, and there was an acrid smell of burning. He continued to take labored breaths as his body cooled before the doctors could check his heartbeat. Then they juiced him again.

"People who commit murder better not do it in Florida," remarked Attorney General Robert Butterworth, in the wake of Medina's death. "Because we may have a problem with our electric chair."

After a flood of media coverage highlighted the horror of this event, Butterworth retreated and announced that he favored a change in method of execution to lethal injection.

With much of 1997 already behind us, Judge Bagley suggested that if we could wait another year, there might be funds in the 1998 budget to pay for Kris's hearing. Meanwhile the prosecution had all the resources it needed. Only the defendant's lawyers would not be paid or receive any expenses for witnesses. We reminded the judge that twelve months had passed—the Florida Supreme Court had ordered the hearing to take place within 90 days. I was getting desperate. I approached the British government and suggested that it might help Kris fund his case, but nothing came of that either. In the end, we felt we had no choice. We decided to go forward with what we had; we felt we could not wait any longer for funding that might never materialize.

As I sat in a rather sordid motel across the road from the Dade County Courthouse, the television somberly reported that Diana, Princess of Wales, was feared to have died in a car accident in Paris. It was Monday, August 31, 1997. Diana's funeral took place on September 6, and I was one of the two and a half billion people who watched it on television—albeit with only one eye, while preparing Kris's case. The hearing was set to begin two days later. Notwithstanding our lack of resources, we still had more evidence to prove an unfair trial than I had ever seen in a capital case.

I hoped that Judge Bagley would act to offset our lack of money. He might press the state to concede issues that were not really in contention, like whether the experts had written their polygraph reports, or whether the person in the British television video was really Prince Ellis. He might agree to waive formalities such as bringing a witness across the Atlantic Ocean merely to ratify the authenticity of a particular document.

Unfortunately, when the time came, he did the opposite. Prince Ellis had recanted his trial testimony. As part of our cost-cutting effort, we had had Ellis's statement filmed for free by a British television cameraman in a hotel room in the Bahamas. I thought the fact that the statement had been filmed by an independent reporter would actually lend it more credibility. We did not have the money to go and take a sworn deposition from Ellis in the Bahamas. We suggested that Judge Bagley admit the videotape into evidence. He said that he could do so only if the cameraman appeared in court to testify that he had filmed it. We suggested that perhaps a telephone call would suffice. Bagley said that was not good enough. We told the judge we would need funds to fly the man over. He said there was no money. He excluded the videotape and so refused to consider a statement from a man who had testified against Kris at trial but now said that Kris had been framed.

The state lawyers seemed intent solely on winning—they must have believed Kris was guilty; perhaps they could not bring themselves to consider otherwise. Sally Weintraub was the lead prosecutor for the hearing, since the original trial lawyers (Ridge and Kastrenakes) were to be witnesses. Local members of the bar told me that she had come out of retirement because she missed the excitement of being mean to people in criminal trials. I thought they were being unkind, but it soon became clear that they were merely being descriptive.

One of our contentions was that Kris had passed a polygraph test and Neville Butler had in large part failed his. Weintraub could simply have agreed that the experts' reports said what they said, nothing more. Instead, she made us pay for the two polygraphers, George Slattery and Dudley Dickson, to come to Miami. Only when she knew that they were on their way—Ben Kuehne had shelled out a thousand dollars of his own money for less expensive, nonrefundable tickets—did she back off and agree to admit their reports as evidence.

And so it went. For a week. It was unpleasant at the start, and it got progressively worse.

Nonetheless we made a lot of headway. We were able to destroy much of the prosecution's case. For starters, we proved that everything Eslee Carberry had ever said about Kris was a lie. Carberry told the jury about a fictional call to an officer at Scotland Yard. We proved that the British authorities had actually approached Kris some years before about two very minor matters: whether his company had paid the right import duty on a shipment of bananas, and the origins of a silver teapot he had purchased. It had all been resolved in Kris's favor long ago.

Carberry had accused Kris of defrauding Derrick Moo Young by trying to steal the *Caribbean Times* from him. ("Mr. Moo Young told me that he discovered the *Caribbean Times* was not a registered paper and that he had, in fact, registered the paper and he was the rightful owner of the paper," Carberry told the jury.) The prosecution had allowed him to say this, even though a trail of documents in the police files—taken from the Moo Youngs' briefcase—showed that Derrick and Duane were actually trying to surreptitiously and illegally take over Kris's business. They had registered a nonexistent paper called the *Caribbean Times International* at their own address, which differed from Kris's home by only one numeral, and then started writing to Kris's bank trying to get access to his account.

Carberry had further suggested that Kris had forged a check to Duane Moo Young. We showed that precisely the opposite was true: Duane had given Kris two checks that were supposed to cover the $443,000 or more that Derrick had stolen from him, but both bounced. These provided the basis for the civil law suit Kris filed and won. We then went on to prove that Carberry himself had written a number of bad checks—once in 1982, in a case that had come before none other than Judge Gross, and a second time a year after the trial.

Then there was a memo about Carberry I had found in the police file that I referred to as the "crooked thief" statement. It was yet another document that the prosecution had failed to reveal to the defense at the trial. "This crooked, notorious thief and con and fraud artist from the island of Grenada," it began, "came to the USA via Texas, then he quickly opened up his paper, then robbed everyone." The author, a police informant, accused Carberry of involvement in drugs. "In '82 & '83 he lived off drug money in Miami, got so rich and took off to Grenada." By the time Ben and I had inherited Kris's case, Carberry had been deported back to Grenada, but even without having him there in court, we felt we'd done enough to eliminate him entirely as a credible witness.

We were allowed to present some of the alibi evidence, although Judge Bagley excluded one witness—George Bell—for reasons I could not comprehend. Contrary to Hendon's assessment, the witnesses appeared voluntarily, and came across as very credible. Detective Buhrmaster testified and, while he tried to smoothly pass off everything as a misunderstanding among professionals, he had to admit that he'd had all the Moo Young documents detailing their business dealings in his files, and that he'd written the note where Kris described owning a Smith & Wesson pistol and having it stolen from him months before the trial. Nobody denied that Judge Gross had been on the take, or disputed Hendon's assertion that Gross became hostile to the defense after Kris refused to pay the bribe. Kastrenakes testified that he had done no wrong but was forced to confess, rather sheepishly, that he had written Judge Solomon's order sentencing Kris to death. His fellow prosecutor, Paul Ridge, candidly admitted that he had "mischaracterized" the result of Neville Butler's polygraph test, when he had asserted to Judge Solomon that their lead witness had passed.

We could not do close to everything that we wanted. We did not have enough money to do a crime scene reconstruction to show how Neville Butler's version of events was inconsistent with the physical evidence of how the bullets had been shot. Ron Petrillo, Hendon's investigator, had agreed to testify about his review of the crime scene, giving his opinion based on years of experience, without charging us anything. Judge Bagley excluded his testimony altogether, saying that we needed a crime scene expert. He then refused to pay for one.

Laura Snook, the forensic accountant from Ernst & Young who had evaluated the documents in the Moo Youngs' briefcase pro bono, was prepared to testify that Derrick and Duane were laundering drug money all around the Caribbean. She agreed to testify for free, but she needed her flight covered. Judge Bagley refused to hear her testimony unless we paid to fly her over from London. We couldn't afford the airfare, so her valuable insights were excluded from consideration.

As the week wore to an end, Ben Kuehne presented the first half of our closing argument to the judge. He focused on our contention that Hendon's assistance had failed to meet the legal standard of effective counsel, leaning heavily on the trial lawyer's failure to respond to Judge Gross's midtrial arrest, to present a single one of his alibi witnesses, to question Neville Butler or point out the inconsistencies in his story, or even to get a copy of Butler's polygraph report. Ben was used to a far higher level of practice—he mainly worked in federal court—and he was genuinely astounded at Hendon's lackluster performance. I did the second part of our closing argument, describing how evidence suppressed by the prosecution—particularly the material in the briefcase concerning the Moo Youngs' apparent money laundering—would have changed the jury's entire perception of the case.

The hearing was frustrating and deeply flawed. Nevertheless, as Ben kept telling me in an effort to buck up my spirits, we'd managed to put forward plenty of evidence, on the basis of which Judge Bagley should throw out Kris's convictions.

Kris had watched the week's testimony and was optimistic. He was now confident that he really would be home by Christmas 1997—one year later than he'd recently hoped, but at this point he wasn't complaining. I did not disabuse him, though by now I had modified my opinion of Bagley. I had been doing death penalty work for thirteen years, and an elected state trial judge had *never* granted a new trial to one of my clients challenging a death sentence—in dozens of cases, no matter how strong the evidence.[2]

Judge Bagley issued his opinion several weeks later—in time for Christmas, but Kris would not be spending it at home. My first reaction was that it had been very badly typed. But I realized that criticism was petty when it came to the content. There was one bright spot: Judge Bagley had thrown out the death sentence, since the order sentencing Kris to death had been written by the prosecutor rather than the judge. But that was of little solace to Kris or, by now, to me. To an innocent person it can make little difference if he dies in prison of natural or unnatural causes.

As for the overwhelming evidence that cast the original verdict into doubt, Bagley glossed over the facts or dismissed them out of hand. Of the hundreds of pages of incriminating documents in the Moo Youngs' briefcase, he wrote that Kris was "procedurally barred" from addressing them as his lawyer had known about the briefcase prior to the trial and had not asked the court to compel its production. This was absurd. Neither Kris nor his lawyer had had any reason to suspect that the briefcase held a gold mine of information, because they knew only of its existence, not what was in it. Ron Petrillo, Hendon's investigator, had asked to see it, but Detective Buhrmaster had told him that it had been returned to the Moo Young family. From this he had concluded that it was not relevant. Buhrmaster never told anyone he had retrieved it, assuming he had actually given it up in the first place. I happened upon its contents years later, and there was no question but that they were highly relevant to the case.

Judge Bagley was of the view that Hendon had done an adequate job and concluded that the conviction should be upheld. Kris should have a new sentencing trial limited solely to establishing the proper punishment—whether he should be executed or held in prison until after his hundredth birthday.

Everyone who had worked on the case was crushed by the decision. So much work had gone into the hearing, with so little to show for it. But somehow Kris brushed himself off, announced that we would win next time, and asked that we move forward and contest Judge Bagley's decision, calling on the Florida Supreme Court to toss out the conviction as well. So we were off on appeal again, another exercise in futility that would take three more years. Kris continued to live on death row, even though he was no longer under a death sentence. Ten more men were taken to Florida's execution chamber as we waited for the court to rule.

I wrote our brief to the Florida Supreme Court and led it with Judge Gross's arrest. Surely the judges would take note of a case in which one of their own had been hauled off in shackles on the third day of trial. Even if they could not bring themselves to denounce Howie the Mouse himself, his outrageous actions must provoke them to consider the other issues more carefully and reverse the conviction.

I was very wrong. The appeal decision, issued on November 30, 2000, made my blood boil. It summarily affirmed Judge Bagley's decision. "These murders," the court repeated with the certainty of the zealot, "occurred as a result of an ongoing dispute between Derrick Moo Young and Krishna Maharaj." The court had no pause for consideration, no moment of doubt.

We had claimed that the hearing before Judge Bagley was flawed because we had not had the funds to call the vast majority of the witnesses who could have proven Kris's innocence. Kris had waited a year, constantly asking for money to pay for the expenses. The court blamed Ben Kuehne and me, suggesting that we were somehow trying to sandbag Judge Bagley by forcing him into an error. The funding issue was barred, the court said, because we had decided to move forward with the case in September 1997—nine months after the deadline that the court had set. "Postconviction counsel, for strategic or other reasons, chose to proceed without the funds being available. Had Maharaj's attorneys chosen to continue his hearing until October and funds had not been forthcoming, he would have a better argument before this Court on this issue."

This was hard to take. What possible strategic reason could we have had for choosing to forgo possible funding? And why October? There were no more funds in October than there had been in September—the entire budget for 1997 had been exhausted long since. The only reason we had gone forward was that, after waiting for a full twelve months, we saw no prospect of any resources being forthcoming before Kris's sixtieth birthday two years later.

If that ruling was disingenuous, then the court's treatment of Judge Gross's arrest was even worse. Here, we were told, Kris had failed to prove that Gross had actually solicited a bribe. "Maharaj has not demonstrated that Judge Gross was in fact involved in a bribery solicitation in this case," the justices wrote. "We cannot base our conclusions on such a serious matter on the fact that the judge was involved in bribery in some other matter."

Kris had complained about the bribery attempt to his lawyer, before Gross's cankerous proclivities had become public knowledge. How could he have made that up? Hendon had passed the complaint on to the prosecutors, who had seen no reason to act. Hendon later testified that Gross's rulings had become hostile after Kris spurned the solicitation. Short of inducing Gross to volunteer his criminality, what more could we have done? Meanwhile the court failed to mention that we had asked the FDLE to disclose material from its investigation of Judge Gross, and our request had been refused.

The justices repeated their mantra: the issue was "procedurally barred," because Kris had "waived" it by agreeing to go forward with the trial before a new judge. But in fact, Kris had simply taken his lawyer's advice. Hendon had admitted under oath at the hearing that at the time he had never put two and two together. Only later did he link Gross's arrest with Kris's earlier report of the attempted bribe. So his "advice" had clearly been inadequate. Regardless, surely there was a societal interest in refusing to allow a trial to go forward when the original judge was prevented by malfeasance from hearing out the case.

And what of the simple claim that Kris was innocent? Surely the courts would hear that. But the response was not just *no*, but *never*.

At this point, as far as the State of Florida was concerned, Kris had a valid conviction, and all that remained was to resentence him. That would involve a complete trial before a new jury. Both sides had a choice to make. Kris wanted to continue with the challenge to his conviction, taking his case to federal court. I agreed with him: I remained convinced that a court with judges who were not elected would be more likely to toss out the guilty verdict, so I felt it was pointless to proceed with another sentencing trial founded on the quicksand of a flawed conviction.

The prosecution had two options. It could simply forgo a new penalty trial—Kris would automatically be given another life sentence, at which point he would have been ineligible for parole until after his hundredth birthday—or it could hold its ground and demand that it be given a second chance to argue for the death penalty. Ben and I told the prosecutor—Sally Weintraub again—that to go back to another jury on sentencing was a waste of everyone's time and an inordinate amount of the state's money. The original death sentence had been imposed by the slimmest of margins, a seven-to-five jury vote. A great deal of new evidence had come to light, and this, combined with a much better prepared defense, would make it very unlikely that Kris would be sent back to death row.

But Weintraub was insistent: the State of Florida wanted to sentence Kris to death again, and it wanted to do so now. Ben and I did everything we could to stop the case going forward to a new sentencing trial before the federal courts had reviewed the conviction, but we were unsuccessful. We asked the state court not to waste money and to allow us to challenge the convictions first. Judge Bagley refused. We asked the federal court to proceed with the habeas challenge anyway. The federal court of appeals ruled that respect for the state court compelled it to allow the state proceeding to putter on to a conclusion before it could intervene. This was really a delaying game by the prosecution. It meant that Kris would have to wait months or years more before the federal courts could either validate or overturn his conviction. So we moved on to the next farcical procedure in front of Judge Bagley: preparing for a full jury trial on sentencing only, in which another twelve jurors would recommend whether Kris should be sent back to death row.

A reasonable person might think that the mountain of new evidence we had collected that cast into doubt Kris's involvement in the murders would be sufficient to carry the day. In the real world, any doubt surrounding the defendant's guilt is the most important factor that impels a jury to vote against the death penalty. This is particularly true in Florida, which has been home to many highly publicized miscarriages of justice—indeed, the state leads the league table. Eleven people sentenced to death had been exonerated since Kris had been sent to Starke.[3] A study of Florida juries revealed that lingering doubt is the most frequent factor that compels jurors to shy away from a death sentence: 69 percent of the jurors interviewed after capital trials said that they still had some doubt about the guilt of the accused, and this was their main reason for recommending life. Like any sane person, the average juror in Florida worries about condemning someone to die who may be innocent.[4]

But Judge Bagley told us that we were not allowed, under any circumstances, in any way, to suggest to the jury that Kris might not be guilty. This is Florida law: if you have been found guilty, then you are guilty. Evidence challenging it is not admissible at a sentencing (or resentencing) trial. Indeed, proof that someone else committed the crime would, the Florida Supreme Court has held, be "misleading" and might "confuse the jury."[5]

The idea that a juror should not be permitted to consider the prisoner's innocence when deciding whether he should die invites every hackneyed expression of incredulity from "Kafkaesque" to "cuckoo." In a resentencing trial such as ours, the argument for allowing evidence of innocence was even stronger. Kris had been convicted in 1987. The original jury had heard the evidence as to his culpability, and Kris had even been allowed to insist on his innocence at the penalty phase. The five jurors who had voted for life were clearly able to take into consideration any reservations they might have had. Now fourteen years later he was to face twelve more jurors, when a vast amount of new material had come to light casting doubt on his culpability. To proceed as if nothing had changed would be a fraud on the new jury.

But Judge Bagley was emphatic: Florida law was Florida law.

That did not mean we had to accept his verdict without a challenge. So we set about trying to encourage Judge Bagley to face the logic of his ruling in every way we could imagine. We filed a "Notice Of Intent To Prove Mr. Maharaj Innocent Of These Charges, Or To Allow The Jury To Hear The Evidence That It Considers The Most Significant In This Capital Case Where Life Is At Stake" before Bagley, so he would be forced to reconsider his ruling. In addition to arguing that the Florida rule was plain silly, we pointed out that one of the listed mitigating factors under Florida law was that the accused had no significant prior history of criminal activity.[6] Here, because Kris was innocent, we should be allowed to show that he had no criminal history at all. Judge Bagley ruled that this was improper.

Another listed mitigating factor was that the victim was partially to blame for his own death.[7] We asked for permission to prove that the Moo Youngs were actually killed in a Colombian hit that had been provoked when they tried to skim 1 percent off the cartel's money. While this in no way justified their murder, nobody would rip off the drug barons without expecting consequences. Judge Bagley excluded the evidence.

We offered to prove another mitigating factor—that Kris would not be a future danger[8]—because he had never been a danger in the past. We wanted to prove the mitigating circumstance of Kris's good character,[9] by showing that he had never committed a crime at all. We lined up an expert who was prepared to testify that Kris suffered from a serious mental problem—clearly a mitigating circumstance under Florida and federal law. Kris was, the expert said, suffering from post-traumatic stress disorder. The cause? Suffering for so many years on death row for a crime he did not commit. Judge Bagley, increasingly irritated, shook his head vigorously at all of it.

We filed a modestly styled "Notice That Mr. Maharaj Intends To Testify To His Innocence." At the first trial, Hendon had inexplicably advised Kris to testify to his innocence at the penalty phase, after the jury had convicted him. But at least Kris had got to say his piece. In the re-sentencing trial, Bagley said this would not be allowed.

Eventually Bagley grew impatient and told Ben and me that if either one of us allowed the word *innocent* to come out of our lips during the trial, we would be held in contempt of court.

We picked the jury in mid-March 2002, more than fifteen years after Detective Buhrmaster had arrested Kris at Denny's Restaurant and taken him to jail. Once we had our twelve jurors and had done brief opening statements outlining the testimony expected over the ten days to come, the state called Neville Butler to testify. I was not allowed to cross-examine him to reveal that his story was a lie, let alone to inform the jury that he had failed a polygraph on some of the very "facts" he was again telling a new jury.

We were reduced to presenting a case for mercy that focused solely on Kris as a person. This was compelling in itself. Four death row guards voluntarily testified for him, risking the opprobrium of their employers, who did not think they should take the side of a condemned prisoner.

They all believed in the death penalty, and none had ever been moved to testify for a death row prisoner before.

"If'n all the prisoners were like Kris Maharaj," testified one gruffly, "we wouldn't need all of us guards."

"The only danger I see in setting him free," said another, "is the culture shock . . . he's been locked away so long."

All the guards, after being around Kris and studying his character for years, thought he was probably innocent, but even though this was a large part of their reason for testifying, they were not allowed to say so.

Various of Kris's friends testified by satellite from London. I had warned each person that we were banned from suggesting that Kris had not committed the crime. A British member of Parliament, Sir Peter Bottomley, who had been a senior minister under Margaret Thatcher, was outraged and nearly got me thrown in jail.

"Why are you testifying for Mr. Maharaj?" I asked him, expecting a testament to Kris's good character.

"Because his case is a miscarriage of justice!" Peter responded vigorously.

Judge Bagley started in his chair, and sent the jury from the room, before giving Peter a lecture about what he could and could not say. He assured me that I would be facing jail myself if any other witness made a similar comment.

The zeal with which the prosecutor, Sally Weintraub, argued for Kris's execution should not have surprised me, but all in all this was one of the most bizarre capital trials I have ever defended. Little of the normal pressure was there. It didn't seem to matter what the jurors decided to do, because Kris might strategically be better off with another death sentence. He was now sixty-two years old and in bad health. The courts give the impression that a death row prisoner who later receives a life sentence has already used up his stock of good fortune—glossing over the notion that he might be innocent.[10] The courts look more closely at a case that involves the death penalty, and back in Britain it would be easier to get people interested in Kris's plight if he were awaiting execution rather than "merely" serving another three or four decades in prison.

The looming execution might provoke someone to help pay for a full investigation. Unless we could get his conviction reversed, one thing was certain: Kris would die in the Florida state prison system, either at the hands of the executioner, or when his battered body could take no more of prison life.

A death sentence, we agreed, would be no big deal." Of course, it was impossible for Marita to take such a view, after all her nightmares of his execution over many years. Even now, she would wake up in the night with visions of the electric chair, and flames licking around her husband's head.

When the closing arguments were over, as the jury listened to Judge Bagley intone the interminable instructions, I watched them, with an arm over Kris's shoulder. I did not feel there was much chance they would come back against us. It was difficult to believe that anyone could take seriously the idea of sentencing a man to death who didn't commit the crime, even though the jury had not heard any of our evidence about his innocence.

The tension soon began to rise. I had thought, optimistically, that it would be a simple matter for the jury to go back to their deliberations, check with one another, and come back with a verdict of life. Not so. After a few hours they said they wanted to quit for the night and to start again in the morning. They had to go to a motel, and Ben Kuehne joked that perhaps they wanted one more free meal at the county's expense for all they had been forced to endure.

It was going to be a difficult evening for Marita, home alone, waiting to hear if her husband would go back to prison with a death sentence. And for Kris in his cell, waiting to hear if another group of jurors would decide he was not fit to live. I went out to the county jail to see him. The guards had come to like him there, too, and they treated me well on visits. We talked about the challenge to his conviction, and Kris put on a brave face about the twelve jurors, now probably back in their motel rooms contemplating what they should do in the morning.

After an unsettled night, everyone reassembled in the courtroom to do some more waiting. There was a clock on the wood-paneled wall. It slowed time down. I had my laptop with me, and tried to do some work on another urgent case, in between telling Marita periodically that everything was going to be fine.

Nothing ever prepares you for that knock on the door, when the jury slips a note out to the judge announcing they have a verdict. It is an amalgam of excitement and dread.

The jurors filed into the courtroom. The foreperson handed a piece of paper to the bailiff, who studiously did not look at it, walking ponderously up to the bench to hand it to Judge Bagley. The judge glanced at it, his face giving nothing away, before he handed it to the court clerk.

"Please publish the jury's recommendation as to punishment," he said.

They were eleven to one for life. The tension suddenly gone, I was unreasonably angry at the one juror who had voted to kill Kris.

15

The Federal Appeal

From the perspective of the State of Florida, Kris now had two totally valid life sentences (plus several more years on top, just in case) and would die behind bars unless, by some miracle, he lived to be older than 101 and was successful on an application for discretionary parole. The time had come to go to federal court. Here at least the judges were not elected but were appointed for life. I managed to recover some optimism; once you got past the first appeal, historically most reversals have happened at the federal level rather than in state court.

Ben and I filed Kris's application in federal district court on July 26, 2002, as soon as possible after Judge Bagley's sentence. By now Kris was coming up on his sixteenth anniversary in prison. The petition we filed was 334 pages long and included the full array of Kris's claims: Judge Gross had been arrested midtrial, Hendon had been inept, the prosecutors had covered up favorable evidence, several key witnesses had lied on the stand, and Kris had five alibi witnesses all willing to testify that he had been miles away at the time of the crime, all in full detail, with scores of documents attached to prove the point.

The prosecutors took ten months to file a brief that could have been written overnight, essentially regurgitating everything they had said in state court: that all of Kris's claims should be procedurally barred from review. These were ten long months, during which Marita was allowed to see Kris for just three hours every two weeks. We responded to the prosecution within days with 103 more pages to show how very wrong they were.

A federal district judge has incredible authority to right wrongs.

Various presidents, from Richard Nixon to Bill Clinton, have been on the receiving end of federal judicial power. It is the essence of a democracy—particularly one with a bill of rights—that the judiciary can intercede between a citizen and government officials seeking to punish him. Federal District Judge Paul C. Huck was a Clinton appointee and seemed to be the kind of judge who would finally bring justice home to Kris.

Huck assigned the case to a federal magistrate, William C. Turnoff, for a preliminary review. This is often the way things are done. Unlike a federal judge, who is appointed by the president for life after confirmation by the Senate, a magistrate is generally a lawyer who has been selected by the local judges and serves an eight-year term. Magistrates don't have the same authority as judges, whose power comes from Article III of the constitution—indeed, their decisions are only proposals that have to be ratified by the judge. But because of his workload, a federal judge often uses a magistrate to recommend what should be done with a case. Ben and I asked Turnoff to give us funds for a proper investigation and help us pay for various experts. For example, we wanted to test the fingerprints from the hotel room that had never been matched to anyone. It was unconscionable that the prints had not been checked in all these years, despite our effort to get proper access—perhaps we could find physical proof that Jaime Vallejo Mejia or Adam Hosein had been in the room. After all, Mejia had been fingerprinted when he was arrested in the United States and, as a foreigner who must have applied for various visas, Hosein probably had a full set on file with the Immigration and Naturalization Service (INS). We couldn't just demand to see copies of these print cards, but if only the magistrate would help us with a couple of court orders it might be a simple matter to link them both to the crime scene.

Nothing happened for a long time. It does not do to harass a federal magistrate, and I was hoping that, while the wheels of justice grind slowly, they would ultimately grind fine, and reach the correct result. A year and a half later, on February 23, 2004, Turnoff issued a proposed order denying all of Kris's claims. He refused us funds to investigate further. He wouldn't let us test the unmatched fingerprints that had been found in room 1215, any of which might have pointed to the real killer. He wouldn't let us summon any of the witnesses whom we had not been allowed to call in state court—Prince Ellis, who had recanted his earlier testimony, Laura Snook the forensic accountant, George Bell (the alibi witness), and a number of others.

It was depressing. I told Kris there was still hope, but it was seeping away fast. Judge Paul Huck could refuse to go along with the magistrate's recommendation, but sometimes the arrangement between a judge and his magistrate is rather cozy, and Turnoff's report would not be rejected out of hand. Still, we had a telephone conference with the judge on June 23, and it seemed that someone—probably his clerk—was going through the record quite carefully. I thought it was possible that we would be granted a proper hearing where we could present the new evidence.

Kris's case had gone nowhere up until now, and he had himself not moved far in any physical sense. He was no longer on death row, but he was still a high-security prisoner, still held in the same prison complex, just a different cell. I sometimes paused to compare his life to my own. As we waited on Judge Huck's decision, my own life took another big shift. After eleven years in New Orleans, my wife and I decided to head back to England in mid-August to be there in time for my aunt and uncle's fiftieth wedding anniversary. We were going to move to England permanently, as both of us had parents there who were getting older, and we wanted to start a family of our own. My father was about to hit eighty and was in bad health; my mother was seventy-nine, though fitter.

Two weeks after we arrived in London—on August 30, 2004—Judge Huck's order came through. The first question he addressed was whether he should allow funds for us to conduct the investigation in several countries that we had previously been unable to visit. The state court's refusal to provide Kris with any funds to present his defense had been "unfortunate," Judge Huck thought, but he would not reverse the decision. He might have been inclined to allow funds, he wrote, if Kris were still sentenced to death, but as this was no longer a capital case, he felt he had no right to intervene.

As I had feared, Kris would have been better off on death row.

Judge Huck recognized that he could still order an evidentiary hearing, allowing us to present the witnesses who had been excluded from the state court hearing. He accepted that Ben and I, working pro bono as Kris's lawyers for more than a decade, had "diligently" tried to secure the witnesses we needed, without any funding. But then, just when I thought he was coming to a sensible conclusion, he stood logic on its head. Based on the case of *Murray v. Giarratano*, he concluded that there is no "right to adequate funding in state post-conviction proceedings." Because the lack of funding meant that Kris could not demonstrate that the witnesses would actually say what we claimed they would, Kris could not have a hearing. That was some catch-22: Kris needed funds to prove his innocence, so if he did not have the funds, he could not have a hearing to prove his innocence.

Lawyers like to set themselves apart from the rest of the world, sometimes perhaps to justify their fees. They do so in various ways. One of the most fraudulent is to hang a certificate on the wall that boasts to prospective clients that they are members of the bar of the United States Supreme Court. This impressive credential implies membership in a most exclusive club. I have such a document stashed away somewhere, and it cost me $130. I did not even have to go to Washington to get it. It does not mean that you have ever done any work in the court; it only means you've practiced law for three years, got a couple of friends to say you're okay, and paid your money.

A second stratagem is to hurl around phrases in Latin—a series of things that could perfectly well be said in English, from *respondeat superior* and *non compos mentis*, all the way to *de minimis non curat lex* (which I had begun to think should, in the context of Kris's case, be amended to *de maximus non curat lex*—"don't bother the law with any serious thing").

The final frontier in this legal apartheid is the use of case names as shorthand for broad principles. They mean nothing to the rest of the world, and yet they allow lawyers to speak in code. Thus we have *Murray v. Giarratano*, the case Judge Huck relied on in his ruling against

Kris.[1] Permit me to translate. Joseph Giarratano, who was on death row in Virginia, submitted a radical proposition to the courts there: that he should be allowed a state-funded lawyer to help him with his capital appeals. The district court and the notoriously conservative Fourth Circuit Court of Appeals had sided with Giarratano, ruling that death row prisoners could not be expected to represent themselves. However, this did not stop a majority of the Supreme Court from deciding otherwise, with Chief Justice William Rehnquist writing yet another opinion that belied common sense.

According to Rehnquist, a prisoner on death row—whether adult or juvenile, whether accomplished scholar or mentally disabled, whether sane or mad—has no constitutional right to the assistance of a lawyer paid by the state to help him with appeals in the most complicated field of law imaginable.[2] The Supreme Court felt that it was justified in this rule because no prisoner would actually be left to die—a lawyer would step in and offer to work for free, as Ben and I had done. This was charity run riot: the government was in the business of killing people, but felt it could depend on some do-gooder volunteering time to provide a basic defense to the condemned prisoner.

As I kept reading Judge Huck's decision, I fell into deep despondency. I knew which way he was going to go on our evidence that Kris was not guilty of the murders of Derrick and Duane Moo Young.

"Although [Mr. Maharaj] vigorously resists clear legal precedent," the judge wrote, "claims of actual innocence based on newly discovered evidence have never been held to state a ground for federal habeas corpus relief." In other words, Judge Huck agreed with the Florida attorney general that Kris's proof of innocence was simply not an issue under the federal Constitution. The reason for this apparently unassailable rule, he went on to explain, was that "federal habeas courts sit to ensure that individuals are not imprisoned in violation of the Constitution—not to correct errors of fact." Kris's innocence was an error of fact, not a constitutional matter, and thus it was beyond the purview of the federal court.

At the resentencing trial, Judge Bagley had threatened to throw Ben and me in jail if we mentioned the word *innocent* to the jury. That was bad enough. But now Judge Huck had ruled that proof of Kris's innocence was not a reason to set him free.

To understand how Judge Huck could have come to this deeply counterintuitive conclusion, we need to understand the shameful hidden meaning behind another case he cited: *Herrera v. Collins*. Leonel Herrera had been convicted of the murder of two policemen in the Rio Grande Valley, in Texas, in 1981. Later, four witnesses came forward with proof that Leonel's brother Raul had actually committed the crime. Leonel's lawyers argued that, because he was probably innocent, he should not be executed. This argument, when taken to the Supreme Court, left the majority of the justices unmoved.

"This proposition has an elemental appeal," Chief Justice Rehnquist piously opined. "After all, the central purpose of any system of criminal justice is to convict the guilty and free the innocent. But the evidence upon which Petitioner's claim of innocence rests was not produced at his trial, but rather eight years later. In any system of criminal justice, 'innocence' or 'guilt' must be determined in some sort of a judicial proceeding."

Rehnquist acknowledged that Herrera was prohibited from bringing his claim of innocence in the Texas courts by an arcane rule that required the prisoner to present evidence of innocence within thirty days of conviction or be forever barred from introducing it at all. This may seem extraordinary, but similar rules apply in forty-one of the fifty states. You may be a teenager when you are convicted, but if you fail to provide proof of innocence within thirty days of your conviction, you may be forced to spend the rest of your life in prison (or even be executed), however strong a proof of innocence you may later assemble.[3]

Why, Rehnquist queried, should the federal courts take a step that the state courts refused? "Claims of actual innocence based on newly discovered evidence have never been held to state a ground for federal habeas relief," wrote Rehnquist in his majority opinion. You might get your case reversed on any number of technical legal grounds, then, but not based on proof that you didn't actually commit the crime. That is the law of the land today in the United States, reaffirmed by the highest court.

Herrera's lawyers retreated a step: how about agreeing that the constitution bars the *execution* of an innocent person? At a minimum, they suggested, the prisoner should not be killed. At least then he might find someone to listen to his proof of innocence at a later date.

"Petitioner urges not that he necessarily receive a new trial, but that his death sentence simply be vacated if a federal habeas court deems that a satisfactory showing of 'actual innocence' has been made," Rehnquist went on. "But such a result is scarcely logical. . . . It would be a rather strange jurisprudence . . . which held that under our Constitution he could not be executed, but that he could spend the rest of his life in prison." Indeed, that might be strange, but not half as strange as a system that positively allows the innocent to be put to death at the hands of the state.

A minority of three justices out of nine disagreed. They felt that a conviction should be overturned if the prisoner could show that he was "probably" innocent. But their argument carried no weight with the chief justice and the other members of the court. "The dissent fails to articulate the relief that would be available if petitioner were to meets its 'probable innocence' standard," wrote Rehnquist. "Would it be commutation of petitioner's death sentence, [a] new trial, or unconditional release from imprisonment?" Surely to ask the question is to answer it: if someone is "probably" innocent, then no sensible person could find him guilty beyond a reasonable doubt, and he would have to be released.

Common sense is, unfortunately, not so common in some of the opinions of the United States Supreme Court. The court has never accepted in any case, either before *Herrera* or since, that the "mere" fact of a prisoner's innocence should be a constitutional basis for ordering his release—or even a retrial.

Over the years, I have been charged with contempt of court on more than one occasion. While I have always been acquitted, I sometimes find it difficult not to have disdain for judges who come up with this kind of nonsense, whether they are the Supreme Court justices who lay down the precedent, or the lower court judges who meekly parrot it. Yet for all the folly of denying Joe Giarratano the right to counsel, or of ignoring Leonel Herrera's evidence of innocence, at least these are human issues that can inspire anger, action, and ultimately perhaps reform. *Giarratano* is still the law, but gradually the states are providing more resources for those appealing a sentence of death. While the Supreme Court still applies the rule of *Herrera*, commentators have disparaged it, and one day surely good sense will prevail.[4]

But far more insidious rules are at play in capital cases, rules so convoluted that they lead to no headlines. Indeed, most of the 1,227 people (and counting) who have been executed in the United States since Kris Maharaj went to prison fell victim to procedural rules that were better suited to medieval law courts than to the twenty-first century.

The American legal system uses various pretexts to prevent judges from deciding the merits of any prisoner's claim. One is the perceived need for "finality" of judgments. Endless appeals, we are told, diminish citizens' regard for the legal system. They are also expensive. Yet it is generally cheaper to have appeals and exonerate someone than it is to hold him in prison unjustly for the rest of his life. It is also worth noting that when we incarcerate the innocent, the real perpetrators are left free, perhaps to wreak havoc in other people's lives. All in all, the state should presumably be allowed to impose a punishment only if the punishment is just and the defendant is in fact guilty.

A second excuse is highly political and is dressed up in a dubious characterization of the relationship between the federal government and the states. We are told that the federal courts must respect a state court judgment. But why defer to a judgment if it is wrong?

In denying Kris Maharaj a new trial, Judge Huck deployed a number of procedural weapons from this armory. One was the "procedural bar." The British government intervened in the case only belatedly for the simple reason that Florida had failed to notify Kris's foreign government of his arrest. There is a treaty between Britain and the United States that requires either country to notify the other immediately if the police hold one of its citizens. This agreement is designed to work to the benefit of everyone: Americans detained in Britain should have access to the U.S. Embassy for help in understanding the weird ways of British barristers with their funny wigs, and British citizens arrested in the United States should enjoy a similar right as strangers in a strange land.

Had the British government known about Kris's plight from the start, the local consulate would have ensured that he had competent legal assistance, and could have helped him gather evidence from various places around the world; he might never have been convicted. But Judge Huck ruled that Kris was "procedurally barred" from arguing this point because his trial lawyer did not raise it. Unless you are a member of the legal profession and enjoy debating the number of angels who may dance on the head of a pin, it is difficult to comprehend how Kris could have "waived" his right to be told that the British consul could help him: the very purpose of the consular notification rule is to alert a foreign prisoner to this right. Obviously Kris did not know about it: if he had, he would not have needed to be told. The law has the cat chasing its tail around and around. It does not contribute to the reliability of the verdict; it merely denies the prisoner access to justice. This procedural bar was just one of many legal loopholes that Judge Huck relied on to ignore the merits of Kris's case.

Other such rules of procedure were derived from the Anti-Terrorist and Effective Death Penalty Act of 1996. Throughout the 1980s the death penalty became increasingly politicized; indeed, crime itself became a political football in many countries, not just the United States. Many valid criticisms of the U.S. system were raised, from the sluggish way it delivered justice, to its failure to correct errors that came to light. As previously noted, in 1995 Jim Liebman, a professor at Columbia Law School, published the results of a study he had conducted of all 4,578 capital appeals that came to a conclusion between 1973 and 1995. He found that serious error, resulting in a new trial, occurred in 68 percent of the cases. He identified two major structural flaws in the process: the systemic mistakes that infected the trials, and the length of time (an average of ten years) that it took to identify those blunders.[5] If politicians had accepted Liebman's analysis, they would have looked to cure both the glacial pace of the system and the grotesque error rate (with a fifty-fifty coin toss, the process would be more likely to reach a reliable verdict). As Liebman explained, "judicial review takes so long precisely *because* American capital sentences are so persistently and systematically fraught with error that seriously undermines their reliability."

But rather than addressing both ills, Congress decided to correct only one: it sought to speed up the process with the Effective Death Penalty Act. The effect of this legislation was to ensure that the judicial system reached the *wrong* conclusion faster, because it made no effort to address the root causes of the errors.

Nowhere did the Effective Death Penalty Act address the notion that a court might make mistakes. The act did not make innocence a substantive federal issue, or mandate that particular procedures should be used to assess the reliability of, for example, eyewitnesses or informants. Instead, it merely imposed harsh deadlines: defendants now must bring their cases before the federal courts within one year or they forever lose their rights to federal habeas review. The federal courts of appeal and the U.S. Supreme Court have since been enforcing the new rules with rigor—to the point that death row prisoners are deemed to have "waived" their entire right to seek a remedy in federal court if their lawyer is only a day late in filing their appeal.[6]

Judge Huck, in his ruling against Kris, cited several aspects of the Effective Death Penalty Act. The question before him was no longer, he wrote, whether the state courts had been wrong in interpreting the law. Rather, it was whether they had been *unreasonably* wrong. What does this mean? They could be wrong but not awfully, awfully wrong? They could make a mistake, but the result would be good enough for government work—adequate to send someone to prison forever or to death?

Again, to illustrate how bizarre his ruling was, consider what he said about the Florida Supreme Court and Eric Hendon's supposed knowledge, at the time of the trial, that the prosecution's star "eyewitness," Neville Butler, had failed a polygraph. Judge Huck accepted that we had presented plenty of evidence to show that Hendon had not known this and that he only came to learn about it years later, when Ben and I told him about it. While the Florida Supreme Court had been wrong on this issue, Judge Huck wrote, the court had not been "unreasonable" in its wrongness. Quite what this means is difficult to divine: the state was either right, or it was wrong. If it was wrong, that meant it had over-looked or misunderstood a significant issue in Kris's trial.

Everyone agreed that Butler had originally told a false story, but he told the jury half a dozen times under oath that he had come forward of his own accord to change his testimony. This obviously made him look good. Judge Huck believed that Butler had in fact changed his testimony because he had been threatened with the negative results of his poly-graph. Logically, this meant that Butler had perjured himself at least six times—a crime that could have put him in prison. But again the state court had not been "unreasonably wrong" in failing to recognize this, and so, according to Judge Huck, the federal courts simply would not consider the issue.

And so it went, on and on. The state court blamed the defense inves-tigator, Ron Petrillo, for not learning about the contents of the Moo Youngs' briefcase, even though Detective Buhrmaster had explicitly told him that it had been returned to the family. Again, the state's decision might have been wrong, but it was not unreasonably wrong.

Any notion that Adam Hosein or Jaime Vallejo Mejia might have been involved in the case was no more than "speculative," and while the state courts probably should have given us the funds to seek and present further evidence to support our contention of their involvement, their failure to do so was not sufficiently wrong to require a new, fair hearing.

Perhaps I should not have been surprised when we lost Kris's case in federal court. Judge Huck dismissed most of Kris's claims without even discussing their merits. I was in the English countryside when the deci-sion was published, staying with my family. I printed out the decision and retired to read it in the solitude of the garden. As I worked my way through it, my hands compulsively crumpled the pages of disingenuous legal waffle.

It wasn't over yet. There were still two courts to come—the Elev-enth Circuit Court of Appeals and the U.S. Supreme Court. I was par-ticularly familiar with the former. When I worked in Atlanta—eleven years earlier—our office had been directly across the street from the massive concrete edifice that housed the judges. There are twelve circuit courts around the United States, each one with a particular geographical responsibility. The Atlanta federal appeals court oversees cases from Alabama, Georgia, and Florida; in the early 1930s, when Al Capone was housed in the Atlanta Federal Penitentiary, his lawyers brought habeas writs to this court twice. This was the next stop on Kris's legal railroad.

The Eleventh Circuit was created in 1981, when the old Fifth Circuit (which also covered Mississippi, Louisiana, and Texas) was split down the middle, to help deal with its crushing workload. In the 1960s the Fifth Circuit had a reputation for showing courage—many of the famous civil rights cases were decided—which was one reason for the long delay in giving the judges more resources. Senate Judiciary chairman James Eastland, a staunch segregationist from Mississippi, had long turned a deaf ear to any plea for funds to expand the court, since he was none too keen on the work it was doing.

"The Southern institution of racial segregation or racial separation was the correct, self-evident truth which arose from the chaos and confusion of the Reconstruction period," Eastland had opined angrily in the Senate, in the wake of *Brown v. Board of Education* in 1954. "Separation promotes racial harmony. It permits each race to follow its own pursuits, and its own civilization. Segregation is not discrimination . . . it is the law of nature, it is the law of God, that every race has both the right and the duty to perpetuate itself. All free men have the right to associate exclusively with members of their own race, free from governmental interference, if they so desire."

"Jim Eastland could be standing right in the middle of the worst Mississippi flood ever known," President Lyndon Johnson once said, "and he'd say the niggers caused it, helped out by the Communists."

By the time I first visited the Eleventh Circuit as a lawyer, in 1984, the court had undergone a sea change. Now the judges were enforcing civil rights in fewer cases and upholding the death penalty in more. Some of the judges had liberal leanings, but they were bound by the pronouncements of the Supreme Court—and with the Rehnquist court ever more dominated by conservatives, even the sympathetic judges in the court of appeals veered away from enforcing the rights of prisoners, anticipating the next restrictive ruling from Washington.

I remain permanently scarred by the first time I had to argue a prison conditions case in the court, in 1986. Judge Gerald Tjoflat had yelled at me for thirty minutes, trying to get me to agree with him that the prisoner should lose his appeal. The judge asked the same question thirteen times, and I gave the same answer thirteen times, to his escalating displeasure. It was not a courtroom that I enjoyed visiting.

But that was the court to which Kris now had to appeal. Ben and I filed his brief on January 3, 2005. We were limited to three issues—the state's suppression of favorable evidence, Eric Hendon's bad advice to Kris not to testify at the culpability phase of his trial, and the failure to tell the British government that one of its citizens had been arrested. We were not permitted to raise other issues, such as Kris's claim of innocence, Hendon's failure to present the alibi witnesses, or whether it was okay for a judge to be arrested for bribery in midtrial, as these issues had been deemed to be frivolous, as far as any "jurist of reason" was concerned.

Indeed, the lawyers for Florida's attorney general—then Charlie Crist—argued that Kris "should understand the limitations on the issues on appeal." We were told that Kris's innocence was not relevant, so our insistence that the court consider it was "disingenuous." The court should not address such piddling questions.

The panel of three judges who would decide Kris's fate was chosen from the eleven full-time judges and various others who had reached an age when they could take senior status. Not long before the oral argument, we learned their names. They made for depressing reading: Judge Stanley Marcus, Judge James Hill, and Judge Frank Hull. I had previously appeared before the first two, and while both were perfectly polite, they were deeply conservative. But it was the last in the trio who concerned me most. Judge Frank Mays Hull, who is a woman, had been a Georgia state trial judge before being appointed to the federal bench. I had offered to help out a friend on a capital case in front of her, and she had been unremittingly rude and unpleasant over several days, once summoning me up to the bench in order to give me advice on how I should wear different shoes the following day. She might be a Democrat, appointed by President Clinton, but she was a member of the Georgia elite, and I did not trust her to have any sense of justice.

In the end, while I worried that Kris might think I was letting him down, I was quite glad that I could not be in the United States for the argument. I thought Ben, with his bow tie and his studied South Florida charm, would have a better chance of bringing the judges around. Ultimately, it made no difference. On December 15, 2005, the court unanimously affirmed the conviction. The judges announced that they were limited to the issues set out by Judge Huck, "and we decline Petitioner's invitation to consider any others." They then explained why they did not even have to reach the merits of most of the claims they did consider, as they owed deference to the state court's judgment.[7]

Once more, I received notice of the decision in England, and once more it was maddening. How would I explain to Marita what had happened? It was impossible to get through to Kris in prison, so Marita would have to take the news to him on her weekly visit, just before Christmas. I tried to be as positive as I could be, though by now that record was scratchy and worn. We had one more place to go, the United States Supreme Court. The probability that it would hear a criminal case, brought by someone without money who was not on death row, was roughly one in a thousand. I had been fortunate in the past: the Supreme Court had granted a hearing in four cases for which I had written the application. In each instance the prisoner had ultimately won. But they had been four cases out of perhaps fifty, and all had involved the death penalty. The Supreme Court was less likely to take Kris's case now that he "only" had a life sentence. I knew it was virtually hopeless.

I spent a lot of time putting together as good a petition as I could, but my pessimism turned out to be realism. On October 2, 2006, the Supreme Court refused to hear Kris's case, *Maharaj v. McDonough*. Kris's appeal to the American judiciary effectively came to an end. He had spent two weeks short of twenty years in prison for a crime he did not commit, and he had exhausted his legal options. We had reached the end of the judicial road.

The U.S. Supreme Court's stated purpose is to ensure the safety of society, and the legitimacy of the legal process, by imprisoning only those who have committed a crime. To accuse the nine justices of maintaining a system whose goal is quite at odds with that purpose is a serious charge. But the catalog of errors in Kris Maharaj's case must be understood as a reflection of a systemic problem if we are to remedy that system and reform the process.

Let us consider who becomes a Supreme Court justice. The candidates are drawn from a shallow, privileged pool of people who tend not to experience the vicissitudes that beset the everyday lives of many American citizens. None of the current crop of Supreme Court justices has ever spent time defending criminal cases, so they have never experienced the human impact of the laws that they interpret from the other side of the bench. The applicant who wants to become a justice must meet a clear set of criteria, and anyone with even marginally "radical" views need not apply. The Senate confirmation hearings provide a stringent vetting procedure, where those nominated for the job promise under oath that they will respect the prevailing interpretation of the law and refer only to the will of the elected legislature in applying statutes passed by Congress.

Most nominees to the U.S. Supreme Court adhere closely to the establishment line. Most have gone to top law schools. (There are two hundred accredited law schools in the United States, but the nine current justices attended just three among them—Harvard, Yale, and Stanford.) They clerk for other judges who teach them how it *has* to be done. They work for government, and then they are appointed to lower courts, where their many judgments provide material for public vetting. Fearing the consequences of future scrutiny, they tend not to take risks. If they are not already predisposed to walk in the footsteps of their predecessors, the shoehorn of their experience soon squeezes them in.[8]

Once on the bench, the doctrine of stare decisis keeps them conservative—*stare decisis* means literally that judges should "leave standing that which has been decided." This chains a judge to a past decision because of the simple fact that the decision was made, not because it is correct. Thus, for example, currently no Supreme Court justice has publicly stated that the death penalty might be unconstitutional, because thirty-six years ago a narrow majority thought it legal.[9]

Shackled in this way, the best that the supposedly liberal wing of the Supreme Court has been able to offer has been to suggest, in 2003, that gay people should not be imprisoned for consensual sexual acts performed in the privacy of their bedrooms.[10] Six years later, when Troy Davis (who had been convicted in 1991 of murdering a police officer) continued to insist that he did not commit the crime, the "liberal" wing of the court proposed a discussion of whether this might be a bar to execution. Nothing came of this discourse, and Troy Davis was executed, loudly proclaiming his innocence with his last breath, in September 2011.

Stare decisis recently found its ultimate expression in the opinion of Justice John Paul Stevens, who decided at the end of his long tenure that the death penalty was—under all circumstances—cruel and unusual punishment and therefore a violation of the U.S. Constitution. Yet notwithstanding his conclusion that capital punishment involved the "pointless and needless extinction of life," he still determined that the particular method of execution in the case before him (lethal injection) met the requirements of earlier Supreme Court decisions.[11] I have the greatest respect for Justice Stevens, but if this is the way stare decisis operates, then it needs serious reconsideration.

In the notorious case of *Herrera v. Collins*, Chief Justice Rehnquist justified the refusal to admit new evidence of innocence in part because the condemned man had the option of seeking a pardon if the courts got it wrong. Pardon was the valve that was to alleviate any mistakes the courts made. The State of Texas moved quickly to prove Rehnquist wrong. The Texas Pardons Board did not recommend clemency for Leonel Herrera, which meant that the governor could not grant a pardon even if he had been inclined to do so.[12] Texas executed Herrera on May 12, 1993, just four months after the Supreme Court ruled that his putative innocence could not save him. He refused the ritual of a last meal, but he did take the opportunity to make a final statement shortly before his execution.

"I am innocent, innocent, innocent," he said. "Make no mistake about this: I owe society nothing. Continue the struggle for human rights, helping those who are innocent, especially Mr. Graham. I am an innocent man, and something very wrong is taking place tonight. May God bless you all. I am ready."

"Mr. Graham" was Gary Graham, another young man on Texas's death row with a strong claim of innocence. Graham had been eighteen when he had committed a spate of robberies. He admitted to the robberies but always denied shooting Bobby Lambert in the parking lot of a Safeway supermarket in Houston. Ballistics later proved that the gun found on him could not have fired the fatal bullet; four witnesses established an alibi placing him far away from the scene at the time of the crime, and his conviction hung on the tenuous thread of one person (out of six eyewitnesses) who identified him as the killer.

The State of Texas got him all the same. In the heated final months of his first presidential campaign, Governor George W. Bush denied clemency, saying he was confident they had the right man, and Graham was put to death on June 22, 2000. "This is nothing more than pure and simple murder," Graham said, using the last words allowed to him by the State of Texas. "This is what is happening tonight in America. Nothing more than state sanctioned murder, state sanctioned lynching, right here in America, and right here tonight."

For Kris, once we had lost in every court in the land, the only place left to turn was the governor of Florida. The quest for executive clemency was not a game on which I wanted to bet much money, but at this point we could gamble at no other table. Decades before, we might have had a chance. Between 1924 and 1966, nearly a quarter of those on Florida's death row received some form of mercy from the governor—some had had their death sentences overturned, and the lucky ones had even had their convictions thrown out. But then came forty years when the death penalty was intensely and increasingly politicized: by now, Florida had issued no positive clemency decision to a death row prisoner in twenty-seven years. While statistics do not tell the whole story, no number is quite so emphatic as zero.[13]

The Republican former state attorney general, Charlie Crist, was now Florida's governor. He was the very man who, for the previous four years, had been defending Kris's conviction on appeal: the briefs in the Eleventh Circuit and the Supreme Court had been filed in the name of Charles J. Crist, Jr., opposing Kris's request for a new trial. Even so, in June 2008, as the date for Kris's clemency hearing approached, we had cause for some optimism. A major law firm in London, Freshfields Bruckhaus Deringer, had volunteered pro bono assistance for Kris. The firm took the lead responsibility for his clemency appeal, since here their gravitas and respectability could make a big difference. They had been working the political side as effectively as anyone possibly could— coordinating with the British government and making appropriate contacts with some of the power players in Florida. A partner at the firm, Paul Lomas, and his colleague Clarissa O'Callaghan were slated to fly to Tallahassee to put Kris's case to the Clemency Board.

I got a call from Marita just a few days before the hearing. Her voice was trembling with excitement. The British consul had stopped by to visit Kris the day before, and he had told Kris to get ready to leave prison before the end of the week. The plane, she said, should be flying out of Miami. The consul had assured Kris that he had a valid passport ready to go. I was initially skeptical, but I got caught up in Marita's enthusiasm; she seemed very certain. She had begun to make arrangements to put her few remaining possessions in storage so that she could fly back to Britain at Kris's side.

The news was surprising. It had to mean that the British government's interventions had finally paid off. I found that hard to believe, as I'd never known a state official to agree to any such thing, but I passed Marita's message along to the other members of the legal team, and it buoyed Paul and Clarissa as they left for Tallahassee to make their pitch. When Tim Samuels, a BBC reporter, telephoned me to ask whether it was true, I called Marita back and begged her to be more circumspect. If it came out in the media that a decision had been made to grant clemency before the hearing was complete, the deal would be squashed, no matter how much influence the British government might have.

While I am generally uncomfortable with such backroom deals—uncomfortable and unfamiliar, since lawyers for indigent prisoners do not get to hobnob with those in power—it was paradoxical to think that, twenty-one years after the prosecutors had written the judge's order sentencing Kris to death before the hearing had begun, perhaps someone had written the final order ending Kris's nightmare before the clemency hearing had begun. Such symmetry would be perverse yet somehow appropriate.

I was in London when the hearing took place. The time difference meant that much of the day in England had passed before we heard the result of the hearing. I was busy, caught up on another case, and had almost managed to stop worrying when the e-mail came through.

"Denied," wrote Paul.

We later caught up on the phone. Derrick and Duane Moo Young's family had turned out in force and told the board how important it was to them that Kris Maharaj should serve the rest of his life in prison. Governor Crist had not even bothered to consult with the other members of the board and summarily cast his vote against commutation. Crist was, after all, still holding out hope that he might be Senator John McCain's vice-presidential running mate in the November 2008 election.

Marita's account of what the British consul had told Kris came into belated focus. The official must merely have told him that they were prepared, should the miracle occur. Kris had heard what he had so desperately wanted to hear and relayed it, thrilled, to his wife.

Instead of enjoying freedom, Kris Maharaj heard the door to his prison cell slam firmly and finally shut.

16

The Victims

Whoever killed Derrick and Duane Moo Young, there can be no doubt that their murders had a deep and devastating impact on the rest of the family. While the term *crime victim* is often used to refer only to the person who is left dead or injured, violent crimes leave an indelible mark on whole families and communities.

The grief and anger that the Moo Youngs expressed at the clemency hearing was understandable. No one should have to lose anyone they love in such horrific and terrifying circumstances. But what had the criminal justice system offered to support the Moo Youngs in their ordeal? When the trial was concluded and Kris was found guilty and sentenced to death by electrocution in 1987, the family was told to stand by for closure, in the form of Kris's execution. More than a decade later, the death sentence was overturned, and the family was told that they would have to come and support the prosecution's demand for the death penalty anew. The second jury had been of the view that life in prison was sufficient punishment, so the Moo Young family were told they would have to make do with that. This was followed by more years of appeals. Finally, they were told that the Clemency Board might let a man whom they believed had killed their father and brother and husband walk free. They trekked to Tallahassee to relive their grief all over again in front of the board.

If this is what "victims rights" get you, all the more the reason to pray that your loved ones are never the victims of a violent crime.

A leaflet called *A Walk Through the System* that I came across in a recent Texas case details the rights that victims and their families are typically told to expect in criminal cases. They have the right to know where the convict is being held. There is a twenty-four-hour hotline that they can call to check whether he is seeking parole. They can seek assistance in preparing a Victim Impact Statement, detailing why a particular punishment should be imposed, or a "protest letter" if the prisoner is being considered for release. Indeed, they can preempt the prisoner's request for freedom. "As often as you wish," the leaflet assures, "you can send protest letters to our office to be included in the inmate's file."[1] Virtually all these rights assume that the victim's only interest is in keeping the prisoner locked up for as long as possible. In a capital case, members of a murder victim's family are given the explicit right to watch the execution.

Why has inspiring a victim to find solace in retribution become a primary focus of criminal justice in America? This phenomenon is an inversion of the previous trend, where the law had been evolving to replace blood feuds and retribution with a more consistent and less socially damaging arbitration of justice. The movement away from revenge echoed the messages of all major religious traditions. Christianity suggests that we should bless the merciful, and Jesus taught us to turn the other cheek. The ninety-nine names of Allah include The Exceedingly Merciful, The Exceedingly Compassionate, The Subtly Kind, and The Much Forgiving. Nowhere will we find "hatred" or "vengefulness" in the list of virtues prescribed by any god since Thor. Similarly, most secular parents encourage their children to resist the urge to hit back.

The retributive interpretation of what is "best" for crime victims was, indeed, a U-turn. In the 1970s a movement had arisen for "restorative justice," which sought to educate perpetrators to appreciate the impact of the offense that they had committed, and to make inroads into repairing the damage by allowing the victims to meet them, so that everyone could better understand what happened and why.[2] But inspiring hatred is politically expedient, a powerful tool of distraction: the more we are taught to hate criminals, the less time we have to look around for complex explanations and difficult but more effective long-term solutions.

The restorative justice movement was a threat to those who would rather trade in the debased currency of hatred and retribution. Politicians—including many elected prosecutors—elbowed psychologists and therapists aside, concerned that an emphasis on healing would deprive them of an opportunity to parlay the politics of fear to their advantage. Those who push for the death penalty, or other harsh punishment, doubtless believe that they are helping the victims of crime, but they are also using these vulnerable people, forcing them into confrontation both with the defendant and the judicial system, and profoundly damaging their chances of ever beginning to recover from the trauma of bereavement.

I have met with many family members of murder victims. Sometimes it has been to deliver my client's apology for the horror he wrought; sometimes it has been to share new facts that have come to light; sometimes it has simply been a matter of courtesy, to listen to what they have to say. Unfortunately, in the case of the Moo Young family, that has not been possible. I tried to arrange a meeting, but the extremely hostile prosecutor—Sally Weintraub—told me in no uncertain terms that she would view any such approach as harassment and, if I initiated any contact, would take it upon herself to seek appropriate sanctions. That is a great pity.

The Moo Youngs, shattered by the murders of Derrick and Duane, were promised the false catharsis of revenge. The family's pain, lasting for a quarter century and passed down through generations, is patent in their submissions to the Clemency Board.[3]

"This man murdered my father and brother," wrote one family member. "MURDERED. This man used up his one life when he had his sentence reduced from death to life imprisonment. I had hoped prior to that that he would be put to death. For people who have not lived through family members being murdered, they will not be able to comprehend the feelings I have, so be it. This man should have been put to death, as was the original sentence. I want this man murdered for what he has done to my family and I. Clemency should never be granted.

What has changed over 20 years? Nothing. This man has never shown any remorse, and I certainly have never been able to find any for him. If he is destined to live out the rest of his life in prison, it will be too long. This man needs to suffer as much as possible until the day he takes his last breath, which will never come soon enough."

"Every time the phone rings," wrote another family member, "or an envelope arrives at my office with the address of the State of Florida Victims' Advocate or State Attorney's Office, a cold sweat runs down my entire body as I think, 'What else is he claiming?' I implore you to please find it in your hearts to make this hearing today the last of my family's seemingly endless tragedy. Enough is enough. Mr. Maharaj had drained our family enough over the . . . years. He has exhausted enough of our State's resources on pointless, ridiculous appeals."

A third wrote: "Repentance and the admission of guilt and unchangeable exile is the beginning of hope. The least Mr. Maharaj could do is pay with his own life for the lives he has taken."

"The psychological effect already pervades and affects our lives," wrote another. "It reveals itself in the way we handle problems in our everyday living and relationships. We have been demoralized, lacking confidence, devoid of trust, and often experience periods of depression, mood swings, and impulsive behaviour as well as angry outbursts of indelible anger, trying as we may to remove the hurt from our hearts. He betrayed our kindness and acceptance of him into our family. This is the man the children once called 'Uncle.'"

For twenty-six long years, a specter has haunted the Moo Young family, of a maniacal Krishna Maharaj, released and hell-bent on exacting his own revenge. The saddest of the statements to the Clemency Board came from one of Derrick Moo Young's grandchildren. "Although I never met my grandfather," wrote the child, born at least a decade after the crime, "his death has not only affected my mother or anyone else who knew him, it has affected me and all my cousins—even the little ones, they will never know their own grandfather. I dread the thought of Mr. Maharaj's release, if he may come after me. I often have dreams about my grandfather being murdered, I see the killer's face and feel as if I were to scream, but I know it is just a dream."

———

The justice system encouraged the Moo Young family to proceed down a particular path. It is not the only course available. Some families have been allowed to respond to murder in a way that is very different, one that seems more likely to lead closer to peace, even when the person in prison is clearly guilty of the crime.

Paula Kurland's daughter Mitzi was murdered in 1986. In September 1998, Paula was able to meet with Jonathan Nobles, the man who had taken her daughter's life. She favored the death penalty, she said, and did not oppose his execution. But she wanted to tell him that she forgave him—largely, she said, because this was the only way to get back her relationship with her other children. She said she had been so filled up with hatred that she needed to let go of it to have space for anything else. Nobles was also able to apologize to her for what he had done.

"It taught me to breathe again," she said. Nobles died two weeks later. She attended the execution, and before he died, Nobles told her how grateful he was to her.[4]

However, the justice system is so structured as to make it very difficult for victims' families to seek anything other than retribution. In Texas, where Mitzi Kurland was murdered, the Texas Department of Criminal Justice (TDCJ) provides for the training of mediation facilitators to work with the victims of crime. The TDCJ does not allow violent offenders to begin mediation until after their legal challenges to their conviction and sentence are completed. I have been told that it takes four to six months of training in the Victim-Offender Mediation (VOMD) program before the victim and the offender can expect a first meeting. A condemned prisoner almost always continues with appeals until the eleventh hour. As a result, it is normally not possible for someone on death row to ever speak to the victim's family. This forces victims who want mediation to shove their way into the process without official aid as best they can. A small number of those who know what they want seek out the organization Murder Victims' Families for Reconciliation,[5] but most must make up their own rules as they go along.

Take the remarkable example of Rais Bhuiyan, who came to the United States from Bangladesh in 1999. I came to know Rais when I was helping to represent Mark Ströman, the man who indubitably tried to kill Rais and managed to take the lives of two other victims. Rais was twenty-five, a former pilot with the Bangladesh air force. He arrived in New York, saw the Statue of Liberty, and was thrilled by the prospect that stretched before him. His plans were flexible, but he hoped to pursue further education and to bring his fiancée to the United States. They had both applied for a green card. In the meantime he had to earn some money to make the dream possible, and a friend told him to try life in Texas. Another Bangladeshi contact offered him a job at a filling station, the Buckner Food Mart in Dallas. In July 2001 the filling station was robbed. Rais was not unduly intimidated—he was not hurt—but he began to see that the American tableau had dark shadows. Two months later came 9/11, and with it a surge in Islamophobic attacks. Now Rais was nervous, but he could not make do without the job.

Shortly after noon on September 21, 2001, Ströman walked into the store and put a shotgun in Rais's face. Ströman's rap sheet listed an astounding array of minor crimes stretching back to his childhood. Now, though, he was stepping up a league. He had decided that the Bush administration was cowardly, unwilling to exact revenge on the "towelheads" who had attacked America, so he took the task upon himself. Rais Bhuiyan had brown skin and spoke a funny language, so Ströman thought he must be from the Middle East.

Rais thought it was another robbery, but it soon became clear that money was not the intruder's motive: "He didn't even look towards the money," Rais told a journalist, "rather he asked me a question." Ströman appeared to be drunk or high on drugs, and he was mumbling. Rais could not understand what he said. "I asked him, since I didn't understand the question, I asked him, 'What was that?' And then he shot me."

Rais felt a pain "like a million bee stings." He heard the echo of the gun blast, and blood poured out of the side of his head. He thought he was going to die. "I saw images of my parents, my siblings and my fiancée and then a graveyard and I thought, 'Am I dying today?' I screamed, 'Mom!' I looked, and he was still staring at me, and I thought he might shoot me again if I don't fall, he doesn't think I'm dead. The floor was getting wet with my blood. Then he left the store. I could not believe he shot me. I thought I was dreaming, going through a hallucination. I didn't do anything wrong. I was not a threat to him. I couldn't believe someone would just shoot you like that."[6]

When Ströman left the store, Rais discovered that he was still conscious and struggled to his feet. He went to the barbershop nearby. "They ran away. They saw me full of blood running like a slaughtered chicken and they thought the guy was behind me. I saw my face in the barbershop mirror and I couldn't believe it was me." The journalist who was drawing this story out of Rais noted that he began to cry at this point as he talked. "A few minutes before, I had been a young guy in a T-shirt and shorts and tennis shoes." The tears came harder. Rais briefly apologized for his emotion. "I was lucky because there was an ambulance in the area."

Rais survived, with the scars of shotgun pellets down the side of his face. Over a three-week period, two others were not so fortunate. Indeed, Mark Ströman had already committed one murder before he came for Rais. On September 15, 2001, four days after the terrorist attack in New York, he had walked into the Mom's Store, where Waqar Hasan had recently invested his savings. The forty-six-year-old Pakistani immigrant was cooking hamburgers. Ströman simply shot the man and left. There was money lying around, but none was taken. Detective Daniel Wojcik was perplexed. Robbery did not appear to be a motive of the crime. The original police report on the Hasan murder was stark: "No motive, no robbery, no suspects, no witnesses."

Rais came next. Then, on October 4, 2001, Ströman walked into the Shell Station on John West Road and Big Torn Boulevard in Mesquite to murder once more. This time the victim, Vasudev Patel, pulled a gun, but the magazine was not locked in, so the weapon could not fire. Patel was left dying on the floor. Ströman was now responsible for leaving two widows without husbands, and several children with no father.

Rais had survived, but he was learning what it meant to be a victim of crime in America. He needed multiple operations to try to save some of the sight in his right eye, as well as protracted medical assistance with his other injuries. He was constantly sent bills for his treatment. His doctor did apply to the Texas Crime Victim Compensation Program, but the request languished without approval for two years. Rais, still a recent immigrant, was trapped between his fear of the debt collectors who appeared on his doorstep, and his fear of forgoing the care he needed. Some of the time he treated himself as best he could with drug samples that he begged from doctors.

Two days after Rais was shot, his father—back in Bangladesh—suffered a stroke. Rais could not return to Bangladesh since he was in and out of the hospital himself. Later he did not have the money. He slipped into a deep depression. His fiancée severed their engagement, feeling estranged by the distance and his impenetrable melancholy. In early 2002 the friend who had let Rais share an apartment asked him to move out, suggesting that he needed to be in a nursing home. He was reduced to sleeping on couches and staying as long as each friend would tolerate, until he felt bound to move on.

Mark Ströman, the man who had destroyed Rais's life, was certainly a racist. When he arrived at the jail, he penned a form of poetry: "Here sits the Arab Slayer. For what he did, we should make him mayor," he wrote. "Patriotic, yes indeed, a true American, a special breed."[7]

The state prosecutor met with Rais. He did not explain any of his rights and stated that the death penalty was essentially a fait accompli; Ströman would become the twentieth photograph on the trophy wall of the district attorney's office. Rais had little comprehension of the legal process. He thought the determination to execute Ströman had already been made and that he had no role in it. He didn't realize that he was being asked to play a part in producing that result.

"This man needs to die, pure and simple," said assistant district attorney Bob Dark in his argument to the jury. Rais was called as a witness at the penalty phase of the trial. He was told only to answer the questions he was asked. Ströman's defense lawyer had not even had the courtesy to contact Rais. At the end of the trial, with Ströman on death row, the judge entered an order forbidding any contact between Rais and the man who had tried to kill him.[8] The Texas Department of Criminal Justice had the same rule, and it also barred Ströman from all contact with Rais Bhuiyan.

While Mark Ströman waited to die, Rais gradually pulled his life back together. In June 2003 he got a job at an Olive Garden restaurant.

In 2005 he became aware of a private charity, the Pathways Clinic, that could offer him therapy for his trauma. Meanwhile he trained in computers, so he would be able to move on from work as a waiter. He was able to pay for a trip with his mother to go on hajj to Mecca.

By 2011, Rais was thirty-seven. He was effectively blind in one eye, and the right side of his face was pockmarked, as if he had suffered from smallpox: "I'm still carrying more than 35 pellets on the right side of my face. If I touch my face, my skull, I can feel it's all bumpy." It was increasingly clear to him that he should take affirmative steps to understand what had happened to him and why. However, he did not know how to engage with the legal system. The trial seemed far in the past.

It all suddenly began to come into focus in March 2011, when Rais read that a date had been set for Mark Ströman's execution: he was to die on July 20, 2011. Rais was horrified. He asked around to see what, if anything, might be done to prevent it. For the first time, he learned that his status as a victim gave him rights. How, though, was he to assert them? He went to the media. On May 16, 2011, he did an interview with the *Dallas Morning News* in which he stated publicly for the first time that he wanted to work on reconciliation with Mark Ströman. "There are three reasons I feel this way," he said. "The first is what I learned from my parents. They raised me with the religious principle that he is best who can forgive easily. The second is because of what I believe as a Muslim, that human lives are precious and that no one has the right to take another's life. And, finally, I seek solace for the wives and children of Vasudev Patel and Waqar Hasan, who are also victims in this tragedy. Executing Ströman is not what they want, either. They have already suffered so much; it will cause only more suffering if he is executed."

Now I was based in England, I was working with a London charity, Reprieve. Because Ströman had German connections, Reprieve was brought in to help mount his last ditch appeal, and we worked closely with Lydia Brandt, Ströman's Texas lawyer. She had previously wondered whether it was permissible to contact Rais, given the prison rules, but the *Dallas Morning News* article satisfied her that such an approach would be welcome. She delivered a letter from her client expressing his deep remorse for his crimes. Rais soon learned more about the man who had shot him. While perhaps typical of many prisoners on death row, Ströman's history was nevertheless shocking, and revealing, to Rais.

From the moment he was born, Mark Ströman's mother, Sandra Baker, had rued the fact that she had ever had a son, remarking that she had only been fifty dollars short of an abortion. She said this in front of Mark. She said it to anyone who would listen. "She wished she had had a dog," reported her sister. "That it would have been better if she'd had dogs instead of children." When Mark was a small child, Sandra married Doyle Baker, who became Mark's stepfather. They were both heavy drinkers and seemed to be well matched. At the age of eight, Mark rode his bike thirty miles to escape briefly to his grandparents' house. If ever Mark came home from school complaining that he was being bullied, Doyle sent him back to fight the other children. The alternative was a whipping at home. Mark was required to be in his room at all times when the parents were downstairs, including Christmas Day. And so it continued.

There is no such thing as a dog born bad, thought Rais, but there are certainly bad dog owners. It seemed to Rais that his terrible experience was gradually becoming more comprehensible. He had heard stories of how much Mark had changed in ten years on death row: a bevy of pen pals vouched for his efforts to improve himself. He had been a white supremacist, a racist, but now he rejected this creed. "It's not been easy to unlearn everything my stepfather taught me," Mark wrote. "And I'm not there yet. I may not have time ever to get there. But I'm trying."

Rais publicly dedicated himself to working on Mark Ströman's rehabilitation. *Rehabilitation?* That was the wrong word, he thought; perhaps he should call it *habilitation,* since Mark never received a decent upbringing in the first place. Rais wanted to meet Mark in person. He still felt it was important for his own recovery that they should talk, so he could hear directly from Mark why that shotgun blast had shattered his new life in America. Mark confirmed to the prison authorities that he was willing to undergo mediation with Rais.

"I requested a meeting with Mr. Ströman," said Rais. The prison authorities told him that various officials had to approve his application, and the attorney general (the person trying to ensure Mark Ströman's execution) would have the power to veto any mediation. "I'm eagerly awaiting to see him in person and exchange ideas. I would talk about love and compassion. We all make mistakes. He's another human being, like me. Hate the sin, not the sinner. It's very important that I meet him to tell him I feel for him and I strongly believe he should get a second chance. He could educate a lot of people. Thinking about what is going to happen makes me very emotional. I can't sleep. Once I go to bed I feel there is another person that I know who is in his bed thinking about what is going to happen to him—that he is going to be . . . killed. It makes me very emotional and very sad and makes me want to do more."

Nobody from the department of corrections got back either to Mark or to Rais about their mediation request—ever. Rais Bhuiyan and the other victims who were supposed to have rights became the only people in the world who were formally barred from meeting with Mark Strö-man. As the execution date loomed, some of Mark's pen pals had traveled from as far away as Europe to spend time with him through the last days of his life. They were allowed into the prison. Rais was not.

Next, Rais decided he wanted to address the Pardon Board, so he could explain why he wanted them to show mercy—or at least a delay in the execution long enough for him to seek mediation with Mark. The board rules specifically provide for a victim's right to speak, but apparently that only applies to victims who want to make a case for the death penalty. Rais never received a call, a note, or even an e-mail in response to his request. Twenty-four hours before the scheduled execution, the board summarily denied clemency.

Rais turned to Governor Rick Perry who could, independently of the board, stay the execution long enough for Rais to meet with Mark. Rais never received a reply from the governor either.

Rais had expected to be treated with some dignity or at least basic politeness. After a decade of Islamophobia, an opportunity had arisen for reconciliation and understanding. Rais had been the victim of a "hate" crime. In the wake of 9/11, such offenses against Muslims in the United States had leaped from 28 in 2000 to 481 in 2001—a sixteenfold increase.[9] Here was a victim trying to repay hatred with mercy, just as his parents and his religion had taught him.

Rais would quote Koranic verses to anyone who would listen: "If anyone kills . . . it would be as if he killed all people. And if anyone saves a life, it would be as if he saved the life of all people." He explained that charity and forgiveness were essential to his own salvation: "If a person forgives and makes reconciliation, his reward is due from Allah." Under Islamic law, Rais would undeniably have had the power to extend mercy or forgiveness. Because he did not want the death penalty—and he was supported in this by the widows of Hasan and Patel—there could have been no execution. In whose name, Rais asked, was the State of Texas planning to kill Mark Ströman?

But nobody in Texas was listening.

Finally, Rais found he had drained the considerable reservoir of his patience. He set out to sue the State of Texas. He did not have the money to pay, but Khurrum Walid, a Muslim lawyer from Florida who supported what Rais was trying to do, agreed to represent him without charge. Rais's lawsuit sought to enforce the Texas Constitution, which imposed a duty upon government officials to treat a victim with respect.[10]

"All we are seeking is an injunction to stop Mr. Stroman's execution so that we may grant an American victim of violence the same rights under the law as are granted to many other Texan victims," Walid told the media assembled outside the courthouse. "This is not about Mr. Ströman. It's about victim rights. Do we believe they exist or not? Because if we cannot enforce them they don't exist for any of us."

The spotlight swung back around to Governor Rick Perry, who even then was dipping his toes in fresh electoral waters, gearing up to run for president. Rais found Perry's conduct particularly galling. Perry had recently declared Victims' Rights Week in April 2011. "I encourage all Texans," the governor had proclaimed, "to join in this effort by learning more about victims' rights and supporting victims of crime whenever possible. We can help our fellow Texans on the road to recovery with compassion and respect."

Rais felt that this statement was pure hypocrisy, and he named Perry as the first defendant in the complaint. The case would be styled *Rais Bhuiyan v. Rick Perry*. It was filed in state court, since it primarily involved victims' rights under state law. Texas state court was surely where Governor Perry would want to resolve the issue: he held himself out to be a vehement advocate of states' rights, a critic (in the Tea Party vein) of the intrusion by federal courts into Texas affairs. Indeed, he had recently complained that the federal courts were "oppressive."[11]

Even after all these years, I was surprised at Perry's response. Through his lawyers, he moved the case to federal court, where he could argue that the State of Texas had immunity from being sued. If this did not work, his lawyers were to argue that the Texas Victims' Bill of Rights was merely "symbolic" and unenforceable. There is no right without a remedy; if there is no remedy, there can be no meaningful right; so Perry was saying that victims' rights were not rights at all.[12]

Perry's actions might have underlined his hypocrisy, but the governor won, and Rais's case was dismissed.

Meanwhile Mark Ströman was in his prison cell, waiting to die.

"I sit here with a Cup of Coffee and some Good ole Classic Rock playing on My radio, how Ironic, the song 'Free Bird' by Lynyrd Skynyrd," he wrote, the grammar and spelling all his own. ". . . Yes, Mr Rais Bhuiyan, what an inspiring soul . . . for him to come forward after what ive done speaks Volume's . . . and has really Touched My heart and the heart of Many others World Wide. . . Not only do I have all My friends and supporters trying to Save my Life, but now i have The Islamic Community Joining in . . . Spearheaded by one Very Remarkable man Named Rais Bhuiyan, Who is a Survivor of My Hate. His deep Islamic Beliefs Have gave him the strength to Forgive the Un-forgiveable . . . that is truly Inspiring to me, and should be an Example for us all. The Hate, has to stop . . .

"Texas Loud & Texas proud . . . TRUE AMERICAN . . ." Mark Ströman signed off. "Living to Die—Dying to Live."[13] There was a brief stay, which extended his life by three hours before he was executed.

Rais felt that he had failed. But he had not. He had upheld the principles his parents had instilled in him. It was the criminal justice system of the State of Texas that had failed him, just as the Florida system has been failing both Kris Maharaj and the family of Derrick and Duane Moo Young for twenty-six years.

17

The Battle Continues

On January 26, 2009, Kris turned seventy. Since his trial in 1987, every court available to him has rubber-stamped the original verdict, refusing even to consider his claim of innocence. By his birthday he had served twenty-three years in prison for a crime he did not commit. I wouldn't say he celebrated, as he had nothing to be joyous about, but at least he had made it that far. Life expectancy in prison is far lower than in the free world. Kris was now considered a geriatric prisoner, and as such he was transferred to another prison, in Miami. That made travel easier for his wife, Marita, who, steadfast as ever, continued to visit Kris as often as she could. Now she could see him for three or four hours on Saturdays. The rest of the week she devoted primarily to preparing for the next visit, and to taking brief calls at night, when he was given access to the phone.

I had moved back to England in 2004 and started working full time with Reprieve in London. I missed New Orleans and my old creaky house, which I never did get around to fixing up quite as I'd wanted, though I managed to straighten out the plumbing and get roughly the right number of columns holding up the front deck. I'd been lucky, as I'd sold it shortly before I left, before Hurricane Katrina inundated the city. Every once in a while, though I was now an ocean away, Marita would call me to find out whether there was any progress. Her calls had a predictable effect, making me feel guilty about Kris's situation, and spurring me on.

In theory, the courts had essentially closed the door on Kris, but those of us who had battled for him for fifteen years could not bring ourselves to give up on him. The law says that innocence is not an issue, but the law is an ass and has to be changed. I passed through Florida every few months on the way to Guantánamo Bay, where I was representing a few inmates. Every now and then I would stop in on Marita and, when the prison visitation schedule allowed, on Kris. From time to time when something came up, Ben Kuehne or the other lawyer now working with him on the case, Susan Dimitrovsky, would pitch in.

Equally sporadically, back at the Reprieve office in London, we would plan investigative forays in the hope that something would break in his case. I hoped a witness might come face to face with his conscience as he thought of Kris as an old man wasting away in his cell. Generally, I was disappointed. We tried to locate more material on the drug prosecution of Jaime Vallejo Mejia in Oklahoma, but documents relating to his guilty plea and sentence had been placed under seal. Jim Drummond, a kindly local lawyer who was generous with his time, agreed to press for access, but progress was slow.

In 2006 the Colombian authorities conducted a raid on a property owned by a man by the name of Rodrigo Tovar Pupo. All manner of information about the inner workings of the cartels had by then started seeping out through the U.S. courts, and it was possible to get a much better sense of the complex structure of their organization. Tovar was the real name of "Jorge 40," the notorious leader of the AUC, a paramilitary group that controlled drug trafficking in the eastern half of Colombia. A quick search revealed details of 558 murders he had ordered in one region alone, hits that had taken place even as he had been negotiating an amnesty for himself and the AUC. Tovar was in the blackmail business, and his computer also offered up a catalog of individuals—from high-ranking politicians to dealers—with connections to the drug cartels and the paramilitary. One name on the list was J. Mejia V. I suppose there is a tiny possibility that this was not Jaime Vallejo Mejia, who had happened to be across the hall in the DuPont Plaza hotel at the time of Derrick and Duane's murder, but it seems unlikely, particularly since Mejia's business partner, Ramiro Betancourt, was also on the list.

Every few years one of our investigators would reach out to Neville Butler, who was now pushing eighty but still refusing to talk. But in time one focus of our work started to bear fruit. It involved the curious flip-flopping testimony of Tino Geddes.

As Kris sat in prison, the life of his trial lawyer, Eric Hendon, had also moved on, just as had my own. Hendon achieved his goal of becoming a county court judge, which is a step down from the circuit court, where Kris was tried. Hendon was initially appointed by Governor Jeb Bush in 1999, but was unseated in the first election he had to face, in 2002. The reason, according to various commentators, was that his opponent had looked around to find the person she could most readily beat and thought Hendon, as an African American, would be the easiest target. Soon afterward, in what is almost a unique occurrence, he was reappointed to a vacant post, again by Governor Bush. He finally won an election, and retained his judgeship, in 2008.

From my interactions with Hendon, I suspect he is a better judge than he was trial lawyer. His instinct was to be fair, even if he did not do the right thing by his former client. One of the most glaring flaws in Hendon's representation of Kris had been the alibi. If Kris was truly forty miles away at the time of the crime—if there had been even a doubt in a juror's mind that he might have been—he should have been acquitted. Key to the alibi was the turncoat witness Tino Geddes, who testified under oath that he had concocted the original defense at Kris's request and that it was false. Five other alibi witnesses had steadfastly stuck to their original story and, when confronted with Geddes's testimony, insisted that he was lying when he claimed he had hoodwinked them into saying Kris was elsewhere at the time of the crime. For this reason, Geddes had always been at the heart of our investigation.

Geddes stood an inch over six feet tall and had a dark complexion. He had a reputation as a smooth talker, a ladies' man. I got the sense he had a bit of a crush on Marita, though she was certainly never going to see him as anything other than the man who had betrayed her husband. At the time of the Moo Youngs' murder, Kris had recently given him a job working for the *Caribbean Times* and treated him as a friend.

Several people who were present in the courtroom told me that Geddes was the most persuasive of all the prosecution witnesses. He was glib, his story was shocking, and it painted Kris in a very poor light. According to Geddes, Kris had enlisted him in a series of attempts to kill Derrick Moo Young. His testimony also managed to turn Kris's solid alibi on its head.

"Why, Tino?" Marita had cried as Geddes had walked back through the courtroom after leaving the witness stand. "Why?"

Over the years, he had never given a good answer.

I had pored over his trial testimony a number of times and had no doubt that he was being deceptive about a number of things. But it was important to work out precisely how he was lying and, more important, *why*. The trial record was not much use since Eric Hendon had conducted such an anemic cross-examination. When I first took up Kris's case, I gathered up a number of statements that Geddes had made— something Hendon appeared not to have done. On the day after the crime, Geddes had told the *Miami Herald* that Kris was totally innocent and that he could not imagine why his boss had been arrested. About a week later he told Ron Petrillo in a sworn statement that he had been with Kris on the morning of the crime, miles north of Miami. Yet eight months later his entire story changed: now, appearing for a deposition, he claimed that the alibi had been concocted and that Kris had connived with him in bizarre attempts on the lives of Derrick Moo Young and Eslee Carberry. His sworn testimony at trial was again different in some key respects from the deposition. When some British journalists interviewed him in 1995, the details varied some more on significant points.

At the time of the trial, some useful facts had emerged in Geddes's testimony. "The name Carberry never appeared on the pages of the *Caribbean Times*," Geddes conceded. Neither did that of Derrick Moo Young. He explained that Kris did not want to sink to Carberry's level. On the face of it, it struck me as improbable that a man would be motivated to kill two people on the basis of their scurrilous articles if he would not even resort to defaming them in his newspaper.

But most of what Geddes said at trial was devastating to Kris's chances of acquittal. As with so many witnesses in this strange case, my initial reaction had been to stand back and assess the overall plausibility of their story: did Geddes's testimony make sense? He said that Kris had hired him away from the *Echo* to work on the *Caribbean Times*. After Geddes took the job, by his account Kris began to hatch plots against Carberry and Derrick Moo Young. First Geddes had described a midnight plot to shoot Eslee Carberry as he took the *Echo* to the printer. "Mr. Maharaj told me that he was going . . ." Geddes had paused, perhaps for effect. "He was going . . . to blow away Mr. Carberry." Geddes said he saw Kris buy two crossbows, which were to be used against Carberry. He said Kris also had two hunting knives, Chinese throwing stars, and camouflage gear. As I read this, I could imagine the way one might cross-examine such a witness, with a rising inflection of incredulity: *How was Mr. Maharaj going to carry out this homicide? Was he going to use the bow like William Tell? The hunting knife like Jim Bowie? Or the Chinese throwing stars like Bruce Lee?*

Geddes testified that he and Kris had gone up together to West Palm Beach, where Carberry was at the printer. The plan was to kill him on the "lonely stretch of road which runs from Wellington down to Ft. Lauderdale." At trial, Hendon did not press Geddes on where exactly the crime was slated to take place. A journalist had later asked this question in an interview.

"You must understand where this is," Geddes replied. "You would drive for miles and see no sign of life or light." It took me only a moment on the Google maps to prove that this description was bogus. The Town Crier printer was, and still is, in the same building as the Publix supermarket in Wellington, Florida, a suburb of West Palm Beach. The road was solid with houses between there and Fort Lauderdale: it was hardly an ideal venue for an assassination. According to Geddes, this plot petered out when they got bored and hungry and went looking for a deli. If this was true, they would not have had far to go: there was a deli right in the Publix.

Then, there was the "dry run," perhaps the most vital episode from the perspective of the prosecution. Geddes described a plot that was remarkably similar, in every detail, to Neville Butler's version of the actual murders on October 16. It was obvious how he might have concocted it; he was friends with Neville Butler, and they had concededly spoken about the crime. The question was whether it was true. The "dry run" supposedly took place in room 408. Once Derrick Moo Young arrived, the plan was for Kris to burst in from the adjoining room. In the early years of our investigation I had taken the simple step that Eric Hendon should have followed before the trial: I went to the DuPont Plaza, met with Ken Kalish, the hotel manager, and asked him to take me to room 408. The room was occupied, but those on either side were not. It did not take long to determine that there was no connecting door between 408 and the adjoining rooms. There never had been. A maintenance man in the hall said that rooms 400 and 401 were the only ones with a door between them on that floor.

There were plenty more problems with Geddes's testimony, but he had faced barely any challenge from the defense at trial. I found a letter in Hendon's file. Not long after he was convicted, Kris had written to Hendon asking him why he had seemed to be in a "frozen stupor" throughout Geddes's testimony. The lawyer had not replied, and Kris had fired him soon afterward.

Why did Geddes flip to become a witness for the prosecution? He told the jury that what made the difference to him was learning the "real" timing of the murders.

"Did you know, in fact, that the murders were committed between 11:30 and 12?" Kastrenakes asked. No, Geddes said, and suddenly he realized how important his alibi evidence was, and he felt a duty to set the record straight. I dismissed this explanation. It was just silly. If Geddes had been asked to create an alibi for his boss, then he would have had to know when the crime had taken place. This, then, could not be his true motive for changing his story.

An alternative reason for working with the prosecution had been put forward at the trial: the chief prosecutor had threatened to charge him with perjury. Geddes reported that Kastrenakes had promised him complete immunity if he would testify against Kris; if he did not cooperate, Kastrenakes said he would make life difficult for him. During Geddes's pretrial deposition, Kastrenakes essentially confirmed this story:

"I would interrupt that," the prosecutor said, as Eric Hendon elicited the witness's testimony, "with saying that we did advise Mr. Geddes that he could not be prosecuted for perjury because he has, in fact, recanted and I advised him of Florida law with respect to that."

Imagine the power of those words. The state prosecutor told Geddes that if he upheld Kris's alibi, he would be deemed to be perjuring himself. In a capital case, lying under oath can get you locked up for fifteen to thirty years.[1] Kastrenakes was insisting that he—the prosecutor—could divine truth from falsehood and it was, he had decided, perjury to claim that Kris was elsewhere at the time of the crime. By contrast, if Eric Hendon—defense counsel—had plucked up the courage to tell Detective Buhrmaster that he had better change his story or he would face prosecution for perjury, Hendon would have been charged with intimidating a witness, for which he could have received life in prison.[2]

The prosecutor also told Geddes he could go to prison even under his new account of events leading up to the murders. "Because I had been with Kris on a number of occasions," Geddes told one of the British reporters, "even if no criminal activity took place, there was criminal intent which I think ... um ... could be looked at as, you know, conspiracy or aiding and abetting." So if he was telling the truth, he was involved in conspiracy to commit murder. But that was okay, as Kastrenakes gave him immunity for that as well.

If the prosecution used a stick, they also held out a carrot. Not long before Kris's trial, Geddes had been arrested in Jamaica on a weapons charge. He downplayed its seriousness—there was no gun, he told the jury, he'd just forgotten to take some ammunition out of his suitcase when he flew back from Miami. Nevertheless, it was a serious offense: under Jamaican law, Geddes could—once again—have faced a stretch in prison.[3]

At Kris's trial, Geddes placed the blame for this arrest on his former employer, saying that the bullets were for a weapon that he had recently bought in Florida. "I purchased that gun because I had become involved in these escapades which I have already described with Mr. Maharaj," he told the jury, "and I was, in fact, fearful for my own safety, and this is why I purchased this firearm."

Geddes got off very lightly in Jamaica—with a $1,000 fine—in part because not one but both Florida prosecutors flew to Kingston to support him. "They simply produced a public document before the Court in Jamaica," Geddes testified, trying to downplay their role. This made no sense. What was the point of traveling all the way to Jamaica simply to bring a piece of paper that could have been mailed for a couple of dollars? It turned out, yet again, that Geddes was not telling the whole story. Before the trial, Paul Ridge had written to Hendon to inform him that he and his colleague John Kastrenakes had gone to Jamaica to testify at Geddes's trial.

Geddes later painted it all as something of a social occasion. "For a time when they came over to interview me, I took them over the north course and I took them around Jamaica," Geddes told a British journalist. "I think they had a wonderful time." The *Caribbean Echo* carried a picture of the two prosecutors and Geddes drinking at a bar. They also accompanied their star witness to a lap-dancing establishment.[4]

When Geddes said he had bought the gun "a couple of weeks" before the murders in response to Kris's homicidal escapades, this was demonstrably false. The supposed plots he described all occurred—by his account—in the two or three weeks leading up to the Moo Youngs' deaths. In other words, they took place either in late September or early October 1986. But a receipt produced by the prosecution at trial proved that Geddes bought the gun on July 19. For once, Hendon had noticed this and brought it up.

"A couple of weeks, like eight," Geddes had explained. "And when I say a couple, I do not necessarily mean two. This is how we speak. This is standard Jamaican." Eight? More like eleven.

All this we knew in 1997, when Ben Kuehne and I filed Kris's state petition for a writ of habeas corpus. Was it sufficient to explain Geddes's about-face? After all, who among us would not do as a prosecutor told us to avoid fifteen years in prison for perjury?

Regardless, something told me this was not the full story. How could a man who was once close to Kris have concocted such deliberately damning testimony? Marita told me she'd heard that Geddes had received $50,000 for his amended testimony. She could not remember the name of the man who had told her this, so it was not much use.

By 2010 Geddes was suffering from cancer. The smart suits that had once fit snugly to his heavy frame now hung on him like sacks. He was sixty-two, but he looked twenty years older. I had learned of a miniscandal that had broken in the local media: Geddes had been fired from his job as a journalist in Kingston because of associations with an infamous gangster, a member of the Jamaican Shower Posse.

When someone first mentioned the Jamaican Shower Posse, I thought I had misheard: the name seemed a rather wet sobriquet. But then I was told that it came from the Posse's penchant for showering people with bullets. They controlled much of the island's drug trade and were closely linked to narco-associates in Colombia.

At this point, an investigator we will call Ken agreed to help us with the Jamaican end of the case. That's not his real name, but it's safer not to say who he is. He gradually pulled together a slew of interesting information. He learned that while Geddes primarily covered sports media, he also did gritty "in the streets" reporting. Younger journalists would be surprised at Geddes's bank of contacts in some of the roughest parts of Kingston, particularly in the Tivoli Gardens area—home to the Shower Posse.

Geddes, it turned out, was very well connected in the Jamaican underworld. He had grown up with the most disreputable of all the Shower Posse members, Carl "Bya" Mitchell, and let slip in a moment of braggadocio that he hid Mitchell out for a year in his home during the 1970s state of emergency. The violence had been so bad then that the government had cracked down heavily on the gangs. While Jamaicans were used to a bit of wild talk, Geddes's admission that he had conspired with one of the island's most dangerous criminals proved to be too much, and he lost his job.

With his health in rapid decline, Geddes finally agreed to an interview. He and Ken, the investigator, met at a bar in Kingston. Ken called me to run through what he should ask. At last, I thought, perhaps Geddes would come clean. But he still had survivor's hope—the optimistic sense that cancer could not take him, no matter what the doctors were saying. He was surprisingly forthcoming about his connections to the underworld, but he would not elaborate on his testimony at Kris's trial.

Geddes maintained his party lifestyle almost until the day he died in 2011. Ken continued to trawl around Jamaica. Churchill Neita, a local attorney of repute who had represented Geddes at the trial on weapons charges, had never spoken about his client before, but after Geddes's death he revealed facts that were rather different from the story Geddes had relayed to the jury in Miami a quarter century earlier. It was not just a matter of a bullet or two in his suitcase. Geddes had been arrested at the Norman Manley International Airport in Kingston with several guns, plenty of ammunition, and a silencer. The lawyer said Geddes was facing a long stretch in jail. As Neita understood it, Geddes had a contact in customs who was going to let him get through with the hardware, but the man got cold feet. Neita said Geddes was mixed up in something much bigger than just the gun charges, but his client pleaded guilty, and instead of being given a custodial sentence, he was simply fined—largely due to the intervention of the American prosecutors.

While Geddes was alive, it had been impossible to get information about him from any member of the Shower Posse, past or present, but with his death the doors began to open. A veteran gang member who went by the name Cowboy[5] was shocked to learn that Geddes had been a witness for the state. He said that if he'd known, he would have "paged" Geddes—in Posse argot, this word covers anything from a strong reproach to causing serious physical injury. Cowboy could not understand how a man who was considered a "hard rock" could switch and become a "stool pigeon." He said there was no way his old friend would have done it unless someone had a hold on him. Thinking back over their long association, he wondered aloud whether Geddes had been involved in importing drugs into America, and guns back to Jamaica.

Ken then tracked down Peanut, a Posse "legend" who by his own admission had been involved in "a lot of things" over the years. Peanut, Geddes, and various Posse dons would regularly go clubbing at two bars in Kingston, Epiphany and Exodus. In the 1990s the police had wanted Peanut "dead or alive," and that normally meant dead. Extrajudicial killings were just a lot quicker than trials. But Geddes had arranged a meeting with the senior superintendent of police; Peanut was held for forty-eight hours and then was released. Peanut described how Geddes had achieved the same thing for Bya Mitchell in the 1970s, albeit after hiding his gangster friend at home for a year.

Peanut agreed that the guns Geddes brought into the country were likely for the Posse, but he declined to go into further detail. He said he had always assumed that Geddes had "bought out of the case"—local slang for paying off the relevant officials. He was shocked to learn that his old friend had testified for the prosecution. He never thought that a man like Geddes would go to "Babylon" (a euphemism for the government). He was even firmer than Cowboy: if the Posse crowd knew Geddes worked the other side, he would have ended up dead. Peanut thought the feds must have had a hold over him.

Meanwhile, if we wanted to know the links between Jamaica and South Florida, a good place to start was John Hodgson, a radio presenter at station WAVS, who goes under the name " John T. " Hodgson knew Geddes from the early days, when Geddes was a journalist and he was a Jamaican police officer. They would go drinking together in Tivoli Gardens. Hodgson met many of the Shower Posse's dons through Geddes—Carl "Bya" Mitchell, Claudius Massop, and Posse hitman Lester Lloyd Coke, aka "Jim Brown."

Ken talked to Hodgson, and the radio host said he had met Kris Maharaj on a number of occasions as well. They would run into each other at the Carib 420 Club. When he'd heard about the murders, he'd been shocked; the story did not fit with the man he knew. He told Ken that Geddes later told him he'd testified against Kris because he was afraid he'd end up in the dock himself: the prosecutors told him he would have to testify or face being charged with conspiracy to murder. Despite being a "hard core" man, Hodgson said, Geddes had a mortal fear of jail. Hodgson also thought the prosecutors must have known about Geddes's involvement with Carl Mitchell's gang, running drugs into the United States and guns back to Jamaica.

I wondered at it all. It suggested that our speculation was correct, and that the authorities knew Geddes was part of a Jamaican crime ring. That would have upped the ante for Geddes considerably. That a silencer had been involved in the gun charges was particularly significant, since it would certainly imply criminality.

As Ken relayed information to me back in London, I felt we were edging toward a fuller picture of Geddes and his motivation, but we weren't there yet. I hoped against hope that his conscience had got the better of him before he died, and he'd made a confession to someone close to him. Under the rules of hearsay, a so-called "dying declaration," a statement made by someone who knows he is close to death, is admissible. If he had made a deathbed confession that he had lied at the trial, that could really help Kris's quest for justice.

Not long afterward, Ken managed to track down Tino Geddes's brother David at the Jamaica Water Board, where he worked. The two brothers had been close, and David knew intimate details of Tino's life. Ken asked whether any pressures had been weighing down on Tino that might have persuaded him to change his statement about the murders.

"Yes," David replied simply. Initially, he would not elaborate. Ken pressed him, reminding him that it could do Tino no harm now, but an innocent man was in prison in Florida. David thought about it and went a little further at a second meeting. He explained that his brother had testified against Kris because he had been told by the prosecutors that if he did not, he would be on trial himself. Then David clammed up again.

"What was Tino mixed up in?" Ken asked.

"My brother was always mixed up in things," David said evasively.

"Well, there's mixed up and then there's mixed up."

"My brother knew a lot of people especially in the garrison areas," he said, referring to the Shower Posse's stronghold.

"What criminal activity was he mixed up in?"

"I don't see what the relevance is of that," David replied testily.

"If the prosecutors had known it, they could have used it to make him come testify."

"I don't know what they knew and didn't know," David said. "I was told certain things by my brother in confidence, and I'm not going to reveal them even after he's dead."

He would go no further. It was bitterly disappointing. David did concede that Kris's case had affected his brother badly. When Tino came back to Jamaica, he had gone into a depression and was taking medication for it. "He was having nightmares," he said. His family saw a man who was deeply traumatized. Tino told them about his alcohol abuse, his abuse of prescription drugs, and the nightmares that plagued him. He told them he felt he was being watched. With others—especially those in the Shower Posse—he insisted he was strong and loyal, giving no hint that he had become a stooge for the prosecution. As a journalist, Geddes was used to juggling stories. That was his talent.

Uncovering Geddes's links with the Jamaican Shower Posse and unearthing the facts surrounding the weapons charge were both significant breakthroughs. Geddes clearly had had a great deal to fear, both from the Jamaican prosecutors and from the drug trade. The Posse had close connections with the Colombian cartels. They did a lot of business together, and while there was never much trust among drug lords, they knew they had common enemies: the DEA, prosecutors, and snitches. But was Geddes an "authorized snitch," giving out a story he had been encouraged to tell by the lords of the drug domain? Had Geddes received a visit from a middleman who was eager that Kris should be the fall guy for the Moo Youngs' murders?

Tino Geddes carried many secrets with him to his grave. And yet if people began to talk so soon after his funeral, there remains hope that we will learn more in due course. Tino lived life to the fullest and was close to many people in his community. While witnesses sometimes do speak ill of the dead, they are unlikely to do so while the funeral eulogies still hang in the air. In time, perhaps they will come to see that helping the living is more important than worrying about the dead.

I hope Ken will be able to find out more in Jamaica. And who knows whether something will bubble up from Colombia? Some big names from the drug business are currently in federal prison, and perhaps one will start talking.

I also wonder about the police. The Miami-Dade Police Department was clearly eaten through with corruption in the mid-1980s. Plenty of players are now in prison, with less to lose by being forthright. Someone out there knows precisely why the Moo Youngs were murdered, and who did it. But will Kris still be alive by the time we find out?

Regardless, we cannot give up on Kris.

Epilogue

For a quarter century now, prison guards have dictated what cell Kris Maharaj inhabits, and when he can eat and shower and brush his teeth. He has been allowed a maximum of a few hours a week with his wife, when she can travel to see him. When he is seriously ill, prison administrators tell him when he can (and cannot) see a doctor.

Meanwhile, my own work has changed a lot. I've been working on blasphemy cases in Pakistan, where you can be executed for saying something disrespectful about the Prophet Muhammad; I've worked on mandatory death penalty cases, trying to help prisoners accused of carrying small quantities of drugs across Asia; and I have represented detainees at Guantánamo Bay. More recently, I have been obsessed with challenging the use of Predator drones to rain Hellfire missiles on people in Pakistan. The CIA calls each victim a "bugsplat."

I have not given up on Kris. The law has let him down, and I can't escape the feeling that ultimately I have, too. In all of my years representing prisoners on death row, his has been my most frustrating case.

It is August 2011, and I'm headed to Florida. I have made arrangements to visit Kris for the first time in a while. Though we are in frequent communication through Marita, ever more months seem to pass between each visit to Kris in prison. I am keen to update my client about progress on our ongoing investigation in Jamaica. Marita tells me that he has been seriously ill. He is seventy-two, and I worry that if and when our investigation bears fruit, it will be too late.

I arrive in Fort Lauderdale late in the evening. Marita pours me a drink, and we sit in her small living room, talking. She tells me that she was burgled a few weeks back. It was early afternoon, and she had stepped out briefly. Someone must have been observing her house. Her eighty-year-old neighbor saw two well-dressed young men at the door and assumed they were guests. They broke in through the dining room window, opened up the front door, and started loading their car.

When she returned home, Marita was heartbroken. On her four-teenth birthday, in 1953, her father gave her a gold bracelet that had belonged to her grandmother. For more than fifty years, she wore it almost every day. As she was heading out, she noticed she had forgotten it, and she nearly went back. Now it has been stolen, along with a five-year-old computer that contained all the files she held for Kris. The machine was ancient in computing terms, worth little to the thieves, but it was her only contact to the outside world. Perhaps, Marita reflects, she was lucky. Her neighbor's appearance on the scene may have scared the men off before they took the last of her possessions.

Marita has visited Kris almost every Saturday, fifty-two weeks a year, for a quarter century. That's more than thirteen hundred weekends, and she's hardly missed one. Recently, Kris has been allowed to call her every evening for a maximum of fifteen minutes. He never uses the whole time, she says. He doesn't want to be cut off, to be told by a guard to end the call. And there are other prisoners to think of, since there are only two phones for forty-six men. Still, the phone calls are their lifeline.

But then in June 2011, suddenly . . . nothing. The telephone sat on her bedside table, silent. Marita called the prison. Initially she was told only that Kris was sick.

"What's wrong with him?" she asked.

"We cannot tell you," she was told.

"Where is he?" she demanded to know.

"We cannot say," she was told. Security.

This brave woman who has stuck by her man for a quarter century was not allowed to know whether he was dying or just had a cold.

In the wake of the burglary, friends bought her a new computer. She contacted us in England with her concerns about Kris and his health. When I got her e-mail, I was consumed by another crisis—we had two months from start to finish to try to stave off Mark Ströman's execution in Texas, and I had little time for anything else. When he was finally executed, I was fit for nothing. I had to quit the world for a while.

For several weeks Marita had no idea how ill Kris actually was. Finally a prison staffer let it slip—he was at the Kendall hospital with bacteria eating the flesh off his leg. But even then the authorities would tell Marita nothing about her husband's condition. And according to someone's uncivilized rules, she was not allowed to visit him.

As she pours out the story of how difficult it has all been, I think of a capital case Reprieve is working on in Yemen: Sharif Mobley, an American, was shot while he was being arrested by the security service in Sana'a. He vanished. His wife had no idea where he was. Eventually we learned he had been in a hospital run by a German company. Pressure applied back in Berlin got us a few meager details: there was a secret ward where Sharif was labeled "Prisoner X." We derided President Saleh and his totalitarian regime. Yet here, in metropolitan Miami, the State of Florida has "disappeared" Kris for ten weeks.

As his lawyer, I was the only one who could get in to see Kris, and then only if it was an emergency. Sitting on the sofa opposite Marita, I feel a surge of guilt that I hadn't come sooner. Marita has shed so many tears that she looks utterly drained.

I am up the next morning at six, bleary with jet lag. Marita sits across the breakfast table from me, reliving her fond memories of life in Britain, with toast and Robertson's Original English thick-cut marmalade. I drive away from her house in my rental car, promising to report back as soon as I emerge from the visit. I arrive at the hospital far too early, but I do not want to be late. Kris has waited a long time.

I park at the Kendall Regional Medical Facility. It takes me a while to settle on a space, as there are signs that threaten to tow unauthorized vehicles but give no indication of which places might be authorized for visitors. The front desk looks like that of any other hospital, but when I announce the purpose of my visit, the receptionist summons three burly corrections officers, who lead me through several security doors into the prison section of the hospital. One guard takes me to a bed, but Kris is not there. He must have been moved. We circle around a dozen cubicles, each with a hospital gurney, each open at the front so that the guard in the center can observe them all. The patients are all old men, lying prone. One has a bandage wrapped around his head. Most look close to death.

The guard points at another bed. For a moment, I wonder whether it can be Kris. The man is clearly asleep, quietly snoring, his mouth open wide to the ceiling. He has a beard, something I have never seen on Kris. But then I realize it is my client. The guard asks what to do. I reply that I am sure Kris won't mind me waking him. I gently press his shoulder. He opens his eyes. He is confused. He tells me later that nobody told him I was coming. For ten weeks he has not had any contact with the outside world.

I think of the vigorous man I first met in 1994. I sometimes wonder at the gray hair those years have put on me, but they are nothing compared to Kris's decline. His hair is very thin now, though the gray beard has come in full. One of his lower teeth is missing—if he were free, he'd have the dental work completed; as it is, he just has a gap. He is breathing with a little difficulty, so I move the oxygen tube until it reaches him. It doesn't fit properly, so I can get only one jet into his nose. At the foot of the bed, a fancy electronic readout purports to tell his weight and monitor various vital signs. It is obviously not working, as it weighs him in at 200 pounds: he was 180 when he arrived at the hospital and can't be more than 160 after weeks of barely eating.

Kris is uncomfortable and wriggles. He needs to move his foot, but when I lift up the sheet, I see that he is shackled to the bed. His left ankle, so emaciated, is wrapped in bandages to limit the chafing. It makes me angry to see this. Here is a man who is barely alive, who cannot walk and is surrounded by half a dozen guards, behind several locked doors, chained down. What is the point? Wilfred Owen's poem "Futility" intrudes on my mind: "Was it for this the clay grew tall?" The toenails on Kris's right foot are crumbling, fragmented, orange, like the sandstone that collapses to the foot of the cliffs near my home. On the inner shin there is a foot-long gouge where the bacteria have been scraped away. It is currently taped up, with a tube dripping antibiotics directly into it.

"My God! I am glad to see you!" Kris exclaims. He leans back in momentary pain, closing his eyes again briefly. A tear runs trembling down the side of his eyelid.

It's been ten weeks, I think to myself.

"I asked to see you, my lawyer," he says. "They said no lawyer, I couldn't even write. I asked to see the British consul, they said no consul. I asked to see Marita. No visit from my wife. Paper. No. Television—just to watch the news. No. Letters. No. Writing letters. No. Books. No. The only thing except the Bible I can have is some Christian thing, something written in 1994."

1994? I wonder, abstractly, at his mention of a date. *Would not 1984 have been more appropriate?*

The neon strip lighting above the bed is his only companion. I am concerned at the flickering and ask whether it is affecting him. Kris says it's all right, that's the least of his concerns.

"For weeks, I cried," he admits uncharacteristically. He does not willingly share emotion. "I felt like they put me here as the final act to kill me. Back in the prison, I was in South Unit. There were forty-six people in the dorm, and they put me in bunk 2106. The last two people who'd had that bed had had an infection. The man next to me, only three feet away, had an infection, too. It came on all of a sudden, one morning, June first, I think. I asked to see medical."

The prison doctor came and looked at him. She recognized the problem at once: a flesh-eating bacteria with the alarming name *necrotizing fasciitis,* and said he'd need surgery right away. They took him to the Kendall hospital. They treated the move like a presidential trip to Afghanistan, as if someone might attack the prison van at any moment. Kris was unconscious for most of the first few days on the ward and is not sure whether the operation was June 1 or 2. Since the initial operation, the hospital staff have been opening the wound up every two days to clean it out.

At one point, the surgeon said they might have to amputate. "I nearly gave up. When the doctor said she might have to take my leg off, I nearly gave up," Kris says, grimacing in pain once more. "I prayed that they would save my leg. It was like an elephant's. But I want to be able to walk normally when I get back home to England. I'd never been in hospital before I was in prison. Not as a patient, though I'd visited a few people there. But here, it's two hours of begging for a cup of water before a nurse will bring it. One of them said she'd slap me if I complained. Slap me!"

By and large the nurses seem to like him more than the other prisoners on the ward. It makes me wonder how the other prisoners get on. Kris does not complain much, and he is unfailingly polite to everyone.

A nurse interrupts. Kris has pointed her out as one of the difficult ones, but she is civil enough with me there. She injects him with his four-hourly painkiller, and it eases his discomfort. She also checks his blood sugar, which is just within normal limits.

Sometimes, Kris says, the nurses have shown some kindness. "Yesterday the nurse made me sit up on the side of the bed," he explains. This was the first experiment in physiotherapy. "It made me feel like a human being for the first time in weeks."

Did they take the shackle off his leg for that? I ask. "No, no!" he exclaims, surprised I would think anything so foolish. Letting him sit on the side of the bed in chains once in ten weeks hardly defines human kindness, I think, but I keep my opinion to myself.

Kris is due for a skin graft on the leg today, at three o'clock. I agree to be gone by then to speed his chances of recovery. He has not been able to eat or even drink water, in preparation for the operation, which worries me. I know I wouldn't be able to talk for four hours without a sip of water. Kris is not bothered. He's just happy to have the chance to talk at all. One of the female guards provides him with two cold flannels to mop his face.

I try to do most of the talking for an hour or so. I fill him in with messages from Marita, catch him up on world events, and update him on our investigation into his case. But our conversation doesn't get far before he starts insisting, as he does on every visit, that he did not do it. He does not have to win me over, but he knows he still has to convince the world, and there is frustration in his voice.

"I didn't kill the Moo Youngs," he begins, as he always does. "I didn't pay someone to kill them, I didn't do a bloody thing. What I'm saying is not ninety-nine percent true; it's one hundred percent."

Kris has had a quarter century to try to puzzle out what happened in room 1215 of the DuPont Plaza on October 16, 1986. He's shared his theory before, and I suspect he is right. "I was meant to be dead that day. I would have been another body in the room. They would have killed me, too, to make it look like I killed the Moo Youngs and then committed suicide when I realized what I had done. They'd have left the gun in my hand." It seems as if the Moo Youngs were late for the rescheduled meeting.

"Neville Butler tried to make me stay," he says. "But I wouldn't. I had another appointment. I don't like to be late for appointments, so I insisted. I had to go."

After a while, I worry that I'm not going to be able to think of enough things to say to fill the four hours. I'm not very good at just talking, but I want to stay the full time available to me, and Kris has no intention of letting me go early. The kinder of the guards takes me out to the toilet— you have to go through the prison doors—and that gives me a moment to remember how to keep Kris chattering happily for hours. I can't have been thinking straight. It's the jet lag. All I have to do is get him to tell a few stories about how he outmaneuvered a business rival.

When I go back into the ward, the guard asks if I would like some coffee. I hate to drink it while my client is barred from a sip of water, but Kris insists, and I am grateful. Tiredness is catching up. I start on a large cup as Kris takes us back to when he was fifteen, in Trinidad in 1954. It was his first employment outside the family shop, at a car dealership. All the other salesmen were in their thirties and forties. When Kris applied for a job, the owner initially sneered, but eventually he took him on a three-month trial, no salary, just a promise of a 5 percent commission.

"The other salesmen were given their own car, a basic two hundred dollars a month, and a two percent commission on top," Kris recalled. But he went to a family friend, a banker who acquired cars for a large corporation. Kris gave him a good price, expecting several sales, and cut him in for 2 percent for each car sold. "In the first month, I took in fourteen hundred dollars. The other salesmen were angry. I was making a lot more than them, and I only just started." In the second month, Kris promised the receptionist her own 2 percent on any calls that came into the dealership that resulted in a sale. He sold even more and made $2,000—a fortune for 1955.

"I've never had one week of unemployment in my life," Kris says. It's a work ethic that was drilled into him by his father. "When I first got to England, I went down to the Labour Exchange for five weeks looking for work. They said I could get ten pounds a week on the dole, but I refused. I didn't want something for nothing."

Kris tells me the story—for the tenth time—about his stallion, King Levenstall, and how he beat the queen's horse, Parnell, at Royal Ascot. I like to see him removed from his current situation, but my attention wanders a little from stories of the past to the grim present. Kris's universe is daubed in grimy orange-yellow paint. There are no pictures hanging on any wall. There is a small closet behind me, which I take to be a toilet that I am not allowed to use, and Kris cannot get to. I adjust the pillow behind his head, and he shifts in pain again. I notice that there is no sound from any of the other beds. No movement either. It is as if they have all been drugged into oblivion—perhaps the kinder alternative.

Kris drifts back to his case.

"I didn't believe they were serious about having me killed until after the trial," he says. "When I got up in the morning after I was sentenced, I felt it was my last day on this planet. I felt I had lost my mind. I thought I may as well be dead."

I tell him again that I would like to talk to the jurors, but I cannot, unless they come forward. "The jurors had their minds poisoned by the prosecutors," Kris says. He does not blame the twelve people who condemned him. He sees their verdict as almost inevitable, given what he has learned about the process. "In a way I think the death penalty is more humane than what I have suffered. Many days I have woken up saying to God, take me home. It's only because of Marita that I am still here.

"My advice to jurors in future is that they need to demand the facts," he says. "Don't accept it if you're not told. And you've got to be sure beyond a shadow of a doubt."

It's been a long time, almost twenty years, since we first met. When we get to talking, Kris and I are comfortable, like an old couple. We can discuss difficult things. I ask him about the impact that a quarter of a century behind bars has had on him.

"What have I missed? My wife. My freedom. But what is freedom? To me, it would have been the chance to open up a few more businesses. To try to help people have some jobs they need, jobs they like."

I ask him whether he would have done other things—travel, maybe get involved in sports. He reminisces briefly about his passion for cricket. "But I probably wouldn't have played cricket again if I'd been freed. It would have been going backward, and I don't go backward. Besides, I always want to be the best at what I do, and I wouldn't have been the best at cricket.

"I'd like to have taken Marita traveling. I always wanted to go to Red Square in Moscow, because I read about it as a child. I was planning to go there once, but the *News of the World* ran a story just before I was about to leave. Some British businessman had been arrested for spying. That was enough for me." Kris can never stay long on the subject of what might have been. He prefers to paint a picture of what is to come. "I'd like to take Marita to South Africa. I wouldn't go when there was apartheid. But I'd like to see Nelson Mandela." He repeats an old story about how Larry Constantine, a famous cricketer and a member of Britain's House of Lords, persuaded him to give a large donation to Mandela's defense fund, back when the South African leader was imprisoned by the apartheid regime on Robben Island. He gave the money simply to please his friend. Back then, he says, he was very naïve about prison, and he would have assumed that Mandela was probably guilty.

Kris and Marita married in 1976. "We went to Paris after we got married. I never spoke French, but I loved Paris," Kris recalls. As usual, it is almost impossible for him to reminisce without reverting to a business opportunity. "I went there one other time, went to La Coupole, the famous restaurant on Boulevard Montparnasse. I'd taken someone there, a business contact, and he ordered something fancy. I just wanted something I knew. I saw this thing on the menu called Pied au Porc. I thought that meant pork pie, so I ordered it. The waiter came up with a big tray, and it had two pig trotters on it. I tried to send it back. That wasn't what

I ordered. But he explained to me that it was. I was shocked. Here was this expensive dish, and I was selling pig trotters in Africa for two shillings each at the time. It was done in white wine, with butter beans, it was delicious. I took the recipe home with me. Dorothy from Jamaica was our housekeeper at the time. She was a wonderful cook, and she used to do it after that."

There is certainly one difference between today and my early meetings with Kris: whenever he finishes a story about a business deal now, he will always turn back to his wife.

"Between you and me and God," he says, looking up at the neon lights, "I didn't expect her to stay with me. She was beautiful, educated, speaks six languages. I thought she would move on. But she didn't. 'You're the man I married,' she said. 'I agreed till death us do part.' Not one in a million women would have stayed through all this."

He is reflective again. I wonder if this unburdening—rare for him—is provoked by his most recent close encounter with death. "Perhaps I can fool you, and perhaps you can fool me, but we can't fool God. And I have to be honest. If this had happened to Marita back in 1986, would I have stuck by her like she did me? The straight answer is no. I would have paid whatever it took, given her money. But I'd not have stuck by her all these years. Now it's different, and that's one thing I've learned. Now, if she needed a heart transplant, I'd give her mine. Not a second thought. May God take me home before her, that's all I want. Don't leave me on this earth without her."

Kris and Marita have not been able to pass a single word in the past ten weeks. He asks me to take a message back to her. "I love you till the day I die. I've been crying for you until today, when I learned that you were okay. I miss your voice every night, but I look forward to being out of here soon, so I can see you every Saturday."

I ask Kris what keeps him going, when he can't do anything in the hospital. He responds by quoting Psalm 23, the entire thing from memory. " 'Surely goodness, mercy and love shall follow me all the days of my life,' " he intones. I look at the grubby wall again and wonder.

We talk about how things have changed for him since we met back in 1994. "Well," he begins, with a slight hesitation, "I suppose you could say I've lost my hair. Right now I feel like I've lost my brain. Here in this hospital bed I'm ruined completely." He pauses briefly again, before the true Kris reappears. "But I'll get it back. I'll get it back. I'm not afraid of this. They've tried to kill me for twenty-five years. I can't allow them to finish killing me."

I tell him I have to leave soon. He looks up at me. "When you get up in the morning, just remember me and Marita. Remember we're suffering."

He wants to return to the South Unit, at the prison, where there is a three-mile concrete track. Now that he is in a different institution, with other old men for prisoners, at last Kris is willing to go outside. The rules are less strict. Kris is already planning how he will use his wheelchair as part of his rehabilitation. On a good day, he hopes for eight hours outside, even in the South Florida heat. He describes the regime he has in mind. Perhaps a mile in the chair, to strengthen his arms; followed by a mile behind the chair, using it as a walker; then another mile in the chair, followed by another mile behind the chair.

"I can't allow them to finish killing me," he says again. "I want to be the best bloody wheelchair man in the whole place."

ACKNOWLEDGMENTS

First I must acknowledge that this book is about a case in which I have thus far failed. Kris Maharaj remains in prison, and while I've tried to show how the justice system is designed to let people like Kris down, what matters most to me is that he be freed before he dies.

Therefore, in acknowledging failure, I must also ask for help—first and foremost for the help of those who have yet to come forward and tell us what really happened in this case. Justice for Kris Maharaj will never be achieved if we don't hear from you. You may have heard someone talking about the case. You may have access to the records that with a few keystrokes would show the historical connections behind the murder. You may know the people described in these pages. It's not too late and it won't be while Kris is alive. Everyone now knows that Miami was riddled with Colombian cartel corruption in the 1980s, but we are not asking you to bring down any institutions—legal or otherwise—with the information you may have. We just need to know who knew what when the Moo Youngs were murdered.

Anyone who has information that might relate to the case in some way, however seemingly distant, can write to me at clive@reprieve .org.uk, or contact me at *Reprieve*, PO Box 52742, London EC4P 4WS; phone: +44 (0)20 7353 4640.

The case also needs funding. Kris is in prison in part because we have never had the money needed for a full investigation. This case spans continents. We need cash for airfares, gas, accommodation, copies of old files that might contain the key to the case—the list goes on and on. To date, the investigation and litigation have cost tens of thousands of dollars in direct costs, as well as tens of thousands of hours of pro bono work. Yet the battle is far from over.

I must also acknowledge that the publication of this book is going to magnify the pain experienced by the victims' family. They have been told that Kris Maharaj killed Derrick and Duane Moo Young, and they believe this. The justice system left them awaiting the "closure" of an execution for many years, and now all they are told to hope for is that Kris never leaves prison. This book may stir up more questions, and dredge up additional anguish for the family. For this, I am truly sorry, but I must also beg the family to consider, in light of the evidence presented in these pages, whether their certainty that the right person is in prison for this crime is not misplaced, and whether they remember anything about Derrick's and Duane's business activities in the months before they were killed that might suggest someone other than Kris Maharaj had a motive to see them murdered.

With these grim but necessary acknowledgements made, there comes the happier task of recognizing the extraordinary work of Kris's dedicated but entirely ad hoc defense team.

For reasons of space, the impression this book leaves is that I somehow did all of the work on Kris's case myself. But I want to undo that impression here, as it is false. It has been a challenge to find a sufficiently clear narrative in the maelstrom of facts that surround the murder of the Moo Youngs to make a readable book, and it would have been too distracting for the reader to introduce each person who has worked on this case at the appropriate moment in the text. But these people are legion. If you have worked on this case but are not listed here, please forgive me, but a quarter of a century is a long time.

The state has never provided Kris Maharaj with the resources required to bring his claim of innocence fairly before the courts, and he has never had more than the part-time assistance of a motley crew of overworked volunteers, but they have all done their damnedest to make the courts see that a terrible mistake has occurred.

White-collar criminal defense lawyer Ben Kuehne, his law partner Susan Dimitrovsky, and others in Ben's law firm have been lynchpins in this case. Ben signed on to help for a reduced fee on one element of the appeal nineteen years ago, and has remained loyal to the cause ever since, though he was never paid again.

The UK law firm Freshfields Bruckhaus Derringer has acted as British liaison on the case for almost as long. I'll mention by name Paul Lomas, Clarissa O'Callaghan, Malindi Durrant, Florence Brocklesby, Patrick Doris, Peter Turner, and Mark Boyle, but there were many others at the firm who dedicated their time to this case on a purely pro bono basis. Most recently, Paul and Clarissa had the task of pleading for clemency for Kris in Tallahassee; tragically, their plea was rejected by an unreceptive governor and his panel.

I was director of the Louisiana Crisis Assistance Center in New Orleans for eleven years, and during that period many of the staff and volunteers there dedicated their "spare" time and effort to this case. Richard Bourke, Frieda Brown, Chris Eades, Joe Hingston, Malkia Johnson, 'Mwalimi Johnson, 'Mlinata Johnson, Shauneen Lambe, Simone Leijon, Dale Long, Beth O'Reilly, Lynne Overman, Gary Proctor, Bart Stapert, and Kim Watts all somehow squeezed time for Kris into their already full caseloads, poring over the documentary evidence, tracking down witnesses and records, working overnight to get exhibits ready for hearings, liaising with British government officials, and generally keeping alive a man whom the State of Florida would much rather have seen dead.

Ron Petrillo, the investigator originally hired by Kris's trial lawyer, has refused to let this case die, and has made himself available to every subsequent investigator, lawyer, and journalist who has attempted to retrace his footsteps. He remains convinced to this day that the wrong person is in prison for this crime. Another South Florida private investigator with an Achilles heel for wrongful-conviction cases has provided vital local advice and assistance on Kris's case more recently, at considerable cost to his solo practice.

Sir Peter Bottomley has been the most dedicated of the British parliamentarians to support Kris, although a hundred others signed onto Kris's brief before the Florida Supreme Court. Barristers have come out from the UK to Florida to help on the case, including Geoffrey Robertson QC and Philip Sapsford QC. And I am grateful to various journalists who have brought the case to public attention, including (but not limited to) Tim Samuels and Ian Katz.

Since I returned to the UK in 2004 to work with the charity *Reprieve* (www.reprieve.org.uk), staff on the death penalty team there have all pitched in to support Kris and Marita, including Zachary Katznelson, Marc Callcutt, Caroline Morten, Clare Algar, and Fatou Kane. Most recently, Chris Chang has the taken on the investigation, assisted by Chinua Brown, operating on a shoestring budget but achieving results that are deeply disturbing for anyone who thinks the Florida criminal justice system generally gets it right.

Other friends, troubled by Kris's story, have helped out in other ways, including Sue Carpenter, Ben Rich (and his colleagues at Luther Pendragon), as well as Kris's old friends Thelma and Tom Wade. I am particularly grateful to the two anonymous benefactors who have helped Marita survive and support her husband, under particularly dire circumstances.

I also wish to thank the many consular officials at the Foreign & Commonwealth Office (FCO) who have had contact with Kris and Marita over the years. When this case began, the UK had a rather lackluster policy on helping Britons facing the death penalty—and Kris suffered specifically because of this absence of support. However, much has changed, and today's FCO is vastly more proactive. This has been a very positive evolution that has received too little recognition; long may it continue to develop.

When it comes to the book, my thanks to my agent, Patrick Walsh, for his constant encouragement, along with everyone at Conville & Walsh; and to Joy de Menil at Viking, whose vigor with the red pen subjected me to the kind of editing I have often longed for (and always needed). I am also grateful to the team at Viking, especially Christopher Russell.

A thank-you to my mother, Jean, who proofread the book, and to my wife, Emily Bolton, who has worked on the case for many years, and has helped shape both the litigation and the writing.

NOTES

Preface

1. Ernst van den Haag, "The Ultimate Penalty: A Defense," *Harvard Law Review* (1986), n12, at http://www.pbs.org/wgbh/pages/frontline/angel/procon/haagarticle.html.

2. Of course, much more fundamental questions could be asked about judicial systems generally, such as why we imprison people for crimes, what motivates us to designate only certain acts as criminal, and so forth. Although they are important, there is not room to debate them in this book, which is a discussion of how the American system does or does not work in actual practice.

Chapter 1: The Trial

1. I have taken the prosecutor's comments essentially verbatim from the prosecution's opening statement in the trial. *State v. Maharaj*, No.86-030610 (Dade County Circuit Court), Transcript at 2151–76. I have added minor matters necessary to a full understanding of the case (e.g., the location of the DuPont Plaza Hotel—in Miami) for those to whom this would not be immediately obvious. And I have done what all trial lawyers wish court reporters would do—fix basic grammar in a few places where the speaker lost his way.

2. Joanne Green, "British Ex-Millionaire Fights for Freedom: Krishna Maharaj Went from the High Life to a Life Sentence—For a Crime He Might Not Have Committed," *Miami Times*, September 27, 2007.

3. The indictment originally contained two other counts that were not submitted to the jury. One involved the alleged kidnapping of Neville Butler, which the prosecution chose to dismiss when Butler changed his story. The other was a burglary count, which the prosecution also withdrew.

Chapter 3: The Defendant

1. See *Maharaj v. State*, 597 So. 2d 786 (Fla. 1992).

2. The Florida Department of Corrections photograph of Kris reflects how he looked when I first met him.

3. See "Death Row Fact Sheet: The Daily Routine of Death Row Inmates," Florida Department of Corrections: "Inmates may receive mail every day except holidays and weekends. They may have cigarettes, snacks, radios and 13-inch televisions in their cells. They do not have cable television or air-conditioning and they are not allowed to be with each other in a common room. They can watch church services on closed circuit television. While on Death Watch, inmates may have radios and televisions positioned outside their cell bars."

4. Kris's battle is discussed in Gordon Myers, *Banana Wars: The Price of Free Trade: A Caribbean Perspective* (London: Zed Books, 2004).

5. "Cockfield Defeated in Green Bananas Trade Battle," *Daily Telegraph* (March 5, 1983), 3.

6. Surprisingly perhaps, Britain has been the largest foreign investor in the United States consistently since 1803 (when it took over from the Dutch). See "Foreign Investment in the United States," *Gale Encyclopedia of US History*. During the 1980s, British investment in the United States rose from $11.3 billion to a staggering $119.1 billion. See Joseph A. Grundfest, "Internationalization of the World's Securities Markets," in Marvin H. Kosters and Allan H. Meltzer, eds., *International Competitiveness in Financial Circles* (Norwell, Mass.: Kluwer Academic, 1991), 355–56.

7. I am obviously bound by legal privilege not to reveal the identity of this person. Suffice it to say that this individual had serious mental health issues; likely he believed what he said to me, even though I found his denial implausible.

8. The issue of the alibi is discussed in much greater detail later in Chapter 8.

9. This is not always true. As we will see in Chapter 5, in the case of Shareef Cousin, a dedicated prosecutor may overcome even the most ironclad alibi.

10. The "guilty" person is of much greater assistance. His help is unlikely to get him an undeserved acquittal but culpability comes in a thousand shades, and where a witness exaggerates or falsifies his testimony to enhance the prosecution's case, the defendant may be able to warn the lawyer.

11. My longer conversations with him came when he volunteered to be a witness for Kris at his resentencing trial in 2002.

12. See Florida Department of Corrections, "Execution List (1976–present)".

Chapter 4: The Witness

1. Ben Kuehne remains a very fine lawyer in private practice, perhaps best known for his involvement in the case where Al Gore and the Democratic Party were pitted against the Republicans in the famous Florida "hanging chads" litigation that ultimately resolved the presidential election in 2000. George W. Bush prevailed in a narrow and arguably ideological decision in the Supreme Court: *Bush v. Gore*, 531 U.S. 98 (2000).

2. Butler's continual confusion concerning whether Kris accused him of involvement in the extortion plots may just illustrate the truth of the adage attributed to Winston Churchill: "If you tell the truth the first time, you don't have to remember what you said." Throughout his testimony before the jury, Butler's story leaped from one version to the next. One time he said Kris "never did express concern that I . . . knew anything about it," directly contradicting his earlier story. But later he changed again: "And indeed at some time later on, he said to me he thought I was involved . . . because in fact, my name was the one being used in Trinidad as having been behind the extortion. He told me that on a number of occasions." *Trial Transcript*, at 2759. He had been similarly inconsistent in his pretrial deposition, where somehow his involvement hinged on whether the name Butler was easier to remember than Carberry. See *Second Deposition of Neville Butler* at 12 (March 30, 1987, 14:15pm) (108911-983): "He [Kris] never said that he knew that I contributed. But the fact that my name was much more easier to remember than Carberry, and I believe his people in Trinidad told him Butler was suppose to come, and he sort of tied Butler because he know I worked for the *Echo* and the assumption was drawn at that point that I did all the talking on the telephone or I wrote the articles." Compare ibid., 9–10: "He felt all along that I may have been part of it, but after meeting with me and getting to know me that three or four weeks, he was satisfied that I had no participation in the extortion." Bizarrely, in his deposition, Butler admitted that he actually had been involved in the extortion: "Calls had been made from my home." Ibid., 11. Supposedly, Kris complained that "they had extorted from his uncle [Ramsook] $160,000 using my name and that it would be in my best interest to assist him to set up this meeting." Ibid., 9. It was all very muddled, something that Kris's lawyer should have hammered home to the jury.

3. Even at trial, Butler was not able to maintain consistency about who Kris Maharaj supposedly wanted to meet—Moo Young or Carberry. "He kept saying, well, Carberry is involved in it and I think I would like to meet with him, and if you would help me set up—he couldn't talk to me," Butler explained at one point. "He said that, 'I will have evidence, I will have documents to prove where he received the money, because the money was gotten from some bank.' I think he mentioned the Landmark Bank, and this was the story that he gave me." *Maharaj Trial Transcript* at 2756.

4. Butler remained confused as to whether he and Kris Maharaj were meant to be meeting Eslee Carberry or Derrick Moo Young—a rather crucial point in a murder prosecution, where the state made much of Kris Maharaj's motive to kill Derrick Moo Young. Butler went on to say he had already talked to Derrick Moo Young about some extortions, and Derrick was apparently the one to tell him that his name was linked with the crime: "Before he even suggested that, I tried to speak with Mr. Moo Young and became very concerned what he told me about my name being used in Trinidad as a person who is extorting money from his relatives. The reason I became very concerned, before I came to the United States, I was working with the Prime Minister in Trinidad and Tobago and I was publishing articles and well known and the president and everyone know who I was. And this would be a calamity as far as my name was concerned." *Maharaj Trial Transcript* at 2759.

5. *Maharaj Trial Transcript* at 2758–59. Although Hendon did not discuss this at trial, Butler had previously said that Dames wanted to get some restaurant equipment. See *Initial Deposition of Neville Butler* at 45 (13 January 1987, 15:30–18:30) (108736-860): "We spoke of a specific project, the supplying of items that Eddie Dames may be interested in." See also *Second Deposition of Neville Butler* at 17-18 (March 30, 1987, 14:15pm) (108911-983).

6. Detective Buhrmaster made a statement to this effect himself. "Sometime prior to October 15, 1986," he explained, "a man named Dames . . . had attempted to contact the Moo Youngs to arrange for shipment of equipment he had purchased in the Florida area." *Maharaj 3.850 Clerk Tr. 2446*. Shaula Nagel had likewise told Buhrmaster that "her father had mentioned that he received several messages from a Mr. Dames, who he did not know, and did not bother returning the calls." Ibid., 2453; *Maharaj 3.850 Exhibit OC* at 9.

7. In her initial statement, Rivero seemed very certain—indeed, 100 percent certain—that Kris Maharaj had been the person reserving the room. *Maharaj Record No. 044_105518-525* at 524 (initial sworn statement of Arlene Rivero to John Buhrmaster, March 3, 1987): "Q. You are one hundred percent sure that this was in fact the man? A. Yes." She had been shown only one photograph and had signed the back of it attesting that it was the person. Prior to making the identification, she had given no description of the person—age, height, weight, unique features, and so forth. In other words, it was about as suggestive an identification as one can imagine, and Eric Hendon should have asked the court to exclude it from the trial. As the Supreme Court has held, "suggestive confrontations are disapproved because they increase the likelihood of misidentification, and unnecessarily suggestive ones are condemned for the further reason that the increased chance of misidentification is gratuitous." *Neal v. Biggers*, 409 U.S. 188, 198 (1972).

8. *Maharaj Trial Transcript* at 2724. Rivero testified that the person was five eight, five ten, or taller, thereby including a large proportion of the population. Her colleague Inez Vargas put the man's height at five five, *Maharaj Trial Transcript* at 2658—far from Kris Maharaj but close to Neville Butler. Vargas was another witness who identified Kris as the person who made the reservation. Her identification was much more equivocal from the beginning—she said only "I think that he was the one that made the reservation." *Maharaj Record No. 044_105542-554* at 549 (initial sworn statement of Inez Vargas to John Buhrmaster, March 3, 1987). Again, Buhrmaster had shown her a solitary photo and had taken no prior description of the individual beforehand. Intriguingly, Detective Buhrmaster asked both Rivera and Vargas whether anyone paid them to make sure that nobody else took rooms on the twelfth floor, based on information he had apparently received. Ibid., 105553. This information had never been turned over to the defense, but it would clearly have been helpful, as it would explain that whoever wanted to use room 1215 wanted nobody snooping around. Of course, one room on the floor was permanently occupied—the room across the hall, which was registered to Jaime Vallejo Mejia, from Colombia.

9. In his first police statement, Butler told Buhrmaster he got the room. See *Initial Police Statement of Neville Butler* at 4 (17 October 1986, 00:50 –01:30) (118882-99): "Q. When did you get that room? A. The morning he was due to arrive. Q. And that was Wednesday? A. Wednesday, yes." He repeated this in his first deposition: *Initial Deposition of Neville Butler* at 9 (13 January 1987, 15:30–18:30) (108736-860). Only later did it change.

10. By the time of trial, Butler had elaborated on this story. To cover for all the times he said he had made the reservation, the prosecutors now led Butler to say that he did not know that Maharaj had actually already done it. This time it was John Kastrenakes who was asking the questions—or rather, telling Butler what might have happened. "Did you know [Maharaj] had already registered into the room in the name of Eddie Dames?" Kastrenakes asked. "No, I was not aware of that," said Butler. *Maharaj Trial Transcript* at 27. Kastrenakes drew out of the witness that Kris was in the hotel at the time Butler paid for the room: *Second Deposition of Neville Butler* at 24-25 (March 30, 1987, 14:15pm) (108911-983). But Butler could not keep his story straight. He slipped up and said once again at trial that he had made the reservation: *Maharaj Trial Transcript* at 2767. When the trial was over, and he again had no prompter, he reverted to his original story—that "I had booked a room in his [Dames's] name." *Maharaj 3.850 Exhibit HP*, at 6 (1995 Channel 4 interview with Neville Butler).

11. *Maharaj Trial Transcript* at 2803. It did not make much sense that Derrick would only now be recognizing Butler—in setting up the Dames meeting, Butler would have clearly explained who he was and how they had previously met.

12. Even Patton's guns—originally a pair of Colt revolvers—were not actually white but had white ivory handles. He carried two because in his first taste of violence in 1914, in a punitive foray into Mexico chasing Pancho Villa, he had emptied the only handgun he carried and had never again wanted to be without a backup. He gave one of his pair of Peacemakers away to a Hollywood star who came to the fore in World War II and thereafter substituted a Smith & Wesson .357 Magnum. See Masaad Ayoob, "Why Patton Carried Two Guns," *Guns Magazine*, August 2003.

13. At the first deposition, frustratingly, Hendon had noticed the discrepancy and rubbed in the folly of Butler's effort to explain the change away: "Q: My question to you is what color was the gun? A: Silver or white or something like that was what I saw. Q: Do you recall telling Detective Buhrmaster that the gun was white? A: Well, I am not familiar with guns. I may have said that. Q: Color has nothing to do with guns. I am asking do you recall telling him that the gun was white?" *Maharaj 3.850 Tr. 1455, Initial Deposition of Neville Butler* at 106 (13 January 1987, 15:30–18:30) (108736-860).

14. When he first talked to Detective Buhrmaster, Butler said Kris Maharaj confronted Derrick and Duane Moo Young over money, bandying about various large but uncertain sums. His original sworn statement was: "I can only hazard guesses. That one had to do with moneys that apparently Moo Young spent that was belonging to people who Maraj [*sic*] introduced to him; or else some sums of money he claims, Maraj claims, was extorted from Maraj's family." *Maharaj 3.850 Exhibit FCW*, at 6, *Statement of Neville Butler* (October 17, 1986, 00:50am). By the time of his second deposition, and later at trial, Butler had settled on a rather precise amount that was in dispute: $160,000. *Maharaj Trial Transcript* at 2806, 3124; *Second Deposition of Neville Butler* at 38–39 (March 30, 1987, 14:15pm) (108911-983). Two checks were to be written to cover the $160,000, and Butler was to take them to Fort Lauderdale to be certified. Butler was actually conflating two issues here. The Moo Youngs wrote two checks to Kris for $200,000 and $241,000 to cover their debt to him. The $160,000 figure came from an altogether different story. In July 1986, three months before the murders, Eslee Carberry and the *Echo* had published an article that made vague allegations of bribery in precisely that amount, $160,000: *Maharaj Trial Transcript* at 2753. See "The *Echo* Will Not Be Bought," *Caribbean Echo* (July 25, 1986). But there is strong independent reason to suggests that Butler made it up. The figure in the paper ($160,000) was itself a mistake, as I later found out from records that had been in the police file. On July 21, 1986, a payment of $150,000 (not $160,000, as alleged in the paper) was made by bank transfer from a Sun Bank Miami account, in the name of Hance and Sam Persad, to a Moo Young account. This proved two things: One, that the Moo Youngs were extorting the money, not Kris; and two, that number that Butler came up with for his testimony was the same erroneous number as had been published in the paper, and it was wrong. That is obviously where he got the number. However, once more, at trial the prosecution used the newspaper to "corroborate" his story.

15. Initially, Butler said the gun was not muffled at all: *Maharaj 3.850 Exhibit FCW* at 14, *Statement of Neville Butler* (October 17, 1986, 00:50am). In his first statement, Butler told Buhrmaster that none of the shots had been muffled: "Q. Any of the shots sound different to you, like the sounds being muffled? A. No. Q. All the shots downstairs sounded pretty much the same? A. All the same. Q. How about the shots upstairs? A. The shots upstairs may be a little muffled. It's only because it's upstairs it sounded a lesser noise to me." By the time of trial, he had come up with a story to explain why nobody heard the shots—Maharaj had allegedly brought a pillow with him to muffle the sound. See *Maharaj 3.850 Exhibit FCW*, at 13-14, *Statement of Neville Butler* (October 17, 1986, 00:50am) (118882-99): "A. [by Butler] He had a pillow ... as part of whatever he had in his bag and—Q. Are you saying that you thought he brought the pillow with him? A. Yes. As he walked around, all the time it was in his left arm. I cannot say whether he used it when he was firing or not." Notably, he could not stay consistent about this, as he said one time at trial that there was no muffling. *Maharaj Trial Transcript* at 2814. By 1995, when he was interviewed by a television station, he had gone back to saying there was no muffling. *Maharaj 3.850 Exhibit HP* at 15 (1995 Channel 4 interview with Neville Butler): "Well, I can't understand why nobody heard with all these gun shots going off, but apparently the hotel room is very airtight, you know, soundproof. However, nobody knocked on the door or anything of that sort." Ibid., 39: "They were loud, they were loud shots so if there was anybody within earshot they ought to have heard it." Ibid., 40: "I can't imagine anybody can hear argument and not hear gunshots."

16. In his first deposition, prosecutor Paul Ridge led Butler into the prosecution's backup theory—that there were two pillows, one left at the scene and one apparently taken away—which was the best that they could do to neutralize his obvious muddling of stories. See *Initial Deposition (Part 2) of Neville Butler* at 39-40 (January 16, 1987, 08:00am) (108861-910): "Q. [by Ridge] I will ask you do you recognize the pillow contained in these photographs? A. [by Butler] This doesn't appear to be the pillow. Q. Why do you say that? A. Because of the color. Q. The pillow you saw appeared to be brownish in color? A. Yes. Q. Could you be mistaken as to the color? A. I could be, but it is very doubtful." More recently Butler reverted to his original story. When I cross-examined him in 2002, Judge Bagley barred me from questioning him about most issues, but because Butler mentioned the pillow in passing, I was allowed to ask him questions about it. Despite being shown a picture of the sofa in the room which had pillows identical to the one he had identified, he continued to insist under oath that Kris had brought the hotel's pillow in a brown bag to the room to use as a silencer, and then took it away again.

17. The prosecution went on to argue that the print technician did not tell Detective Buhrmaster which of Maharaj's prints had been matched until four days after Butler gave his initial statement, so the witness had to be telling the truth. *Maharaj Trial Transcript* at 3185.

18. "The next thing I heard was boom!" Butler now describes it. "He shot the boy in the back of the head": *Maharaj 3.850 Exhibit HP*, at 19 (1995 Channel 4 interview with Neville Butler). How would he know that the bullet was in the back of the head, if he was downstairs where he could not see?

19. When asked why he did not run, Butler replied, "Very simply, sir. I cannot move faster than a bullet." *Maharaj Trial Transcript* at 3079. But this was fatuous. He would have been out of the room long before anyone could have fired a bullet at him. *Maharaj Trial Transcript* at 3790.

20. *Maharaj Trial Transcript* at 2839. See also *Second Deposition of Neville Butler* at 67-68 (March 30, 1987, 14:15pm) (108911-983). "In no uncertain terms," interjected Paul Ridge. "Mr. Butler has absolutely not been promised any immunity from prosecution for the perjury or the alleged perjury in this case. We made that clear to him in no uncertain terms. At this moment he does not know whether or not he will be arrested for the murder or whether or not he will be arrested for any possible perjury in this case."

21. In many states, for reasons that are difficult to comprehend, before trial a defense counsel may have only a very general sense of what the government's star witness is going to say. Most southern states do not require the prosecution to turn over previous statements of witnesses, and even the federal courts require disclosure only after the witness has testified and before cross-examination (i.e., not just in midtrial but in the middle of the witness's testimony). Florida is one of the few states that allow the defense to take statements from all the witnesses. Butler gave several sworn versions of his story before the actual trial. On the night after the murder, he gave a lengthy taped statement to Detective Buhrmaster. In January 1987, over two days, Hendon questioned him in a deposition. As a result of the changes in his story, Hendon deposed him again for much of a third day. Finally, a year after the crime, he testified to the jury over two days. Hendon had access to all this material.

22. One of the very few legal ethicists to have addressed the issue is Monroe Freedman of Hofstra University Law School. See Ralph J. Temple, "Monroe Freedman and Legal Ethics: A Prophet in his own Time," *Journal of the Legal Profession* 13 (1988) 233, 237n22. Temple notes that Freedman was "the first to analyze the ethical issues in preparing witnesses" and cites Monroe Freedman, "Counseling the Client: Refreshing Recollection or Prompting Perjury?" *ABA Litigation* 2 (Spring 1976), 35. Although Freedman raised these issues for the first time many years ago, it remains true that "little is said about what an attorney should not do when preparing a witness, except for the obvious warning to avoid suborning perjury. Tension exists between an attorney's ethical duty to proffer only truthful evidence and an attorney's duty to represent his client zealously, because under the latter an attorney's allegiance is to the client, not the truth." Liisa René Salmi, "Don't Walk the Line: Ethical Considerations in Preparing Witnesses for Deposition and Trial," *Review of Litigation* 18 (1999), 135 (footnotes omitted). In one case, the U.S. Equal Employment Opportunity Commission gave advice to witnesses in a sexual harassment case. The EEOC put it in writing, so that the other side would know what was said: "The letter included 'memory joggers' that advised the women: 'Try to remember whether or not you have experienced or observed' various incidents, such as 'sexual jokes,' 'unwelcome touching' and 'circulation of pornographic photographs.' " The defendant corporation, Mitsubishi, complained that this letter was unethical, but the judge disagreed, ruling that "suggesting subject matters to focus on in telling [the client's] story is surely what every competent lawyer, including the Mitsubishi lawyers, does to prepare clients . . . for a deposition." See Michael Higgins, "Why the Fine Line Between Preparing Witnesses and Suborning Perjury Is More Than an Affair of State for Lawyers," *ABA Journal* 52 (May 1998), 56. See also W. William Hodes, "Seeking the Truth Versus Telling the Truth at the Boundaries of the Law: Misdirection, Lying, and Lying with an Explanation," *South Texas Law Review* 44 (Winter 2002), addressing "yet another intractable boundary-line dilemma: insufficient preparation of a witness is malpractice, while preparing 'too well' can degenerate into subornation of perjury."

23. While academics debate ethical issues at great length, they rarely cite any instance where a lawyer has been sanctioned for coaching a witness. Richard C. Wyrick, "The Ethics of Witness Coaching," *Cardozo Law Review* 17 (September 1995), 1120, discusses many hypotheticals but cites no real-world examples of sanctions. W. William Hodes details his own experience as an expert witness with respect to the Baron & Budd asbestos memorandum, where a detailed memo, written by the lawyers, was used to go over the testimony of each witness. Hodes vigorously defends the ethics of counseling witnesses on what they might say—indeed, he notes that the lawyers representing the authors of the memo prepped Hodes himself (or to use his quaint term, "horse-shedded" him). See Hodes, "The Professional Duty to Horseshed Witnesses—Zealously, Within the Bounds of the Law," *Texas Tech Law Review* 30 (1999). The Baron & Budd lawyers were not sanctioned for what they did. Indeed, Hodes describes as normal the kind of misleading strategies that most lay people might well condemn. See W. William Hodes, "Seeking the Truth versus Telling the Truth at the Boundaries of the Law: Misdirection, Lying, and Lying with an Explanation," *South Texas Law Review* 44 (2002): "the boundary lines . . . are relatively well defined, relatively stable, and drawn in about the right place. In criminal cases almost certainly, and probably in many civil cases as well, it ought to be open to lawyers to make misleading arguments during litigation, so long as the underlying evidence presented in court is factual. But actively contaminating the proceedings with evidence that is known to be false has always been forbidden, and should always remain forbidden."

24. There were various suggestions in the Clinton case that witnesses had been leaned on, heavily, in order to say one thing or the other. For example, a "talking points" memo, prepared presumably by someone in the White House, seemed to give instructions to a potential witness concerning what she

should say about former White House aide Kathleen Willey, who accused Clinton of sexual harassment. The memo said: "You never saw [Willey] go into the oval office, or come out of the oval office. You have never observed the President behaving inappropriately with anybody." This could be read in two ways: one, it was merely a reflection of an earlier interview; and two, it was basically telling the witness what to say. Higgins concludes that the difference between preparing a witness and suborning perjury is in the eye of the opponent. Higgins, "Why the Fine Line," 52, 53.

Chapter 5: The Prosecutor

1. Even then there are exceptions to the prisoner's rights, under the Freedom of Information Act. The state is allowed to claim exemptions for various materials, including the prosecutors' own work product, various information about informants, and so forth.

2. I am referring primarily here to the selection (and self-selection) of prosecutors in state courts. Federal cases represent fewer than 5 percent of criminal prosecutions, so cases in state courts constitute the overwhelming majority of prosecutions. Of the death sentences imposed in U.S. courts, under 2 percent—as of 2010, just 59 out of 3,268—were imposed in federal court, with an additional 8 in military courts. See "Death Row Winter 2010," NAACP Legal Defense and Educational Fund, 36, http://naacpldf.org/files/publications/DRUSA_Winter_2010.pdf.

3. For the figure of 2,341 local offices, see U.S. Department of Justice, "Prosecutors in State Courts, 2001," *Bureau of Justice Statistics Bulletin*, July 1, 2002, 1, 2, cited in Ric Simmons, "Election of Local Prosecutors," *Election Law @Moritz*. There are an additional six million misdemeanors, which can also carry prison sentences up to one year. Simmons, "Election of Local Prosecutors," 2. More than half the states elect prosecutors by county; some elect them by judicial district (which may include several counties or, in Louisiana, several parishes). Notably, the attorneys general for the states are also elected: "The Attorney General is popularly elected in 43 states, and is appointed by the governor in five states (Alaska, Hawaii, New Hampshire, New Jersey and Wyoming) and in the five jurisdictions of American Samoa, Guam, the Northern Mariana Islands, Puerto Rico and the Virgin Islands. In Maine, the Attorney General is selected by secret ballot of the legislature, and in Tennessee, by the state Supreme Court. In the District of Columbia, the Mayor appoints the Corporation Counsel whose powers and duties are similar to those of the Attorneys General of the states and jurisdictions." See "How Does One Become an Attorney General?" *National Association of Attorneys General*. Attorneys general are normally responsible for appellate litigation in the state. Thus, when Kris's case was on appeal, the work was generally done by the office of the attorney general rather than the office of the state attorney (who is called, in many states, the district attorney).

4. Simmons, "Election of Local Prosecutors," citing Abbe Smith, "Can You be a Good Person and a Good Prosecutor?" *Georgetown Journal of Legal Ethics* 14 (2001), 355, 389.

5. Kenneth Bresler, "'I Never Lost a Trial': When Prosecutors Keep Score of Criminal Convictions," *Georgetown Journal of Legal Ethics* 9 (1996), 537, 541n18; and Catherine Ferguson-Gilbert, "It Is Not Whether You Win or Lose, It Is How You Play the Game: Is the Win-Loss Scorekeeping Mentality Doing Justice for Prosecutors?" *California Western Law Review* 38 (2001), 283. According to Mike Tolson and Steve Brewer, "Harris County Is a Pipeline to Death Row," *Houston Chronicle*, February 21, 2001, 1, the district attorney of Harris County, Texas, campaigned on his record of having put fourteen murderers on death row "where they belong." According to Daniel S. Medwed, "The Zeal Deal: Prosecutorial Resistance to Post-Conviction Claims of Innocence," *Boston University Law Review* 84 (2004), 125, "there are a series of political incentives for prosecutors to resist post-conviction innocence claims, even potentially meritorious ones, with zeal. Candidates vying for the office of chief prosecutor typically campaign on a general tough-on-crime platform, strewn with references to their overall win-loss record and reminders about specific successes in high-profile cases. Appearing 'soft' on criminals, such as by accepting the possible validity of a prisoner's innocence claim, detracts from that tough-on-crime rhetoric and is largely an anathema to prosecutors." One notable exception to this rule was the 2006 district attorney election in Dallas County. Craig Watkins ran for the position promising to clean up the ethics of the office and review doubtful convictions. See website of the Dallas County District Attorney, http://www.dallasda.com (accessed October 31, 2010): "Committed to the concept of "doing the right thing," our talented and diverse staff prides itself on seeking justice not on high conviction rates." Watkins even called for jail time for unethical prosecutors who secured convictions against the innocent. See Jennifer Emily and Steve McGonigle, "Dallas County District Attorney Wants Unethical Prosecutors Punished," *Dallas Morning News* (May 4, 2008): "The Dallas County district attorney who has built a national reputation on freeing the wrongfully convicted says prosecutors who intentionally withhold evidence should themselves face harsh sanctions—possibly even jail time. 'Something should be done,' said Craig Watkins, whose jurisdiction leads the nation in the number of DNA exonerations. 'If the harm is a great harm, yes, it should be criminalized.'" However, I have some familiarity with the Dallas office, since I

have worked on two capital cases there, and while I have no doubt of Watkins's good intentions, the general mindset of the assistant prosecutors there remains similar to the one discussed in this chapter. An organizational culture is not easily transformed, and whether Watkins will be DA long enough to achieve it remains to be seen.

6. "The taxpayers don't pay us for curiosity," said one senior prosecutor. "They pay us to get convictions." See Andrew Martin, "The Prosecution's Case Against DNA," *New York Times Magazine*, November 25, 2011, quoted in Richard Lewontin, "Let the DNA Fit the Crime," *New York Review of Books*, February 23, 2012, 29. The more senior the prosecutor, the more likely he is to take this position, perhaps partly because he has internalized the attitude, and partly because those who disagreed have moved on, out of the role. See Medwed, "Zeal Deal," 125, 138, 140: "One study demonstrated that assistant district attorneys articulating a primary focus on convictions had, on average, roughly twice as much experience as those who displayed a deep concern for justice"; "the police only arrest guilty people in the first place [which] reinforces the belief that the right person was charged and later convicted." Medwed cites George T. Felkenes, "The Prosecutor: A Look at Reality," *Southwestern University Law Review* 7 (1975), 98, 111. At some point, as many as half of all prosecutors may renounce the presumption of innocence, notwithstanding strong pressure to agree with it. Felkenes, "Prosecutor," 112, says that more than 50 percent of prosecutors surveyed did not presume a man innocent until proven guilty and that many believed that the screening processes of the police and prosecutor prior to trial determined guilt. See Smith, "Can You Be a Good Person," 355, 384: "Notwithstanding the legal presumption of innocence, the cultural and institutional presumption in most prosecutor offices is that everybody is guilty." See generally H. Richard Uviller, "The Neutral Prosecutor: The Obligation of Dispassion in a Passionate Pursuit," *Fordham Law Review* 68 (2000), 1695, 1702: "Even the best of the prosecutors—young, idealistic, energetic, dedicated to the interests of justice—are easily caught up in the hunt mentality of an aggressive office.... I know that the earnest effort to do justice is easily corrupted by the institutional ethic of combat."

7. This issue is not as simple as it may first appear. Culpability has many shades. If a perpetrator killed when he was provoked, the act may be deemed manslaughter; if it was a moment of panic, he might not have had a specific intent to kill (the active desire that a death should take place). After immersing myself in the facts, I have generally concluded that a partial defense is often closest to the truth. But if my experience is anything to go by, the defendant will probably be found guilty of the most serious charge, regardless.

8. Bill Foster prosecuted John for the death penalty, and John was sentenced to die. It was small wonder: Bill was well attuned to the local jurors. I was wet behind the ears. I was immensely grateful when, some months later, we got the case reversed on appeal: *Pope v. State*, 256 Ga. 195, 345 S.E.2d 831 (1986). On retrial, thankfully Bill agreed to a plea, and John was sentenced to life. Before I left the United States in 2004, I hoped to go back to visit my first client, but when I called the prison to make arrangements, I was sorry to learn that he had died in prison.

9. When I ask prosecutors to meet with my clients, they sometimes point to an ethical rule that, they think, forbids them from taking such a step: if they speak to the accused and learn something that makes them a witness, they are forbidden to be both the advocate and a witness. See, e.g., *United States v. Hosford*, 782 F.2d 936 (11th Cir. 1986): "It is clear that a prosecutor must not act as both prosecutor and witness." But this problem is readily soluble: there could be another person in the room as well, who could be the witness if necessary. Thus, this argument is a pretext for not meeting the defendant rather than a genuine obstacle.

10. The Louisiana Capital Assistance Center (LCAC) used to work closely with the office of the district attorney in Orleans Parish to ensure effective assessment of cases before they went to trial. Such cooperation as we briefly enjoyed is rare, and the problem becomes greater once the trial process has been set in motion—and again when someone has been convicted and sent to prison. It is not the case (obviously) that prosecutors never admit mistakes; my thesis is that prosecutors are selected and self-select from a group whose attitudes make such an admission far less likely—and if we are serious about remedying mistakes, we need to recognize this problem and take affirmative steps to put a very different institutional culture in place.

11. Shareef was convicted despite the videotape evidence and the testimony of various witnesses. In addition, "two recreation department supervisors, Cousin's coach, and an opposing team's player testified that the game had started late and ended late, and the coach testified that he dropped Cousin off at his house at approximately 10:45 pm." *Cousin v. Small*, 325 F.3d 627, 629 (5th Cir. 2003). This time frame was well after the murder took place.

12. One of the statements was sent to the trial lawyers—too late—in a brown manila envelope, presumably by someone in the police department with a conscience. We turned up the rest gradually, as the police were forced to allow access to the rest of their files. The Louisiana Supreme Court later characterized these statements as "obviously exculpatory" and held that they should have been turned over.

State v. Shareef Cousin, No. 96-KA-2973 (La. 4/14/98), 710 So.2d 1065: "The prosecutor did not disclose this obviously exculpatory statement to the defense prior to the trial, as required by *Brady v. Maryland*, 373 U.S. 83 (1963), and *Kyles v. Whitley*, 514 U.S. 419 (1995)." However, I suspect that Jordan thought (or convinced himself) his witness was telling the truth now, rather than in the earlier versions, so did not think the statements credible.

13. Small's colleague Detective Mims received this Crime Stopper tip: "The form was dated 3-10-95 and the anonymous caller named Antonio Harper, Derrick Smith and a subject known only as 'Brandon' as being the subjects responsible for the robbery/murder which occurred in the 1300 block of Dauphine." This lead fit snugly with the evidence that had been developed on the night of the crime. Jonathan Webb, an eyewitness whose name was kept from the defense by the prosecution, watched the killers leave in their car and, because he was a bird-watcher by habit, used his binoculars. Within minutes of the crime, he had called in the license plate of the rapidly departing vehicle. The police ran a printout for BVG456 at 11:39 p.m. on the night of the crime—less than two hours after the murder. This gave the police the name Christell B. Baham. The car was a red 1989 Ford four-door. Based on other evidence, on March 13, 1995, at 10:50 p.m., Detectives Mims, Zenon, and Lawless went to 3244 Desaix Street to find Antonio Harper. Detective Mims noted in his report that parked outside the address was the car he had tried to find earlier in the week: a red Ford Escort registered to Christell Baham with plate BVG456. Christell Baham, he learned, was the mother of Derrick Smith. In other words, the police put a compelling case together against three other suspects soon after the crime—but none of this was disclosed to Shareef's trial lawyers, because Detective Small had already decided that Shareef would be convicted of the crime.

14. Shareef had also been charged with four armed robberies, and when his lawyer insisted that he was looking at ninety-nine years, he entered a guilty plea. Shareef was no angel, which was ultimately perhaps part of Detective Small's motivation for putting together the murder case against him. But neither was Shareef the one-person crime wave portrayed by the prosecution: when we subsequently investigated the robbery cases, we found that, while Shareef got in with a bad crowd, he had never used a weapon himself. He was sentenced to twenty years for those other offenses—extremely harsh for a juvenile first offender by any standards.

15. Sad to say, life in prison for a juvenile was not uncommon then and remains available as a sentence today. See "No Way Out," *New York Times*, November 22, 2005. Outside the United States, only three countries had any juveniles serving life without parole, seven in Israel, four in South Africa, and one in Tanzania. Thankfully, in *Graham v. Florida*, 130 S. Ct. 2011 (2010), the Supreme Court decreed that life *without parole* was an unconstitutional punishment for juveniles who commit a crime less than murder. On the other hand, at the time of writing, it is still possible for a juvenile to be sentenced to life without parole for murder (it cannot be a mandatory sentence), or to life with the possibility of parole for a lesser offense.

16. Rowell said the earlier statement was false, but he admitted that he had made it. He said he had implicated Shareef only to save himself from criminal charges that he was facing himself. Thus, legally, he could not be "impeached" with the substance of the prior statement, since he had not denied making the statement. While this is black-letter evidence law, the prosecutor went through the entire statement with Rowell, then argued to the jury that the prior statement was evidence of Shareef's guilt. See *State v. Shareef Cousin*, No. 96-KA-2973 (La. 4/14/98), 710 So.2d 1065. Jordan later admitted that this procedure is not allowed: *State v. Cousin*, 710 So.2d at 1072, reversing in part "because of [Roger Jordan] the prosecutor's flagrant misuse of that evidence for purposes that the prosecutor himself admitted was an improper use of that evidence." While the conviction had involved a number of other highly prejudicial issues, in reversing it the Supreme Court chose to address only this one.

17. I believe that, in prosecuting Shareef Cousin, Roger Jordan took steps that were profoundly wrong and that are the antithesis of what the judicial system purports to mandate. But what he actually did is rather human and sadly typical of how the system operates in the real world. Jordan believed that he did not make mistakes. He believed that essentially everyone brought to trial—particularly on his watch—was inevitably guilty, and that slippery defense lawyers were trying to help them avoid their just deserts.

18. *Louisiana Revised Statutes* 15:572.8(c)(3): Compensation for wrongful conviction and imprisonment "shall be calculated at a rate of fifteen thousand dollars per year incarcerated not to exceed a maximum total amount of one hundred fifty thousand dollars." Thus the prisoner receives no compensation for the time he spends in prison over ten years.

19. *Cousin v. Small*, 325 F.3d 627, 631 (5th Cir. 2003) notes that there is no official codification of the "doctrine of prosecutorial immunity" but quotes the Supreme Court for the assertion that Congress must clearly have intended to adopt such a rule, as it existed in the common law, as developed by the courts; quoting *Kalina v. Fletcher*, 424 U.S. 118, 123 (1997). See also *Imbler v. Pachtman*, 424 U.S. 409 (1976), the seminal Supreme Court decision recognizing prosecutorial immunity.

20. *In re Roger W. Jordan*, No. 57,734 (La. October 8, 1979).

21. "Neither are [prosecutors] realistically subject to criminal sanctions," the Louisiana Supreme Court acknowledged in *In re Roger W. Jordan Jr.* (La. 06/29/2005), 913 So.2d 775. "Our research reveals only one instance in which a judge held a prosecutor in contempt of court for failing to disclose evidence," the court went on. This solitary case was *In re Burns*, 2001-1080 (La. 11/28/01), 800 So.2d 833. It involved misconduct again in Orleans Parish and a finding by the trial judge that an assistant district attorney had actually planted evidence in addition to failing to notify the defense of hugely important evidence. While it may be the only case where a judge has convicted a prosecutor of contempt, the conviction was reversed in large part: the Supreme Court found the proof that the evidence had been planted was insufficient and ordered only a $500 fine with regard to the failure to notify the defense of the evidence.

22. The central allegation against Ben Kuehne did not even involve fees that would be paid to him, but rather his investigation into the validity of fees that were being paid to another lawyer, and his determination that the lawyer could agree to be retained without fear of violating the law. After the federal judge threw most of the case out, the government took the case on appeal to the Eleventh Circuit in Atlanta, where it lost again. Ultimately, that court dismissed the charges. See Jennifer Forsyth, "DOJ Gives Miami Lawyer Ben Kuehne Happy Thanksgiving, Drops Charges," *Wall Street Journal* (November 26, 2009).

23. The charge and ultimate acquittal are detailed in the court record of *State of Louisiana v. Marcel O'Connor*, No. 07-98-62 (19th JDC, East Baton Rouge).

24. I should underline that this is not actually the legal test for the prosecutor's obligation to disclose "exculpatory" evidence: evidence does not have to prove the suspect innocent but rather may be of material assistance to his defense, in any number of ways. For example, a suspect may actually have committed a homicide, but evidence of provocation might reduce the crime from murder to manslaughter. However, some prosecutors have a very narrow interpretation of the test.

25. *Berger v. United States*, 295 U.S. 78, 88 (1935).

Chapter 6: The Police

1. An apologist for the lie detector would say that this is not possible, or else label me as part of the "sociopathic segment of the population," capable of lying without emotion. See "How Can You Beat a Polygraph?": "How can you beat a polygraph? You can't. If the examinee KNOWS they are lying [*sic*], the polygraph will detect the lie. Unless the examinee is part of that tiny sociopathic segment of the population that can tell a lie *and honestly believe it*, they cannot beat the polygraph. Most *experienced* polygraph examiners can detect deception" (emphasis in the original). However, others agree that the polygraph can quite readily be beaten. See Anti-Polygraph.Org: "Liars can beat the test by covertly augmenting their physiological reactions to the 'control' questions. This can be done, for example, by doing mental arithmetic, thinking exciting thoughts, altering one's breathing pattern, or simply biting the side of the tongue. Truthful persons can also use these techniques to protect themselves against the risk of a false positive outcome. Although polygraphers frequently claim they can detect such countermeasures, no polygrapher has ever demonstrated any ability to do so, and peer-reviewed research suggests that they can't."

2. For a limited sample of these studies, see Taiping Ho, "The Interrelationships of Psychological Testing, Psychologists' Recommendations, and Police Departments' Recruitment Decisions," *Police Quarterly* 4 (2001), 318–42; J. Zhao, N. He, and N. P. Zovrich, "Individual Value Preferences Among American Police Officers: The Rokeach Theory of Human Values Revisited," *Policing* 21 (1998), 22–37. There are many other interesting discussions concerning the psychological testing of officers, indicating that those rejected for police jobs include people with a problem with authority figures. See, e.g., http://forums.officer.com/forums/showthread.php?t=56663 (accessed September 12, 2008), where we read that an applicant apparently failed because of MMPI results "in the areas of respect of authority figures."

3. These terms come from the literature. See J. E. Teahan, K. M. Adams, and E. C. Podany, "A Comparison of the Value Structure of the British and U.S. Police," *International Journal of Social Psychiatry* 26 (1980), 246–54. The word *authoritarian* has been applied to different police recruits. See, e.g., Alexander B. Smith, Bernard Locke, and William F. Walker, "Authoritarianism in Police College Students and Non-Police College Students," *Journal of Criminal Law, Criminology, and Police Science* 59 (1968), 440. It is difficult to say which is chicken and which is egg in terms of the development of the "values" of police. Teahan, Adams and Podany question "whether the characteristics found are due to the kind of men attracted to police work, or whether, instead, they result from the occupational stress of the work itself." However, it is clear that those hiring do not emphasize protecting the innocent. For a typical description of the job of an officer, taken from a federal government website, see U.S. Department of Labor, Bureau of Labor Statistics, "Police and Detectives: Nature of the Work," *Occupational Outlook Handbook*, 2008–9. See also "Online Police Officer Education and Criminal Justice Degree Programs": "In local, state and federal police related departments a police officer's career description includes maintaining law and order, collecting evidence and conducting investigations" (with no mention of doing justice).

4. In the Vietnam War, 58,148 Americans were killed out of 2.59 million who served, or one in forty-five. The war lasted perhaps fifteen years in total. While it is obviously a very rough approximation, the fatality levels were not far off the murder rate in the St. Thomas Housing Projects.

5. The phrase *thin red line* originally referred to the line of British soldiers who faced down charging Russian Hussars at the Battle of Balaclava in the Crimea in 1854. It later became a general term for British sangfroid in battle. American police adopted the label *thin blue line* to denote their role in protecting society from an overwhelming threat. It is also the title of a 1988 film about the wrongful conviction of Randall Adams, which led to his spending years on Texas's death row.

6. *Serpico*, a 1973 film starring Al Pacino as Frank Serpico, was based on the true story of a New York police officer who tried to expose corruption in the NYPD. In 1971 he testified before the Knapp Commission on police corruption, which had been set up in large part because of his public allegations. See Martin Arnold, "Serpico's Lonely Journey to Knapp Witness Stand," *New York Times*, December 15, 1971. The commission identified two categories of corrupt police: A "Grass Eater" is an officer who "accepts gratuities and solicits five, ten, twenty dollar payments from contractors, tow-truck operators, gamblers, and the like but do not pursue corruption payments." Grass eating was a rite of passage for many police, to prove their loyalty to the brotherhood, and was treated like a job incentive. "Meat Eaters" were officers who "spend a good deal of time aggressively looking for situations they can exploit for financial gain." For example, they shake down pimps and drug dealers for money. The officers not only profit, but they can neutralize their guilt by convincing themselves that the victim deserves it.

7. "Jury Convicts 5 on Multiple Counts in Danziger Trial," WDSU.com (2011). All four officers (and a fifth) were ultimately convicted of violating the victims' civil rights.

8. See *Maharaj 3.850 Exhibit P*, Tr. 114. At a subsequent hearing on this issue, when his superior officer John Buhrmaster was accused of perjury, Romero tried to wriggle out of what he had said. However, when originally made, his answer to the question could not have been clearer.

9. At a later hearing, the state made no denial that this note was accurate, and *Edwards v. Arizona*, 451 U.S. 47 (1981) had long ago made clear that all subsequent statements would have had to be suppressed. The only question that remained was at what time Kris had asked for counsel. Naturally, when this note came to light, Buhrmaster tried to suggest that anything he had quoted from Kris at trial had been said before midnight. However, given the time of his arrest at Denny's, this timeframe was improbable. Regardless, the intentional suppression of this information reflected very badly on the integrity of the prosecution. I came across a similar note that Detective Buhrmaster had apparently written. First Buhrmaster noted that Kris had said, "That's all I have to say about today's activities." But this line was scratched out and replaced with Buhrmaster's observation, "That's all he was able to tell me about the days activities." The difference was critical: the first was the suspect's assertion of the right to remain silent, which would have barred the police from asking further questions; the second carried no such implication. See *Maharaj 3.850 Clerk* Tr. 2034. At the hearing, the prosecution tried to make out that they, rather than Buhrmaster, had made this change in order to prevent the detective from commenting on the accused's assertion of his rights. It is true that in *Griffin v. California*, 380 U.S. 609 (1965), the Supreme Court laid down the rule that no comment might be made on the accused's assertion of his right to remain silent in court. *Griffin* was then expanded to include a prohibition against commenting on the defendant's refusal to talk to the police, so the prosecutors would not have wanted Buhrmaster to mention this before the jury. The crucial issue, however, from the defense perspective, was that the notes had not been turned over to Hendon, so he did not know that there was independent proof that Kris had asserted his rights. All of this must also be read in light of the fact that John Buhrmaster insisted that he did not record Kris's supposed statements in any format.

10. *Maharaj 3.850 Exhibit FAO*.

11. In April 1986, Gordon Daskowski supposedly wrote to Dr. W.C. Bryant regarding $134,872,546.66 worth of gemstones in the possession of the Los Angeles Church Loan Corporation. *Maharaj 3.850 Exhibit OCY* at B002193. The Moo Youngs had all the gemstone documents in their files, indicating an effort to use them as collateral for other transactions.

12. Key man insurance is designed to protect a business financially from the effects of the prolonged illness or death of staff who are central to its prosperity. The insurance is meant to buy time, to cover the costs of temporary staff, recruitment, or loss of profits, or to provide a cash injection.

13. *Maharaj 3.850 Exhibits OAY, OAZ*. In the month of September, someone got careless and allowed the account to rise briefly to $66,688.23.

Chapter 7: The Expert

1. Sadly, the doctor's admission that he would change his testimony depending on who was footing the bill comes from a real case in New Orleans: *Ladner v. Higgins*, 71 So.2d 242, 244 (La. App. 1954). The appellate judges introduced this quote, rather incredulously, with the following observation: "of vast

significance in our judicial determination of the serious medical issues involved herein, we find these pearls of wisdom emanating from the mouth of one whose testimony was being adduced to assist the court and whom we must presume, from the very nature of his profession, has accepted the Hippocratic Oath which, as we all know, is the foundation of medical ethics."

2. See generally Jenny Uglow, "The Other Side of Science," *New York Review of Books*, June 24, 2010, 31.

3. The various attributes of hair that a technician considers are set out in U.S. Department of Justice, FBI, *Handbook of Forensic Science* (1981). More recently, after being thoroughly embarrassed in court, hair analysts have taken to referring to "European Origin," "African Origin," and "Asian Origin." However, even here the definition is fairly meaningless: If someone has one grandparent each from England, Russia, Thailand, and Ghana, how do we categorize him?

4. See C. A. Stafford Smith and P. D. Goodman, "Forensic Hair Comparison Analysis: Nineteenth Century Science or Twentieth Century Snake Oil?," *Columbia Human Rights Law Review* 27 (1996), 227.

5. Raulerson is not his real name. I have also changed the name of the victim and other players in the case.

6. Forensic hair analysis continues to play a key role in serious cases. In the following decisions from the past ten years, courts have reviewed and upheld death sentences based in part on expert testimony concerning a hair "match." *Allen v. Secretary, Florida Department of Corrections*, 2010 U.S. App. LEXIS 14570 (July 2010), which affirmed the death sentence, since the relevant hair could have been one victim's; *Duckett v. McDonough*, 2010 U.S. Dist. LEXIS 38440 (M.D. Fla. March 25, 2010), which affirmed the death sentence, against a challenge that the state had searched out a hair expert who would testify unfavorably to the defendant; *West v. Ricks*, 2010 U.S. Dist. LEXIS 1119 (W.D. Ct. January 7, 2010), which affirmed a life sentence in a capital case against a challenge on the use of hair analysis; *Manning v. Epps*, 695 F. Supp. 2d 323 (N.D. Miss. 2009); *Blankenship v. Hall*, 542 F.3d 1253 (11th Cir. 2008); *Storey v. Roper*, 2008 U.S. Dist. LEXIS 46662 (E.D. Mo. 2008); *Green v. Quarterman*, 2008 U.S. Dist. LEXIS 11459 (S.D. Tx. 2008), all of which affirmed the death sentence; *Berryman v. Ayers*, 2007 U.S. Dist. LEXIS 51738 (E.D. Ca. 2007), which upheld the conviction in a capital case, rejecting a challenge to hair analysis; *Thomas v. Beard*, 388 F. Supp. 2d 489 (E.D. Pa. 2005), which upheld the conviction but reversed the sentence on other grounds, *death sentence reinstated*, Thomas v. Horn, 570 F.3d 105 (3d Cir. 2009); *Bryan v. Mullin*, 100 Fed. Appx. 783, 2004 U.S. App. LEXIS 11172 (10th Cir. 2004), in which a motion for stay of execution was denied and the death sentence affirmed; the court noted that since "the evidence relied upon by Bryan to assert the unreliability of the bullet comparison and the hair analysis did not exist until well after the completion of Bryan's direct appeal," the state was not in a position to ensure its accuracy at trial; *Bagwell v. Cockrell*, 2003 U.S. Dist. LEXIS 16107 (W.D. Tx 2003), which affirmed the death sentence and vacated a stay of execution; and *Crawford v. Head*, 311 F.3d 1288 (11th Cir. 2002), which affirmed the death sentence. Hair analysis is still being widely used, notwithstanding the possibility, in some cases, of doing DNA testing on the hair. The latter is much more expensive.

7. See B. D. Gaudette and E. S. Keeping, "An Attempt at Determining Probabilities in Human Scalp Hair Comparison," *Journal of Forensic Science* 19 (1974), 599; and B. D. Gaudette, "Probabilities and Human Pubic Hair Comparisons," *Journal of Forensic Science* 21 (1976), 514. Since even hair analysts agree that scalp hair and pubic hair are very different, this really means that only one study has been done on either. Gaudette published a subsequent article further discussing his own studies: B. D. Gaudette, "Some Further Thoughts on Probabilities in Human Hair Comparisons," *Journal of Forensic Science* 23 (1978), 758. Two other hair analysts published a later review of these materials: Ray A. Wickenheiser and David G. Hepworth, "Further Evaluation of Probabilities in Human Scalp Hair Comparisons," *Journal of Forensic Science* 35 (1990), 1323.

8. To be more precise, the actual number he came up with was 1 chance in 65,000,000,000,000,000, 000,000,000 of a false match. Given that the population of the world was roughly 6 trillion, if this was true, then James Raulerson had to be the perpetrator and no other evidence was necessary.

9. I phoned the Royal Canadian Mounted Police (RCMP) to get a copy of Gaudette's hair analysis data, but they said that the original materials had been destroyed.

10. In the retrial, James was acquitted of capital murder but was convicted of the lesser crime of simple murder—which meant that the jury did not believe he had raped Annie Martin, the victim in the tragedy. Given his prior history, he was sentenced to life imprisonment. Very rarely does a prisoner receive two reversals of a conviction, and James did not.

11. *Williamson v. Reynolds*, 904 F. Supp. 1529, 1554-58 (E.D. Okla. 1995), *aff'd Williamson v. Ward*, 110 F.3d 1508 (10th Cir. 1997). The court of appeals refused to ratify Judge Seay's finding that the hair analysis should have been excluded as a matter of law. The court held that while it did not "review the merits of the court's ruling [in that respect], we note that some of the authorities it cited view hair analysis as highly subjective and unreliable. It is undisputed that hair analysis . . . is not conclusive." Ibid., 1520.

12. Gore was sentenced to death, but the case was reversed on appeal, and he ultimately received life imprisonment. Williamson's freedom was short-lived. He received compensation from the State of Oklahoma but was dead within a year from liver disease.

13. P. L. Kirk and J. I. Thornton, *Crime Investigation* (New York: Wiley, 1994), 143, quoted in Max M. Houck, "Hair Bibliography for the Forensic Scientist," *Forensic Science Communications* 4 (2002).

14. The crime laboratories that do this work have other problems as well. Many of their flaws—low standards of staff competence, low salaries that do not attract better staff, inadequate budgets for the caseloads, pressure to produce results too rapidly, and so forth—are detailed in Craig Cooley, "Forensic Science and Capital Punishment Reform: An 'Intellectually Honest' Assessment," *George Mason University Civil Rights Law Journal* 17 (2007), 299. In one capital case, hair analysis was brought directly into question: *Miller v. Anderson*, 162 F. Supp. 2d 1057 (N.D. Ind. 2000) (affirming the conviction), *rev'd Miller v. Anderson*, 255 F.3d 455, 457 (7th Cir. 2001). Judge Posner reversed both the conviction and the death sentence, based in part upon erroneous hair analysis. Notably, the original hair analysis was disputed not by an independent scientist but by another hair expert. The case must, then, go down as an example of one expert challenging the competence of another, rather than anyone challenging the reliability of the "science" itself.

15. Nowhere in criminal law is the hubris of pseudoscience more dangerous than in the notion of "shaken baby syndrome" (SBS). Over the years I have represented a number of prisoners who have been charged with the murder of a child in this context. The issue is worthy of a book to itself and cannot be addressed properly here. Suffice it to say that when pseudoscience is presented by neurologists ("brain surgeons") as a medical diagnosis that proves a defendant guilty, the danger of a wrongful conviction is frightening.

16. See, generally, Solomon Moore, "Science Found Wanting in Nation's Crime Labs," *New York Times*, February 4, 2009.

17. Cooley, "Forensic Science and Capital Punishment Reform," 299n200-2. The rather greater but still small proportion (12 percent) of exonerations where DNA was implicated is probably a reflection of the fact that it is much harder to secure an exoneration without a much-touted DNA result.

18. One example of the prosecutor's statistical fallacy is the notion that, if the odds of a chance match to a DNA profile are one in a billion, then the odds that the accused is innocent are one in a billion. In truth, even accepting the demographic DNA data, the likelihood of a mistake by a technician (which might be 1 in 100 or even 1 in 10) easily swamps the mind-boggling number that the prosecution would rather tout to the jury. The many other flaws in these statistics are beyond the scope of this book.

19. On the license to carry a concealed weapon or firearm, limited concealed-carry rights, etc., see *Florida Statutes* §§790.001(17), 790.06, 790.253.

20. Philip J. Cook and Jens Ludwig, "Guns in America: National Survey on Private Ownership and Use of Firearms," *National Institute of Justice Research Brief* (1997), table 4A (1994 data).

21. *United States v. Glynn*, 578 F.Supp.2d 567, 569 (S.D. N.Y. September 22, 2008), quoting *United States v. Hicks*, 389 F.3d 514, 526 (5th Cir. 2004), stated that "the matching of spent shell casings to the weapon that fired them has been a recognized method of ballistics testing in this circuit for decades"; and *United States v. Foster*, 300 F.Supp.2d 375, 377 n.1 (D.Md. 2004) stated that "ballistics evidence has been accepted in criminal cases for many years." See Dr. Adina Schwartz, "A Systemic Challenge to the Reliability and Admissibility of Firearms and Toolmark Identification," *Columbia Science and Technology Law Review* 6 (2005), 1-42. See also National Research Council, *Forensic Analysis: Weighing Lead Bullet Evidence* (Washington, D.C.: National Academies Press, 2004) : "Ultimately, as firearms identification is currently practiced . . . the decision of what does or does not constitute a match comes down to a subjective determination based on intuition and experience." The Browning nine-millimeter is a famous and widely circulated pistol, seemingly more common than the Smith & Wesson described by Quirk. Millions of them have been made. While I have not been able to find precise numbers for the whole period, 251,000 were manufactured between 1954 and 1969. The Sig Sauer, used by the U.S. military and numerous American law enforcement agencies, also seemed to be an intensely popular gun in the trade; I could not find precise numbers on sales, but a dealer described it to me as selling out the moment he got some in.

22. Although the ballistics evidence in *Riechmann* was effectively irrelevant, the Florida Supreme Court opined: "The expert also testified that the bullet that killed Kischnick could have been fired from any of three makes of guns. Riechmann owned two of those three makes of weapons." *Riechmann v. State*, 581 So. 2d 133, 136 (Fla. 1991).

23. See *Brief of Appellant, Riechmann v. State*, S. Ct. Fla. No. SC37-060, at 22 (filed March 15, 2005). See also *Riechmann v. State*, 966 So. 2d 298 (Fla. 2007).

Chapter 8: The Defense Lawyer

1. All this appeared in his statement, taken one week after the crime: *Statement of Arthur McKenzie* (October 23, 1986, 15:15), File 044-101625-28. Some years later we called him as a witness, and he testified consistently with his statement: *Testimony of Arthur McKenzie, Maharaj 3.850 Hearing Tr.* at 836.

2. *Statement of George Bell* (October 24, 1986, 19:17), File 044-101579-85.

3. Bizarrely, Judge Bagley, who was sitting on Kris's post-conviction hearing, would not allow George Bell to testify based on the prosecution's objection that Hendon had specifically withdrawn him as a witness at the trial. *Maharaj 3.850 Hearing Tr.* at 861. The issue before Judge Bagley was whether Hendon had acted appropriately in making this decision—so of course his testimony was relevant.

4. *Statement of Douglas Scott* (October 29, 1986, 14:35pm), File 044-101620-24.

5. Ramkissoon knew Kris very well and would have been able to provide other important testimony. He had been present when two women from Trinidad were meeting with Kris about Derrick Moo Young ripping them off for a total of $135,000. Kris's response had not been to get angry—he had the money, so he reimbursed them what they had lost. As many other witnesses could have confirmed, Kris simply brought a lawsuit to get the money back.

6. We ended up not calling her as a witness in the post-conviction hearing because of some choice things that she said about her views on law enforcement during her deposition: *Maharaj 3.850 Hearing Tr.* at 942-47. Notwithstanding the fact that she did not like the police, I believed what she said, and her statement corresponded to what all the other witnesses were saying.

7. These verbatim quotes from Hendon are taken from his testimony later (in 1997) when we called him as a witness at a hearing challenging the quality of his representation. For the most part, his earlier statements to Ben and me were similar to his later statements in court, but I have relied on the transcript as a more reliable rendition of what he actually said rather than the notes we took at the time. I should make clear that no court ever found Hendon to be legally ineffective. I strongly disagree with the courts' ruling in this regard, but when I refer to his work on the case as inadequate, I am expressing my opinion rather than stating a finding by a court.

8. Jack P. Friedman, "Criminal Procedure—Alibi Instructions and Due Process of Law," *Western New England Law Review* 20 (1988), 342: "An 'alibi instruction' informs the jury that the prosecution has the burden of disproving the defendant's alibi beyond a reasonable doubt and that the defendant does not have the burden of proving the alibi."

9. American Bar Association, "Guidelines for the Appointment and Performance of Defense Counsel in Death Penalty Cases, rev. ed. 2003," *Hofstra Law Review* 31 (2003), 913, 952: "The defense team should consist of no fewer than two attorneys qualified in accordance with Guideline 5.1, an investigator, and a mitigation specialist." The guidelines refer to "the four individuals constituting the smallest allowable team" in a capital case (at 957), yet Eric Hendon was sailing solo.

10. See, for example, Peter Lattman, "Lerach's Enron Class-Action: The First $1 Billion Fee?," *Wall Street Journal* (June 1, 2006): "Class-action king Bill Lerach could be on the verge of winning the first billion-dollar award of attorneys' fees in the history of American securities litigation." Lawyers' fees are often shockingly disproportionate to the relief they win for their clients. In a settlement against the brokerage firm A.G. Edwards, each of the plaintiffs received only about $24 worth of coupons toward mutual fund fees, to be used over three years—while their lawyers split $21 million in fees. In a case against headset makers, claiming their products carried insufficient warnings about potential damage to hearing, the only relief to the client was a rewording of the manual, while the lawyers got $850,000 in fees and expenses.

11. Nationwide, a lawyer immediately out of law school expects to be paid $151 per hour, ranging up to $224 after twenty years of practice. See "Hourly Billing Rate Survey Report for Job: Attorney / Lawyer," *Pay Scale.*

12. *Martinez-Macias v. Collins*, 810 F. Supp. 782, 786-87, 796-813 (W.D. Tex. 1991), *aff'd*, 979 F.2d 1067 (5th Cir. 1992); Gordon Dickinson, "Man Freed in Machete Murder Case," *El Paso Times*, June 24, 1993, 1.

13. See *Wilson v. State*, 574 So. 2d 1338, 1340 (Miss. 1990); *Pruett v. State*, 574 So. 2d 1342 (Miss. 1990). All the lawyers in these two cases received less than the minimum wage. The two attorneys for Wilson documented 779.2 and 562 hours, and the two attorneys for Pruett documented 449.5 and 482.5 hours. Thus, the rates ranged from $1.28 per hour to $2.22 per hour. Ibid., 1348n7 (Anderson, J., dissenting). By the time one has paid administrative staff, paralegals and others, and rent, every hour that an office remains open costs more than $25. Long ago, I wrote something on this matter. See Anthony Paduano and Clive Stafford Smith, "The Unconscionability of Sub-Minimum Wages Paid Appointed Counsel in Capital Cases," *Rutgers Law Review* 43 (1991), 281. So have many others. In November 2010 the Iowa Supreme Court struck down the $1,500 fee cap that was then applicable in all felony appeals. The court did simple arithmetic: if an appellate lawyer does the maximum number of cases permitted each year (25) and receives the maximum amount ($1,500), he or she will be paid $37,500. Since running a law office in Iowa costs an average of $70,000 per year, this would entail a loss of $32,500 before considering paying the lawyer a salary. The lawyers in the relevant appeals kept time sheets, and they were being paid between $12.27 and $12.56 per hour for their work. *Simmons v. State Public Defender*, No. 07-0870 (2010).

14. See Thomas L. Jones, "The O.J. Simpson Murder Trial," *CrimeLibrary*. The prosecution spent $4 million, using as many as nine lawyers in court. The county spent $3 million, mainly on the costs

associated with jurors. "O.J. Simpson Double Murder Trial Cost Taxpayers in Los Angeles County $9 Million," *Jet Magazine* (December 25, 1995). The precise cost of the defense has never been made known, but it was certainly considerably more than the prosecution, with as many as eleven lawyers appearing in court for Simpson.

15. Guerinot represented thirty-eight clients charged with capital murder in a career from 1980 to 2003. Twenty received the death penalty. Three were dismissed by the state for lack of evidence; five pleaded guilty to life in prison; in six cases the state took death off the table, and they were convicted and sentenced to life. The remaining four received life at trial. Lisa Olsen, "Hundreds Kept Jailed for Months Pretrial; Lawyers for the Poor Have High Caseloads, But Little Oversight, Analysis Shows," *Houston Chronicle* (October 4, 2009). The American Bar Association allows lawyers to have no more than 150 cases going at any one time, which is itself an extraordinary number.

16. Ultimately, much of the work we did was incorporated into a report by Michael M. Kurth, Ph.D., and Daryl V. Burckel, D.B.A. and C.P.A., *Defending the Indigent in Southwest Louisiana* (2002), whence I have derived the facts in the following paragraphs, except where noted. Each resident of Calcasieu Parish paid the equivalent of $6.65 per year toward the local indigent defense system, which worked out at $110 per criminal case. The prosecution also complained of a lack of funding. In 2001 the Calcasieu Parish district attorney's office had a budget of $4.2 million and a staff of eighty-eight employees, including twenty-one attorneys—each with their own investigator and secretary—as well as access to forensic testing, expert witnesses, and of course the entire police force. By comparison, the public defender's office had a budget of just $1.2 million and a staff of eighteen, including nine attorneys, no assistants, and just two investigators to cover all the cases. Even excluding the work that the police did on the cases, the prosecution was funded almost four times as well as the defense was, with five times the number of personnel.

17. *Pope v. State*, 256 Ga. 195, 345 S.E.2d 831 (1986); *Gamble v. State*, 257 Ga. 325, 357 S.E.2d 792 (1987).

18. For an excellent discussion, see Stephen B. Bright, "Counsel for the Poor: The Death Penalty Not for the Worst Crime But for the Worst Lawyer," *Yale Law Journal* 103 (1994), 1835. Illinois's record is particularly bad: "Illinois Suspends Death Penalty," CNN, January 31, 2000: "We have now freed more people than we have put to death under our system—13 people have been exonerated and 12 have been put to death," Governor Ryan told CNN. "There is a flaw in the system, without question, and it needs to be studied." I must emphasize that the number of those exonerated does not accurately reflect the frequency of error. For reasons I will discuss later in this book, the appellate process is structurally organized to *avoid* identifying mistakes. Thus, actual number of errors is likely to be much greater than the figures reflect.

19. See *Coleman v. Kemp*, 778 F.2d 1487 (11th Cir. 1985). One attorney who had been appointed to defend a capital case claimed that the appointment was "the worst thing that's ever happened to me professionally"; another stayed on the case because "to refuse would be contempt of court". A judge in a Florida case took a defense lawyer into chambers during the penalty phase to explain what it was about. The lawyer responded: "I'm at a loss. I really don't know what to do in this type of proceeding. If I'd been through one, I would, but I've never handled one except this time." *Douglas v. Wainwright*, 714 F.2d 1532, 1556 (11th Cir. 1983), *vacated and remanded*, 468 U.S. 1206 (1984), *on remand*, 739 F.2d 531 (11th Cir. 1984), *cert. denied*, 469 U.S. 1208 (1985). An Alabama defense lawyer asked for time between the guilt and penalty phases so that he could read the state's death penalty statute. Record at 1875-76, *State v. Smith*, 581 So. 2d 497 (Ala. Crim. App. 1990). See Bright, "Counsel for the Poor," n50.

20. Record Excerpts at 102, *Dungee v. Kemp*, (11th Cir.) No. 85-8202 *decided sub nom. Isaacs v. Kemp*, 778 F.2d 1482 (11th Cir. 1985), *cert. denied* 476 U.S. 1164 (1986). Sadly, this case was not unique. In *Goodwin v. Balkcom*, 684 F.2d 794, 805 n.13 (11th Cir. 1982), the defense counsel called the defendant a "little old nigger boy" in closing argument. In *Ex parte Guzmon*, 730 S.W.2d 724, 736 (Tex. Crim. App. 1987), the defense counsel referred to his Mexican client as a "wet back" in front of an all-white jury.

21. *People v. Garrison*, 254 Cal. Rptr. 257 (1986). The defense counsel, an alcoholic, was arrested en route to court one morning and was found to have a blood alcohol level of 0.27. The court was unwilling to assume that the lawyer was incompetent, even when he was under the influence of alcohol at breakfast time.

22. The state court judge predictably found the practice of napping during a capital trial acceptable. The case arose out of Houston, famous for having more people on death row than any other jurisdiction in the country and for being not too concerned with how they got there. See John Makeig, "Asleep on the Job; Slaying Trial Boring, Lawyer Said," *Houston Chronicle*, August 14, 1992, A35. The federal court of appeals also initially found no error in Calvin Burdine's lawyer sleeping during the trial, before the full court changed tack. See *Burdine v. Johnson*, 87 F. Supp. 2d 711, 713 & n.2 (S.D. Tex. 2000), *rev'd*, 231 F.3d 950 (5th Cir. 2000), *vacated en banc*, 262 F.3d 336 (5th Cir. 2001), *cert. denied*, 122 S. Ct. 2347 (2002). Ultimately Burdine avoided the death sentence on his retrial. Defense counsel was also found to have slept during a capital trial in *Harrison v. Zant*, No. 88-V-1640, Order at 2 (Super. Ct. Butts County, Ga. Oct. 5, 1990), *aff'd*, 402 S.E.2d 518 (Ga. 1991). See also *Tippins v. Walker*, 77 F.3d 682, 685–90 (2d Cir. 1996),

which found Tippins's attorney to have been "repeatedly unconscious . . . when Tippins' interests were at stake"; and *Javor v. United States*, 724 F.2d 831, 832–35 (9th Cir. 1984), in which Javor's attorney slept through a substantial part of a two-week trial.

23. *State v. Leatherwood*, 548 So.2d 389 (Miss. 1989). On retrial, Leatherwood pleaded to time served (meaning that he was freed immediately) to avoid the possibility of his facing another death sentence. Notwithstanding substantial evidence of his innocence, he went on the sex offender registry. More than twenty years later, he is still on it. Similar stories abound. In *Bellamy v. Cogdell*, 952 F.2d 626 (2d Cir. 1991), a seventy-year-old defense counsel had been found incompetent prior to the trial; a second counsel was promised, but nobody told the client. In *Waterhouse v. Rodriguez*, 848 F.2d 375 (2d Cir. 1988), the defense lawyer was in the midst of disbarment proceedings at the time of the trial. In *House v. Balkcom*, 725 F.2d 608, 612 (11th Cir. 1984), *cert. denied*, 469 U.S. 870 (1984), the court-appointed lawyer cross-examined a significant witness, although he had not heard the man's direct testimony to the jury because he had been outside parking his car.

Chapter 9: The Other Suspects

1. While the Florida Supreme Court ruled that Hendon should have objected to the use of the *Caribbean Echo* articles, the court thought the jurors would have considered them for the limited purpose for which it might be legally admissible—to show that Kris Maharaj had a motive for being angry at the Moo Youngs. But the jurors had no reason to think that any of the articles were false, and the notion that they could carefully delimit the relevance of the material for one purpose alone, and otherwise ignore it, is the kind of fiction that gives courts a bad name.

2. On drug corruption in the Bahamas generally, see Ethan A. Nadelmann, *Cops Across Borders: The Internationalization of U.S. Criminal Law Enforcement* (Pennsylvania State University Press, 1993), 277 and n50. See also Carl Hiaasen and Jim McGee, "A Nation for Sale: Corruption in the Bahamas," *Miami Herald* (September 23, 1984); and U.S. Senate, Committee on Foreign Relations, Subcommittee on Terrorism, Narcotics, and International Operations, *Drugs, Law Enforcement and Foreign Policy* (Washington, D.C.: Government Printing Office, 1989), 18.

3. For much of the background on both Pindling and the Bahamian drug scene, I am indebted to Paul Eddy, *The Cocaine Wars: Murder, Money, Corruption, and the World's Most Valuable Commodity* (New York: W. W. Norton, 1988).

4. By 1984 the Medellín cartel controlled 80 percent of the world's cocaine. However, it went too far even for its crooked supporters in the Colombian government. Lehder was believed to have been at least partially behind in the 1985 Palace of Justice siege, which resulted in the death of eleven supreme court judges and eighty-four others, as well as being responsible for the death of Justice Minister Rodrigo Lara in 1984. The government cracked down, and many of the Medellín cartel fled to the protection of Manuel Noriega in Panama. Lehder mistrusted Noriega and went instead to Nicaragua, then returned to the Colombian jungle, where he was eventually caught and extradited to the United States in February 1987.

5. Alan A. Block, *Masters of Paradise: Organized Crime and the Internal Revenue Service of the Bahamas* (New Brunswick, N.J.: Transaction, 1998).

6. *United States v. Lehder-Rivas*, 955 F.2d 1510 (11th Cir. 1992). Lehder consciously imitated Hitler's "organizational genius" in structuring his smuggling operation. Later, he would strike a deal and testify against Manuel Noriega in order to reduce his sentence—since he is still in prison many years later, he insists the United States has not respected the deal. *United States v. Lehder-Rivas*, 136 Fed.Appx. 324 (11th Cir. 2005).

7. U.S. Senate, *Drugs, Law Enforcement and Foreign Policy*, 19, citing INCSR, Department of State, at 123 (March 1989). The Senate report notes that "the United States has for more than three years sought extradition of Nigel Bowe, a Bahamian lawyer with strong ties to the PLP and the Bahamian government." It goes on to observe that "U.S. law enforcement authorities believe Bowe has played a key role in organizing smuggling throughout the Caribbean." See *United States v. Bowe*, 221 F.3d 1183 (11th Cir. 2000).

8. There were other indicators of how important Hosein might be to the case. One of our investigators talked to another witness who relayed some important hearsay: Hosein had confessed his own involvement in the murders to a third person, divulging gruesome details and confirming that Kris was innocent. This evidence was obviously crucial, but the third person refused to discuss it. Thus we could neither present it nor rely on it. Because of a promise made at the time, I am not at liberty to elaborate on this highly relevant point.

9. Mark Fineman, "Triple Hanging Returns Death Penalty to Trinidad," *Los Angeles Times*, June 5, 1999. Shortly before I arrived in Trinidad, Ramesh offered to take the case of one of those he would later see hanged, Russell Sankerali, for $5.5 million in Trinidad dollars, which comes to around $850,000 U.S. The fee proved too much for Sankerali's family, so Ramesh did not defend him. On the day before the execution was scheduled to take place, Amnesty International provided Ramesh with a tape

that purported to prove Sankerali's innocence; the hanging went ahead anyway, and Amnesty accused Ramesh of using the case for his own political purposes. In many ways, this was a small-town mirror of similar events in the United States where, in January 1992, former death penalty opponent Bill Clinton, in a blatant act of political opportunism, flew home to Arkansas during the presidential campaign to oversee the execution of the lobotomized Ricky Ray Rector.

10. Much of my information is derived from U.S. Senate, *Drugs, Law Enforcement and Foreign Policy*, a comprehensive report that states, "Between 1979 and 1983, the PDF [Noriega's party] helped the Medellín cartel launder billions of dollars through Panama"; "between 1970 and 1987, Noriega's name appeared in more than 80 different DEA files."

11. Derrick's passport reflects that he arrived in Panama City on April 10, July 21, August 20, August 28, September 8, September 15, and September 26, his stays varying from one to five nights. His visits rapidly accelerated as the day of the murder—October 16—approached. The "business" being conducted in Panama seems to have been picking up.

Chapter 10: The Money Trail

1. U.S. Senate, Committee on Foreign Relations, Subcommittee on Terrorism, Narcotics, and International Operations, *Drugs, Law Enforcement and Foreign Policy* (Washington, D.C.: Government Printing Office, 1989), 9. See also Jeffrey Robinson, *The Laundrymen: Inside the World's Third Largest Business* (New York: Simon & Schuster, 1994), 224, 235.

2. William R. Long, "Colombia Drug Lords Find Fugitive Life Erodes Power," *Los Angeles Times*, October 22, 1989), in "Noriega and Key Players in the Drug Trade, Part 1," *Historical Text Archive*. For a fuller discussion of the differences between Cali and Medellín, see Misha Glenny, *McMafia: Crime Without Frontiers* (New York: Bodley Head, 2008), 287–88.

3. Douglas Farah, "Cali Drug Cartel Avoids Crackdown, Powerful Traffickers Operate Differently from Medellín Rivals," *Washington Post* (October 5, 1989), A1, in "Noriega and Key Players in the Drug Trade, Part 1."

4. "Noriega and Key Players in the Drug Trade, Part 1": Flavio Acosta was "formerly commander of the Medellín Metro Police and considered to be in the traffickers' hip pocket. He never made an important narcotics arrest. Medellín police are known to frequently make multi-million peso bank deposits. Their arrest of Pablo Escobar in 1986 was a mistake."

5. Glenny, *McMafia*, 290–91. See also U.S. Senate, *Drugs, Law Enforcement and Foreign Policy*, 28.

6. Peter Ross, "DEA Scam Hooks a Drug-Cartel Money Man," *Washington Post*, August 27, 1989, A01: "The trade is so successful that its biggest problem is not the threat of arrest or the seizures of drugs, but how to move vast amounts of money. Annual sales revenues are estimated at $100 billion, and almost all of it begins as cash. Managing that volume is extremely difficult, since federal law requires reporting of cash transactions or bank deposits in excess of $10,000. Some of the currency is used to purchase cars or small businesses, airplanes and real estate. But most of it must be converted into another form for return to the drug lords." See also "Anderson Warns Against Powerful Medellin Drug Cartel," UPI, November 1, 1988, in "Noriega and Key Players in the Drug Trade, Part 1."

7. Robert Sherrill, "Stalking International Drug Traffickers," *Washington Post*, January 6, 1986, A04, a review of James Mills, *The Underground Empire* (New York: Doubleday, 1986), in "Noriega and Key Players in the Drug Trade, Part 1."

8. Ross, "DEA Scam," A01.

9. Paul Eddy, *The Cocaine Wars: Murder, Money, Corruption, and the World's Most Valuable Commodity* (New York: W.W. Norton, 1988), 34–36 (emphasis in the original).

10. This process, along with many others, is described in Robinson, *Laundrymen*.

11. As of 2008, the Baptist Church Loan Corporation offers loans of $25,000 to $5 million.

12. According to Bryant, the LACLC was based at the Euclid Street Baptist Church, 1408 South Euclid, Anaheim, California 92802.

13. All quotes from W.C. Bryant come from his deposition in *Shaula Ann Nagel and DMY International Inc. v. William Penn Life Insurance Company of New York*, No. 87-0786 CIV (S.D. Fla), taken on October 31, 1988. I received a copy of this document from Brenton Ver Ploeg.

14. Originally, Bryant said they were worth $500 million. In documents that Ver Ploeg had found, he put the second valuation at a very specific $94,488,614. Ibid., 29, and *Exhibit 2*. I located a third valuation, a letter in the Moo Youngs' briefcase from someone called Gordon Daskowski to Dr. W. C. Bryant regarding two sets of gemstones worth $9,310,401.06 and $134,872,546.66, in the possession of the LACLC (for a total of $144,182,947.72). *Maharaj Exh. OCY* at B002193. This reference to different sets of gems was consistent with the itemization that was included in one of Bryant's documents.

15. See *Kazanjian Bros.*, http://www.kazanjianbros.com/history.htm: "The most famous of all Queensland sapphires is the 733 ct Black Star of Queensland. Found on Klondyke Ridge in 1935 by

14 year old Roy Spencer, it was allegedly used as a door stop for many years by his father Harry Spencer." "Mining Sapphire in Australia," *GemSelect.com* (May 9, 2008). The original uncut crystal was 1,156 carats. Jeweler Harry Kazanjian purchased it in 1947. It was then cut and polished, revealing a six-ray star. While estimates have varied, and there are suggestions that it has been sold for as much as $100 million, it seems to have been valued at least at $50 million.

16. In the later 1980s, in the Japanese asset price bubble, some banks granted increasingly risky loans. DKB apparently financed crime organizations in order to invest its capital resources more easily than its competitors were doing. After the bubble burst, the bad loans were poor value for money. A raid by Tokyo prosecutors in 1997 relating to the loans to *sōkaiya* (local racketeers) laid DKB open to public criticism. Kuniji Miyazaki, former president and the then-chairman of DKB, faced severe pressure over a series of alleged misdeeds and committed suicide by hanging himself at his home.

17. The documents purported to come from Rex C. Jensen (vice-president) and Dennis L. Walker (president) of the International Bank of the South Pacific (Kingdom of Tonga). There were various such letters of credit. Some had the names whited out, and some names had merely been marked through so you could not read who the beneficiaries were. The Moo Youngs seem to have got their hands on some (possibly genuine) letters of credit, whited out the names of the real beneficiaries, and then made up a substitute beneficiary with the same number of characters as the original—the name *Cargil International* was not long enough to fill the space, so they had to put both *Cargil* and *Amer Enterprises* in.

18. R. T. Naylor, *The Wages of Crime: Black Markets, Illegal Finance, and the Underworld Economy* (Ithaca, N.Y.: Cornell University Press, 2002), 170. See also *United States v. Bell*, 27 F.Supp.2d 1191, 1196 (E.D.Ca. 1998), a case assessing tax liens on Glen D. Bell and his wife for $3.6 million plus interest: "The beneficiary [of the property] was an apparent creation of Mr. Bell, known as the 'International Bank of the South Pacific.'"

Chapter 11: The Colombian Connection

1. Pereira has also long been in the area of influence of Carlos Mario Jiménez (alias Macaco), one of fourteen paramilitary leaders finally extradited to the United States on drug charges in May 2008.

2. The address on Mejia's card was listed as All Leather Import and Export Inc., 100 S.E. 1st Street, #42, Miami, Fla. 33131. A leather company was such an archetype for drug dealers in the early 1980s that the DEA set up a sting operation using a phony company called Green Ice, importing leather goods. Jeffrey Robinson, *The Laundrymen: Inside the World's Third Largest Business* (New York: Simon & Schuster, 1994), 250.

3. Pérez was allegedly involved in the second-largest drug seizure that has ever taken place worldwide. "On 30 April 1983, 667 kilos of high purity cocaine was seized which had been found inside a small plane that had landed in Charallave, near Caracas. This plane came from Colombia and was owned by Lizardo Márquez Pérez, a retired military officer living in Estado Táchira. One of Márquez Pérez's partners was the Regional Commander of the Venezuelan army at the Colombian frontier, General Ital del Valle Alliegro, who later became Minister of Defense.... This was the largest seizure of cocaine in Latin America and second in the world, surpassed only by the 800 kilos captured a few months earlier in Miami. Márquez Pérez fled to Medellín and was arrested in the USA on 10 November 1984..." See Pedro Grima, *Narcotráfico S.A. La nueva ruta del Opio.*

4. "Noriega and Key Players in the Drug Trade, Part 1," *Historical Text Archive.*

5. Mejia never did his community service because the U.S. embassy in Colombia refused to allow him a visa to reenter the United States. *Letter of Manuel Fente, counsel for Mejia, to Philip French, Department of State* (September 20, 1989) (File 044-132837). Being banned from the United States upset Mejia considerably. He wrote to the Oklahoma magistrate about his treatment when he went to get a visa. "I found myself in front of a person who didn't have the least consideration and respect toward me," he complained in a letter. "He thought he was talking to a criminal or a delinquent . . . when I expressed my admiration and respect for your country, he had the impudence to suggest that he didn't believe the explanation that I gave him relating to my case, and also that Colombians had a bad prestige." *Letter of Jamie Vallejo Mejia to Hon. Robin J. Cauthorn, U.S. Magistrate* (July 12, 1989) (File 044-132839). Mejia submitted a letter from the Pereira branch of Colombia Red Cross, suggesting that he be permitted to do his community service for them—in between "looking after his 85 year old mother." *Letter of Yaneth Ch. De Jaramillo, President, Red Cross of Colombia, to Hon. Robin J. Cauthorn, U.S. Magistrate* (July 12, 1989) (File 044-132840). But eventually his lawyer worked out a deal whereby he was forgiven the two hundred hours of work. *Letter of Manuel Fuente to Maci Almon, U.S. Probation Service* (July 27, 1989) (File 044-132842). Ultimately, then, he got off without any punishment at all.

6. Paul Eddy, *The Cocaine Wars: Murder, Money, Corruption, and the World's Most Valuable Commodity* (New York: W. W. Norton, 1988), 291. Around the same time that Mejia was purporting to run a leather goods concern in Miami, his compatriot Francisco Torres was also operating an "import-export

336 | *Notes*

business in Miami." On November 22, 1983, Torres—a Medellín businessman—tried to buy thirteen hundred fifty-five-gallon drums of ether in New Jersey. The company reported it to the government, which then launched a sting operation. Torres candidly told the FBI agents who posed as ether dealers that it would be used for processing cocaine. Ibid., 295–96.

7. James Kelly, "Trouble in Paradise," *Time*, November 23, 1983.

8. Eddy, *Cocaine Wars*, 231.

9. Ibid., 71, 92, 201. As the MDPD website explains, the Centac 26 bureau still exists. "The team, which eventually became the Specialized Investigations Squad, has evolved through the years. The investigations have also expanded to include organized crime, home invasions, complex murder cases, police sting operations, and other acts of domestic street-style terrorism. Through the development of many confidential informants and after numerous investigations, the squad has been credited with not only convicting various previously 'untouchable' criminals, but also with the seizure of millions of dollars in cash and property."

10. Eddy, *Cocaine Wars*, 194ff, 243, 256, 281. At their first trial, the jury could not agree on a verdict for the police officers on trial—mainly thanks to the best narco-defense lawyers money could buy. The legal teams received at least $1.6 million in fees. Eventually, once most of their profits were in the pockets of their attorneys, their united front cracked, and they pointed fingers at one another. The prosecution went on to secure some convictions.

11. Ibid., 202.

Chapter 12: The Judge

1. Swickle's downfall was particularly sad, as his career had included various interesting criminal defense cases, including one that went to the Supreme Court, albeit ultimately without success. See *Murphy v. Florida*, 421 U.S. 794 (1975).

2. Hendon also said he was anticipating "other witnesses who would be called by the state whose testimony would be . . . contradicted by the state's earlier witnesses." He was referring to Prince Ellis, who had already testified. He thought that Ellis's testimony would prove inconsistent with that of Eddie Dames, who he had deposed prior to trial, and he worried that if the case started over again, the prosecution would not call Ellis. It apparently did not occur to him that the prosecution would not call Dames—which is what happened.

3. *State v. Riechmann*, 777 So. 2d 342, n.12 (Fla. 2000): "Section 921.141, Florida Statutes (1985), require the trial judge to independently weigh the aggravating and mitigating circumstances to determine what penalty should be imposed upon the defendant. This section also requires the trial judge to draft the order," citing *Florida Statutes Ann.* 921.141(3) (1999). "The court is overwhelmingly compelled to conclude," the prosecutor had written, that the death penalty was appropriate, that the aggravating circumstances outweighed the mitigating, and so on, discussing at least eleven different issues. *State v. Riechmann*, Record of Trial, at 593–600. As time went by, further examples of Judge Solomon's abdication of his role came to light. Rickey Roberts had been sentenced to die in Judge Solomon's courtroom. Like Kris's case, Roberts's had been the narrowest of jury verdicts, seven to five for death. The governor had signed two warrants for his execution, and the second time, after Roberts had run through one set of appeals, he had been set to die in the electric chair. Roberts's lawyers figured they should make the same requests that we had made, to see whether Solomon ever wrote his own orders. This time, instead of turning the material over, the prosecutor's office refused the request for public records, and it took an order from the Florida Supreme Court to stay his execution and produce the records. *State v. Roberts*, SC92496, at 6 (Fla. Dec. 5, 2002): "During the hearing on the 'Motion to Get the Facts,' Roberts's counsel also questioned Judge Solomon about who had prepared the original sentencing order in Roberts's trial . . . Judge Solomon revealed that the State had drafted the sentencing order and the judge had merely signed it and read it in court."

4. Stephen B. Bright and Patrick J. Keenan, "Judges and the Politics of Death: Deciding Between the Bill of Rights and the Next Election in Capital Cases," *Boston University Law Review* 73 (May 1995), 759n87, n165, citing Bill Poovey, "Hooper Criticizes Chief Justice for Soliciting from Lawyers," *Tuscaloosa News* (July 20, 1994), B8; and Phillip Rawls, "Justice Race Another Political Brawl," *Columbus (Ga.) Ledger-Enquirer* (December 10, 1994).

5. In *Bracy v. Gramley*, 520 U.S. 899 (1997), the Supreme Court traces the sordid history of Operation Greylord, which exposed corruption in the state judiciary of Chicago. For other cases where judges have been caught accepting bribes, see also, e.g., *Ohio v. McGettrick*, 40 Ohio App. 3d 25, 531 N. E. 2d 755 (1988); and *In re Brennan*, 65 N.Y. 2d 564, 483 N.E. 2d 484 (1985). See generally Geoffrey Hazard and Angelo Dondi, *Legal Ethics—A Comparative Study* (Stanford, Calif.: Stanford University Press, 2004), 82–83. With respect to federal judges, see Mary L. Volcansek, Maria Elisabetta De Franciscis, and Jacqueline Lucienne Lafon, *Judicial Misconduct: A Cross-National Comparison* (Gainesville: University Press of Florida, 1996), 9.

6. During the time that Rose Bird voted to reverse every case, a majority of the court voted to overturn fifty-eight of the sixty-one death sentences (95 percent). See Patrick K. Brown, *The Rise and Fall of Rose Bird: A Career Killed by the Death Penalty*, M.A. thesis, California State University at Fullerton (2007). See, generally, "Guide to the Californians to Defeat Rose Bird, 1985-86," Online Archive of California, California State Library.

7. Maura Dolan, "State High Court Is Strong Enforcer of Death Penalty," *Los Angeles Times* (April 9, 1995). See generally Bright and Keenan, "Judges and the Politics of Death," 759.

8. In slightly fuller detail: "Presidential candidate Bill Clinton demonstrated that he was tough on crime in his 1992 campaign by scheduling the execution of a brain-damaged man shortly before the New Hampshire primary. Clinton had embraced the death penalty in 1982 after his defeat in a bid for reelection as governor of Arkansas in 1980. In his presidential campaign ten years later, Clinton returned from campaigning in New Hampshire to preside over the execution of Rickey Ray Rector, an African-American who had been sentenced to death by an all-white jury. Rector had destroyed part of his brain when he turned his gun on himself after killing the police officer for whose murder he received the death sentence. Logs at the prison show that in the days leading up to his execution, Rector was howling and barking like a dog, dancing, singing, laughing inappropriately, and saying that he was going to vote for Clinton. Clinton denied clemency and allowed the execution to proceed, thereby protecting himself from being labeled as 'soft on crime' and helping the Democrats to take back the crime issue. Clinton's first three television advertisements in his bid for reelection—already begun a year and a half before the 1996 presidential election—all focused on crime and Clinton's support to expand the death penalty." Bright and Keenan, "*Judges and the Politics of Death*," n70. See also Leslie Phillips, "Crime Pays as a Political Issue," *USA Today* (Oct. 10, 1994), 11A.

9. U.S. Constitution, Article II, Section II, Clause 2. The Constitution defines the selection only of Supreme Court justices, but Congress has applied the same rules for lower court federal judges.

10. Sometimes both senators in a state will be from the opposing party. Nevertheless, during the tenure of President Franklin Roosevelt, more than 90 percent of the nominees were Democrats.

11. The death penalty continues to play a significant role in the confirmation hearings of Supreme Court justices; in some quarters any hint of opposition to the death penalty is cause for concern. See Julie Davis, "Sotomayor's Confirmation Hearings to Begin July 13," Associated Press, June 8, 2009; and Benjamin Weiser, "In '98, Hints from Sotomayor on Death Penalty," *New York Times*, June 24, 2009.

12. In *Bracy v. Gramley*, 520 U.S. 899 (1997), a corrupt judge's compensatory bias was the precise issue. Bracy had not bribed a judge himself, but he claimed that the judge would have imposed harsher penalties on all others, to cover for the fact that he periodically let someone off who paid him money. While the Supreme Court viewed this as a difficult burden of proof for him to carry, the court held that he had a right to discovery on the issue, to have a chance to make his case. This is precisely the discovery that we demanded on Kris's behalf, citing to *Bracy*, but no court was willing to order it. There has never been a hearing of any kind on the question of Judge Gross's attempt to solicit a bribe from Kris.

13. In terms of procedures intended to ensure a more reliable outcome, I suspect that *Miranda* warnings do help prevent the police from overreaching, although some will disagree on this point. Various rules that the Supreme Court has not yet adopted are surely vital to a fair outcome—for example, banning gruesome photographs of dead bodies from the courtroom, since these only inflame jurors to convict someone (anyone) even if the man before them had nothing to do with the crime. In a capital case in Lake Charles that I was doing around this time, in which the killer cut up two dead women, some truly horrendous pictures had been taken. We conducted a study with the pictures, showing them to fifty volunteers. At the start, we asked whether any of them had an opinion as to whether the person on trial was guilty—and none did. But merely viewing the photographs made a large number of these mock jurors think that the client was guilty, although the pictures themselves were no evidence against him at all. Such is the true nature of prejudice, and this is why procedural rules are needed to ensure fairness.

Chapter 13: The Jury

1. The genesis of the legal term *voir dire* is debated. In modern French, it literally means, "to see, to say," which is a good description of the process: observing the prospective jurors speak, and listening to what they have to say. However, one school of thought suggests that it comes from old Anglo-Norman, in which *voir* (or *voire*) is derived from the Latin *verum* ("that which is true"), so the phrase would mean "to speak truthfully."

2. A juror must also swear that they will not *always* impose a death sentence, should the defendant be found guilty. However, most defense lawyers are not good at rooting out and removing the "automatic pro-death penalty" jurors. As the American public generally becomes less strongly in favor of the death penalty—a shift that has gradually taken place over the past twenty years—the elimination of jurors becomes increasingly damaging to the defendant: there are fewer people who will always vote for

death, and more who have qualms about the death penalty. When the United States was in a more liberal phase in the 1960s, this meant that as many as 50 percent of jurors would be removed from the case because of their opposition to capital punishment. Thus, in the seminal case of *Witherspoon v. Illinois*, 391 U.S. 510 (1968), "the prosecution eliminated nearly half the venire of prospective jurors by challenging . . . any venireman who expressed qualms about capital punishment."

3. The best solution to these problems is to ensure that everyone in the voir dire process speaks out. However, this is not possible in the federal system (where the judge conducts much, and sometimes all, of the voir dire) and in some state systems. For example, in Mississippi the questioning is sometimes done collectively—with one hundred people in the courtroom. The chance of getting jurors to speak their minds openly in front of ninety-nine of their neighbors is zero.

4. *Turner v. Murray*, 476 U.S. 28, 30–31 (1986). The court held that a capital defendant accused of an interracial crime is entitled to have prospective jurors informed of the race of the victim and questioned on the issue of racial bias. But this ruling applies only to capital cases, and only to interracial crimes, and is deemed to have an impact only on the penalty phase of the trial—in other words, Turner's conviction was left undisturbed by the refusal to allow this line of questioning. All three of these caveats would seem to be unjustifiable: an African American defendant is surely likely to suffer discrimination at the hands of a bigot regardless of whether his trial is capital, regardless of whether the victim is white. And how could the court conclude that bigotry affected only the sentence and not the conviction? Mind you, *Turner* was a step in the right direction, particularly when compared to the systems in other countries (including, for example, Britain), where the racism of the potential juror is never exposed.

5. Either party may move to exclude an unlimited number of jurors who are biased because they have already formed an opinion about the case. According to *Murphy v. Florida*, 95 S. Ct. 2031, 2036 (1975), the "constitutional standard of fairness requires that a state defendant have a panel of impartial, indifferent jurors." And according to *Irvin v. Dowd*, 81 S. Ct. 1639, 1641-42 (1961), "In essence, the right to a jury trial guarantees to the criminally accused a fair trial by a panel of impartial, 'indifferent' jurors. . . . 'The theory of the law is that a juror who has formed an opinion cannot be impartial.'"

6. After both sides remove jurors for clear reasons, there are peremptorily challenges, which also can be made by either party and for which they generally do not have to articulate a reason. Depending on the jurisdiction in the United States, the parties have a variable number of such strikes. In many states, the parties have an equal number, varying according to the seriousness of the case.

7. See John Schwartz, "As Jurors Turn to Web, Mistrials Are Popping Up," *New York Times*, March 17, 2009. In a major federal drug trial in Florida, nine out of twelve jurors used Google during breaks to check out facts. While it led them toward acquittal of the accused, it thoroughly perverted the trial, as the jurors skirted the judge's ruling on admissibility of evidence by simply reading that material on the Internet. In another trial, a juror from a panel that awarded $12 million against a building materials company tweeted the result.

8. Generally, for cases I tried myself, my colleagues would do the first post-conviction interviews, allowing the jurors to be more honest in their criticism of the lawyering than they might be if they were talking to me to my face (and criticism can be hugely beneficial). However, in cases where I was not the trial lawyer, I would often do the interviews myself, getting fascinating insights into what really happened.

9. Securing Sam Johnson a new trial was a long battle. With the help of the New York law firm Cahill Gordon, we persuaded the court in New York to throw out Sam's prior conviction, which had been used at his penalty phase. Then the U.S. Supreme Court ordered a new sentencing trial based on the Mississippi jury's consideration of the unconstitutional prior conviction. See *Johnson v. Mississippi*, 486 U.S. 578 (1988).

10. See *Brief of Amicus Curiae of Kathleen Hawk Norman in Support of Petitioner's Application for Supervisory Writs* in Orleans Parish Case Number 375-994 "F," Hon. Dennis Waldron, Presiding. The brief argued that the jurors had been "deceived, duped, and denied critical evidence necessary to complete their civic responsibility."

11. One study was conducted in Michigan, where the jurors' educational background was higher than the U.S. average. See Alan Reifman, Spencer M. Gusick, and Phoebe C. Ellsworth, "Real Jurors' Understanding of the Law in Real Cases," *Law and Human Behavior* 16 (1992), 539, 546–47. The researchers studied 224 real jurors in Michigan, finding that 97 percent had high school diplomas, 53 percent had finished college, and 22 percent had graduate degrees. "Jurors were more often wrong than right," they concluded, "in their answers to questions about their right to ignore irrelevant instructions, the difference between direct and circumstantial evidence, the fact that the prosecution had the burden of proof (less than a third of those who served on *criminal* juries got this right), the prohibition against inferring guilt if a defendant did not testify, and their freedom to reject expert testimony" (emphasis in the original).

12. Jack Davis is not his real name; I have changed it for legal reasons.

13. The Florida rule on juror testimony means that jurors generally cannot testify to anything they think, only to what they see. *State v. Hamilton*, 574 So.2d 124, 125 n.3 (Fla. 1991)

14. In *Tanner v. United States*, 483 U.S. 107, 117 (1987), the insanity of a juror was considered irrelevant, as an "internal consideration," citing *Sullivan v. Fogg*, 613 F.2d 465, 467 (2nd Cir. 1980). What the Supreme Court meant is that anything that is deemed to be properly inside the jury room (be it evidence that has been admitted, or a mentally imbalanced juror) cannot be the basis for the reversal of a conviction; whereas anything that has been improperly brought in (a dictionary to check the meaning of a word, the Bible to determine whether God would vouchsafe the death penalty, and so forth) can. The rule was originally set out in *Remmer v. United States*, 347 U.S. 227 (1954), where someone allegedly made a statement, in jest, to a juror that he could profit by bringing in a verdict in favor of the taxpayer, where the man who was on trial for evading income taxes. This case has been applied in various cases, often because the jurors felt the need to consult a book in order to understand the judge's instructions.

15. Rush's letter reads as follows (the spelling and grammar are her own):

> Dear Mr. Dioguardi,
> Under the situation and such circumstance I hope that I have made the right decision. I talk to my friends Bertha and her husband Olive about this, Olive agree that I write to you. Bertha, however, was against it. Nevertheless, I felt I had to write you. I cannot omit what I have seen. When I saw the good within you and how hard your wife was trying; I prayed about it. One word appear before me *repent*. If you repent and run a clean business it is the good within you that will save you, and you will gain what you have lost. Before I continue I must explain something to you. I have eyes and ears that I can see things before it happen. I can tell you about other and what they are thinking and doing. If I am wrong about this it is the first time.
> I would like to visit you. I would like to talk to you about what appear before me. I would like to do so when my eyes fully open. They are only partly open. I don't know at the present when they will open. Unfortunate, a curse was put upon them some years ago. I have some people working on them. Everything is being done that can be done. So we will have to wait. As I stated I cannot omit what appear before me, when I was on the jury bench. You feel that this is the end for you. However, it is not. Something appear before me that I must do. It is the good within you that I must use and within that good, you will gain what you have lost. If, however, I am wrong it is the first time.
> Why, you let such a relationship exist between you and a man like Hellerman? When I think of the good that I saw within you it does not add up. Where did Hellerman get those fur coats? Does he have any for sail? Omit the question. I really can't afford one, and if I could I probably be afraid to wear it.
> Why persecute your wife? Your mistake your guilty then take it out on her. The ordeal you put her through I wonder how she survive through it. One word appear before me brave. She is a brave girl. She love you. She never stop loving you not a single moment. Tell her to please be careful. From what I can see she is still in business. I suggest it is not wise at this time. I believe she is being watch.
> That was a good lawyer you had. I entain to send him some custom as soon as my eyes open. Tell [your co-defendant] Ostrer I am praying for him.
> Mr. Dioguardi, I want to ask a favor of you please. I want you to look upon me as a woman and I look upon you as a man and not white man and black woman. Olive agree with me. Let's leave color out, OK.
> I was told you will only have to serve one third of the time given. So relax this is not the end. Soon you will be free. When I call the Federal information center and the record room yesterday they all know you. They all seem to have it in for you. Its seated deep within them like a personal matter.
> Sincerely, Genena

The letter sheets were printed with the word "LIBRA" and a picture of a woman with scales. On the last page of the letter, under the picture, Rush wrote: "The sign Libra is the heavenly house of the zodiac under which I was born." See *United States v. Dioguardi*, 492 F.2d 70, 75 n.7 (2nd Cir.1974).

16. *Tanner v. United States*, 483 U.S. 107, 115 (1987). Hardy was the second juror to come forward unsolicited. Earlier, Juror Vera Asbul had described the same kind of conduct, although not in the same detail. Ibid., 113.

17. On remand from the Supreme Court, the Eleventh Circuit Court of Appeals held that neither criminal law was applicable to either Tanner or his codefendant, William Conover, so they both walked free: *United States v. Conover & Tanner*, 845 F.2d 256 (11th Cir. 1988). Four of the justices in *Tanner* felt that evidence of drug abuse and alcoholism was an outside influence that should have resulted in reversal: *Tanner v. United States*, 483 U.S. 107, 140-141 (1987, dissenting opinion): "I would nonetheless find the testimony of juror intoxication admissible under the Rule's 'outside influence' exception. As a

common-sense matter, drugs and alcohol *are* outside influences on jury members" (emphasis in original; footnote omitted).

18. See James Liebman, Jeffrey Fagan, and Valerie West, "A Broken System: Error Rates in Capital Cases 1973-1995," *Columbia Law School* (2000). In Florida, the figures were slightly more extreme: 73 percent of cases did not survive review.

19. After Congress enacted the 1996 Anti-Terrorism and Effective Death Penalty Act, designed to expedite the legal process, Liebman presented another study that sought to identify solutions. See James S. Liebman et al., "Getting to Death: Fairness and Efficiency in the Processing and Conclusion of Death Penalty Cases After Furman, Final Technical Report," National Institute of Justice, U.S. Department of Justice (2004). Liebman's proposals suggested requiring "proof beyond *any* doubt that the defendant committed the capital crime" before a death sentence can be imposed; making it clear that the alternative to death is life without parole; preventing judges from overriding a jury verdict of life; and so forth. None of the proposals has been adopted across the United States, and the Supreme Court has explicitly determined that several are not constitutionally required.

20. Of course, these numbers are affected by the fact that many of these prisoners would have entered a guilty plea—the general estimate is that 95 percent of U.S. cases are settled by a plea bargain. However, they arguably cannot be discounted, as each person would have made an assessment as to whether he or she would have been convicted at trial.

Chapter 14: The Road to Nowhere

1. See Stephen B. Bright, "Counsel for the Poor: The Death Sentence Not for the Worst Crime but for the Worst Lawyer," *Yale Law Journal* (1994). In the lead Supreme Court case on the issue, the Supreme Court said that the prisoner had "advanced no explanation whatever for his failure to object at trial." See *Wainwright v. Sykes*, 433 U.S. 72, 91 (1977). There is a good reason for this failure: it was not the defendant's job to object, but his lawyer's.

2. My own experience is not so different from the nation as a whole. Over the years, roughly 90 percent of cases have been affirmed in state post-conviction. See James Liebman, Jeffrey Fagan, and Valerie West, "A Broken System: Error Rates in Capital Cases 1973-1995, National Composite Capital Punishment Report Card," *Columbia Law School* (2000). Of those reversed, the overwhelming majority would have come at the direct appeal and federal habeas levels.

3. Florida leads the nation with twenty-three death row exonerations to date. See "Exonerations by State," Death Penalty Information Center.

4. William Geimer and Jonathan Amsterdam, "Why Jurors Vote Life or Death: Operative Factors in Ten Florida Death Penalty Cases," *American Journal of Criminal Law* 15 (1988), 1, 28 See also Arnold Barnett, "Some Distribution Patterns for the Georgia Death Sentence," *University of California at Davis Law Review* 18 (1985), 1327, 1338–45; Michael Mello and Ruthann Robson, "Judge Over Jury: Florida's Practice of Imposing Death over Life in Capital Cases," *Florida State University Law Review* 13 (1985), 31, 59–60; Lawrence T. White, "Juror Decision-Making in the Capital Trial," *Law and Human Behavior* 11 (1987), 113, 123–26. Even the Supreme Court has ruled that certain evidence of innocence must be admitted at the penalty phase. See *Green v. Georgia*, 442 U.S. 95 (1979). However, more recently, the Supreme Court has backtracked on the issue. See *Franklin v. Lynaugh*, 487 U.S. 164, 174 (1988): "Our edict that, in a capital case, 'the sentencer . . . [may] not be precluded from considering, as a mitigating factor, any aspect of a defendant's character or record and any of the circumstances of the offense,' in no way mandates reconsideration by capital juries, in the sentencing phase, of their 'residual doubts' over a defendant's guilt. . . . This Court's prior decisions, as we understand them, fail to recognize a constitutional right to have such doubts considered as a mitigating factor."

5. See *Darling v. State*, 808 So.2d 145, 162 (Fla. 2002): "We have repeatedly observed that residual doubt is not an appropriate mitigating circumstance." See also *Brief of Appellee* (the State of Florida), *Merck v. Florida*, No. 91,581 (filed Sept. 1999): it is inappropriate to "turn a penalty phase proceeding into a guilt phase proceeding . . . or . . . permit[] evidence to confuse or mislead the jury, in the performance of its responsibility of returning a sentencing recommendation, or . . . subvert[] a long line of precedents of this Court that residual or lingering doubt is not a non-statutory mitigating factor." Troy Merck's case was reversed because of the failure to consider mitigating evidence of intoxication; it was okay, apparently, to exclude evidence that he did not commit the crime. *State v. Merck*, 763 So.2d 295 (Fla. 2000). This was the third trial of the Merck case; in the first, the jury had been unable to agree as to conviction. At a fourth trial, Merck was sentenced to death again. He remains on death row. See *State v. Merck*, 975 So.2d 1054 (Fla. 2007).

6. *Florida Statutes* §921.141(6)(a): "has no significant history of prior criminal activity."

7. *Florida Statutes* §921.141(6)(c): "[t]he victim was a participant in the . . . conduct" leading to the murder.

8. It may generally be aggravating that the prisoner is likely to pose a danger in the future: *Jurek v. Texas*, 428 U.S. 262 (1976). But it is equally mitigating to prove that this is not the case: *Eddings v. Oklahoma*, 455 U.S. 104, 108, (1982).

9. *Tyler v. Kemp*, 755 F.2d 741, 745 (11th Cir. 1985), recognizing as a mitigating circumstance that the defendant's "character and reputation . . . were good."

10. In 1994 DNA cast doubt on the guilt of Earl Washington, a mentally disabled prisoner on death row in Virginia, after which the governor commuted his sentence to life without parole—as if this were the appropriate response in a case where there was a strong case for innocence. Washington's able and extremely dedicated lawyer, Jerry Zerkin, continued to fight for his client. Only some years later did new DNA tests prove him conclusively to be innocent, at which point he was released from prison.

11. Bagley made enough mistakes in the resentencing trial that we were confident we would get the death penalty reversed. The only disadvantage of a death sentence was the requirement that we appeal again to the Florida Supreme Court and go through years more of state appeals before we could go to federal court to challenge the conviction. Indeed, if the state courts sent us back for a third sentencing trial, we could be on the merry-go-round for another twenty years before getting out of state court for the first time. For this reason, life would be preferable to death, but only marginally so.

Chapter 15: The Federal Appeal

1. *Murray v. Giarratano*, 492 U.S. 49 (1989).

2. Not until sixteen years after *Giarratano* did the Supreme Court finally determine that executing juveniles was unconstitutional. See *Roper* v. *Simmons*, 543 U. S. 551 (2005). Now someone who has just reached his eighteenth birthday can be required to represent himself in a capital case. However, children as young as thirteen may still have to fight their own appeals against a sentence of life without parole. See "Children in Adult Prison," *Equal Justice Initiative*.

3. *Herrera v. Collins*, 506 U.S. 390, 410 (1993). Only nine states out of fifty allow newly discovered evidence of innocence to be presented at any time; forty-one have time limits, with seventeen allowing only sixty days after trial.

4. The Supreme Court recently took a tentative step toward overruling *Giarratano*, recognizing a very limited right to effective assistance of counsel (if you have one) in state post-conviction proceedings. See *Martinez v. Ryan*, No. 10-1001 (March 20, 2012).

5. James S. Liebman, Jeffrey Fagin, and Valerie West, "*A Broken System: Error Rates in Capital Cases* 1973–1995," *Columbia Law School* (2000). Liebman did not take into account the fact that prisoners would not be allowed a federal hearing on the issue of innocence. In other words, for simplicity's sake, his analysis accepted some aspects of the system that most people would disavow. In this sense, his conclusions almost certainly underestimated the scope of the problem.

6. This kind of hypertechnical rigor has been applied for quite some time, even before the Effective Death Penalty Act made it statutory. For example, in *Mann v. Lynaugh*, 840 F.2d 1194 (5th Cir. 1988), the lawyer for the petitioner was one day late in filing his notice of appeal in a capital case, so the court simply did not consider the merits of his appeal. See also *William Davis v. Gary Johnson, Director*, No. 98-20507 (5th Cir. 1998); *Thomas James Fisher v. Gary Johnson, Director*, No. 98-50566 (5th Cir. 1998).

7. The Eleventh Circuit Court of Appeals in Atlanta behaved in a way similar to Judge Huck. See *Maharaj v. Secretary for the Department of Corrections*, 432 F.3d 1292, 1312 (11th Cir. 2005), *cert. denied*, 549 U.S. 819 (2006): "As for the finding that the defense had knowledge of the polygraph results, the district court noted that there was substantial evidence in the post-conviction record to indicate that the defense was not aware of the fact that Butler's answer to one of the questions was indicative of deception. But, the district court observed that even if it were to disagree with the Florida Supreme Court's conclusion, the state high court's finding was not an unreasonable one." If the Florida Supreme Court said the polygraph results were not withheld from the defense, and this was patently false, how could its conclusion that the prosecution did not withhold evidence be "reasonable"?

8. Justices Roberts, Scalia, Ginsburg, Breyer, and Kagan went to Harvard; Thomas, Alito, and Sotomayor, to Yale; and Kennedy, to Stanford. (Some secured other degrees from other high-powered law schools as well.) Most followed a well-beaten path—clerking for judges, then taking jobs in government and academia, followed by appointment to a lower court—before nomination.

9. In *Furman v. Georgia*, 408 U.S. 238 (1972), five justices declared the death penalty statutes then in existence were unconstitutional. Four years later, under heavy political pressure, the court reversed itself, in *Gregg v. Georgia*, 428 U.S. 153 (1976). By then, only Justices Brennan and Marshall dissented, finding the punishment per se illegal. Since that time only two justices—as they verged on retirement—have decided to no longer, as Justice Harry Blackmun put it in 1994, "tinker with the machinery of death." *Callins v. Collins*, 114 S.Ct. 1127, 1130 (1994), Blackmun, J., dissenting from denial of certiorari:

> From this day forward, I no longer shall tinker with the machinery of death. For more than 20 years I have endeavored—indeed, I have struggled—along with a majority of this Court, to develop procedural and substantive rules that would lend more than the mere appearance of fairness to the death penalty endeavor. Rather than continue to coddle the Court's delusion that the desired level of fairness has been achieved and the need for regulation eviscerated, I feel morally and intellectually obligated simply to concede that the death penalty experiment has failed. It is virtually self-evident to me now that no combination of procedural rules or substantive regulations ever can save the death penalty from its inherent constitutional deficiencies. The basic question—does the system accurately and consistently determine which defendants "deserve" to die?—cannot be answered in the affirmative.

At the time he had his Road to Damascus moment, Justice Blackmun was eighty-six years old and had been on the court for twenty-four years. He retired five months later. When his turn came, Justice John Paul Stevens was four days shy of eighty-eight years old, had been on the court holding the opposite opinion for thirty-three years, and he also retired two years later. Their change of heart came too late for many prisoners; both justices were part of the majority that upheld the death penalty in 1976.

10. *Lawrence v. Texas*, 539 U.S. 558 (2003). The liberal wing also called for a debate on whether innocence might act as a bar to execution *In re Troy Davis*, 130 S.Ct. 1 (2009). However, when the lower court declined to enunciate a clear standard, the Supreme Court denied review without a dissenting voice: *In re Troy Davis*, No. 08-1443 (March 28, 2011). The vigorous right-wing justices, by contrast, have no compunction in overruling earlier decisions with which they disagree. Justice Antonin Scalia has written, "I do not myself believe in rigid adherence to *stare decisis* in constitutional cases"; see *Lawrence v. Texas*, 539 U.S. 558, 587 (2003) (Scalia, J., joined by Rehnquist C.J., and Thomas, J., dissenting). While I disagree with most of what Scalia writes, on this point he must surely be correct.

11. *Baze v. Rees*, 170 L.Ed.2d 420 (2008) addressed the issue of whether the drug-injection protocol for executing prisoners was sufficiently painless to pass constitutional muster. Justice Stevens began by writing that "the imposition of the death penalty represents the pointless and needless extinction of life with only marginal contributions to any discernible social or public purposes. A penalty with such negligible returns to the State [is] patently excessive and cruel and unusual punishment violative of the Eighth Amendment." Ibid., 454. However, while he would have ruled that the death penalty was unconstitutional in *all* cases, because of *stare decisis* he went on to determine that the lethal injection protocol was legal here. "The conclusion that I have reached with regard to the constitutionality of the death penalty itself makes my decision in this case particularly difficult," he concluded. "It does not, however, justify a refusal to respect precedents that remain a part of our law. This Court has held that the death penalty is constitutional, and has established a framework for evaluating the constitutionality of particular methods of execution." Ibid., 455 (2008) (Stevens, J., concurring).

12. In that case, Chief Justice Rehnquist observed that "in Texas, the Governor has the power, upon the recommendation of a majority of the Board of Pardons and Paroles, to grant clemency." *Herrera v. Collins*, 506 U.S. 390, 416 (1992). The governor was then Ann Richards, who did nothing to stop Herrera's execution. The chances of anyone receiving clemency dipped when George W. Bush became governor in 1994. While he allowed 152 prisoners to be executed on his watch, he granted clemency to one person—confessed serial killer Henry Lee Lucas. Although Lucas was thought to have killed as many as 350 people, he had apparently not committed the crime for which he was on death row. Lucas died of natural causes three years later, while other states lined up to execute him. Lucas is the *only* person to have received clemency in Texas in the two decades since the reintroduction of the death penalty in 1977. To date, Bush's successor as governor, Rick Perry, has never granted clemency to anyone.

13. Austin Sarat, "Governor Perry, Governor Ryan, and the Disappearance of Executive Clemency in Capital Cases: What Has Happened to Mercy in America?" *FindLaw* (December 29, 2004). In the thirty-two years since 1976, only six Florida death row prisoners have been successful in their clemency applications, all between 1979 and 1983.

Chapter 16: The Victims

1. *A Walk Through the System*, Texas Department of Criminal Justice, Victim Services Division (undated).

2. See, e.g., Richard Burr, "Expanding the Horizons of Capital Defense: Why Defense Teams Should Be Concerned About Victims and Survivors," *Champion*, December 2006, 44, 45; and Pamela B. Leonard, "All but Death Can Be Adjusted: Recognizing Victims' Needs in Death Penalty Litigation," *Champion*, December 2006.

3. I am painfully aware that the publication of this book may only add to the Moo Young family's grief. It is not my place to speak for them. All I can say is that if the courts had ever given Kris Maharaj a

full hearing, this book would not have had to be written. I have rendered anonymous all the statements that I have reproduced, although all are public record. I should also underline that nothing in this book should be read as implying that any surviving member of the family knew or had any involvement in any of the dealings that Derrick and Duane were, according to the evidence as it has developed, apparently involved in.

4. *Reprieve* investigators interviewed Paula Kurland on July 16, 2011, as part of work on a Texas case. She is one of the only victims in Texas who has been able to meet the person who killed her loved one. See also Ken Camp, "Two Mothers Find Grace to Forgive the Men who Killed Their Daughters," *Texas Baptist Communications*, April 21, 1999.

5. Murder Victims' Families for Reconciliation, http://www.mvfr.org/.

6. While Rais said similar things to me, both this and the following quote are taken from Timothy Williams, "The Hated and the Hater: Both Touched by Crime," *New York Times*, July 18, 2011.

7. Paradoxically, Mark Ströman's racism could have saved his life. Under Texas law, he could not have been executed for murder alone: the crime had to have been committed in the course of another felony, an armed robbery. So evidence that Ströman planned a robbery was necessary to support the death penalty. The prosecution went to trial first on the Patel murder, as it was the one where the racial motive was least clear.

8. *Defendants' Answer, Affirmative Defenses and Motion to Dismiss*, at 11, *Bhuiyan v. Perry*, Travis County Civil District Court No. 1:11-CV-00603 (July 18, 2011).

9. For the FBI statistics, see Tanya Shevitz ("FBI Sees Leap in Anti-Muslim Hate Crimes," *SFGate*, November 26, 2002.

10. "A crime victim has the following rights: the right to be treated with fairness and with respect for the victim's dignity and privacy throughout the criminal justice process." Texas Constitution, Article 1, Section 30(a)(1).

11. On April 9, 2009, Governor Perry issued a statement concerning his perspective on the federal courts: "Gov. Perry Speaks in Support of States' Rights," *Office of the Governor*, April 9, 2009.

12. *Defendants' Supplemental Memorandum of Law in Support Of Defendants' Motion to Dismiss*, at 8-9, filed in *Bhuiyan v. Perry et al.*, Civil Action No. 1:11-CV-00603 (W.D. Tex. July 19, 2011), citing *Martinez v. Texas Dept. of Criminal Justice*, 300 F.3d 567, 575 (5th Cir. 2002). The memo claimed that Governor Perry had "immunity [against being] sued in federal court for state-law claims." See also the argument that the victim had no rights, made in *Defendants' Answer, Affirmative Defenses and Motion to Dismiss*, at 12, *Bhuiyan v. Perry*, Travis County Civil District Court No. 1:11-CV-00603 (July 18, 2011): "Even through Art. 56.13 suggests that TDCJ 'shall . . . provide mediation services' as described in Art. 56.02, it is undeniable that a crime victim has Plaintiff has a right to request victim-offender mediation; he does not have a right to have victim-offender mediation. In any case, the 'right' is essentially symbolic where Art. 56.02(d) effectively eliminates any recourse in the event the 'right' is denied."

13. Williams, "Hated and Hater."

Chapter 17: The Battle Continues

1. *Florida Statutes* §837.02(2) defines perjury in a capital case as a second-degree felony, which is punishable by at least fifteen years in prison or, with certain enhancements, thirty years. See also *Florida Statutes* §775.083, 083, 084.

2. *Florida Statutes* §914.22(2)(e) provides that witness tampering in a capital case is punishable by *life in prison.*

3. In 1974, in an effort to stamp out violence with firearms, the Jamaican government introduced some draconian laws. Under the Firearms Act, Geddes, for importing ammunition into Jamaica illegally, was "on conviction before a Circuit Court [liable] to imprisonment for life with or without hard labour." *Firearms Act of Jamaica*, §4(2)(b)(2). Furthermore, his case could have been heard before one of the so-called gun courts, which severely restricted his legal rights and his right to appeal. See *Gun Court Act of Jamaica*.

4. Geddes also admitted in his interviews with British journalists that shortly before he testified at Kris's trial, he was arrested for drunk driving in Miami. The prosecutors arranged for him simply to pay a fine, he said.

5. These are not the real names of the Shower Posse members. I have changed them because the investigation continues, and I do not want to burn our limited entrée into the Jamaican underworld. I hope that further information will be forthcoming. These names are not atypical, though: in a recent "wanted" notice, the nicknames of gang members included Dutch, Winter Fresh, Popcorn, and Cornflakes. See "St. James Police Releases Most Wanted List," *RJR News* (January 3, 2010).

INDEX